REGULATION AND ECONOMIC ANALYSIS

Topics in Regulatory Economics and Policy Series

Michael A. Crew, Editor
Graduate School of Management
Rutgers University
Newark, New Jersey, U.S.A.

Previously published books in the series:

Rowley, C., R. Tollison, and G. Tullock:
  Political Economy of Rent-Seeking
Frantz, R.:
  X-Efficiency: Theory, Evidence and Applications
Crew, M.:
  Deregulation and Diversification of Utilities
Shogren, J.:
  The Political Economy of Government Regulation
Hillman, J., and R. Braeutigam:
  Price Level Regulation for Diversified Public Utilities
Einhorn, M.:
  Price Caps and Incentive Regulation in Telecommunications
Crew, M.:
  Competition and the Regulation in Telecommunications
Crew, M., and P. Kleindorfer:
  Competition and Innovation in Postal Services
Thompson, H.:
  Regulatory Finance: Financial Foundations of Rate of Return Regulation
Crew, M., and P. Kleindorfer:
  Economic Innovations in Public Utility Regulation
Crew, M., and P. Kleindorfer:
  The Economics of Postal Service
Crew, M., and P. Kleindorfer:
  Regulation and the Nature of Postal and Delivery Services
Oren, S. and Steven S.:
  Service Opportunities for Electric Utilities: Creating Differentiated Products
Kolbe, A. Lawrence, William B. Tye, and Stewart C. Myers:
  Regulatory Risk: Economic Principles and Applications to Natural Gas Pipelines
Pechman, C.:
  Regulating Power: The Economics of Electricity in the Information Age

REGULATION AND ECONOMIC ANALYSIS

A Critique
over Two Centuries

by
Richard L. Gordon
Department of Mineral Economics,
College of Earth and Mineral Sciences,
The Pennsylvania State University,
University Park, Pennsylvania

KLUWER ACADEMIC PUBLISHERS
BOSTON / DORDRECHT / LONDON

338
.973
G664r

A C.I.P. Catalogue record for this book is available from the Library of Congress.

ISBN 0-7923-2790-X

Published by Kluwer Academic Publishers,
P.O. Box 17, 3300 AA Dordrecht, The Netherlands.

Kluwer Academic Publishers incorporates
the publishing programmes of
D. Reidel, Martinus Nijhoff, Dr W. Junk and MTP Press.

Sold and distributed in the U.S.A. and Canada
by Kluwer Academic Publishers,
101 Philip Drive, Norwell, MA 02061, U.S.A.

In all other countries, sold and distributed
by Kluwer Academic Publishers Group,
P.O. Box 322, 3300 AH Dordrecht, The Netherlands.

Printed on acid-free paper

Printed in the Netherlands

To the memory of my parents

Table of Contents

Foreword: The Road to the Study

This book is a survey with selected illustrations of the economic debates about regulating markets in nonsocialist economies. A full examination of the deficiencies of specific regulatory practices would be as massive as an unabridged encyclopedia. Therefore, I stress general principles illustrated by examples with which I am particularly familiar, primarily uncorrected defects in energy-related regulation.

This book was written because of a critical gap in the vast literature. Those who closely study specific regulatory practices deem them unsatisfactory. The discord concerns the best remedy in each case. One side sees the need for government action as so great that improved regulation is the preferable goal. The other side contends that some combination of the undesirability of intervention and the barriers to amelioration makes deregulation preferable. Observers, moreover, differ about which policies are best improved and which are best removed.

This skepticism about regulation is inadequately conveyed. All sides contribute to the misunderstanding. Proponents of wide-scale deregulation exaggerate their uniqueness by claiming opposition from many other economists. Proponents of the removal of a specific regulation often fail ever to indicate that their complaints illustrate a wide-scale problem. Those adopting the better regulation posture understate the concerns shared with deregulators. "Better" regulation usually involves lessening what is covered (i.e., partially deregulating). Even those who want reform recognize it is difficult to effect.

Periodically, some observers of the debate suggest that its most interesting aspects are those, the complaints against regulation, where agreement is widespread. However, none of the many broad discussions of regulation documents this argument. This book tries to do so. It seeks to show how the theory and practice of economics inspire skepticism over intervention. It further endeavors to demonstrate that the discords over key areas are less than the tone of the discussions indicates.

Criticisms of intervention are the unique contribution of economics to the debate. Too many noneconomists support too much intervention and remain impervious to the unfortunate experiences that have occurred. Economics long has been the principal profession devoted to exposing and seeking to thwart harmful protectionist instincts. The threat comes from many directions. Protectionist instincts often are more important than conscious ideologies. The true beneficiaries of actual policies regulating markets are mostly affluent, politically powerful groups. If recognized, such outcomes would be politically unacceptable.

The stress here on principles reverses the process by which I reached the conclusions. Recognition of the breadth of discontent with regulation began with research on energy, expanded with work on related areas such as public utilities and public land, and culminated with examination of the literature on many other regulatory experiences. Only then did examination of general principles seem appropriate.

This book began as an attempt to suggest that discussions of energy and mineral policies concentrate more explicitly on the need for lessened intervention. It quickly became evident that I was dealing with the special case of a more general argument against regulation. Turning to the broad issues seemed preferable. Study for over thirty years of theories of intervention determined which theories warranted stress and how to present the analysis. An applied economist's perspective on intervention is helpful. The subject seemed too important to be left to theorists, ideologues, and interest groups and their apologists.

During the long period of writing and rewriting, public discussion on dirigisme evolved considerably. The Bush administration showed lesser resistance to regulation than the Reagan administration. The Clinton administration seems confused about intervention. Its international trade policy continues the uneven approach of past administrations. The Clinton administration is determined to impose another massive new intervention--universal health care. This may lead to a revival of concerns over excess regulation. It has already produced reinforcements of my arguments. For example, Clinton selected as head the Council of Economic Advisers, Laura d'Andrea Tyson, an economist who advocates what she dubbed "cautious intervention in world trade." Theorists who had praised intervention then became more outspoken in arguing that free trade, in practice, was the best policy. The theoretic cases for intervention are more often misused than correctly applied.

Another interesting development was the spread of discussions criticizing environmentalism. That market-oriented groups showed more concern was surprising only for its belatedness; that *The New York Times*, long highly supportive of environmental arguments in news stories as well as editorials, should run articles on doubts about aspects of environmentalism was more surprising.

The treatment should be helpful to a variety of audiences. It seeks to encourage experienced economists of all orientations to rethink the issues. Theorists may learn more about practice; practitioners, more about principles. Believers in very limited government may be convinced they exaggerate the unpopularity of their arguments. Those who dismiss advocacy of limited government as extremism may similarly realize how much they agree with many of the specific proposals of the anti-government writers.

Students can get a perspective different from that of most textbooks. General readers can receive an overview of these debates. Specialists can benefit from realizing that the issues they treat are special cases of long-extant general problems. Everyone will benefit from being reminded how difficult it was to establish many critical economic conclusions now considered "obvious." The primary problem in reaching all these audiences is the wide and growing differences in what they know. An effort was made to find the level of discussion that best served all the targeted readers.

Throughout this book, claiming knowledge of the consensus of economists on anything is avoided. While often made, such assertions are presumptuous. It is possible only to view published work. Its tone can be assessed. Such appraisals are extensively made here. Surveys are not available about the knowledge and opinions of other economists on these writings. Many writings on policy or policy-related theory, as noted, fail to make the authors' positions clear. Another distinction among economists concerns which parts, if any, of economic theory are employed. The variety and ambiguity of these approaches preclude full characterization.

Difficulties arise in identifying economists. Even the most obvious test of a doctorate in economics has drawbacks. Proficiency without the doctorate is possible. An economist must possess thorough knowledge and acceptance of economic theory. Some graduate programs fail to inculcate the knowledge, and some students choose to reject the principles.

Too many observers seem to lack views. Such people soberly report the arguments on both sides and cannot reach conclusions of their own. This characteristic is particularly rampant in texts for the introductory courses in economics. The more advanced texts remain more forthright. Since their writings are so vast and scattered, even greater restraint is maintained here about evaluating work by noneconomists and economists before Adam Smith.

Acknowledgments

This book was written without any direct external support. The College of Earth and Mineral Sciences at The Pennsylvania State University provided me with the time, a liberal book-buying and personal computer budget, some part-time research assistance to comb the libraries, and adequate physical resources to undertake extensive research. These were more than enough for the task. Many people supported the prior research upon which this book draws. They were thanked previously, and full reiteration is not necessary here. I received a fellowship endowed by a distinguished alumnus who wishes to remain anonymous. The funds from the fellowship enabled me to purchase the books I needed.

An extra special debt is owed Walter Mead who spent many hours pouring over the manuscript and making valuable comments. Helmut Frank provided invaluable general suggestions that inspired a pruning of inappropriate digressions and a better organization. The text was self-typed on a microcomputer through all but the last draft. It then was thoroughly edited by Kathryn Al-Halool.

Heavy use is made of what I learned in extensive work on federal coal leasing. This included membership on a U.S. Department of the Interior Commission to study policy in the area. The experience provided insights few academics ever secure into the inefficiency of regulatory processes and the narrow-mindedness of advocates of intervention. The literature suggests that the experiences were all too typical of regulatory practice. Thus, the material seemed to provide appropriate illustrations. The insights are employed in a discussion of U.S. public land policy suggesting the perils of excessive retreat from reliance on markets. The review synthesizes several articles that I wrote on the subject including one written for a Resources for the Future project funded by the J. Howard Pew Freedom Trust.

Material was extracted from my writings on other matters. The basic market failure portions of chapter 3 expand on an earlier article (Gordon 1987b). The monopoly discussion of chapter 4 and chapter 6 on transactions costs are new. The treatment of natural monopoly in chapter 7 draws on my prior writings in that area (Gordon 1982, 1984a, 1986, 1990, with much of the last incorporated directly). Chapter 11 was initially pasted together from several articles on public land and coal policy (1984b, 1985a, 1985b, 1987a, 1988, 1992c). Gordon (1992b) provided the basis for decisions on the national-security argument for regulating energy. By the time all these were extensively edited, much of the original was lost.

Timing made it appropriate to dedicate this book to the memory of my parents. In some senses, this book is not the best one in which to make this acknowledgment. The views here are not ones that either parent would necessarily endorse. In other senses, the choice is apt. The discords are typical of those between economists and noneconomists that are the subject of this book. Moreover, this book is motivated by recollection that all my grandparents and my father were immigrants before restrictions were imposed. I resist ideas whose purported nobility masks efforts to limit the opportunities such as were available to my family. Another alternative would have been to acknowledge three economists--Stigler, Mason, and Hayek. Although I never met them (I did hear the first two speak), they had an enormous influence and died while I was editing the book.

Note on the Literature and its Citation

Having encountered so many unsatisfactory citation practices in my research, I chose the standard approach that seemed most convenient. I use name-date citation in the text and a unified bibliography.

The works cited here include much material with complex pedigrees. Important articles may be reprinted in several places. Many useful anthologies of economic articles have appeared. Many economists have had volumes of their collected articles published. An article can have at least four incarnations--the original appearance in a journal, publication in anthologies devoted to the author, and appearance in two or more anthologies devoted to a special topic. Books can go through many editions and change publishers, particularly, but not invariably, with a paperback edition. An emerging trend seems to be the republication by university presses of titles abandoned by commercial publishers. Another problem is that the translations often appear long after the original book and in an order different from that of the original publications. English language rights often are given to different publishers in different countries.

Another concern is that the bibliography has three purposes--documentation of citations, listing of further material consulted, and guiding the interested reader to other material. Often, particularly with multi-edition books, the last goal may conflict with the other two. No consistency seems to exist about citing any type of multiple incarnations. Cases arise in which authors citing themselves in different places in the same book cite different incarnations of a work.

The works of Stigler and Mises epitomize citation problems. Stigler's essays from many places, including a few in obscure publications, have appeared in many types of anthologies. Mises's *Socialism*, for example, had several German editions, was published in English and is most readily available in a version that includes extensive additional material added by the editors. His *Human Action* had at least three different publishers and was based on an earlier book in German. Many of his books written before *Human Action* appeared later in English.

I attempted to provide citations of both original and at least widely cited anthology publications of critical articles. Citation here of original versions generally is limited to the main articles that appeared in journals likely to be available in research libraries. Obscure pedigrees are noted when the date of original publication is relevant. Given the vastness of the literature, the incompleteness of reporting, and the ease of letting errors slip by, this effort undoubtedly also is incomplete. To facilitate location of material, citations are presented in the text of most entries in the bibliography.

My inclusion procedures involve a few idiosyncrasies. The out-of-print American Economic Association (AEA) series of reprinted articles on various areas is cited, but the outflow of new anthologies from the British publisher, Edward Elgar, is ignored. The AEA series was priced to encourage inclusion in personal libraries and thus became widely cited. The Elgar series seems designed for university libraries, and its accessibility remains to be proved. The collected works of economists noted only in passing were not examined. Given the problems of checking for publishers in the United Kingdom, the citations here are mainly to U.S. publishers. The edition I possessed was cited when the choice did not seem vital.

This book sometimes cites more than one person with the same last name. I try to distinguish which one is meant. This is done even in cases of some widely known economists. The main exception is that no such distinction is made when I cite myself. The context will make clear that none of the surprisingly large number of other Gordons, none of whom are known relatives, practicing economics are meant. (Despite snide remarks to the contrary, self-citation arises, not from vanity, but from the rules of attribution that require indicating the prior work on which reliance inevitably occurs.)

I do not claim that I have thoroughly read and digested everything I examined. Conversely, not everything of relevance that I have read is cited.

Chapter 1

Introduction: Governments and the Marketplace in Economic Analysis

As the deficiencies of intervention became more evident during the 1970s, criticism of the excesses of government in the leading industrialized economies became more fashionable. The traditional economic concern with excesses of government received more attention in policy debates. Economists led the attack.

This book seeks to explain and illustrate the economic principles used in developing a critique of market regulation. The economics literature is full of heated debates on the proper role of government. Differences of opinion center on the best reforms and about what policies should be retained. This book does not seek to resolve these debates, but to expose the critical open questions. Balance is sought. I consider the range of viewpoints prevailing about public policy. This book differs from other critiques of intervention in a sampling from the vast empirical literature on the subject without allowing the case studies to dominate the contents.

That the extent of criticism of intervention is understated even by economists is the principal theme and justification of this effort. Stress is on showing that discontent with regulation occurs among many economists. Specialists in regulation agree that much should be eliminated and the rest radically reformed. Noneconomists involved in regulation also share this dissatisfaction with prevailing practice. The difference is that they believe that the difficulties would vanish if only they were in charge. This is precisely what all economic analyses deem unrealistic. One problem in communicating this view is that specialization limits awareness of how massive is the accord. This discussion seeks to provide outsiders and perhaps even many insiders a sense of this breadth.

The task of persuading skeptics to reject obviously bad policies seems more than enough to try and is emphasized. My focus is limited to distrust of the government as either regulator or as provider of services that have been effectively supplied by the private sector. Stress is on the more complex policies that purportedly seek to eliminate some evil rather than on the more clearly protectionist practices. While the latter type of intervention remains rampant, refutation only requires showing that the programs are subsidies for the unworthy.

Anticipating a subsequent discussion, I deal neither with whether the state should only be a constable nor with how that constable should behave. These are issues no one has satisfactorily resolved. While I discuss other people's cases for greatly narrowing the role of government, improvement in traditional government services is not a concern here. Little danger exists that critical needs for government action will be neglected.

What is argued here is that, despite the uncertainties, much government intervention, including many programs with impregnable political support, lack economic justification and are widely attacked by economists. The specific policy proposals made here are not extreme and going too far would invite the usual dismissals.

Writers on economic issues disagree about how best to approach intervention. The view that warnings about the drawbacks of governments are more critical seems most valid and is adopted here. Stress is on the consensus toward lessened statism. The critical problem is that governments intervene excessively rather than insufficiently. The defects of dirigisme are ancient and unchanging. With the increased integration of the world economy because of improvements in transportation and communications, private monopolistic forces have weakened. Analyses showing the strength of competition and the defects of government need the greater emphasis. Even those who want a more active government should better recognize the deficiencies of statism.

Too much enthusiasm exists for statism. Noneconomists inadequately appreciate the well-established drawbacks of interference. Neglect of the defects of regulation has far more public policy impact than excessive fear of intervention. Warnings about limitations are much rarer and much less likely to be heeded outside economics than cheering for regulation. Strong regulatory instincts prevail among politicians. They have inadequate respect for markets but little need for instruction about opportunities to intervene. Similarly, economic illiteracy among too many of those who enter policy debates is appalling. The pages of leading newspapers and magazines and television news programs contain little understanding of economic principles. Discussions of how intervention could be beneficial thus are widely available. Their elaborate reiteration here seemed unnecessary.

Many modern economists recognize that the valid justifications of interference are more often misused than properly applied. Economic studies identify many bad government policies that can only be reformed by repeal. Much regulation cannot be excused by any economic guidelines about what constitutes a potentially desirable action. Even the "market failure" arguments designed to determine when intervention is desirable ultimately reinforce the case against statism. To be sure, invalid claims that the criteria for efficient regulation are met are routinely made by interest groups seeking government protection. This phenomenon regularly occurs in all areas of policy debate and, consequently disfigured the energy debates in which I have long engaged. These misuses, in turn, cause analysis of market failures to recognize the limited practical relevance of theory. Moreover, as many observers stress, the benefits may be given to inappropriate groups. Policies advocated for allegedly helping the poor often have the opposite effect. Economic analyses of government actions toward markets predict that the political process inevitably leads to such results (see chapter 6). These concerns over misuse are another inadequately documented aspect of economics.

Many other examples could be provided. Rent control and minimum wage legislation are prime examples. These policies are widely considered bad economics but are politically untouchable. Farm subsidies are only slowly moving from a similar status. Inordinate attention is given dubious protectionist arguments. The errors of energy policy were inadequately reported. Strong criticisms of environmental policy making long went unreported. Suggestions are being made (Gore 1992) that it is immoral to report reservations about environmental policies, but at least part of the press responded by being more critical.

A secondary concern, which is too fascinating to ignore, is that many commentators on all sides of the general debate on intervention exaggerate prevailing differences. Often what is presented as an issue of substance proves only one of form. Sweeping attacks, in particular, are easily misunderstood. They appear to display excessive certainty. Yet, the stronger arguments are too influential and less extreme in substance to ignore totally.

My choices deliberately focused on areas in which vigorous debates prevail among economists and about which noneconomists seem unaware. The examples are ones that both illustrate some critical points and are familiar to me. The covered topics include such perennials as antitrust, public utility regulation, the use of price controls, international commodity price "stabilization" schemes, environmental policy, the use of market regulation to promote equity and macroeconomic stability, and property rights economics.

Then a case study on an area about which I am particularly experienced, coal leasing policy for federal lands, is provided. The inclusion seems worthwhile because the policy is such a graphic example of a program that is economically unsound and politically popular. As the discussion shows, the defects of coal leasing practice are illustrative of problems of federal land mismanagement probably best corrected by turning the land over to the private sector.

Before turning to a more detailed overview of the content of the book, comments on guiding principles are made. A comprehensive survey of the literature on regulatory practice would require thousands of pages. Instead, lessons drawn from reading key parts of that literature are presented, and illustrations from areas with which I am most familiar are provided. No effort is made to provide a complete list of desirable reforms. Chapter 13 attempts a partial recapitulation.

Mineral experiences and appraisals are drawn upon throughout the book to illustrate the continuing debates on statism. I contend that the calls for intervention are only sanitized versions of some of the worst protectionist arguments. Among the many causes of a disastrous World War was belief that political hegemony was needed to maintain access to "essential" commodities. Thus, the Japanese were fascinated with creating a coprosperity sphere. Sanitized but no more defensible vestiges of this argument for protectionism persist. Similarly, raw material exporting countries are so obsessed with reaping the benefits of selling more processed forms of the goods that the costs of processing are ignored.

This book similarly does not try to duplicate the enormous literature on the failures of economic planning in both the communist world and most less developed countries. The difficulties of showing the defects of more modest actions are more than enough for one book to cover. Moreover, these deficiencies are more insidious and less fully discussed than those of comprehensive planning. While many serious policy defects are in taxation, this subject is better left to the others who have competently treated tax issues.

Similarly, little is said about the issue of aid to the poor. Exactly what governments can do to alleviate poverty is difficult to determine. Discussion is provided on why this is so and on why regulation of markets is an unsatisfactory way to attain fairness.

Regulatory experience tells us little about perennial issues of inflation, unemployment, and poverty. Limits of manageability and knowledge dictate exclusion of a comprehensive appraisal here of such issues. The always great difficulties in dealing with inflation and unemployment seem to have greatly increased for reasons noted more fully in chapter 9. However, long-standing doubts about the efficacy of stabilizing the economy or redistributing income by regulating individual industries have been reinforced.

The selectivity also implies that many major issues such as regulation of financial institutions, international trade policy, and farm subsidies receive little or no attention. One rationale is that these are largely blatant protectionist policies that need less analysis. Another issue not explicitly treated is the proper role of government in fostering new technology and distributing new information. The discussions here provide the principles for evaluating government programs in the area. Review of the practices would require another book.

In this book, political realism is not considered a germane criterion. What is politically feasible is not an area in which economists should claim expertise; it is not even clear that the political professionals know what is feasible. For example, the history of energy policy creation in the 1970s and destruction in the 1980s suggests that many fears may have existed mainly among politicians. Had energy economists accepted the claims of irresistible political forces, they might not have provided the rationales that motivated the reforms that occurred. (This was written long before the August 1991 events in the USSR invalidated expert pronouncements about the invincibility of totalitarianism.)

Political reality can be and has been changed. Protectionism and farm subsidies have lessened in popularity under the pressure of economic criticism. Tenured, independent scholars should propose desirable alterations whatever their present popularity. The growing attacks on tenure arise from recognition that it too rarely is used to promote freer inquiry. Policy leaders should persuade voters to accept desirable changes.

In particular, policy advisers should do all they can to resist efforts to limit the scope of the investigation. All too often, politicians only request proposals for modest change when more radical changes, including deregulation, are needed. To counter this deficiency, the option of filing supplementary opinions should be used more fully.

In developing the discussion, I found it desirable to consult and note several vast but incompletely connected relevant literatures. My position was formed mainly from reading empirical studies of many types of regulation. The burgeoning theoretical writings relevant to the issue were then pursued. Then, the advocacy of and the attacks on the efforts to develop sweeping cases for freer markets inspired extending my familiarity with these works. (Here, as in much of the development of the argument, the defects of the attacks on free-market economics often were more influential on my reaction than the brilliance of the defenses.)

The empirical literature is the easiest to handle. As noted, agreement prevails that actual market regulation is flawed. Those working on policy studies regularly find confirmation of the traditional concerns about inappropriate government actions. Studies exist about the defects of programs in many areas. These include ones in which I have worked such as control of energy and minerals, related areas such as land management, environment, public utilities, and health and safety. Areas such as antitrust and securities supervision are also attacked.

Broad attacks on statism have a bad reputation and often are dismissed as too unacceptably extreme to cite. However, it would be dishonest to ignore these writers here. They are people (such as Hayek, Friedman, Stigler, and Coase) with long experience in economics and merit sufficient to warrant Nobel prizes and high office in professional societies. Their influence has been substantial yet largely benign. They are precisely those who have most inspired the victims of tyranny, particularly in Eastern Europe; many themselves were victims of tyranny. The need for recognition is stimulated by the widespread tendency of friends as well as foes to misrepresent their work. The position here is that these arguments are a natural extension of economic principles. Conventional theory is less supportive of intervention than such critics as Mises and Coase recognize. Conversely, too many prominent economists exaggerate the defects of attacks on dirigisme. Moreover, complaints of extremism are not very convincing when, as often occurs, their authors are more vitriolic than the ideologues being attacked. Insertion in a manuscript of remarks about Mises or Hayek no kinder than those in this book provokes scathing denunciations. Such readers invert my arguments. An unexpected recognition that the facts support the ideology needs admission.

An Overview of the Discussion

My argument is built on three propositions. The first is that the increasingly dominant general equilibrium model defined below is only a useful starting point for understanding economic reality; where it leads depends on how it is used. The model is so abstract and leaves so much undefined that it is used as the base of many conflicting policy conclusions. The proposition developed in chapter 2 is that the theory is most useful in promoting understanding of the virtues of market economies.

The second key point is that the attack on intervention starts with the delineation of the market failures that might justify intervention. As noted, these arguments are viewed here as severely limiting what can be legitimately be regulated. This view deliberately disputes the complaint of strong proponents of free markets that market failure discussions are the basis for excessive intervention.

My contention is an obvious generalization of an alternative view particularly prevalent in international trade economics. Sophisticated arguments for adopting protection actually imply that successful protection rarely can occur. The view here is that this principle applies to many other types of intervention. This proposition is introduced in chapter 3. The market failures considered most critical are the existence of goods such as environmental amenities for which it is difficult to organize markets and monopoly. Chapters 4 and 5 extend the argument.

Chapter 4 deals with the special case of intervention to prevent (or create) monopoly. Monopoly is a central issue and one critical for chapter 7. The monopoly discussion deals with the problems of identifying and controlling monopoly. My basic argument is that the monopoly problem is not a clearly pressing one. It is further contended that the leading observers differ less about the issues than their tone indicates. The evidence suggests that the possibility of monopoly is of much less practical significance than the earlier theoretic literature suggested.

In chapter 5, some implications of market failures for international trade are treated. The discussion examines issues such as infant and declining industries not handled elsewhere. Given the economic tradition of showing that international trade does not fundamentally differ from trade within countries, many points critical to international trade debates are reviewed in other chapters.

The third proposition is that the case is greatly bolstered by extending economic theory to encompass the complications critical for deciding when government action is appropriate. This argument is introduced in chapter 6 and used in chapter 7 to suggest the many ways the private sector can organize to serve customers efficiently.

Chapter 6 explains the key barriers to intervention and the implications of considering them. The focus is on transaction costs, the indirect expenses of learning and the direct expenses of dealing. With such costs, markets may be organized much differently from the idealized forms assumed in verbal discussions of the general equilibrium model. Simpler theories overstate the desirability of organized, centralized markets similar to stock exchanges. Government activity similarly becomes less desirable than when it is costless.

The role of property rights in reducing transaction costs is then treated. Other problems of government are examined. These involve growing efforts to warn of government failures. The arguments indicate that the susceptibility to pressure groups and the bureaucratic desire to extend their activities both lead to excesses of intervention. This chapter thus presents the theories devised to explain long-standing distrust of government.

In chapter 7, the implications of transaction costs, imperfect competition, and supply uncertainty for the conduct of business and public policy are discussed. The objective is to show that well-functioning markets arise under a wide range of institutional arrangements. The goal is to indicate why it is not desirable to make all markets closely resemble those in which transactions occur on organized exchanges. The argument is used to treat proposals for oil-import fees and government stockpiles to protect against supply insecurities, political arrangements to stabilize markets, and regulation of public utilities. The chapter is an effort to integrate and apply the scattered literature on the optimal structure of economic institutions. It is shown that theorists have moved to better appreciation of the many techniques available to facilitate dealing in the market place. The study of alternative methods of transacting proved interesting and in need of more extensive, less abstract analysis.

Chapter 8 deals with the inappropriateness of using market regulation as macroeconomic policy. Discussion begins by examining the erosion of confidence in economic stabilization policy. It is suggested that even those who believe that something can be salvaged from the argument doubt that regulation of industry is the best approach. Proposals to tax oil imports to promote economic stability are used as an example of the problems of stabilizing by using industry-specific programs.

It is further argued that regulation of specific industries is a poor device for attaining a fairer society, however it is defined (see chapter 9). Difficult problems arise in judging and reacting to the fairness of outcomes. A few examples are provided to show the barriers to delineating universally acceptable rules and to demonstrate that regulation of markets is a poor way to promote whatever concepts of fairness may be adopted. Little effort is made to appraise the programs employed. Comments are made about the prevailing agreements, about the obvious failings of existing programs, and of the difficulties in designing effective cures.

Chapters 10 and 11 are case studies in applying the principles. As noted, I have deliberately concentrated on areas in which I have worked and the ones where the conflict between economic analyses and public perception is particularly great.

Chapter 10 treats the special and pervasive issue of environmental policy. The preferences among economists for using financial incentives rather than the detailed regulations actually imposed is emphasized. Attention is given to the theoretic and practical criticisms of the goals as well as their implementation. The thus-far rarely expressed view that environmentalism may not be as noble a cause as widely believed is addressed.

Chapter 11 applies the principle of secure property rights to the evaluation of U.S. public land policy. Public land policy is an example, known to a few specialists, of the disparity between public opinion and economic writings. Attention is also given to the critical issues of granting mineral rights in less developed countries and property rights for mobile resources such as oil and natural gas. I suggest that government land management suffers from two major problems. First is that the government is attempting things best left to the private sector. A second objection is that obsession with avoiding the impression of permitting windfall profits aggravates the inefficiency.

After all this evidence is presented, the penultimate chapter examines generalizations about both economics as a whole and its treatment of intervention. The discussion seeks to explain the eclectic principles guiding the exposition, suggests why the record inspires greater sympathy for market-oriented economics, and uses the experience with energy and mineral policy to illustrate the drawbacks of "indicative" planning. A final chapter sums up the arguments and uses them to conclude that classic ("economic") liberalism is by far the most satisfactory theory for a politically and economically thriving world.

An appendix deals with the curious phenomenon of using discussions of methodology as a disguised way to reiterate ideological debates.

Chapter 2

Choices in a Market Economy: A Prologue

Modern economics uses an abstract general model of an idealized economy as the starting point of analysis. The theory is extended to introduce numerous complications and then combined with observation of experience to produce practical conclusions. Perversely, the basics are much harder to make comprehensible than are the extensions. For the numerous extended discussions, examine the texts devoted to theory. However, comments to suggest the practical relevance of the theory seem necessary here. The basic points are critical and badly abused in many ways. Balanced assessment of the contribution of the central theories is rare. All sides worry too much about what simple theory cannot do. The great contributions made are neglected. Even those familiar with the analysis should reexamine the problems.

The approach employed is termed general equilibrium. It postulates the existence of two types of decision makers, consumers and firms. Consumers are thinking-feeling units who seek maximum satisfaction that is realized by utilization of the resources. Firms are impersonal organizations that seek to maximize monetary gain by securing and transforming resources into more valuable things. These entities interact in markets to attain their goals. This interaction leads to determination of a set of equilibrium prices; i.e., ones establishing a pattern of production, exchange, and consumption that no one wishes to change. (For a lucid survey of the development of the abstract theory, see Ingrao and Israel 1990.)

One perennial area of controversy is the meaning of the principles of consumer analysis. Consumers are considered to be able to compare options in a consistent manner and determine which is the best of the affordable options. Consistency means that all options can be ranked and the ranking between any two options remains the same no matter how many other options are simultaneously considered. This assumption is often described as involving rationality. Consistent ranking can occur without the cool dispassion that often is associated with rationality. For example, fanaticism for some foods, beverages, and various entertainers can be conducted in a logically consistent manner. Likewise, while Iraq risked and endured international retribution, Libya maximized its oil profits to increase its ability to finance terrorism. Systematic also does not necessarily mean materialistic or narrow-minded. The theory can cover more than choices made in the market place. It is applicable to any selection. Every participant in the choice process is capable of systematically valuing every trade-off made in or out of the marketplace.

The principle of economic individualism means that individuals can better choose for themselves than can an outsider what, including helping others, is best to do. This viewpoint is less condescending to the poor than the supposedly more considerate views of those designing welfare policies. The assumption of consumer sovereignty implies the poor generally can better allocate aid they receive than can government agencies. Earmarking aid to the purchase of particular goods and services and tight monitoring of the behavior of the poor are inconsistent with individualism but intrinsic to actual policies.

Extensive work used the theory of rational choice to analyze many nonmarket choices. Even deviant behavior such as criminality and actions of various types of nonprofit organizations is explored (e.g., the work of Becker that earned him the Nobel Prize in economics in 1992). The applications have the same virtue. An effort is made to see if any order can be distinguished in the apparent chaos.

The justification for the expansive view is that presuming rational choice is universally useful in seeing what uniformities, if any, prevail in behavior. Rationality is the only plausible restriction on choice. Any outcome is possible if people or institutions act irrationally and inconsistently. Assuming systematic rational behavior imposes restrictions on the outcome. It is always helpful to see how much behavior can be explained as adherence to such restrictions. This is as true for analyzing those such as criminals who supposedly are highly irrational as for treating business firms that are presumed to be as rational as possible. No one should argue that choices exactly correspond to the idealized model. The issue is how far behavior in different realms departs from rationality.

These extensions have been dubbed economic imperialism--an effort to take over all the social sciences (see, e.g., McCloskey 1985, 76). (See the work of Judge Richard A. Posner, a product of the interchange between lawyers and economists at the University of Chicago, 1986, for one of the most sweeping and interesting applications of economic imperialism.) Economic imperialism seeks less to explain everything than to challenge tendencies to assume total irrationality and the resulting total uncertainty of outcomes (Posner 1986, 266).

An associated theory of welfare economics treats the problems of evaluating the outcomes of general equilibrium. The theory starts first by assuming away all the problems that are the focus of the next chapters. Then, the distribution of assets is made predetermined. It is then shown that under these conditions the general equilibrium is equivalent to attaining every possible transaction that is beneficial to the participants. Even those engaged in developing and presenting the theory feel uneasy about it. The fixation with simplifications is bothersome. Some argue that the dominance of the theory reflects the rise of a sterile formalism in economics. The analysis is viewed as an effort to attain elegance at the expense of fruitful evaluation of actual economies.

The specific criticisms take many forms including two widely-held conflicting views. Critics on the left assert that advocacy of markets over governments arises from the mistaken belief that real economies closely resemble the idealized world of the theory. Advocates of preference for markets counter by arguing that the theory actually leads to systematic underrating of market solutions. Undue devotion to the models leads to basing appraisals of real markets solely by how well they correspond to their idealized theoretic counterparts. While both are flawed, the promarket attack is more accurate than the antimarket.

However, an even better interpretation is that the model is only designed as the starting point for understanding markets. Too much is left undefined or unanswered. Policy appraisals should be delayed until enough extensions of the theory have been mastered *and* applied to specific cases.

Another set of problems involves the relationship of the basic concepts of the analysis to those arising in practice. Critical terms such as consumer, firm, resources, satisfaction, monetary gain, and markets are left undefined in the standard mathematical formulations of the model. The accompanying text may attempt definitions, and often the choice is a narrow one. Thus, satisfaction is often defined as relating to what can be attained in markets. Markets are defined to resemble the purest form of organized markets such as stock exchanges where all the trading in on the floor during market hours. This naturally inspires further criticism of the model. The basic concepts are best kept undefined because it is not possible to determine exactly what forms are consistent with the workings of the model.

All this carping involves misstatement of what theory reasonably can accomplish. Real economies are far too complex to comprehend. A simplification is needed to provide a satisfactory starting point for analysis. This is precisely what general equilibrium and welfare economics (see Little 1957) contribute. The economy of the model is still complex enough to explain the most critical problems of economics--scarcity and the lessening of its impact by specialization, production, and exchange. Scarcity is simply the tendency of desires to exceed the ability to produce. This fact would only be a sad truism without specialization, production, and exchange. These processes lead even in the simplest models to lessening of scarcity. The analysis also raises a series of questions that lead naturally to incorporating essential complications.

The key to the theory is identification of the critical basis of analysis--the valuing of a pair of goods by a pair of individuals. In principle, absolute measures of value might exist, and for many decades efforts were made to define and determine such absolutes. These absolutes are unobservable and irrelevant to practical decision making. Real decision makers effectively trade one good for another. The relevant question becomes the comparative worth between the two potential traders of one good in terms of another. This might be the value in terms of bolts of Harris tweed cloth of Portuguese Madeira wine (a case chosen in tribute to the slightly broader ones used by David Ricardo). Introductory economics texts normally show for the special case of trade among countries that any differences in such valuations create the opportunity for mutually beneficial trade. A higher valuation of Madeira is simply a willingness of one party to offer more Harris tweed for the Madeira than does another party. (See Graham 1933 on the problems of Ricardo's actual analysis.)

General equilibrium and welfare theory use the concept of marginal rates of substitution to extend the argument. The rates of substitution are values by each separate firm and individual of one good in terms of another. Two points arise. The first is from the simple theory and indicates the irrelevance of whether we look at the tweed price of wine or the wine price of tweed. The second is the extension that beneficial trade is possible whenever any pair of economic units differs in the rates of substitution they have for any pair of goods. The pair could involve any of the three logical possibilities--two consumers, two firms, or a firm and a consumer. Given the millions of firms and goods in an economy and the uneven distribution among units, it would be surprising if few rates of substitution differed in the absence of trade. Thus, many opportunities for mutually beneficial trade should exist.

The theories of consumers and of firms add the hypothesis that trading processes are self-limiting. As trading proceeds step by step or, in formal terms, marginally, the differences between valuations narrow and ultimately vanish. As holdings of any good increase, its value in terms of other goods diminishes. Direct dealing between pairs of units is an analytic nuisance for at least two reasons. One is the problem of identifying appropriate trading partners. The other is that direct trading involves comparative bargaining skills that cannot be neatly modeled. The problems are resolved by assuming that everyone trades in markets by reacting to competitive prices. Market determined prices set the rate at which any unit can trade all it desires of any good for any other good. Instead of comparing rates of substitution of every other unit, economic units look at market prices. A good whose value to the individual in terms of another good is greater than market prices of the first good in terms of the second is bought until its value falls to equal the price. A goods whose value to the individual in terms of another good is less than market prices of the first good in terms of the second is sold until its value rises to equal the price.

With the introduction of markets and prices comes the addition of another key concept, equilibrium or market clearing. This is the idea that market processes establish a set of prices that establish consistency among all the trading desires. For every pair of goods, the market clearing price is one at which the total quantity sellers are willing to provide exactly equals the total quantity buyers are willing to acquire.

The theory at least tacitly adds an arbitrage principle that in equilibrium at routes to making a deal involve the same payoff. This is a generalization of the principles observed in financial markets. Commodities or securities selling at the same time in different markets such as Exxon stock in New York, Boston, and London will sell at the same price. If price differences prevailed, those watching the market would buy in the lower priced market and sell in the higher priced market. The process eliminates the difference. The buying raises prices in the lower priced market; the selling lowers prices in the higher priced market. The buying and selling continues until the difference is eliminated.

More elaborate smoothings occur so that no advantage arises between direct and indirect methods of securing goods. The usual example of this process is foreign exchange trading. A holder of U.S. dollars desiring Japanese yens could buy them directly or go through chains of dealings of different lengths--e.g., dollars for British pounds, British pounds for Deutsche marks, and Deutsche marks for yens. The arbitrage principle ensures that exactly the same number of yens is secured on a direct trade and any possible chain of indirect trades.

Exchange means that a sacrifice is made, but arbitrage implies that the exact nature of the exchange is neither knowable nor relevant. In equilibrium, the marginal rates of substitution among any pair of goods actually traded equals their relative market price. Consider a consumer selling tweed and tea and buying Madeira. The Madeira-tweed rate of substitution would equal the market price of Madeira in terms of tweed. The same equality would prevail with the Madeira-tea rate of substitution and the Madeira price in terms of tea. No matter how many more goods are traded, the same equality of marginal rates of substitution to relative prices would prevail. A good is excluded from acquisition if its market price exceeds the marginal rates of substitution of any positive level of consumption.

Thus, the theory develops several basic points about how economic processes lessen the burden of scarcity. The first is the reciprocal or mutual nature of advantageous deals. Cheapness is definable only in terms of relationships among goods. It is near nonsense to talk about the absolute superiority of one producer (company or country) over another. Absolute superiority could exist in principle, but it is very unlikely. Such superiority would mean that under all circumstances the better producer used less of all inputs than did the worse producer.

The critical point, however, is that, even if such superiority exists, it is irrelevant. Producers only sell to reap returns. They must find a commodity to produce that can be beneficially traded for another good. The key to such dealing is differences in rates of substitution, not superiority.

A second key conclusion is that market processes eliminate differences. The arbitrage principle extends to indicate that ultimately everything is smoothed out. Equilibrium prices of goods and payments to those who provide land, labor, and capital resources to producers ultimately become identical everywhere in the world. Everyone ends up with the same standard of living.

The natural question about why this has not occurred has the answer that powerful forces have thwarted the working of the arbitrage principle. The required free trade in goods, people, and ideas is limited everywhere. The argument can be reversed to suggest the superficiality of the concerns over who will be number one. The elimination of differences is equivalent to making everyone number one in equilibrium.

However, this argument alters rather than refutes the concerns. What is most interesting about equilibrium is the gain produced in its attainment. The benefits might be shared in infinitely many ways, and valid, but unanswerable questions arise about whether particular units have secured all they can. A classic analysis by Stolper and Samuelson (1941), for example, demonstrated the inevitability of short-run loss to one factor of production in the two country, two good, two factor version of the Ohlin (1931) factor intensity model of international trade. The Ohlin theory holds that countries will export goods that require relatively more of factors of production in which it is better endowed. The analysis is tractable only in their two good, two factor, two country case. Two types of ratios are considered--the ratios of factor use in different industries and the ratios of factor endowments in the two countries. In the Stolper-Samuelson analysis, the two factors were labor and capital. The country being considered had a higher capital/labor ratio than the rest of the world. One of the goods, wheat, required a higher ratio of capital inputs to labor inputs then the other good, watches; this is the precise definition of using relatively more of a factor.

Instituting international trade would involve increasing the output and exporting wheat, lowering watch production, and importing watches. Given the difference in factor use, the shift of resources from a less capital-using watch production to wheat would release less capital and more labor than the wheat industry wanted at existing factor prices. To restore market equilibrium, real rents to capital and real wages would have to fall. Samuelson (1948b, 1949) extended the analysis to show the restrictive circumstances under which factor-price equalization, elimination of international differences in factor rewards, would occur.

As discussed further in chapter 5, even in the confines of general equilibrium theory, such problems do not imply that it is desirable to restrict trade. The ultimate effect of feasible trade restriction may be worse for everyone than free trade. When key complications are added, the case for free trade strengthens materially. What is left from all this is recognition that the gains from trade can be unevenly distributed, but it is very difficult to determine the actual situation. The deluge of complaints that America is "slipping" can charitably be treated as concerns that the U.S. is not working hard enough and therefore not getting a high enough share of the gains.

The critical points here are that the proofs provided are grossly insufficient and that a charitable interpretation is unwarranted. The first point was already made by noting that it is not that gaps close but how the gains from such closings are distributed that matter. Such distributions are impossible to measure. Reading the literature on international competitiveness inspires skepticism about the validity of the fears. The most obvious concern is that even those who should know better choose to overlook the problems in appraising performance. Beyond that, the complaints are invariably the basis for advocacy of massive government aid to something. The specific points made in this literature inspire concern that the arguments are largely just another in the unending efforts to find respectable arguments to justify unwise intervention

A final major contribution of general equilibrium theory is demonstration that absolute values are unobservable and irrelevant. This is a powerful counter to standard protectionist arguments that a particular industry is so vital that it deserves assistance. At most, special circumstances as discussed in chapter 5 may justify aid.

Having seen what the theory includes, it is time to examine what it omits. The theory neglects but immediately leads to consideration of three other key features of an economy--the use of money, specialization, and technical progress. The first omission is particularly frustrating because the theory comes so tantalizingly close to justifying the use of money. Two of the three key rationales were noted already.

We saw that it was more convenient to deal in a market and that in equilibrium it did not matter what was traded in any deal. It would be even more convenient if instead of markets for every pair of goods, it would be possible to settle on one good against which all other goods are traded. That benchmark good should be stable in value, portable, and storable. That the choice of what to trade does not affect the real pattern of trade means no problems arise from selecting a benchmark good.

The theory discloses a third rationale for a benchmark. Without it, the prices are incompletely defined. Any of an infinite number of price ratios could prevail--no way exists to choose between five to one and ten to two. Defining the units of the benchmark and setting prices as units of benchmarks sets a unique scale. We define what is one unit of the benchmark and select the five to one ratio in the example.

The theory concentrates on the last rationale for a benchmark and leaves tacit the advantage of reducing the number of markets maintained. It also fails to consider the attributes of a good benchmark. Some observers, most vociferously Mises (1980), consider this an undesirable gap. The points are fully taught elsewhere in economics, primarily in discussions of money and the financial system.

Whether this is the best approach is purely a question of form. The justification for exclusion would seem to be that a loss of generality occurs if money is introduced. The counterargument is that the "loss" is a desirable one because no extensive economy is possible without use of a money. It can be argued that the separation was workable when economists could attain adequate knowledge of all branches of the field. Now that the only place that both markets and money always are discussed simultaneously are introductory texts, it may be desirable to add a few words about money to the end of advanced discussions of markets. (Such discussions are emerging.)

Another serious concern is the neglect of division of labor and the resulting stimulus to innovation. The terse statements about these points that comprise the first few chapters of The Wealth of Nations are a major source of the book's continuing influence. Division of labor raises the paradox that to secure more diversity we must become more specialized. We consciously pick an area on which to concentrate and devote ourselves to learning about it. We thus know more about one thing than those who maintained self-sufficiency. Adam Smith (1979a) added that as the market became bigger we could become even more specialized. People could shift from being makers of all four main string instruments to specialists on the violin, viola, cello, or bass. (See below for discussion of Stigler's efforts to extend the argument.) Being very good at one thing generates much more purchasing power than trying to do many things.

Smith (1979a) also observed that specialization inspired efforts to introduce better ways to produce and to improve the product. This idea was extended in the early twentieth century by the Austrian economist Joseph A. Schumpeter (1934). Schumpeter argued that as equilibrium forces pushed down the payoff to existing ideas, strong incentives arose to innovate. This involved the familiar ideas of new products and processes and also new uses of existing products and processes. Schumpeter further distinguished between conceiving the idea and making it a commercial success. The latter, by definition, is the payoff to the effort.

It seems widely agreed that innovation is a critical additional payoff to market processes. It is further recognized that pressures from potential rivals are a great spur to innovation. Thus, for example, many of the short-run concerns about free trade seem less important than the way in which free trade and innovation reinforce each other. A less sheltered industry is less able to protect profits from old operations and is under pressure to generate new ideas. With world markets available, the gains to innovation necessary are greater than if one market is local or national. A further result is that even greater gains to trade accrue to customers everywhere.

Issues arise about the best way to effect innovation. Schumpeter (1934) stressed the role of large firms; critics suggest the case was overstated. Further questions arise about balancing between widening the availability of the innovation and allowing the innovator to make sufficient profits. This leads to questions about how much protection should be provided by patents and similar devices. Yet another concern is what role governments can play.

Much has been written deploring the lack of explicit treatment of innovation in general equilibrium theory. The complaints appear in many places such as much of the literature on economic development and in at least one leading history of economic thought (Blaug 1985).

The self-styled Austrian economists who focus on Mises's emphasis on innovation overstate his contribution. Mises, who was disliked by Schumpeter and may have had reciprocal feelings, attacked any consideration of equilibrium. He argued that attention should be given only to the innovative processes that upset the equilibrium. This contrasts with Schumpeter's belief in the importance of both equilibrium and innovation theory. The prior discussion here sought clearly to support Schumpeter's position on this issue. It can be added that an understanding of the gains of attaining equilibrium assists appreciation of the benefits of innovation.

The one drawback of the theory that is not so easily resolved is that it ignores the existence of any real government. At best, an idealized, all-knowing, benevolent government is introduced as the cure for all problems. As shown in the next chapter, the theory can easily be extended to suggest a justification of one role of government--financing provision of services to all citizens. Later chapters discuss some of the problems of this rationale.

The Nature of Market Prices Further Considered

Economics seeks to correct misunderstanding of market prices. Economics arose to demonstrate that market prices were based on the combined judgment of the participants about the worth of goods and to suggest that these valuations were the most dependable indicators of worth.

Market price setting eliminates shortages and gluts, disparities between desires to buy and desires to sell. A sufficient price rise removes all shortages; gluts end by price cuts. A clear, impersonal solution always emerges. Of course, this process produces winners and losers. This is true of all systems of allocations. The difference between a market solution and a political one is that the former eliminates while the latter perpetuates differences between the desire to buy and the desire to sell. Thus, economic analysis demonstrates that gluts and shortages are signs of interferences with the market. When governments intervene to prevent a market solution, they must devise alternative allocation schemes. In shortages, they must choose who receives and who is deprived. In gluts, the governments must decide who can sell and who cannot.

For example, an often encountered complaint is that people are free to starve under a market solution. The argument invariably is for massive government intervention. Little recognition is shown that some forms of etatism such as Soviet communism can and did vastly increase starvation. Mismanagement is compounded by tyranny. Profit-seekers consider people as potential customers and suffer from their demise. Too many governments consider people dangers to be controlled or killed. The legitimate point is that markets should be supplemented by (not necessarily governmental) assistance programs that prevent starvation. Chapter 9 reviews the problems of devising such a policy.

Similarly, the competitive market process makes goods freely available to all who are willing to pay the price. No political machinations of any sort are needed. Suppliers and customers need not be conquered, flattered, cultivated, appeased, or otherwise given special treatment. Payment usually suffices. At most, skill and politeness sometimes must be demonstrated. All the agonies to which governments and particularly their foreign ministries around the world are prone become mercifully irrelevant. This is the basis for the argument that the market economy eliminates the need for imperialism. The persistence of alternative methods of dealing then is another reflection of distrust of markets and of political barriers to market solutions.

Further issues arise about how to interpret observed prices. The proper prices are ones that are adapted to presently prevailing market conditions. These, in turn, depend on both the current situation and the latest views about probable future developments. (The characteristic of reflecting reality holds for monopoly and competitive prices.)

A somewhat more controversial contention about market prices is that they are the best available epitome of expectations. Puristic theory imposes excessively restrictive requirements about the degree of insight and risk pooling that must exist for prices to be superior indicators. All that is necessary to justify reliance on market prices is that they measure expectations better than other available measures.

This point is often overlooked. Too many observers fault prevailing prices because they reflect a market reality that seems unsatisfactory--usually because it makes them worse off than they hoped to be. Those harmed by a buying price higher than they wished or a selling price lower than they preferred often ask their political representatives to override the market decisions. No basis exists for determining prices better than those arising in the market. Buyers hit with higher prices and sellers facing lower ones complain. Elaborate rationalizations are developed about why the prices are undesirable. Proposals are made that the appropriate prices should be based on subjective criteria of worthiness. These then become the excuse for ill-advised protectionist policies.

Nonmarket valuations, at best, would be based on tradition and at worst on assertions by interest groups. Such subjectively-determined prices thwart shifting resources out of inefficient existing uses (as in farm price supports) or encourage moving resources into less productive new uses (such as motor fuels from grain in the United States). Thus, no one has defined a workable alternative to market prices.

Those familiar with the history of economic thought will recognize the influence on the prior discussion of allegations in the economic literature that ecclesiastic scholars advocated prevalence of just prices, not necessarily determined in the market. Distinguished efforts (see, e.g., Schumpeter 1954) to prove the ecclesiastics had more sophisticated views have not stamped out belief that a just-nonmarket-price concept existed. In part, the contrary vision persists because the germane literature is too inaccessible to evaluate. The more critical rationale, however, is that implied by the prior discussion. The belief in imposing a just nonmarket price, whoever originated or believed in it, well describes protectionism in every era.

More broadly, Schumpeter's (1954) dismissal of Adam Smith's contributions seems inappropriate. Smith is readily available to any who make a modest effort. The prior writings are scattered and, as described by their most sympathetic reviewers, much less coherent and harder to interpret than Smith.

Similarly, the profit motive acts as an effective means of both encouraging attempts at imaginative new ventures and terminating them if they fail. The worst possible outcome is that a large company with high profits in other businesses will be too slow in recognizing a failure. Governments can use tax revenues to sustain favored activities (including subsidizing unprofitable private practices). Government, thus, is more likely than private enterprise to perpetuate inefficient activities.

A second, less widely considered problem is that individual tastes may offend aesthetic sensibilities. Critics of economics often make this argument; George Stigler's ([1962] 1984) discussion seems the best response. He argued that market economies are better viewed as reflecting tastes rather than molding them. Economics cannot ensure good taste or even tell us how it could be defined or developed. Economics warns of the perils of imposing tastes or anything else on the individual. Mises (1956, 52) presented a less well-developed version of this argument.

A key aspect of Stigler's argument is that calls for better taste are a form of advocacy of protectionism. Protectionists seek to make their pleadings more attractive by asserting that some noble purpose is served. However, this is easier to do for culture and nature than for commercial interests. Thus, cultural organizations in the U.S. regularly assert their special merits, and many countries assert a desire to defend their cultures from vulgar American offerings. Those protectionists better able to convince people of nobility may have greater success than those using more traditional arguments.

Further Reflections on the Benefits of Interdependence

The theories sketched above add up to a rousing endorsement of free and unrestricted trade within and among economies. This universalism clearly conflicts with the depressingly widespread belief in the parochial arguments advanced by protectionists. An example so classic that is considered the quintessence of protectionism is restriction of international trade. As often as counterarguments are made, protectionist ideas, based mainly on xenophobia, reappear. For example, the press and politicians fail to recognize that the *primary* victims of policies that either restrict free trade or subsidize exports are the citizens of the countries imposing the policies. This is particularly clear for export subsidies. By definition, the citizens of subsidizing countries are providing aid to foreigners. These aids to foreigners usually are the unintended side effects of efforts to protect some national industry. However, some countries have been of accused displaying a mania for exports. The causes of export subsidies are secondary to their implications to other countries. If the beneficiaries refuse such gifts, they harm themselves.

Charges of predation, criticized in chapter 4, are frequently used to justify thwarting foreign or other sources of vigorous competition. The theory is that the price cuts are temporary expedients to drive out competition and that once the competition is eliminated, prices will be raised to monopolistic levels much higher than those charged by the eliminated rivals. The critical flaw in the argument is the predation usually will do no more than destroy the specific firms presently competing. The resources needed to create new rivals remain. Thus, efforts to charge monopoly prices will be thwarted by creation of new competitors, and the profitability of predatory pricing is questionable even if rivals can be eliminated (see chapters 4 and 5).

Another issue is the fairness of subsidy to those displaced. It is doubtful whether the risks of being subsidized out of existence should be treated any differently from other risks of participating in the market economy. Much of the case is clearly specious. Countries too often denounce foreign actions and ignore the subventions prevailing domestically. Subsidization often is hard to document, and the review process often includes a bias towards uncritical acceptance of charges by domestic industries.

In some ways, attacks on international trade are less insidious than some newer developments. Over two centuries of argument have forced those seeking to secure protection from international trade to seek arguments that better disguise the self-serving nature of their mission. Many comparable attacks on market decisions escape scrutiny because they have been less fully recognized. For example, it has taken several decades for at least a substantial minority of economists to recognize the validity of Milton Friedman's (1962) concerns that licensing rules and his later (1980) observation that the favored position of government-run schools were protectionist devices.

Another example that is still inadequately criticized is the frequent call for simpler more self-sufficient approaches. Twentieth century fads such as Amory Lovins's (1977) *Soft Energy Paths* and E. F. Schumacher's (1973) appropriate technologies are but the latest in a long line of such thoughts. Lovins tries to maintain the untenable position that he can determine from his Colorado workshop which technologies, invariably those that operate on smaller scales than those presently employed, are preferable. Schumacher similarly asserts that "appropriate" technologies should be devised for poor countries. This proposal is either tautological or another arrogant assertion of abilities far beyond anyone's knowledge to determine what is best. It is also wildly incongruous coming from a man whose occupation was an apologist for a bloated bureaucracy--the British National Coal Board.

Chapter 3

An Introduction to Market Failures

This chapter deals with the market failure complications neglected in the simplified model presented in chapter 2. An overview is given first, and then issues related to specific market failures are discussed. The discussion employs the proposition more fully developed in chapter 6 that the market failure argument neglects the difficulties of implementation. These problems are clear enough that they can be sensed before the full criticism is presented.

Market Failure

The chief market failures are inability to supply public goods, monopoly power, and imperfect foresight (see Bator 1958). Another, possibly the most critical violation of the assumptions of idealized general equilibrium is the government failure of distorting taxation. Distorting taxation refers to the way in which most feasible-to-impose taxes interfere with equating rates of substitution. For example, income taxes may discourage work efforts. Chapter 11 discusses some of the many ways that taxes and fees for access to public land have created inefficiencies in mineral exploitation. Before analyzing these concepts, definitions are needed.

Public goods are those simultaneously consumed (as in national defense) or nearly simultaneously consumed (as in roads and bridges) by many individuals. Considerable difficulties supposedly exist in getting the beneficiaries together to contribute the needed funds. Samuelson's (1954) presentation of the theory included an undocumented presumption that government intervention was needed to ensure efficient supply. A group classified as public-choice economists has proposed methods to improve public-good supply decisions (Buchanan and Tullock 1962, Mueller 1989). As discussed below, Coase argues that in many cases, private decisions will be more efficient.

Monopoly power here is a general term for any case in which an individual economic entity has a large influence on market prices. Large, in this context, means the individual recognizes and reacts to the impact. In particular, activity is restrained to reduce price movements unfavorable to the possessor of monopoly power.

Imperfect capital markets refers to an alleged inability of private markets to ensure that risks can be reduced sufficiently that all socially profitable investments are undertaken.

Until Coase's 1960 work on social costs, it was widely believed that another, separate problem was "externalities"--the harm or benefits unintentionally caused people other than those engaged in a particular transaction. Coase proved that the existence of an externality did not inevitably involve market failure. Under favorable circumstances, an efficient market solution could arise.

Coase demonstrated that externalities are not necessarily market failures and if any failure occurs it is a special case of a public-good difficulty. The key to success or failure in dealing with externalities was the cost of implementing a private solution. With low costs, an efficient market solution would emerge. High costs could impede attaining efficiency. Such high costs would occur when the number of affected parties is large. However, the problem of inability to deal efficiently because of large numbers *is* the public-good question.

As discussed further in chapter 10, neglect of this result and Coase's inferences from it have contributed to deficiencies in environmental policies. In particular, Coase's warning that the public solution also may be unattainable is totally ignored by policy makers and too many of the economists who profess to be following Coase.

This stress on market failures has many drawbacks. Criticisms of actual markets generally ignore that the defects reduce, rather than eliminate, the benefits of market economies. Every market failure recognized in economic theory prevents the full attainment of equality of rates of substitution. However, mutually beneficial trades still prevail. It is unwise to abandon the market because it does not produce all that hypothetically would occur in an idealized economy.

As discussed in chapter 2, the general equilibrium model is tacit, at best, about virtues of markets such as technical progress. The market failure argument may suffer from unduly narrow views of the market. Market failure is another economic concept that has more ambiguous implications than its users and critics recognize. Some observers of public policy uncritically seek to develop market-failure justifications. Credulity is pushed excessively. This causes concern that the concept provides too much support for unwise regulation. With proper skepticism, including recognition of the tendency to misuse economic arguments, market-failure analysis can provide the basis for an extensive attack on intervention. The absence of plausible market failure rationales often suffices to demolish the case for many programs.

The Public-Good Problem and its Limitations

The most fully accepted argument for intervention relates to what is variously known as the public-good, collective-consumption, or nonexclusivity problem. Situations arise in which it is impossible or at least infeasible or undesirable to exclude anyone from consumption of a commodity. Both promoting desirable widespread activities and discouraging scattered harms are involved. Goods such as national defense and air pollution are simultaneously consumed by all of society and are classic examples of inherent inabilities to ration consumption.

Uncrowded parks, roads, and other facilities are examples of where exclusion is possible but undesirable. Given these conditions, members of society can use governments to raise the money to ensure that the services are made available. Samuelson (1954, 1955, 1958, 1967a, 1967b, 1969) wrote the classic modern discussions of the problem. He concentrated on the problems of adequate financing of the supply of public goods.

Additionally, governments often regulate the health and safety impacts arising out of direct dealings between employers and employees and buyers and sellers. In these cases the disbursed-impact-barrier-to-transaction problem does not arise directly. The nominal failure is inadequate information about the dangers. It is often suggested that the proper response is to make the facts available. The presumed counterargument that would justify regulation is that education may be more expensive than direct control. Critics of intervention naturally view this argument skeptically (see chapter 10).

Many commentators such as Coase (1988), Buchanan and Tullock (1962), Sugden (1984), and Mueller (1989) have discussed how the publicness question can be resolved. This literature deals both with developing satisfactory rules for whatever the government undertakes and with proposing nongovernmental approaches. For present purposes, it suffices to note that a clear, universally-accepted solution has not emerged. The optimum extent of government and the best way to determine and implement that optimum remain unknown.

Coase (1988) warns that contrary to what Samuelson (1954) suggested, dispersion of benefits does not invariably ensure that a public solution is best. Coase suggests that circumstances often arise when the unwillingness of private parties to participate produces less inefficiency than the unwillingness of legislators to provide assistance.

Most critically, many claims of publicness are invalid. Many clear examples exist of excesses of government provision of services. Many government programs reviewed below involve no publicness (and are lacking other good rationales). Nationalization is undesirable. The management of well functioning industries is not improved; troubled industries are not saved. Excesses of public involvement can occur even in areas where private ownership is often distrusted.

Consider, for example, the traditional case for government provision of park lands. The extent of crowding is the critical determinant of when a zero price is optimal. Once substantial crowding occurs, access charges are needed to limit use. Thus, incomes are generated. It becomes feasible for private owners profitably to own the resource and control use, and no efficiency case can be made for government ownership. Many arguments for retention of public lands for recreation also involve using charges to protect the land from crowding (see chapters 10 and 11).

Examples abound of other defective policies to control market failure. The economics literature on environmental regulation, at least in the United States, attacks the inefficiencies of implementation (see chapter 10). Whether the net effect is positive is unclear. Also, much government support of research is probably misdirected. Aid often goes beyond the support of public-good type knowledge. The standard criticisms relate to government support of "applied" research. This is the type of knowledge production and dissemination that can be marketed and thus needs no subsidy. With the honorable exception of Milton and Rose Friedman, few have challenged the dependence on government aid to "basic" (i.e., unmarketable) research.

American higher education has attained dominance over that in other countries through reliance on extensive government aid. It is difficult to imagine how to retain that eminence without continuing government assistance. However, serious problems are associated with this dependence. Decision making under public scrutiny is excessively timid and too influenced by changing perceptions of what is desirable. Some types of research cannot be supported because they are "controversial." Long before the well-publicized attacks on grants to art that seemed immoral, pressures were exerted to prevent support of policy studies such as of competition in energy that refuted the views of powerful politicians. In short, the system is subject to many undesirable pressures. Similarly academics are too prone to suggest aid to education as a cure and should be more aware, as were Milton and Rose Friedman (1980, 150-

88), of the dangers. The most blatant protectionists are convinced of their importance to the economy and sincerely believe that they deserve aid. Educators should be more concerned that they too will overstate their case.

A final point to note is the difference between financing and supplying public goods. Traditional attacks on government stress limiting what is financed. Recognition has increased that the public-good argument only justifies government financing of activities. The theory provides no rules for determining how the money could be spent. The services could be provided by establishing government agencies or by hiring private firms. The choice would be based on which alternative is cheapest.

Governments often excessively extend their self-production. Critics of intervention have become conscious of inadequate consideration of using private suppliers. These analysts contend that governments should increase their reliance on private suppliers. Private supplies of publicly financed education, garbage removal, prisons, and hospitals are among the proposals. Except in the first case, implementation arose.

An Introduction to the Treatment of Monopoly in Economics

Elimination of monopoly power is a widely recognized rationale for government intervention. Monopoly and monopsony are retreats from the competitive outcome of extending trade to the point at which all mutually beneficial trades are completed. Some mutually beneficial transactions are eliminated and more of the benefits of the remaining dealings are transferred to the monopolist or monopsonist. The destruction of desirable deals is a clear loss. The transfers probably are undesirable.

Consider first monopoly. It involves lowering output of some commodities to raise their prices. The lower output deprives consumers of some of these goods. The resources that would have been used to produce the monopolized product are diverted to less desirable uses. The higher price means that the consumers pay the sellers more for the remaining output. Money is merely shifted around. The destructive impacts, traditionally called deadweight losses, have no offset and are the critical net impacts of monopoly. Each output reduction eliminates a transaction worth more to the buyer than the production cost to the seller. Consumer losses to monopoly exceed the profits to the monopolist by the value of the lost consumption. Under special circumstances, discussed most fully in the literature on public utilities, more complex pricing systems can lessen the loss of output to monopoly.

For example, Middle-East oil prices were about $1.00 per barrel in 1970. Had the oil prices risen only with general price levels, the 1980 price would have been about $2. At their 1980 peak, the price actually was around $35 per barrel. Producers thus gained and consumers lost $33 extra dollars on every barrel sold. Unquestionably, oil production and consumption were extinguished to attain this transfer. Much use of oil that would have occurred at $2.00 a barrel must have become unattractive at $35. (World oil production growth was over 7.5 percent per year from 1950 to 1970 and only 2.7 percent per year from 1970 to 1980.)

(The discussion deliberately abstracts from problems of the existence of many different crude oils, each with its own price, and treats the levels associated with the main suppliers. Also ignored are issues of whether the $1 price itself was above efficient levels and, if so, why this was true and where the price might have been had monopolization not occurred. As discussed further in chapter 7, the exact cause of these price rises is still being debated. Most explanations relate to the success of the governments of some oil-producing countries to effect monopolistic restriction of output. Given the plausibility of this explanation and its convenience to the present discussion, it is presumed correct here.)

As discussed in later chapters, many additional questions arise about monopoly. It is conventional to start the analysis by treating a hypothetical "pure" monopolist that has no rivals. However, such pure monopolies do not exist in practice, at least without government support. Even if only one producer of a commodity exists, as once was the case for nickel, that producer faces rivalry from makers of products able to substitute for its product. Even most government sanctioned monopolies such as electricity, telephone, mail, and cable television have rivals. One has to resort to the older practice of granting monopoly over salt sales to find an example of nearly pure monopoly; even here, rivalry from smugglers arose.

As discussed more fully in chapter 4, actual monopolies involve several powerful producers. The existence of multiple participants severely complicates the analysis. Actions must be coordinated, and the theory shows that the outcome is unpredictable. Given these difficulties, some observers argue that monopolization can only succeed when directed by an all-powerful government.

Monopsony, monopolization of purchasing, involves restricting buying below its efficient level. Again, destruction of desirable trade allows a transfer of wealth. Similarly, avoiding monopsonization eliminates trade destruction. Direct aid can more efficiently provide needed transfers.

When direct aid is hard to secure, people may feel justified in resorting to interfering with trade. Such arguments characterized a call in the 1970s for a new international order. A major component would have been cartels to aid poor countries. It is rarely the deserving who monopolize so the qualification has dubious practical relevance. Critics of visions of a new world order suggest that aid to less developed countries would benefit only the autocratic rulers.

Analysis of these issues has concerned many economists for many decades. Chapter 4 is devoted to presenting a survey of this effort.

Imperfect Capital Markets

A charge that markets do not sufficiently provide for the future is often made by economic theorists and used by business executives seeking subsidies. However, this seems largely another (perhaps the prime) example of how too many economists inadequately recognize how much support for intervention is self-serving. The argument about neglect of the future is repeated incessantly without supporting evidence. Attacks on the shortsightedness of bankers are the predictable outcome of failures to secure financing. It is suggested that some projects are too big or too risky to finance. This is a popularization of the imperfect capital market concept. The record suggests the contentions should be disregarded.

The most frequently encountered theoretic argument about why the market inadequately values the future is wrong. The assertion is based on concern that markets do not exist to permit hedging against all risks. The provision of such markets is optimal only under the invalid assumption that all these markets can be created costlessly (or at least at a cost less than the net benefits). When markets cost money to operate, then they should exist only when the benefits of having a market suffice to cover the costs of running it. (Stigler 1968, 113-22 presents a similar discussion.)

Therefore, the most that can be concluded is that the number of markets available might be significantly different from the optimum. An excess, rather than a deficiency, of markets might prevail. The critics of markets are willing to argue, when expedient, that markets do too much. A particularly popular version of this view is that Wall Street or the Rothschilds needlessly churn up activities (Hobson 1938). As this reference to the Rothschilds was deliberately intended to suggest, anticapitalism often, as discussed below, is tainted by vulgar biases. Such contentions imply that too many markets are created.

Observation of the ingenuity of financial institutions produces grave doubts about the applicability of the contention that the market does not allow enough hedging. Financial institutions have proven adroit at responding to new opportunities. Innovations in financing occur regularly. In the U.S., it is possible for the small investor to buy mutual funds holding almost any type of asset--government bonds, many different types of stock portfolios ranging from things as broad as all 500 stocks in the Standard and Poors Index or as narrow as a single industry, short-term notes, and real estate. Funds specializing in foreign investment proliferated. The upheaval in world oil inspired the rise of many financial innovations including spot and futures markets in selected crude oils (Verleger 1993). Many large, long-lead-time projects around the world are routinely financed by private investors. Even nuclear plants could readily acquire funds until regulators undermined the projects. Knowledge industries, particularly at universities, are politically influential and may not suffer from underfunding.

Conversely, governments too often concentrate their efforts on bad investments such as corporate bailouts and public works that cost far more than the benefits produced. The large number of unwise public investments suggests that major government failures plague political efforts to provide for the future. Examples include waterways and railroads that will never repay the money invested in them and the British-French venture into the supersonic transport, the Concorde. The promotion of Airbus was more successful but still of doubtful worth. The tunnel under the English Channel threatens to become another example. The effort to promote "alternative" energy sources (anything but what we heavily use now) involves many further dubious efforts. The wisdom of nuclear subsidies remains controversial, but the evidence suggests aid continued after private firms became willing to invest (Zimmerman 1987). Synthetic fuels proved difficult to finance, not because of the bigness of the projects, but because the economics are unattractive. Even South Africa with the barriers supposedly imposed by international sanctions is probably worse off for having promoted synthetic fuels. The costs exceed those of getting oil on the world market even with the (ineffective) UN boycott. (See Cohen and Noll, 1991 for appraisal of U.S. government technology-promoting programs; the book provides an overview and six case studies, of which four are in energy.)

Government policy is often the problem rather than the solution. Bans on investments by foreigners hinder development in many countries. This record makes it inappropriate to base public policy on claims of less adequate attention to the future by the private sector than by the public sector.

However, a more sophisticated and even more ambiguous argument treating the impacts of the existence of income taxes can be used to raise concerns about treatment of the future. The appropriate interest rate for society to use may differ markedly from the market rate of interest. What that rate should be is difficult to determine and potentially different for different decisions. Lind (1982) reviews the arguments applied to valuing government expenditures. He proposes a refinement of earlier proposals to use an intermediate rate. The correct value depends upon the nature of both what the use of the resources and how they are obtained. The value can range from below after-tax yields to above before-tax rates. The value depends upon what kinds of spending governments undertake and displace. If government activities are primarily at the expense of consumption, the interest cost is closer to the after-tax yield to individuals. If expenditures are mainly at the expense of investment, the interest charge should be closer to the before-tax interest costs of firms. Lind (1982, 31) notes that severe distortions would justify tax reform. Given the orientation here for suggesting improved government policies, a proposal for really reforming taxes would be appropriate. However, the literature on this area is already well developed by more expert observers.

This suggests that the charges often made about the excessive shortsightedness of American industry are overdone. However, it is probable that the tax laws perniciously affect investment in many ways, most notably the double taxation of corporate profits.

Exhaustion of Mineral Resources

The exhaustibility of mineral resources (Hotelling 1931) does not alter this argument. Extensive economic analysis of the issue has shown no special market failures are associated with exhaustion. Markets can be and are designed to trade in exhaustible resources. The possible barriers to efficient working of the markets for exhaustible resources are identical to those in other markets. A monopoly argument is of limited interest since monopoly output reduction only delays exhaustion. Most concerns about the market solution to exhaustion involve the capital-market failure argument. The same counterarguments, therefore, apply.

Moreover, the often encountered presumption that capital-market imperfection inevitably produces premature exhaustion is incorrect. In the usually employed models, imperfection of capital markets produces higher than efficient interest rates. A classic problem in analyzing the effect of interest rate changes is that results from simple models rarely generalize. Thus, in a simple model of exhaustion, the output-retarding influence of lowering the cost of waiting is the only effect of lower interest rates that occurs. The basic influence is that interest rates are effectively the prices of waiting. Like all lower prices, lower interest rates encourage the activity, in this case waiting. More general models (Gordon 1966) show that lower interest rates also reduce the cost of production by reducing the cost of using plant and equipment and stimulate output increases. The critical effect is that lower interest rates raise profitability and higher profitability increases the desire to produce. This speeds up production and exhaustion. The net effect of the two influences is indeterminate.

The cost impact will predominate when, as appears to be the dominant case in practice, profits are low. Then, discount rates will have more effect on costs than on the difference between price and cost. Moreover, one classic theoretic vision of how best to care for the future, rushing to build up the world's capital stock, would stimulate material use and exhaustion. Extraction is itself a form of investment and thus would accelerate if investment is stimulated.

More critically, historical experience is that minerals have become less scarce. Barnett and Morse demonstrated this in 1963, and subsequent experience has not reversed the conclusion. Similarly, since Malthus, questions have been raised about whether population would grow so rapidly that few people would have rising real incomes. Here factual issues exist about what rate of population change is best. Arguments have been made that at least moderate rises in population further the division of labor and promote the growth of per capita income. Other questions arise about whether people learn to limit population increases sufficiently to permit rising per capita incomes. At the other extreme, proposals are heard radically to reduce world population. The most vigorous ideas propose reduction to very small numbers such as 25,000. This is part of tendency to replace the Biblical view of a humanity centered world with assertions that humanity is an illegitimate part of the world order.

Summary

The main theoretic concerns about markets are failures to provide adequately for public goods, monopoly, and inability properly to invest for future needs. Only those externalities that are public goods might require intervention. The practical importance of all these arguments is unclear. The rationales are often overused, but the exact degree of misuse is unclear. One basis for the attack on regulation is doubt about the applicability of market failure rationales to specific situations.

Chapter 4

Further Problems of Analyzing and Treating Monopoly

Concern about monopoly has long influenced the theory and practice of economic policy. The debates center on what must be done to ensure a competitive economy. The optimistic view is that competitive forces are so strong that all that is necessary is to prevent the government from imposing barriers. It is warned that many government policies claiming to promote competition actually increase inefficiency. The contrary view is that monopolistic forces are so extensive that massive governmental control efforts are needed.

Once again, it is suggested here that economic commentaries differ less than their tone indicates. That some economists have adopted explicitly optimistic views about the vigor of competition and pessimism about the efficacy of regulation is widely discussed. What is less well recognized is that many apparently avid supporters of government policies to promote competition actually do so reservedly and with stress on government-created problems. The belief held in the 1930s that monopoly was widespread has yielded to belief that monopoly is limited but, in some cases, correction is desirable and feasible. The existence of perversion of antimonopoly policy is widely recognized. The optimists think the problem is correctable.

The present chapter seeks to survey this debate. Given the vastness of the subject and the literature, the treatment is selective. As is often done, the antitrust aspects of antimonopoly policy is emphasized. The review of policy is kept general. With so many available surveys, several of which are excellent, a massive review is not needed.[1] The discussion begins with examination of economic approaches to monopoly. I sketch the structure and conduct approaches to monopoly analysis. The contention about structural analyses is that it is now quite widely recognized that no practically applicable methods exist to identify undesirable structures. The conduct section concentrates on practices designed to scare competitors. The conclusion is that the practical importance of these practices is doubted by many specialists and strongly believed by few. A survey of antitrust experience then is given.

Following a particularly strong tradition in economics, this chapter ignores the "problem" of excess competition. Concerns often arise that excess competition

---

[1] At the end of 1980s, many important books appeared on these issues. Scherer acquired a coauthor, Ross, for a third edition (Scherer and Ross 1990) of his classic undergraduate text on industrial organization and two interesting, totally new texts by Carleton and Perloff (1990) and by McGee (1988) emerged. Tirole (1988), Spulber (1989) and Krouse (1990) each produced more advanced texts largely devoted to the relevant theory. Schmalensee and Willig (1989) edited a massive anthology reviewing the literature, again with a stress on theory; key contributions are by Carlton, Eaton and Lipsey, Fudenberg and Tirole, Gilbert, Holmstrom and Tirole, Jacquemin and Slade, Katz, Krugman, Ordover and Saloner, Panzar, Perry, Reinganum, Schmalensee, Shapiro, Stiglitz, Varian, and Williamson.

prevails in the agricultural and to a lesser extent the mineral resource realms. This is the quintessence of the conflict between sound economics and popular policy. Economic analysis has been unable to produce plausible analyses of how competition might be excessive. Discussions usually are presented as examples of the defects of regulation. At best, the arguments to limit excessive competition return us to the conduct arguments criticized here. Claiming excess competition is a typical rationalization of ill-advised demands for protectionism. It is, at best, the predation argument restated. More often, all that is meant is that the industry must shrink to attain profitability, and those who fear they must exit are asking for subsidies.

Economic Views of Monopoly: A Sketch of an Alternative History

The doubts about a market economy inspired by the great depression included suggestions that private monopoly was a serious problem justifying stringent countermeasures such as radically restructuring the economy or implementing some form of planning. The most vigorous calls came from unconventional economists such as Gardiner Means (most famous for Berle and Means 1968, a book that does not deal with monopoly or any other well defined problem). They developed analyses purporting to show why big business harmed the economy.

A response was started by Edward S. Mason (1957) of Harvard. Mason instituted an alternative approach rooted in more traditional economic theory. This effort inspired a less alarmist approach to monopoly and bigness. The responses produced ranged from modest dissents from the Means-type arguments to severe denunciations of Means. Mason's direct contribution to the literature consisted of a few articles dealing with broad issues including the deficiencies of Means's analyses. Mason, however, inspired his students to undertake pioneering studies of the theory and practice of monopoly control. These students became prominent teachers and writers on these issues. By the 1990s, their students' students' students are affecting the debate.

From examination of the writings of Mason and many of his leading students, I conclude that the prior is a more accurate characterization of his approach to industrial organization than that in frequently presented discussions by, e.g., Posner (1979), Adams 1990, Scherer and Ross (1990), McGee (1988), Stigler (1988), and Tirole (1988). These writers suggest the Mason tradition is identical to the Bain structure, performance, and conduct framework noted below. The perpetuation of these distortions is another example of the misstatement of economic views on regulation. Again, the frank enemies of intervention want to exaggerate their originality, and the more cautious want to disguise their distrust of government. Those devoted to the Bain classification enjoy receiving the credit for broad influence. The mathematical theorists use the arguments to indicate their originality.

However, changes at Harvard and Chicago in the 1950s caused Chicago to become the center of an alternative type of monopoly-analysis. Mason's interests shifted radically to such areas as natural resource scarcity and the problems of less developed countries. The Chicago tradition, in contrast, has stressed broad principles, often much more sweeping and unqualified than those in the Harvard tradition, and less detailed empirical analyses.

An Introduction to Monopoly: Structural Analyses

Mason's writings included discussions of the comparative role in appraising competition by viewing structure, i.e., how markets are organized, and performance, i.e., the outcome. Bain (1949, 1956, 1968), particularly in his pioneering textbook extended the argument to suggest that analysis systematically appraises structure, conduct, and performance (the outcome of structure and conduct). Several later writers followed Bain in employing this framework. Others including me feel the divisions are too artificial and restrictive.

The proposals for distinctions among structure, performance, and conduct produced efforts to treat separately each of the three issues. One key deficiency is that most analyses of structure, performance, or conduct are unsatisfactory. Obviously, the sum of deficient parts cannot be a satisfactory synthesis. The structural work includes theoretic models of imperfect competition, efforts to deduce from the theory rules for measuring the degree of monopoly, and attempts--often not grounded in the theory--to estimate how much monopoly prevails.

Diverse views of the nature and importance of monopoly have been explicitly or implicitly expressed in the economics literature. The tension, often epitomized by Adam Smith's (1979a) reflections on the subject, between the desire of firms to monopolize and the difficulty of restraining competitive forces seems widely recognized. (This is a theory that is widely suggested and rarely fully developed in the literature. The present discussion was heavily influenced by the writings and classroom teachings of M.A. Adelman and R. L. Bishop.) The basic idea is too simple to challenge theorists. Once the tension between the desire to monopolize and the formidable barriers to attaining the desire are stated, little more can be added. Theorists too often yield to the temptation to develop more complex, less relevant models. The analysis dates from Cournot's classic study of 1838 and had an explosive growth in the 1980s.

However the analysis is conducted, it produces various policy views. The literature has moved towards greater optimism about the vigor of competition. One polar view is that competitive forces are so strong that actual market economies behave similarly to the idealized economies discussed in chapter 2. The other extreme is concerned with widespread monopoly, usually by a few rather than one firm.

Economic theory distinguishes between natural (inherent) and artificial monopoly. A natural monopoly prevails when the cost advantages of large scale operations are such that only one or a few firms can efficiently serve a market. An artificial monopoly is one where in an effort to restrict competition, the number of independent entities is reduced below the number that could operate efficiently. (Baumol, Panzar, and Willig 1982 provide full, rigorous but technical definitions.)

Natural monopolies allegedly occur mostly in industries such as electric power, gas transmission, and distribution involved in the sales of services from capital assets. Thus, the rationale for electric power and gas pipeline regulation is the existence of large indivisible capital requirements. Natural monopolies are rare in manufacturing or in mineral or agricultural natural resource extraction. Oil once was widely identified as possessing mysterious properties that precluded competition, but Adelman's (1972, 1993a) analyses suggested that the concerns were unjustified. This argument predicted subsequent developments far more satisfactorily than did rival theories. A few commodities with limited demands may be produced under conditions of natural monopoly. For that reason, natural monopoly analysis long was kept separate from general industrial organization economics. The benefits of comparing work in the two areas have caused many newer industrial organization works to include natural monopoly. This is discussed further below in sections on natural monopoly and its control.

Departures from pure competition generally involve the existence of more than one decision maker with a significant effect on price. The economic term for this situation is oligopoly; the alternative name of shared monopoly arose among lawyers. In such a case, the outcome is not readily predicted. It could, in theory, range from attaining a purely monopolistic outcome to behavior approximating that under pure competition. Influences include the ability to create additional competition, the similarity of interests, and the ability to reach and maintain agreement.

As noted, the simplest and, in many ways still the most fruitful, model of oligopoly starts by noting following Adam Smith that every industry wishes to organize as if it were a single-firm monopoly. However, unless a monopoly firm is created by mergers, the desired outcome is unlikely to be attained. Formidable barriers hinder successful cooperation.[2]

Attainment of accord requires, at the minimum, a hard to attain consensus. A complex chain of mutual confidence must prevail. Market riggers must both trust each other *and* believe they are trusted. The firms must agree on what each will do. They must recognize the long-run consequences of keeping and of violating the agreement. They also must be confident that every other firm fully recognizes the consequences of noncooperation and that it desires to maintain the accord. Finally, they must be sure that all the other firms are confident that collaboration will persist.

Absence of mutual confidence is what causes accords to collapse. Failure to understand the consequences of the action is improbable. The more likely problem is that someone begins to fear, possibly incorrectly, that someone else is likely to defect. It only takes one dissident to end the conspiracy, and history demonstrates such deviations usually emerge from panic. Thus, nervousness is appropriate among oligopolists and hinders attainment of the monopolistic outcome.

A critical influence is the difference between the immediate and long-run consequences of violating the market-rigging agreement. The essence of monopoly behavior is that an additional perceptible cost of output increase is a noticeable price effect. The benefit-cost calculation for a monopoly compares the revenue on additional sales to the costs of both increasing production and cutting prices on existing sales. In contrast, the price-cut effect is negligible by assumption for competitive firms.

Those familiar with economic analysis will recognize that this reformulates the presentation. The traditional approach is to compare the net marginal revenue effect to marginal costs. However, that net revenue effect consists of the sales increase benefit less the loss-of-revenue-on-existing-sales cost. The discussion here is

---

[2]The literature is enormous. Key contributors to the older theories include Fellner (1949), Chamberlin (1962), R. L. Bishop (1960), Dewey (1969), and Stigler (1947, 1964). The new approach based on the mathematical theory of games includes contributions in addition to several chapters in Schmalensee and Willig (1989) by Shubik (1959), F. Fisher (1989), James Friedman (1977, 1983), and Shapiro (1989b).

equivalent to the classic one. Those not familiar with the concept stressed by economists of marginal effects should note that these relate to the benefits and costs of changing positions. This emphasis, in turn, is a translation into words the mathematical principle that determination of the best position is best handled by considering the net payoff of each change from the initial position. As long as the changes are beneficial, more moves should be made.

At the monopoly optimum, a disparity prevails between the immediate and long-run consequences for each member of the oligopoly producing more than its agreed output. In the short-run, before others react, the output increase is beneficial. By the definition of an optimum, net industry marginal benefits equal industry marginal costs. By the nature of an output increase by only one firm, the increase will be beneficial to that firm. It has only part of industry output and so incurs only part of the loss on existing sales. The firm also gets all the benefit from extra sales. Thus, the net benefit to the firm exceeds that to the industry by the amount of the losses to lower prices on existing sales borne by the other firms. However, such a breakdown will produce retaliation and leave the firm ultimately worse off. Total industry profits would decline severely, and no firm would be likely to improve its market share sufficiently to offset the impact of a lower total profit.

Recognition of these consequences does not guarantee adherence to the output restrictions. A rush to undermine prices often arises. Producers become convinced that a price drop is coming. They seek to cut their losses by getting a head start and having the higher price and sales that prevail before others retaliate. This is because faith in others is so fragile. As noted, it only takes one person, unaware of the consequences or afraid of others, to start the process. Adelman likes to epitomize the problem as reflecting the cynical life view that, in politer terms than actually used, you should do people in before they do you in. Experience shows that such breakdowns occur frequently. Thus, even the most determined monopolizers fail to maintain collusion. This is why the view that monopoly will not last seems more applicable than Chamberlin's expectation that collusion would persist.

Naturally, the barriers to a monopoly outcome change if other forces further undermine or support collusion. The theorists have examined additional pressures with both effects. One key barrier to collusion is additional potential competition. Some of the devices that may aid collusion are examined below. The basic conclusion is that the barriers make collusion even more difficult than the simple model indicates.

Another problem is that no definitive method is available for measuring the degree of competitiveness. No readily calculable, simply interpretable measure of the degree of competition is available. The textbook definitions stress the absence of a perceptible effect of the firm on price. Practical approaches have stressed various measures of market shares. This approach suffers from many defects. The most fundamental is the difficulty of correctly defining the market. No one, moreover, has determined what constitutes a dangerously high market share. Various proposed improved measures do not fully satisfy the complaints. To effect any computations, a decision must be made about whether given firms are inside or outside the industry. Differences in the degree of substitutability hinder computations of market size.

When the market involves competition among somewhat different goods such as different types of fuels, coals, computers, or packaging materials, share measures cannot be used satisfactorily. The degree of interfuel competition and of the linkages of different sectors of the coal industry is perennially debated. The last two sectors were the subject of major U.S. antitrust cases.

Dupont succeeded in winning acquittal of charges of monopolizing cellophane because claims of vigorous competition from other packaging materials were upheld. This decision was attacked for accepting an unduly broad market definition. Subsequent history showed that the competition ultimately was strong enough to cause the disappearance of cellophane. Whether a decision that Dupont had monopolized would have speeded the rise of competition in packaging or chilled competition elsewhere is a typical area of debate about public policy.

Similarly, IBM's economic defense explicitly emphasized the problems of share measurement. The experts testifying for IBM produced books on the experience. The volume by Fisher, McGowan, and Greenwood (1983) concentrates on the problem of identifying monopoly. The writers argue that the melange of computers of different sizes and vintages is too varied readily to reduce to a simple measure of shares. This analysis antedates the emergence of the boom in microcomputers and the resulting further extensions of competition that greatly weakened IBM.

McGee (1971, 1974, 1988) effectively summarizes the theoretic and measurement problems. He argues that the methods of collecting data give a misleading picture of even the competition prevailing nationally. He believes industries are generally defined too narrowly. He also feels the data use unsatisfactory measures of output. Firms are assigned to an industry on the basis of their principal products. What is reported for each industry then is actually the total value of output of goods of firms assigned to that industry. If a large proportion of output is of goods that compete in other markets, a misleading picture emerges. The contribution to value in the industry to which the firm is assigned is overstated and the contribution to the output of other industries is ignored. While overstatement of concentration is not inevitable, McGee feels that it often occurs. He also reiterates the standard and increasingly relevant reminder that the statistics omit foreign competition.

McGee's discussion (1988, 257-65) of the difference between the cost of monopoly and the degree of monopoly power looks at the role of economies of scale, the cost advantage that may arise from having fewer, larger, and more efficient firms. McGee chastises those concentrating on structures for ignoring these cost impacts. He probably misstates what error prevails.

The limits to structural reform are most obviously recognized in the practice of preserving and regulating natural monopolies. Any rule that makes a specific market share automatic cause for restructuring, however, implicitly assumes scale effects on structure always are irrelevant. Bain (1954, 1956) and others were aware that economies of scale might justify large firms. They believed that they had proved that breaking up large firms would not involve loss of economies of scale. The proper concern then is the adequacy of the proof. At best, the Bain argument proves that many large firms can be broken up without severely raising costs. The possibilities that some exceptions exist and that they may be substantial are good reasons not to adopt purely structural criteria for reorganization.

Bain's evidence on economies of scale was not sufficiently conclusive to disarm critics. The unimportance of size advantages, what constitutes high concentration, and what are the dangers are not firmly established. Policy makers, despite their zeal to regulate, have not been convinced that massive structuring using a mechanical rule is clearly advantageous. Good reason then exists to continue the restrained approach actually employed. Restructuring is considered on a case-by-case basis and rarely attempted. In each case, both sides must develop extensive appraisals of the state of competition. As a result, those restructuring efforts actually litigated often fail.

The proceedings (Goldschmid, Mann, and Weston 1974) of a conference on deconcentration remains the best discussion of the main views. Many leading figures in the study of monopoly participated.[3] In several critical cases, pairs of papers were presented by one of the Chicago economists and someone with a contrasting view. The pairs of most interest were Scherer-McGee and Demsetz-Weiss.[4] In each case, the author presented his interpretation of the available evidence. Scherer suggested Bain's conclusions about economies of scale had been upheld. McGee contended the methodologies used were unsatisfactory. Similarly, Demsetz challenged claims that high concentration produced high profits. Weiss presented extensive data purporting to show a high relationship between concentration and profits.

The summary of the discussions showed that, once again, the discord was overstated. The dialogues about the papers suggest that neither Scherer nor Weiss considered their evidence sufficient to justify a law to break up concentrated industries. Demsetz challenged Scherer on this issue. Scherer's first answer was, "I was not referring to a scheme for deconcentration (108)." When pressed about Demsetz's perception that Scherer thought the costs of deconcentration were slight, Scherer replied, "Okay, that is a fair statement (109)." The discussion moved in other directions so Scherer never amplified how he felt about deconcentration programs. Weiss was favorable about deconcentration (243). Milton Handler, a veteran teacher of antitrust law, then said, "That is based on esthetic instead of economic reasoning (244)." Weiss responded, "I am afraid you're right (244)."

Discussions also stress that competition is furthered by the existence of many actual and potential participants. The meaning of "many" is left undefined. Variant approaches such as Demsetz's (1968) analysis of natural monopoly and the Baumol, Panzar, Willig (1982) model of contestability indicate ways to attain competitive outcomes without large numbers of active firms (see chapter 7 for further discussion). The explosion in the 1980s of development of more formal mathematical models of oligopoly left these conclusions unchanged. The mathematical pyrotechnics supported the previously prevailing conclusion that the outcome depended on the circumstances. Some economists were comforted to see that the theory supported traditions. Others felt the efforts were redundant. A more critical concern is why analysis of oligopoly was considered a pressing problem when expansion of international trade was promoting competition.

---

[3]Others contributing papers or comments beside those cited directly included Donald Dewey of Columbia, Yale Brozen of Chicago, H. Michael Mann of Boston College, Jesse W. Markham of Harvard, Willard F. Mueller and J. Fred Weston of UCLA, Walter Adams of Michigan State, Almarian Phillips of the University of Pennsylvania, and Richard A. Posner of the University of Chicago. The discussion moderators were Adelman, Coase, John Blair (a long-time government economist working on the issues), and Donald Turner. Attendees included Robert Bork, Mark Green (a one-time associate of Ralph Nader and in 1994 an office holder in New York City), Milton Handler, and George Hay. This group thus consisted of economists and lawyers, mostly, but not entirely from academia, who were prominent in the discussion. Some of them are cited later in this chapter.
[4] Weiss is a University of Wisconsin economist with views similar to Scherer.

Thus, the usual inability of economic theory and econometric studies to produce conclusive results has involved particularly severe limitations in the ability to appraise departures from purely competitive behavior. Satisfactory measures of market power have not been produced. Mason ([1939] 1957, 60) noted somewhat confusingly "The theory of oligopoly has been aptly described as a ticket of admission to institutional economics. It is to be regretted that more theorists have not availed themselves of the privilege."

As noted, Mason rejected the antitheoretic approach traditionally associated with institutionalism. Apparently Mason charitably overlooked this aspect of institutionalism and redefined it simply to mean belief in empirical verification. His statement then is simply an argument that facts are needed to settle the debate. The advice remains applicable but must be qualified by recognition that conclusive evidence is difficult, if not impossible, to obtain for reasons illustrated here and further treated below.

Neither theory nor practice gives clear principles for evaluating the extent of monopoly. The search for simple, readily calculated indicators has shown that they do not exist.

The Conduct of Monopoly: The Great Predation Debate and Other Examples

The importance of conduct centers on the relevance of various tactics for enhancing or lessening monopoly impacts. A key characteristic of the Chicago approach is particularly strong skepticism about concerns over anticompetitive conduct. However, few others also are convinced that these tactics are widely employed.

The debate over predation is the most instructive example. The discussion of an intrinsically uninteresting subject was enormously elaborated (in a fashion that dragged in most of the other concepts of monopoly-promoting conduct). At the end, both sides held fast to their views, and the differences were still exaggerated.

A curiosity of the debate is that predation always had a dubious reputation in the economics literature. The idea is that firms sell below cost to chase out rivals, establish a monopoly, and recoup with high future prices. This contention has arisen in discussions of both national industrial organization and international trade. Contributors to the industrial organization discussion show a deplorable neglect of the enormous but apparently now-outdated literature about predatory practices in international trade. (Examination of more recent writings indicates the trade theorists have forgotten the old literature on dumping and also suffer from ignorance of the predation debate in industrial organization.) Numerous examples of false charges of predation by companies facing foreign competition have been provided. Familiarity with this literature (see chapter 5) would have caused greater reluctance to dispute the initial or final skeptical findings of McGee.

By the middle 1950s, predation was considered in both industrial economics and international trade economics primarily as a myth used to justify protectionism. In the days of the robber barons, predation might have been used at times. The charge was more often made by weak firms claiming that their ouster would lead to monopoly. Nevertheless, a long debate subsequently was staged to examine the subject more closely.

Ironically, the new literature was launched from an article by McGee (1958) in which the theoretic criticism of the feasibility of predation was strengthened.

Examination of the historical record showed that predation was rarely, if ever, used. The persistence of concerns, particularly in litigation, produced a second debate in which efforts were made to develop better legal tests of predation. Finally, theorists concerned about the disparity between prior results and the prevalence of charges of predation designed theoretic models in which "predation" might occur. As the discussion unfolded, efforts were made to rescue the argument by broadening predation to include all tactics designed to frighten rivals. These extensions suffered from their own limitations. The tactics were not necessarily undesirable; their detection and elimination involve even greater problems than does regulating simple predation.

Two drawbacks to predatory behavior have produced considerable doubt about the reality of predation. First, success is questionable. Existing firms can be bankrupted, but their physical assets will survive. Efforts to monopolize will be thwarted by reorganization and reentry. Second, as noted, the charges come predominantly from injured competitors. Their inability to compete may arise from their inefficiency. Prices may be below *their* costs but above those of the tough new rivals they face.

McGee (1958) added that the necessity to cover demands at the predatory price meant that the strategy inflicted heavier losses on predator than prey. He concluded that this was not the strategy most likely to be followed since it was cheaper to buy out rivals. He also examined the historical example that previously had often been used to show predation could be a common strategy, the practices of the Standard Oil Trust. He concluded that the results showed Standard had actually bought out rivals at generous prices. Further analyses by Telser (1966), Koller (1971), and Mariger (1978) largely reinforced McGee's conclusion. Yamey (1972) was somewhat more skeptical (and provided the much cited example of shipping cartels in the nineteenth century, in which predation may have occurred). Isaac and Smith (1985) report on work in which subjects competing in market stimulating experiments did not engage in predation.

Much later, Malcolm R. Burns (1986) claimed to find evidence in the record of the American Tobacco case suggesting that American had lowered the cost of buying out rivals by engaging in predation. McGee's (1988) more recent review of predation argues the Burns's results are so uncertain and limited in occurrence that fears about predation still seem unwarranted. Theorists have proposed but not demonstrated the empirical relevance of more complex models in which predatory-like toughness can be an effective strategy for a multimarket firm. McGee's critics stress that his initial argument may have overstated the case. This obscures the more basic point that the possibilities for predation were exaggerated by others. McGee simply indicated further theoretic and practical flaws in the already weak case for arguing that predation is a significant policy problem.

The second debate over predation was initiated by a 1975 article by Areeda and Turner of Harvard Law School. (The two were antitrust specialists at Harvard Law. Turner had served as the U.S. Assistant Attorney General in charge of antitrust.) The dispute continued vigorously into the early 1980s, and was still inspiring work into the 1990s. The discussion attracted the interests of many leading industrial economics specialists and wandered into many other aspects of conduct to further monopoly. Areeda and Turner responded (1976, 1978) to the earliest critics.

Areeda and Turner's initial article discussed how to identify predation if it existed. They proposed using evidence that the standard economic criterion, selling below marginal cost, was met or, as a proxy, selling below variable costs. Variable costs are those whose existence depends upon whether or not production occurs. The idea was developed to indicate the difference between economic and accounting definitions of costs. Accountants always include in costs incorrectly calculated measures of what is required to repay past investments. (All conventional accounting techniques are economically defective because of, among other things, a failure to adjust for changes in the overall price level and the cost of individual goods. Investment cost figures suffer from these defects and omission of the cost of using stockholders' funds.) Sometimes outlays that are actually investments in future output are charged to current output. The variable-cost concept is designed to purge accounting costs of such charges. Those charges persist whatever happens to current operations. What is appropriate for deciding whether any current operations persist is what is actually saved by a shutdown. Variable costs measure that saving.

Numerous criticisms of the Areeda-Turner approach to detecting predation followed from many prominent economists including Scherer (1976a, 1976b), Williamson (1977, 1979b), Baumol (1977), Joskow and Klevorick (1979), and Ordover and Willig (1981a, 1981b). The writings spilled over several law journals and inspired a conference sponsored by the U.S. Federal Trade Commission (FTC), which published the proceedings (Salop 1981). Contributors include Gilbert, Hay, Plott, Michael Porter, and Spence. Brodley and Hay (1981) provide another survey.

Attention quickly turned to the overall importance of imperfect competition. Starting with Scherer's (1976a, 1976b) criticism of Areeda and Turner, the debate began to encompass other tactics to lessen competition, particularly of cases where existing firms had to consider the threat of entry. Ordover and Willig (1981a, 1981b) suggested examining whether excessive innovation thwarted competition. Other debated tactics include the feasibility of using price wars to scare away rivals. Ordover and Saloner (1989) provide a review with extensive citations of writings on scare tactics. Katz (1989) covers cases of the imposing conditions of purchase that reinforce monopoly power.

Ultimately, such critics of concerns over predation as McGee (1980), Easterbrook (1981), and Sidak (1983) produced appraisals reflecting their outlook. In particular, McGee (1980) analyzed all the then extant proposals for more elaborate criteria than those suggested by Areeda and Turner. The debate has several elements. These include the importance of simple predation as defined by Areeda and Turner, the reasonability of their proposed test, the importance of the other types of conduct about which others were concerned, and the importance of nonpredatory efforts to lessen competition.

McGee (1980) naturally inquired why so dead an issue inspired concern. It was not until the later appearance of the proceeding of the FTC conference (Salop 1981) that an acceptable answer appeared. It contained a paper by Hurwitz, Kovacic, Sheehan, and Lande showing that courts still remained concerned about predation. A 1990s update would be that the argument keeps reemerging in international trade debates.

Although the proponents denied the charges, the advocates of more complex procedures were criticized by McGee (1980), Easterbrook (1981), and others for undermining Areeda and Turner's search for clearer legal principles. The Areeda-Turner criterion that predation requires prices below marginal cost seemed (correctly) to McGee (1980) the most reasonable of the proposed approaches. If anything, the rule is too strict. Cases arise in which selling below marginal production cost is justified by future profits generated. Payoffs include learning about the market, making customers aware of the product, and "learning-by-doing" cost reductions.

The critics proposed various, more elaborate tests of which a full review is not necessary here. Some suggested looking at output behavior; others suggested restricting subsequent price changes. The most complex was Joskow and Klevorick's (1979) suggestion of undertaking a "simple" analysis of market conditions. McGee's (1980) complaints about the drawbacks of all these proposed complications raise valid concerns about the difficulties of sensible application. For example, it is difficult to accept the Joskow and Klevorick view that simple analyses were feasible. The pressures for comprehensive analyses illustrated here in chapter 11 are hard to curb.

The most critical defect is one not adequately noted in the debate. (McGee, for example, only hints at it.) The Areeda and Turner variable cost rule cannot be implemented. Variable costs of a product can only be defined meaningfully for a single product firm. All that can be estimated is the saving on shutting down a portion of the business. This is the cost of change, i.e., the marginal cost. Thus, no substitute for marginal cost analysis exists.

The extensions of the discussion to nonpredatory actions are problematic because appraisal is even more difficult than in predation. The possibility that the profitability of the industry would attract new firms and that behavior of existing firms might be modified to lessen this entry had been the subject of considerable prior work. Scherer's (1976a) critique of Areeda and Turner stressed the idea of entry deterrence by "limit pricing" discussed by such prior writers as Bain in the 1950s, Sylos-Labini (1969), Modigliani (1958), and Gaskins (1971).

As is often not made explicit, analyses of limit prices distinguish between cases in which the number of potential rivals is small and those in which numerous entrants may exist. As Gilbert (1989, 478) points out, questions arise about whether the price and output behavior with limit pricing is necessarily inferior to that with entry. Nearly competitive behavior may be required to prevent entry. Cases can be conceived in which the costs of excessive entry or more relevantly, excessive government efforts to preserve inefficient rivals exceed those of the modest or even nonexistent excesses of price over marginal cost needed to deter entry.

The initial emphasis in the literature on entry was on keeping prices down to discourage entry. Later writers have suggested that in some cases waiting until entry occurs and either cooperating with or fighting against entrants might be preferable. Such strategies are most feasible when the number of entrants is limited. Where large numbers of entries are possible, price restraint prior to entry may be necessary.

Thus, Baumol, Panzar, and Willig (1982) developed their analysis of contestability to indicate the circumstances under which the optimal response to the threat of entry is behaving as if the industry were competitive. This was presented as the most competitive of the many possible cases and was related to the whole range including the opposite pole of natural monopoly. The authors, nevertheless, have been criticized as unduly optimistic about the empirical relevance of contestability.

McGee (1980, 1988) argued that forestalling entry was futile since the entrant could contract for sales outlets; therefore, entry limitation has no greater empirical relevance than predation. McGee's discussion refrains from adding either Coase's (1937) point (see chapter 6) that integration is an alternative to contract or the view of Stigler (1951) and others that integration often occurs to bypass monopoly pricing.

Another key area of concern over conduct is the one that worried Ordover and Willig (1981a, 1981b) of efforts by firms to carve special positions by marketing new products, altering the quality of the product and support services provided, and advertising their availability and prowess. When viewed at the FTC conference, the argument for policy surveillance was criticized because of the resulting threat to beneficial innovation. (See the critique of the Ordover and Willig paper by Easterbrook in Salop 1981, 415-46. See further comments by Turner, 675-88 and others, 695-701). All this suggests that although Chicago economists are particularly unsympathetic to the concepts of predation and limit pricing, few others vigorously contend that these are central public policy issues.

As noted, the later theoretic efforts develop models showing under what circumstances "predation" and other forms of aggressive behavior pay off by causing rivals to cede markets. Threats include aggressive preemptive expansion and vigorous response to rivalry. Milgrom and Roberts (1987) provide a lucid, favorable literary summary of the work and an extensive bibliography. The major industrial organization texts and surveys all also review the debate; of particular interest are the chapters in Schmalensee and Willig (1989) on predation by Ordover and Saloner (1989) and by Gilbert (1989) on the related area of mobility barriers. (Other contributions include Easley, Masson, and Reynolds 1985, Fudenberg and Tirole 1984, Roberts 1986, Krattenmaker and Salop 1986, Kreps and Wilson 1982, Saloner 1987, and Milgrom and Roberts 1982.)

Again questions arise about whether this is a challenging extension or repackaging of ideas of limited relevance. The enthusiasts suggest that these subtle pressures may be more effective than the allegedly blunter ones previously discerned. Gilbert's point seems applicable here too; it is not evident that successful maintenance of position is possible without sacrificing almost all the monopoly profits.

Another often discussed tactic is price discrimination. It is well treated analytically by Varian in Schmalensee and Willig (1989) and Varian (1992). This involves selling the same product to different customers at different prices or having the price of each good to each customer differ with the quantity purchased. Discrimination is advantageous to a monopolist because it lessens (and, in the theoretic extreme case, eliminates) the losses on existing sales by cutting prices only on sales to those customers most responsive to price cuts. Discrimination is possible only when high transaction costs preclude arbitrage. Otherwise, the person receiving the lower price would resell to the person paying the higher cost.

This is a tricky area in which to make determinations. Ascertaining whether identical products are involved requires consideration of all the attributes such as support and delivery services associated with different sales. Quantity discounts may reflect the transaction cost savings of large-scale sales. Discrimination is involved only if the price difference is not due to cost differences. Cost differences, in turn, can be difficult to measure. A consensus prevails between Chicago and others that the 1936 Robinson-Patman Act attacked efficiencies of large scale buying through an overly stringent requirement to prove such economies existed (see below).

Even if discrimination arises, its consequences are ambiguous. It has long been known that if discrimination is extensive enough, it can eliminate monopoly inefficiency; the literature on pricing by natural monopolies regularly presents this argument (Berg and Tschirhart 1988). Work in the 1980s centered on discussion of circumstances in which more limited discrimination lessens or worsens the curse of monopoly (Varian 1989, 1992). The simplest cases of discrimination involve segmenting customers in a small number of groups. By definition, at least two groups must exist.

In the absence of discrimination, the monopolist will seek the most profitable uniform price. No profitable opportunities to raise prices will be neglected. In moving from a unified to discriminatory structure, prices are raised for some and lowered for others. The first group then consumes less and loses more from the monopoly. The second group then consumes more and loses less from monopoly. Conversely, the issue then is whether the gains of the second group exceed the losses of the first. Varian showed that the gains of the second could not exceed the losses of the first if output did not rise. However, an output rise did not guarantee a gain. Varian (1989, 1992) developed a formula for determining how high an output rise was required to produce a gain.

An earlier proposition developed by Adelman in his numerous writings about retailing and petroleum is that the ability to discriminate facilitates undermining cartel accords. By extension of the prior argument about why price fixing efforts break down, the individual firm benefits are greater if discrimination allows limiting concessions to new customers. Thus, another problem with regulating discrimination is that it can lessen such incentives to weaken a cartel. Adelman added that the process is accelerated if the buyers are large and sophisticated enough to recognize and exploit weaknesses in collusion. He further observed that the ability to benefit depended on the absolute volume of purchases. The sophisticated buyers had to purchase on a scale large enough that the benefits of lower prices exceeded the transaction costs of securing them.

He further stressed that these buyers need not and in the retail and oil cases did not possess monopoly power. Their markets were large to allow the survival of many firms of the scale necessary to maintain a sophisticated buying organization. Thus, competition among buyers caused the benefits of their actions to go to final customers. As is rarely, if ever, noted in discussions of Galbraith's (1952) vision of countervailing power, Galbraith explicitly indicated that his analysis was adapted from Adelman's. Galbraith did not incorporate the presumption of competition among buyers in the resale market and thus introduced concerns about the outcomes absent from the Adelman analysis. Without competitive pressures, buyer efforts may only transfer monopoly profits.

While the possibility of increased competition is recognized, so is the opposite one of discrimination thus increasing the strength of a company in a fashion making it less vulnerable to attack. We have those who want a policy that can identify and appropriately respond to the type of discrimination being practiced, those who favor banning discrimination, and those who would tend not to prohibit it. This is another case in which uncertainty prevails about what to do. Chicago, however, is not unique in being skeptical about the wisdom of prohibiting discrimination given that the effects are so uncertain.

Yet another conduct issue is the role of diversification. Firms can expand into the production (or sale) of goods used with the goods they presently produce--paper for copiers or disks for computers, for example. Several observers have argued that this can facilitate discrimination. It may be prohibitively expensive to meter use, but paper usage is an indirect indicator and the discrimination in pricing may occur in varying the paper price. (This example and many similar ones have been outmoded by legal bans, the lower cost of metering, changes in the germane technologies, and increases in competition.)

Similarly, entry may be vertical integration. Conditions can occur in which vertical integration can facilitate price discrimination that would not be possible without integration. Conversely, a firm victimized by monopoly in buying or selling can obviate this by vertically integrating. (For a good formal survey see S. Grossman and Hart 1986.)

McGee and Bassett (1976) have pointed out that traditional analysis of vertical integration takes too narrow a focus. The key to monopoly gains is restricting sales to final consumers. Organization to effect such restrictions can involve action at any stage of processing. Analysis should be directed at the best way to monopolize. Control of final sales has the advantage of not distorting the actions in earlier processing stages. In particular, the monopoly price for the partially processed good encourages undesirable reductions in its use. An advantageous situation might be where the raw material production is easier to monopolize than the final product production. Any appraisal is incomplete if it does not compare integration to other methods of monopolizing. Again, questions arise about the practical importance of monopoly through integration. These illustrations suggest that the Chicago skepticism about the relevance of various strategies for monopolizing does little more than codify the warnings in the economics literature that such devices have questionable efficacy.

Antimonopoly Policy

Specialists on monopoly are better able to agree on the drawbacks than on the benefits of intervention. Many views prevail about the extent of monopoly, the degree to which it is natural, and the ability of governments to effect improvements. At least three major subissues about the control of monopoly can be noted--the role of sanctions against market-rigging, the role of efforts to restructure industry, and the role of direct regulation. Here as elsewhere, pessimism about governments is at least as important as optimism about markets in inspiring an anti-intervention stance. The uncertainty produces comparably extensive opinions about what should be done. Many observers are skeptical of both restructuring and direct regulation.

Accord is greatest in opposing government *support* of market-rigging. All recognize that government is a prime source of monopoly. Too much government policy, including many laws ostensibly passed in the name of controlling monopoly, actually promotes monopoly by sheltering firms from competition. Too often, this outcome is intentional. The clearest needs are for removal of monopoly-preserving laws and regulations and for making market-rigging contracts unenforceable.

Government monopoly-creating acts often are justified as protecting the unfortunate from the alleged excesses of competition. The most pervasive and clear-cut example is agriculture. Throughout the industrialized western world, governments have acted for a half century or more to protect farmers from competition. In less developed and communist countries, governments turn their monopoly power against farmers and force prices down below competitive levels. Just as textbook economics predicts, the result is perennial excesses of output over consumption (gluts) in developed countries and less output than desired consumption (shortages) elsewhere. (See chapter 9 for further comments.)

Prointervention sentiment, however, is so powerful that the strongest possible evidence that markets are competitive is ignored. Belief that U.S. oil markets are monopolistic survives extensive evidence to the contrary. Discussion of these controversies appears below.

In short, while theoretical analysis leaves open how big a role the market should play, applied studies show considerable skepticism about the practice of intervention. Even those policies supposedly designed to promote efficiency can be used to increase inefficiency. Again, debate prevails about how best to effect a more clearly efficiency-promoting policy.

The U.S. pioneered a two-phased antitrust program of general rules as an alternative to industry-specific regulation. The stronger element of the policy is that of banning practices that are believed to facilitate monopoly. The second, less effective approach is by controlling existing companies by enforced restructuring to foster competition. The laws started with the Sherman Act in 1890. It forbade various types of actions by existing firms and created power to break up large companies with monopoly power. Later laws increased the ability to block mergers that promote monopoly and banned other forms of conduct.

Given the many discussions available at several levels of complexity, exhaustive review of antitrust is not essential here. The literature is enormous with both economists and lawyers contributing.[5] The critical point is that antitrust enforcement is heavily criticized for frequent anticompetitive decisions. This defect is considered reformable even by the Chicago school and calls for abolition come from elsewhere.

On the rule-making side, the most widely accepted element of the policy is the total ban on cartels that the U.S. Supreme Court long ago said was implicit in the Sherman Act. The Supreme Court believed that the possibility for good was so remote and the monitoring problems so severe that a ban was justified. This conclusion is strongly supported in the economics literature.

Just how far the extensions of the conspiracy concept should go is still being debated. Economic theory indicates that in principle the results of a formal agreement could be produced through signals conveyed by output decisions. Firms could maintain behavior patterns that indicated they would fight price cutting actions and support price raising ones. Without any direct contact among rivals, the results of a cartel agreement could be secured. Courts understandably are reluctant to apply this economic concept of tacit cooperation. The theory fails to provide ways to identify such behavior in a fashion that conforms to basic legal standards of proof.

Conversely, concerns are often expressed by a wide range of observers, including both some advocates of national planning and vigorous critics of intervention, that antitrust policy is overdone. The courts had difficulties

---

[5]The economics texts covering industrial organization and its regulation (e. g., McGee 1988, Scherer and Ross 1990, and Carlton and Perloff 1990) cover antitrust. Numerous law texts such as by Areeda (1980), Handler (1967) and by Posner and Easterbrook (1981) are devoted to the subject. Many surveys are available. Those by Bork (1978) and Posner (1976), both highly critical of existing practice, are particularly widely cited. A review stressing the details is Neale and Goyder 1980. A good brief view of the impacts was prepared by Stigler (1966). Hofstadter (1965) wrote an essay that gives a useful perspective on how inertia preserved enforcement long after the issue lost its popular appeal. Important articles include Baumol and Ordover (1985), Cooper (1974), Landes and Posner (1981), and Easterbrook (1984). Pratt (1980) reevaluates the contribution of antitrust to competition in the oil industry.

distinguishing desirable data collection efforts from those designed to aid collusion. Another concern is restrictions on cooperative research.

A resolute opponent of etatism would contend that refusal of support to cartels is sufficient government action. The inability to enforce accords combined with the tendency to fail would be a sufficient deterrent. Others argue that Section 1 of the Sherman Act has had largely beneficial effects and does not need reform. Other questions include whether there should be penalties for acting and, if so, whether these penalties should be civil or criminal.

The rules for practices by individual firms are more controversial. It is widely recognized that the 1936 Robinson-Patman Act severely and unwisely restricted quantity discounts reflecting cost savings. The law was designed to protect small retailers from chain stores. A cost defense was supposedly allowed. Defenses acceptable to the regulators, the U.S. Federal Trade Commission, could not be devised. However, an alternative defense ultimately succeeded. Meeting offers of rivals was permitted. The courts proved willing to allow widespread reaction to claims of better offers. Firms were not required to obtain conclusive proof that the offers were made. Ability to use this defense lessened the harms from the Act. For the reasons stated above, the result of any rules against price discrimination or other competitive practices is unclear. Thus, so is the wisdom of actual prohibitions.

Section 2 of the Sherman Act has been less influential because of the difficulties already discussed in determining when restructuring is desirable. Enforcement is further complicated by reluctance of the courts to base decisions solely on demonstrations of inefficiency. As all too often occurs, both possible types of rejection of the efficiency criterion are used. Some suggest acceptance of both the excess competition argument and using the laws to preserve inefficient firms. Alternatively, it is suggested that the basis as well as the extent of the inefficiency be appraised.

This view that appraisal of the firm's history is necessary has long been expressed in major Section 2 decisions. The meaning remains obscure. Vague statements and questionable arguments mar the discussions. The point seems to be that the undesirable monopoly power is illegal only if it was consciously sought. The more extreme versions suggest that the efforts must involve aggressive tactics such as predation. The issue originated from the 1911 decision affirming the breakup of Standard Oil of New Jersey. That decision included material, widely and properly criticized for its vagueness, that the reasonability of actions had to be considered. The meaning became only slightly clearer with the 1920 decision that United States Steel was not a monopoly because its behavior was more reasonable. The vigor and success of efforts to monopolize had to be considered. The need for treating such factors nominally was confirmed by the 1945 decision in the Alcoa case. Stress was placed on the large market share of Alcoa and its active efforts to secure position.[6]

These decisions have been widely criticized for both what was decided and for how the decisions were explained. McGee's (1958) critique of predation was inspired by doubts over the widespread belief that Standard Oil was a vicious competitor.

[6]The decisions are reported in all the standard antitrust texts. Extensive commentary and further reviews have appeared. The Alcoa case involves the peculiarity that so many members of the Supreme Court at the time had been Department of Justice officials that the Court could not get a quorum to hear the case. Congress passed a law allowing the Washington, D.C., Circuit Court of Appeals to hear the case.

Others point out that by 1911, the shift of petroleum production from Appalachia to the Southwest had removed much of Standard Oil's power. Thus Standard Oil may not have been a worse offender than United States Steel. They may have been equally deserving (or undeserving) of breakup.

The Alcoa decision simultaneously weakened the behavioral requirements and tended to reinforce the high market share criterion for action. The arguments in the decision have been widely criticized for twisting the facts to correspond to the criteria allegedly used. The decision contended that active pursuit of power had to prevail but need not involve the allegedly ruthless approach of Standard Oil. Others viewing the record concluded Alcoa was less aggressive than the Court tried to suggest. A more critical problem was that the decision argued that monopoly meant a high market share. The decision proceeded to define the market too narrowly. Competition from copper was understated, and Alcoa's ability to affect scrap supplies was exaggerated. Observers sympathetic to the actual outcome complained that the court had used a bad market analysis to correct a bad criterion of excessive market power. Those skeptical of Section 2 actions could conclude that again the drawbacks of restructuring had been demonstrated.

This precedent was to prove problematic in later cases. Dupont succeeded in thwarting breakup of its position in cellophane by convincing the Court that many close substitutes were available. While these substitutes ultimately displaced cellophane, some critics feared that at the time of the case, the competition was weaker. In contrast, as noted above, IBM's successful defense from monopolization charges involved extensive evidence from a team of economists arguing that the competition was vigorous.

The Clayton Act and its amendments have been interpreted as allowing less stringent evidence to justify preventing or reversing mergers. Considerable debate prevails about whether merger prevention rules at any given time are too strict or too lenient. However, it is recognized that antimerger policies up to the Reagan years had involved undertaking cases of little or no competitive significance. For example, Kennecott had to divest Peabody Coal because evidence was provided that Kennecott was considering entry into coal mining.

In 1968, the Antitrust Division of the U.S. Department of Justice developed rules for challenging mergers. Market share tests were established. These criteria proved controversial and were modified in the Reagan administration. The Reagan administration sought to lessen the occurrence of undesirable cases. These modifications were hailed by their advocates as a desirable retreat from excessive belief in the power of simple structural tests. These supporters cite the numerous questionable prohibitions of mergers. Its critics then contended the rules had become too permissive. Predictably, the changes have been described at least by journalists as gutting the antitrust laws. (Porter 1990 also fears the changes were excessive; this is part of a curious belief that vigorous regulations are good discipline.)

The laws did not generate strong efforts to undertake extensive reorganization. Restructuring has not inspired literature as extensive or passionate as that over "socialism." Few long defenses of the desirability of extensive corporate reorganization seem to exist, but a number of attacks on the argument have appeared. Extensive restructuring of firms, at best, has only had sporadic conceptual support by either scholars or politicians. The principal drawback is that restructuring cases consume vast amounts of time and resources with questionable results. The efforts have often failed, and the desirability of some of the successful prosecutions, as noted, remains controversial. The efficacy of restructuring or even preventing mergers is too unclear to enlist enthusiastic support. Thus, even those who believe that the Clayton Act and Section 2 of the Sherman Act should be retained often would not want to see the use greatly increased.

Enthusiastic advocacy of restructuring probably crested with the New Deal of the 1930s. The New Deal has been described by observers such as Tugwell (1957), a prominent New Dealer, as a battle between planners such as himself and restructurers. In various places including his biography of Roosevelt, Tugwell bemoaned Roosevelt's repudiation of planning. Galbraith has regularly argued that planning is preferable to antitrust. Various writers in the 1980s have readvocated planning. Planning to these writers is a vision of a tamed version of the socialist planning board discussed below; the idea resurfaces periodically but never secures implementation. Planning, no matter how tamed from its most intrusive forms, has little appeal; even such small scale planning as regulation of natural monopolies also is viewed with disfavor (see below).

Restructuring meant an increase of antitrust activity and here even the New Deal did little. Subsequent restructuring proposals such as by Bain (1968) and by Kaysen and Turner (1959) were in publications addressed more to economic scholars than to a wider audience. A task force established in Lyndon Johnson's administration proposed a law to effect deconcentration.[7] All advocated using mechanistic rules that could be applied in identifying candidates for break-up. Such proposals, in turn, reflect a long-standing concern in studies of antitrust that too little restructuring has occurred. The conference on restructuring reported above was organized to treat the legislation proposed to implement the task force suggestion of a deconcentration act. Such an act was not passed, presumably because the justification was so weak.

Two histories of the enactment and early history of U.S. antitrust laws by Thorelli (1955) and Letwin (1965) suggest that the motives for enacting the Sherman Act were mixed and unclear but that the legislation was not inspired by a desire for radical restructuring of the economy. Bork's (1966b) article concentrating on expressions by members of Congress of their intents stresses the evidence that, nevertheless, the basic goal was promoting efficient competition. Thorelli's analysis largely supports this view.[8]

In contrast, DiLorenzo (1990) suggests that considerable influence was exerted by business groups fearing new competition. DiLorenzo cites but does not explicitly refute Bork's article. Instead, DiLorenzo embarks on a criticism of Bork's insistence on reliance on original understanding of what the legislation meant. (As is typical of Bork, his analysis is more careful than his critics suggest; he simply proposes avoiding interpretations the legislators could not possibly have advocated.) This is seen as leading to judicial activism. Others contend that Bork took too narrow a view of the goals of antitrust and neglected interest in preserving inefficient competitors.

---

[7]The task force had among others Robert Bork, William Baxter (later to lead the Antitrust Division of the Department of Justice away from mechanistic attacks on concentrated industries), Paul MacAvoy, Lee Preston, and James McKie as members. The last three are leading specialists in industrial organization. Bork attached a dissent to the report disputing the wisdom of the deconcentration law. The report was not completed until the Nixon administration. Its refusal to publish led to insertion in the *Congressional Record*.
[8]Letwin does not deal with this issue.

Earlier in his article, DiLorenzo uses Stigler as the example of how the Chicago school has not applied its usual skepticism to antitrust. With antitrust, the standard Chicago calls for abolition are replaced by more conventional suggestions of better enforcement. Stigler's expositions on the subject (esp. 1966) display skepticism but not rejection. He warns that the virtues of antitrust have not been adequately appraised.

Armentano (1990), a modest update of a book first published in 1972, appears to be a pathbreaking effort. What is most remarkable about the book is how little the substance differs from more standard treatments. For example, the deflating of the cases against Standard Oil and Alcoa draws upon familiar material. The limited success of the electric equipment conspiracy is similarly widely recognized. The fresh feature is one of interpretation, concluding that antitrust is another fatally flawed policy. The DiLorenzo article and those that accompanied it in the Fall 1990 issue of *Regulation* then represents the spread of the view. The abolition approach to antitrust is part of the increasing efforts of libertarians to stimulate the maximum possible contraction of government. While the arguments are inconclusive, they at least expose an asymmetry in Chicago writings. The optimism about reform effectively exempted antitrust from the frequently stated position that when failure persists the policy may be unworkable.

It has already been noted that advocates of planning also oppose antitrust on similar grounds. The difference, of course, is in the proposed cure. The libertarians see no problem and thus, no need to act; the planners think a real problem exists, and they have a better a solution.

Conclusions

The theoretic literature on monopoly indicates that many outcomes are possible depending upon the circumstances but fails to provide specific predictions about what conditions produce what outcomes. Applied studies typically display various degrees of skepticism about claims of rampant monopoly. Some say concern cannot be abandoned totally, but few would vigorously enforce or even retain all the laws. Many and indeed probably most experienced antitrust analysts recognize that anticompetitive administration of antitrust laws is a danger. A few see this as so dominant a force that the laws should be repealed. The critical area of accord is that monopoly is no longer viewed as a clearly pressing concern. This consensus is another example of the area of agreement among economists being more important than the discords.

Chapter 5

International Trade Policy Issues

Another widely supported major point of Adam Smith is that international division of labor is as desirable as intranational specialization. Chapter 2 indicated that much international trade economics demonstrates that the principles of economic efficiency are independent of whether or not the dealings take place across borders.

As protectionism reemerged around the great depression, international trade economists began more systematically analyzing the implication of market failures for international trade policy. The effort dates back at least to a 1950 article by Haberler. This started numerous efforts to develop further Haberler's point; contributors included Bhagwati (1971) and Johnson (1965, 1977); Caves (1960) provided a good literature survey; Meier (1968) provided a clear review of the issues; Kemp (1964, 1969) developed difficult mathematical formulations. Corden (1974) provided an excellent synthesis of the optimal policy issue using mainly geometric analyses of the issues. A new generation of more mathematical surveys emerged in the 1980s (e.g., G. Grossman and Helpman 1991, Helpman and Krugman 1985, 1989, and Krugman 1990.) Bhagwati (1989, 1991), once more accepting of intervention, presents strong nontechnical defenses of free trade.

Protectionism proved no more attractive in an imperfectly competitive world than in a competitive one. For reasons closely related to the arguments made in chapters 2 and 3, these reappraisals largely reinforced the traditional conclusion that trade restriction is usually inappropriate. Even when it might be helpful in the short-run, it will at least ultimately and usually immediately prove dangerous.

This chapter emphasizes these revisions of international trade theory to handle market failures. The key subissues are examined. Discussion begins with an overview of the theory of optimal intervention developed by international trade theorists but applicable throughout economics. The classic "optimum tariff" argument that a country can exploit its monopsony power by imposing restrictions on international trade then is evaluated. The appraisal is related to an example of suggestions for implementing such policies, the calls for taxes on oil imports.

Note is taken of the problems posed by existence of domestic and foreign monopolies. Special attention is given the classic issue of dumping, price discrimination in international trade. Variants on the long-standing, often confused arguments of the role of protection in promoting new industries are examined.

Protectionism and Cures of Market Failures

Another example of how the critical implications of economic principles prove difficult to deduce in practice is provided by the theory of optimal policy. Its close correspondence with traditional economics suggests that the principles should have been obvious. In fact, as so often occurs, the results emerged slowly.

Policy makers often adopt familiar tools to attain their ends, and economists do not always carefully consider how the appropriateness of the choice of instruments should be reviewed. Indiscriminate restriction of international trade is a flagrant example of inappropriate policy selection. Therefore, specialists in international economics found it desirable to develop an analysis of the best way to eliminate different types of market failures. The work showed that regulating international trade was less desirable than policy makers believed, at least before the economic case for free trade again began to influence policy.

The work develops basic economic principles that even theorists previously failed to appreciate adequately. The central proposition is that the preferable actions require precise identification of the problem and the most directly corrective policy. Any policy directed at the secondary impacts of the market failure will be less efficient. An indirect policy would be preferable only if it were much cheaper and almost as effective to implement than a direct one.

The further point that some policies inevitably aggravate some problems is left implicit. Bhagwati's (1971) review of the options ranks effective polices. Understanding of the economics of the options immediately leads to recognition of why he made these choices and why other policies are inappropriate. Nonspecialists may need fuller discussion. The instinct to restrict imports is so great that controls may be imposed even if the results are undesirable.

Tariffs and import quotas, the most widely used trade policies, necessarily have an effect only if the good is imported. The nature of a tariff or quota is to restrict foreign and thus total supply. As basic economics textbooks show, this tends to push up prices, lower consumption, and lessen competition for domestic producers, consequently increasing domestic output. Tariffs and quotas have the right type of effect when the good is imported *and* the appropriate policy goals involve reducing consumption, raising output, or both. The full theory of optimum policy (see Bhagwati 1971) then catalogs the foreign trade interventions that would produce changes in consumption, production, and international trade different from those under tariffs and quotas. It deals with problems with goods that are exported or not traded.

The control of detrimental externalities (discussed in chapter 10) and of their textbook opposite, unconscious benefits of one economic activity to another, can be used to illustrate the points. This example is more complex but probably more realistic than those typically employed. The nature of the appropriate international trade policy to deal with the impacts of an uncontrolled externality differs with the nature of the externality and of the commodity with which the externality is associated. We need production reducing policies for goods whose production produces detrimental externalities and consumption reducing policies for goods whose consumption produces detrimental externalities.

Chapter 10 shows that efficiency requires imposing a marginal cost on the creator of a detrimental externality equal to the marginal cost of damages at the equilibrium level of pollution. If externalities are beneficial, the creator should have marginal income augmented by the benefits to society of the equilibrium level of amenity creation. The charge on harmful externalities would best be levied on the production of harm. As chapter 10 also notes, optimal response to additional charges will involve a combination of possible responses. They include switching to naturally available or manufactured inputs that are less polluting, using control methods to reduce the environmental impact of pollutant use, or lowering output of the product whose production causes pollution.

The adoption of such changes in production practices, in any case, makes output reduction a secondary reaction by raising the cost of production. The output reduction, in turn, produces a drop in use of other inputs. An output fall also involves lower consumption and, if the good is internationally traded, increased imports or reduced exports. Pollution reduction could be secured by imposing a policy that produces one of these secondary effects of the optimum policy. At least four indirect alternatives exist for a detrimental externality. (1) A tax could be imposed on consumption of the output of the polluting entity; e.g., a tax on electricity consumption because electricity production involves producing pollutants. (2) The tax could be on output of the offending firm, a tax on electricity production. (3) The use of polluting inputs such as coal could be taxed. (4) The tax could be on use of non-polluting inputs such as labor. Where the output is exported, a tax on its export could be imposed. If the output competes with imports, an import subsidy could be provided.

Every one of these policies would reduce pollution but in a less efficient way than an emissions tax. In every case, the inefficiency arises from forcing arbitrary choice among the many alternative measures that might have been employed. Thus, a consumption tax, an output tax, an export tax, or an import subsidy discourages production but does not encourage use of pollution controls. The consumption tax has the further disadvantage of reducing imports. Given a nationalistic outlook, increased imports are desirable whatever the pollution control policies abroad. Even if we considered foreign interests, inefficiency is involved in encouraging imports only if pollution control policy abroad is inadequate. If inadequacies prevail, questions arise about the wisdom of seeking to take actions to offset defective policies in other countries. Such action is paternalism at its worst. Moreover, charges of inadequate pollution control easily can become another way to rationalize unwise protection.

While some increase in imports or reduction of exports is desirable, policies such as export taxes and import subsidies produce excessive change. Changing trade patterns are assigned the primary role in stimulating a production shift that should occur through a more balanced mix of domestic and foreign trade impacts.

A tax on nonpolluting inputs depresses output but also fails to provide incentives to employ the use of pollution controls. If a tax is levied only on selected inputs, the tax also inefficiently stimulates substitution of untaxed inputs for taxed ones. If all nonpolluting inputs and no polluting ones were taxed, the output disincentive effect would be offset by an incentive to substitute polluting inputs for nonpolluting ones. If only some nonpolluting inputs were taxed, then an inefficient increase in the use of other nonpolluting inputs also would occur.

Taxes on polluting inputs can be levied in at least two ways. First, consumption of the pollutant itself could be taxed, or equivalently the pollutant content of the purchased input (e.g., a sulfur containing fuel) could be taxed. Second, use of the pollutant-containing input could be taxed independently of its pollutant content. Both types of taxes provide incentives to use less of the pollutant-causing input but only the first provides incentives to use clean-up processes. A tax on input use without recognition of variations in pollutant content has the further disadvantage of encouraging shifts to more pollutant-containing varieties of the input. Those who advocate a tax on gasoline or petroleum production or consumption on environmental grounds ignore the resulting bias against emission controls.

The theory of optimal policy demonstrates the generality of these illustrations. The looser the relationship of the problem being cured to what actually is subject to control, the more inefficient are the control policies. The case chosen is an example of problems arising from inappropriate choice of policies. The problems considered are inefficiencies very indirectly related to production, consumption, or international trade levels and thus not best controlled by a policy that primarily alters production, consumption, or international trade.

Finally, for goods that are not traded internationally, international trade policies can, at best, have circuitous effects. A highly distorting policy would be required if international trade regulation is the sole policy tool. Reducing imports by tariffs on imported products and raising exports by export subsidies would attract resources and depress other outputs. An industry that is not involved in international trade and with too high an output would lower output.

Similarly, it is possible to stimulate one industry by depressing an exporting industry using export taxes or depressing an import competing industry using import subsidies. The resulting declines in domestic output of the other industry make resources available to all other industries in the economy including the one needing stimulus. Thus, inefficiencies are introduced into a large number of industries that did not create pollution. This would be the ultimate in misdirected intervention. A more direct policy avoids this spreading of distortions.

The Optimum Tariff in Theory and Practice

Turning to optimal tariffs, the basic point is that they involve difficult to implement strategies to exploit foreigners. Employment of the optimal tariff concept has several drawbacks. The tariff imposing country does not inevitably gain. Such policies are not even potentially beneficial unless the country restricting trade is a large enough buyer to affect world prices. A successful optimum tariff or export tax amounts to effective use by the government of the monopsony or monopoly power the country as a whole possesses.

The principles of private monopsony remain applicable to government exercise of the monopsony power (see chapter 3). The critical differences between individual and state action are that sovereign states are better able to effect and maintain the coordination that is so difficult for private firms. Governments employ monopsony power in world trade by restricting imports by tariffs or quotas. A tariff or quota necessarily lowers the demand seen by producers. The tariff drains off revenues consumers were willing to pay producers. A quota directly limits how much consumers may buy. If the importing country is a major force in world trade, the result is a lower price paid to suppliers and a lower foreign output and trade level. The price reduction is the benefit to the country imposing the tariff.

Monopoly or monopsony applied through restriction of international trade has particularly predictable effects on where the displaced resources go. A tariff discourages consumption and stimulates production of the commodity involved in the country imposing the tariff. A quota also restricts supply and consumption and stimulates production. Furthermore, the loss of sales by the exporter increases the attractiveness of purchases by consumers in the producing country and third countries not imposing tariffs. This can never offset the loss to the tariff or quota. Without such a tariff or quota, the country restricting trade would have outbid the other customers.

The resulting loss of output eliminates outputs at least as valuable as their cost. Losses are associated with depriving consumers of the additional goods, eliminating producer profits from producing the goods, and causing producers in the importing country to divert resources to a less profitable use.

The tariff transfers income to the importing country. The lower prices finance part of the tariff. The exporters necessarily incur a loss of equal amount on sales actually made. (The full impact involves additional transfers. In particular, domestic consumers pay more for domestic output and possibly also bear part of the tariff burden.) This transfer combined with an inefficient shift of resources reducing the profitability in the exporting country guarantees a loss to the exporting country. The gross gain to the tax-imposing country then is the transfer of income, and it is offset by losses in both countries by transferring resources to less profitable uses. The exporter's loss thus exceeds the gross returns and thus necessarily any net gain by the importer, so the world loses. A further effect is that, unless the exporting country can use discrimination to limit the scope of price reductions, other countries share in the price-decline benefit. Thus, an importer-cohesion problem, analogous to the cartel-discipline conundrum, arises with optimum tariff practice. A quota has less certain effects because if badly designed, it can allow the exporters to raise prices and reap the benefits of trade restrictions.

As usual in price rigging, success depends on choosing the right level of restriction. Severe import restrictions may cause the consumption reduction and production diversion losses in the trade-restricting country to exceed the transfer gains.

First, difficulties prevail in determining what the optimum tariff should be. In practice, the state may overdo the taxation and make things worse. Dangers exist that protectionist sentiments and greed for revenue will lead to too high a tax. Domestic industries' demands for protection influence the outcome. The domestic industries are concerned with the benefits they receive. Higher than optimal tariffs are desirable to producers because they allow their profits to rise even further. The tariff optimal for producers is one that eliminates imports and thus any gains from the foreigner. In the United States, calls for imposing tariffs are too closely linked to efforts to lower the budget deficit and help particular groups. Thus, excessive tariffs are likely. Trade restriction is overdone; trade is reduced below the optimum monopoly or monopsony level.

A second drawback is that the policy can inspire imitation and ultimately lead to damaging everyone. Imposition of optimal tariffs is a game that many can play. The tax can set a bad precedent that will unleash a world trade war. No one country is so important that it can impose these taxes with impunity. Retaliation is a near certainty. If the other country also has monopsony power, the retaliation lessens the impact of the initial tariff. The probable long-run outcome is that both sides become worse off from an endless round of tariffs and countertariffs. Instead of gaining, tariff imposers stimulate a downward spiral of trade from which everyone loses.

This is particularly true in oil where we have what is known in economics jargon as bilateral monopoly, monopoly power by buyers and sellers. Success in imposing an optimal tariff requires that monopoly sellers are convinced of the determination of the taxers and reduce prices instead of trying to force a retreat from taxing. This outcome is far from assured. The retaliation tradition in international trade is that the other side tightens rather than lessens the pressure.

Another view is that when foreigners collude to force up prices the best defenses consist of unleashing competitive forces. Doing nothing may be preferable to erecting retaliatory tariffs. At a minimum, inaction keeps markets open and allows a country to benefit to the breakdowns of collusion that so often occur. The uncertainties that the tariff will be set correctly, the dangers of retaliation, and the difficulties of reversing the restrictions make the optimum tariff less satisfactory than stimulating competition.

The parallel monopoly strategies are export taxes or upper limits of exports. The supply restrictions lower exports, raise prices, and divert production to domestic users. In the case of limiting exports, other exporting countries could gain. As with import controls, a loss of desirable trades, transfers, losses to the taxed buyers, uncertain gain for the exporter, and certain world losses occur.

The stress on exploitation of monopsony power reflects the peculiarities of protectionist traditions. Monopoly power is the greater concern with private actions because in the private sector sellers are more likely than buyers to combine. Monopsony is the preferred route for governments. Protectionists believe exports are good and imports bad, and so import controls are more acceptable than export taxes. The latter are forbidden in the U.S. constitution, but export controls are imposed to evade the restriction. However, such export controls appear to be motivated by goals other than monopoly gains.

Any tariff has the disadvantage of reducing the number of suppliers and increasing the market impacts of disruption of supplies in the remaining regions. Such disadvantages are increased if the tariff degenerates into a means of protecting high cost suppliers. Quotas such as were used to limit U.S. oil imports would be worse. First, the problems of assigning rights would return. The fights over the ability to buy at world prices and sell at protected ones produces battles for access. At best as in U.S. oil and gas experience, this involves unmanageable squabbles; at worst as in many less developed countries, corruption becomes widespread.

The transfer usually is from foreign suppliers to quota holders. The reduction of demand seen by the exporters leads to lower purchase prices than before the quota. The reduction of supplies available to consumers leads to higher resale prices than before the quota. Possibilities for evasion not available under tariffs may arise under quotas. Foreigners can organize so they get the higher incomes. An export cartel might be established. For example, U.S. oil import control may have been an element in the efforts of the members of the Organization of Petroleum Exporting Countries (OPEC) to restrict oil supplies and push up prices.

An Oil Import Tax: The Optimum Tariff Misapplied

As discussed in chapter 7, proposals for oil import taxes were widely advocated in the United States. The anthologies by Plummer (1982) and Deese and Nye (1981) and the surveys by Horwich and Weimer (1984), Bohi (1990), and Bohi and Montgomery (1982) all make the case. These arguments have serious drawbacks. The tax is advocated, in part, because oil is a case in which an optimal tariff policy is believed feasible. The primary objections then are those to any use of optimum tariff arguments.

Among the critical special questions about an import tax is why oil prices slid in the 1980s. The advocates of the tax seem to believe that the slide reflects a weakening of OPEC cohesion. Prices arc below the monopoly-profit-maximizing level, and the tax would restore prices to that monopoly-profit-maximizing level. The consumers then seize the price-raising opportunities before the key OPEC countries do. A contrary view is that the 1979-1980 price increases pushed prices to levels far above the monopoly-profit-maximizing level sustainable as supply and demand adjusted. The OPEC countries then moved prices to more realistic levels. Then, the tax would squeeze the OPEC countries and produce resistance. As the prior section argued, it is also possible that the OPEC countries will retaliate whatever the price level. Yet another point is that the 1980s saw the Reagan era of energy deregulation in contrast to the activism of the 1970s. The differences in price effects seem more than coincidental. This would support the argument that encouraging competition is the best strategy. These special points reinforce the general ones in suggesting that optimum-tariff-based oil taxes have severe drawbacks.

Proponents also hope the tariff will produce a more equitable distribution of world energy supplies. In particular, another benefit of the tax would be lower energy costs for less developed countries. The developed world will restrain its energy use to allow the poor to consume more energy. Income transfers would be preferable. Perhaps if we cannot effect income transfers, low prices are the best available measures. We cannot be sure that transfers are not possible. Moreover, the barriers to equitable transfers may also make low energy prices inequitable. Critics of foreign aid (Bauer 1981) contend it perpetuates an affluent elite rather than aiding the poor. Cheap energy might have the same effect.

Private Monopoly at Home and Abroad

The traditional optimum tariff argument with its emphasis on government use of monopsony and monopoly power has been extended to treat the trade-policy implications of actual or potential private monopoly power at home or abroad. The dominant tradition is that free trade is the preferable policy in the presence of domestic monopolies because free trade increases competition. Modern extensions of this view such as Corden's (1974) add that protection undertaken to attain some valid policy goal must be modified to reduce the possible inefficiencies if domestic monopolies prevail.

Variants on the optimal tariff and retaliation analysis can be used to raise (and ultimately dismiss) the possibility of benefits to trade interference. Countries can benefit by creation of domestic export monopolies or import monopsonies or by destroying monopolies abroad. The basic problem is that seeking to use private firms to create monopoly power is a less satisfactory variant of the optimal tariff approach. All the disadvantages of the optimum tariff and some additional ones prevail. In particular, scattered private efforts may be less effective than direct use of the sovereign power to tax. The usual problems of properly distributing the gains, whatever they prove to be, are likely to be greater when private firms are the initial beneficiaries. Conversely, if foreign monopolies or monopsonies exist, their reversal is not readily effected. As seen earlier, retaliatory actions are risky.

Dumping and the Beneficiaries

A complication that long has fascinated international trade economists is dumping, selling abroad for less than at home. The conflict between economic principles and folklore is sharp. A political tradition has arisen of antidumping legislation. Harm by foreigners is considered somehow worse if it is produced by dumping. Actually, dumping is almost always beneficial to those who are subject to it. The dumping argument is another effort to make classic protectionist arguments sound better.

Dumping usually is the international trade form of price discrimination, varying prices of the same good with the identity of the customer, the quantity purchased, or both. The alternative to discrimination is a single price charged to all customers. This approach is forced on competitive producers by their lack of power over price. Discrimination is possible only if producers can control price and thus by definition have monopoly power.

Not all monopolists can discriminate. An additional requirement is that high transaction costs hinder favored buyers from reselling to disfavored ones. Thus, discrimination is feasible for public utilities if their legal monopolies truly preclude customer resales. Discrimination is possible in international trade when the seller can make availability of a lower price f.o.b. factory conditional on taking delivery at a distant location. The costs of the initial shipment and the return trip limit the ability to undercut the supplier in less favored markets.

If discrimination is adopted, higher prices on some sales and lower ones on others compared to a uniform monopoly price are conventionally expected to occur. If prices could profitably be raised or lowered in all markets, this option is available under uniform pricing as well as discrimination. Choosing higher or lower prices in all markets under discrimination than under uniform pricing then is inconsistent with profit maximization under uniform pricing. Theorists, e.g., Nahata, Ostaszewski, and Sahoo (1990), have found cases, whose empirical relevance is unclear, in which this conclusion does not hold. For present purposes, the key point is that usually importers do pay less than customers in the supplier's home country.

The literature on price discrimination (Joan Robinson 1933, Schmalensee 1981, Varian 1985, 1989, 1992) has devoted considerable attention to the net effect on all customers. The critical question about the net impact is whether the inevitable benefit to those charged a lower price is greater or less than effects on those charged a higher price.

The countries paying the lower price are better off with the discrimination than with uniform monopoly pricing. Consumers have more of the commodity than would have been available under uniform monopoly price. A further benefit to the importing country is that this lower foreign price allows elimination of the higher-cost additional domestic output that would have operated at the nondiscriminatory foreign price.

Only in extreme cases would discrimination lead to higher sales and lower prices in the favored market than if the foreign industry employing dumping charged nondiscriminatory, efficient (i.e., competitively determined) prices. (A further problem, discussed in chapters 4 and 6, is how to attain this efficiency if economies of scale prevail.) With a high enough response of demand to price cuts in the favored countries and a large enough reduction of sales to the less favored markets, this result would occur. Thus, the outcome is more likely from foreign suppliers who constitute a small part of total supply in the favored area and have most of their sales in disfavored areas.

Unless the extreme outcome occurs, the monopoly still makes even the favored buyer worse off than if efficiency could be effected. The discrimination is better than uniform pricing but not as good as prices equal to marginal costs. This comparison is germane only if some method is available to produce efficient pricing. As long as monopoly cannot be undermined, dumping is desirable to its beneficiaries by lessening the burden.

The conclusions are unchanged when a government subsidizes exports. The dumping necessarily is greater than it otherwise would have been. This is a gift from the foreign government to the importer that should be gratefully accepted. The benefits to the buyers are the same as under any other form of dumping and thus increase. The harm again is to the exporting country. A tariff or quota reduces this harm of subsidy. The benefits of reducing dumping if any accrues to the exporting country. It is rescued from some of its folly; it probably will respond with more stupidity.

For example, the U.S. steel industry contends that it deserves protection because it is the victim of ill-advised policies in the rest of the world. As one study (Howell, Noellert, Kreier, and Wolff 1988) commissioned by the leading steel companies argues, steel mills were built with government financing throughout the world. Often the political intervention led to locating the plant inefficiently. In other cases, other types of mismanagement occurred.

While many of these charges about foreign steel are exaggerated, unwise decisions have prevailed. Protection still is not in the interest of the U.S. economy. To the extent that foreigners invested stupidly, they made a gift to the rest of the world. Only that part of the gift that is continuing, subsidies of current operations, can be eliminated by foreign policy reform. Where a plant exists that can sell at high enough prices to cover operating costs, it will do so (see chapter 7). It can be argued that leadership is needed to prevent resorting to unwise subsidy. However, avoiding similar policies is more convincing than protesting the actions of others.

The last resort answer to these defenses of dumping is to claim that the dumping is predatory in the sense discussed in chapter 4. Once the predation has succeeded, prices will be raised well above prior levels. Chapter 4 pointed out this argument is frequently and falsely made in international trade. The assumptions that predation is preferable to collusion, that the capacity shut-down by the price cutting cannot reopen, and that significant new entry can be avoided remain dubious. The OPEC cartel learned that the last was an invalid premise. Moreover, the record of U.S. practice with dumping laws suggest much abuse. Bovard (1991) presents a highly polemic attack; the more dispassionate survey by Destler (1992) tends to support Bovard. The methods used are biased towards findings that dumping has occurred.

Creating New Industries

Promoting new industries long has been a concern in international trade economics. International trade economists distinguish between two types of problems in establishing a new industry (Meade 1955, 119-35; Meade 1955, 254-71). One relates to problems of attaining minimum efficient size and the other involves financing the costs of learning how to operate an industry. Analysis shows that the first problem has no policy implications and the second is of limited validity.

Two logical possibilities arise with an industry with economies of scale. First, the industry might or might not be a natural monopoly. This case further subdivides depending on whether the feasible geographic range of operation is local, national, continental, or world-wide. Only in the last two cases does any international trade effect exist.

It is difficult to see that a policy issue would arise in any case. If it were desirable to replace an existing natural monopoly in one country with one in another, no natural barriers exist to this replacement. If protectionism thwarts the replacement, no good response exists.

The case is even worse for the other, more relevant and more commonly discussed situation of an industry in which several firms can operate. Without trade barriers, market decisions about entry will be efficient. By definition, society receives no benefit from operation at scales below the most efficient level. Such operation undesirably shifts output from existing firms elsewhere operating at efficient scales to the inefficiently small domestic firms. The desirable time for entry is the one chosen by private firms--when the available market allows profitable operation.

When the good is exportable, no problem should ever exist. The firm could attain the required size by selling abroad. Where exports are hindered by protection, export subsidies could be desirable. Retaliation may neutralize such efforts. Where no possibility of exporting occurs, the industry should not exist until it operates at a scale at which its costs are below those of imports. When such costs prevail, the firm will come into existence. No policy problem arises.

A more valid argument relates to problem of the initial costs of establishing a new industry. Even here, the mere existence of these costs is not sufficient to justify intervention. These are real investment costs, and establishment of the industry is socially profitable only if these costs can be recovered through the profits of the new industry. For a subsidy to be justified some market failures that prevent optimum financing must prevail. The possibilities stressed are externalities associated with the generation of knowledge and imperfect capital markets.

The investor may find that others benefit from the knowledge acquired about technologies and markets and from the knowledge disseminated about the ability to supply. Corden (1974) discusses with appropriate skepticism more complex forms of publicness such as a spillover of the benefits of very large investments in knowledge into other industries and situations in which simultaneous actions are required by different firms. Again, Coase's question about whether market failure is worse than government failure applies.

As is so often the case with the writings surveyed here, the ultimate conclusion is that anti-intervention arguments still prove relevant. The barriers to creating the industry arise, not from the existence of foreign rivals, but from domestic market failures. Thus, for reasons suggested earlier in this chapter, trade intervention is not the preferable solution.

The labor market arguments relate to alleged frictions in the labor market that cause inefficiencies. In extreme forms, it is postulated that the agricultural sector in less developed countries subsidizes the employment of workers with zero or low productivity. A more moderate argument is that the flow of workers into more productive sectors occurs too slowly. Whatever the problem, the best cure is assisting the movement of labor to the more productive sector.

A so-called new theory of international trade holds that certain industries can generate extraordinary (presumably monopolistic or externality) gains and public policy should assist formation of such industries. It is similarly argued that a sheltered domestic market may promote more profitable export sales than would otherwise occur. Even the advocates of the view recognize that identification of industries to aid is a formidable task and that competitive industry creation among nations may negate the impacts. Qualified pro-targeting articles by Brander and by Spencer appear in Krugman (1986). Gene Grossman, Carliner, and Yamamura present more critical views in the same book. The call by Tyson (1992) for cautious activism to assist industries asserted without convincing proof to generate large external economies is another example.

Tyson's cautious activism consists of first working to reduce foreign subsidies and barriers to trade. She proposes supplementing this by an agency to identify and assist the development of promising new strategies. Tyson (1992, 292) gives minimal recognition of the barriers to success and swiftly dismisses them. Her optimism relies on the long-cherished and regularly-refuted belief that an impartial bureaucracy can be sheltered from political pressures. The arguments are influenced by the belief that the Japanese government has effected a successful strategic development program. Tyson adds the case of European promotion of passenger airplanes. As Carliner points out, the French experience is much less impressive. The targeted industries ran losses in excess of the subsidies provided. Moreover, the belief that large external economies prevail in technically progressive industries seems based mainly on intuition.

Yamamura argues "I am also persuaded that the effectiveness of Japanese industrial policy was achieved at the cost of economic efficiency and political 'fairness' which was not readily visible while the policy was being pursued (201)." Yamamura's consideration of efficiency and fairness does not indicate the weight of the two forces in his negative appraisal. The critical point is that targeting may have not produced profits sufficient to justify the expenses incurred. Instead of being wily exploiters, the Japanese may have been deluded into subsidizing their foreign customers and inefficient industries. The Japanese certainly have problems recognizing when a sunset period has emerged as has occurred in steel. The Japanese model may be better evaluated by traditional theories of subsidization.

One can go further than Yamamura. Too much attention is given to the cases such as auto-making and various electronics realms in which the Japanese appear highly successful. Only rarely is the profitability of this success appraised. Less attention is given such clear failures as agriculture, coal, and aluminum or early successes such as steel, ship building, and other electronic areas that have not been sustained. Similarly, concentration is on possible new gains while future losses such as those apparently arising in parts of electronics are ignored. Other discussions of Japan such as that by Porter (1990) similarly suggest that the situation is more complex than advocates of planning have recognized. (Other surveys of interest on Japan are Ito 1992, Komiya, Okuno, and Suzumura 1988, Peck, Levin, and Goto 1987a and 1987b, and Woronoff 1990. On Germany, see Giersch, Paqué, and Schmeiding 1992.)

More critically, the whole discussion of economic position neglects basic economic principles. In a mobile world, competition erodes advantages. The differences among countries following sensible policies should decline over time. The valid concern is over whether countries are doing things that unnecessarily retard performance. Again, it is easy to identify many bad public policies at work everywhere. How to improve private practices is harder to indicate.

Summary and Conclusions

The prior discussion has shown that even after considering the complications of international trade theory, trade restriction is a dubious policy. The perils of action and counteraction are likely to offset any initial gains to trade reduction. Severe limits exist to the economic goals attainable by trade policy. Few market failures arise from foreign trade. The theory of optimum policy indicates the best cures are those that directly regulate the source of the problem. Thus, trade policy is rarely the preferable way to correct market failures. Optimum tariff policy is difficult to effect and sustain effectively. Instead of the expected monopsony gains, losses can arise from poor initial application and the retaliation induced. Dumping is more desirable for its beneficiaries than admitted in policy making. Trade restriction rarely, if ever, is the best way to promote new industries because any inefficiencies lie in domestic market failures.

Chapter 6

Transaction Costs, Property Rights, and the Limits of Government

This chapter examines arguments used to contend government failure is a more serious problem than market failure. The review starts by examining transaction costs, the expenses of organizing and participating in a market or implementing a government policy. The principle of property rights is then sketched. The transaction-costs analyses of Coase, Stigler, and Williamson are reviewed in more detail. The goal is to show how transaction costs and property right economies imply drawbacks to reliance on government. Attention then shifts to two examples of direct attacks on intervention--the debate in the years between the two world wars on the possibility of an efficient planned economy and the newer economic theories of political behavior.

An Overview of Transaction Costs

Transaction costs are the barriers to easy private and public decision making. As discussed below, the prevalence of market failures stems from the occurrence of transaction costs. Conversely, little government would be required if transaction costs did not exist. Market solutions could be devised even for situations in which the impacts are diffuse and simultaneous among individuals (the public-good problem).

The expenses that comprise transaction costs are those relating to providing and securing information about what is available, making a transaction, monitoring buyer and seller compliance, and adjusting to drastic, unanticipated changes in circumstances. All the steps require time and other resources; fees may be involved. Information costs, in turn, consist of expenses of broadly defined advertising and market research. Costs associated with transacting include those of transportation to or communications among participants, fees charged by brokers, and the costs of drafting contracts. Compliance costs include expenses of buyer efforts to prevent or remedy failure to provide the promised goods or services, checking on the quality of the goods provided, securing promised special assistance such as service calls on equipment and maintenance services for rental properties, and seller work to ensure payment.

Concern with transaction costs leads immediately to examining property rights. Transactions are impossible without assignment of clear and, in most cases, undivided property rights to everything traded. Such rights are precisely what the usual meanings of property and rights suggest. A property right is the legal grant of control over a specific economic resource. Ownership is the source of such rights. However, often leases are used to allow others to utilize the resource. Such leasing transfers a portion of the owners' rights. Improving the assignment of rights can lower transaction costs. Many market failures may be only defects in assigning property rights. Changing property rights then is the best reform.

Critics of the transaction-cost concept claim it is merely a fancy name for obvious problems, but as is often the case with many critiques of economic discoveries, this is the verdict of hindsight. What seems obvious after the fact took a long time to emerge and an even longer time to be recognized. Others, including too many economists, remain oblivious to the implications of transaction costs. The theory clarifies many issues, and the results may be obvious only to some trained economists. To be sure, as Coase and his admirers admit, the delineation of transaction costs and their implications remains incomplete. (On this, see the symposium on "The Optimal Theory of the Firm" cited here as Williamson and Winter 1991. It contains Coase's original article, his fresh review of his work and discussions by others.)

As Stigler (1987, 117-20), Coase (1988, 157-8, 174-9), and others have indicated, transaction costs are the sole barrier to economic efficiency. This argument develops points that, while tautological, still were long unrecognized. If transactions were costless, every economic inefficiency could be negotiated out of existence (Coase 1988, 175). Monopolists could be bribed to increase output to efficient levels; public goods would be provided optimally.[1]

Restoration of competitive output *could* occur with a gain to consumers without a loss to the former monopolists. The gains to monopoly are less than the losses inflicted on consumers (see above). If that loss were reversed, consumers could profitably compensate monopolists for their profit loss. Consumers would retain the difference between their initial gain and the monopoly profits. Conversely, if transaction costs were low enough, monopolists would be best off adopting a pricing system that captured all the benefits of producing at the competitive level. Such systems are described in the literature on public utilities. One method is to force consumers to use the gains of buying at competitive prices to pay for the right to buy at such prices. With public goods (as defined above), if accurate information could be obtained costlessly, the information needed to attain an optimum would be available.

The feasibility of compensation for removing monopoly or any other act is different from the desirability. Monopoly profits are considered undesirable gains. Return of the money to consumers is preferred. However, transaction cost problems might make this solution prohibitively expensive to attain. Compensation of firms might be necessary as the most practical way to cut losses.

In a world of transaction costs, the costs of action are higher than in the world of costless communication and trading assumed in simple general equilibrium analyses, and behavior must be modified to account for this. Inefficiencies are not so easily eliminated. This general conclusion has several key implications. First, what appear to be inefficiencies may really be ways to adjust better to transaction costs of which the outside observer was unaware. Second, since reforms often require substantial transaction costs, the evils must be large enough to repay the expenditures. Only great inefficiencies justify government intervention. Third, the preferable reform may prove to be eliminating public barriers to efficient private action. Fourth, even determining whether reform is justified involves costs; so, limits must be set on efforts to evaluate claims that action is needed.

---

[1]See Stigler (1988, 73-80) for a discussion of the seminar at Chicago at which Coase convinced his audience of the validity of his analysis.

This last requirement is particularly problematic. It leads to recognition of the difficulties in policy planning. Selection of policy targets proves an example of decision making under uncertainty. Thus, those who set targets must have the same sort of intuition as a successful business pioneer. Therefore, a high level of sophistication is needed. This may be difficult to attain in a political setting. Markets allow many participants. Entrepreneurs prove their acuity by succeeding financially. Those who err vanish unless they can secure government aid. Governments lack comparable devices to test the wisdom of those who set policy priorities. Old policies become sacrosanct. The difficulties are aggravated by the pressures to bias government policies to benefit narrow interests.

These propositions clearly imply greater skepticism about government-imposed reforms of the private sector. Obviously the existence of transaction costs implies that less reform is appropriate than if no transaction costs arose. Such conclusions are useful because prior reform proposals seemed to ignore transaction costs and particularly the severe difficulties of determining where to act. Thus, as this book stresses, the efficacy of governments is overrated.

The analysis also warns that the appropriate degree of modification cannot and should not be fully quantified. Uncertainty must remain about how many apparent problems can be efficiently solved and the best way to effect desirable improvements. We can never be sure whether an interventionist public action is more efficient than one facilitating better private actions.

A major part of evaluating reform prospects is better understanding of public and private practices. As Stigler's analysis discussed below stresses, particular attention must be given to the relationship between the nature of markets and the optimum organization of individual firms. The nature of a firm can be altered in many ways.

Similarly, intervention can take many forms such as continuous regulation, infrequently forcing changes, or instituting government ownership. The first option is typified by the agencies established to control public utilities and environmental problems. U.S. antitrust laws are the quintessence of periodic actions of various types. The meaning of government ownership requires no explanation.

Given the complexity of the issues, it is too demanding to complain that the clarifications have not resolved all doubts. Before and after the rise of transaction costs economics, writings were divided between those that stressed market failures and those that emphasized the superiority of markets. This division started becoming pronounced as support for classic economics waned somewhere around the turn of the twentieth century. Form again is hard to separate from substance. Frequently, the discord is merely over which aspects of largely accepted conclusions are most important. Some stress the residual market-failure problems; others, the need to reform unwise policies.

The discussion gets further biased because market failures historically have posed more analytic challenges. When competitive forces are vigorously at work, few problems can exist. Weak competition can be manifested in many different ways. Study of market failure has prevailed for over 100 years and produced extensive work. Examinations of alternative private solutions to transactions cost problems and consideration of government failure are much more recent (specifically with transaction costs, mainly after the 1960 appearance of Coase's article on social costs) and are still less extensive.

The implications were slowly absorbed; these criticisms of interventionist impulses did not become influential for a decade or more after 1960. Much writing of the 1960s that could have benefited from consideration of Coase failed to do so. Much later recognition of Coase still is perfunctory.

While the antiregulation aspects of transaction cost economics are stressed here, the concept can also support prointervention cases. Writers can and do either stress that, given transaction costs, practice may be not worth regulating or warn that the need for regulation has not been disproved. Thus, one author concludes his survey of potential entry-reducing strategies by noting the "market equilibrium outcomes...may be as good as can be expected...(Gilbert 1989, 531)." Another contribution to the same book has a section on mergers that concludes, "A general presumption in favor of mergers, therefore, does not appear to be justified (Jacquemin and Slade 1989, 437)."

Below, I discuss the criticisms of faith in regulatory reform. They stress the unrealism of a vision of impartial, rational, efficient regulation. The barriers include interest group politics, the impossibility of isolating the bureaucracy from political pressures, the forces that encourage bureaucrats independently to take unwise steps, and that full attainment of stated regulatory goals would involve intolerable levels of expenditures and intrusions into individual activities.

Property Rights and Effective Government

Even arguments that governments should be restrained, as noted above, usually do not call for anarchy. Proponents of heavy reliance on the markets such as Mises and Hayek stress that strong but restrained government is, in fact, critical. When markets are the best way to meet a need, governments should create a climate that prevents public or private actions that hinder markets from operating. The state must maintain the rule of law that is indispensable to the proper functioning of a market economy (see the discussion in chapter 12 of Rothbard and David Friedman for the case for abolishing government).

Following the tradition of John Locke and the contemporary work on law and economics, property-rights economics stresses that participants in markets cannot act without clear, enforceable property rights in the resources they wish to trade. The maintenance of such property rights and the protection of life and property from predators require effective government. (See Furubotn and Pejovich 1974 for an anthology of key contributions on the subject and Bromley 1991 for argument that common ownership can be efficient if a small enough, like-minded group is involved. Bromley's views seem a variant on the arguments by Coase discussed below on the private provision of public goods.)

This argument is largely based upon and best justified by observation of experiences with alternative approaches to property management. Examples of such experiences are provided in chapters 10 and 11. It is argued that many problems with mineral resources and amenity preservation are due to unsatisfactory property right assignment. In particular, greater reliance should have been placed on transferring ownership to private parties and on eliminating inefficient rules defining ownership rights.

The rule is that whenever it is physically possible to assign ownership of anything to a single entity, the legal system should encourage the undivided assignment of that right to an entity. The choice of how to use property cannot be made efficiently unless someone has a clear ability to decide what to do. The more power is divided, the greater the problem. Ill-defined ownership and access available to all at no cost inevitably leads to ruining the resource. This problem, for example, is the cause of the extermination of fish and wildlife and forest depletions in less developed countries such as Brazil. Chapter 11 examines case studies of property right issues stressing U.S. public land policy.

The Coase Analysis of Transaction Costs

Particularly critical work on the implications of transaction costs was done by Coase. In articles written over more than 50 years starting in 1937, he contributed to the development of transaction cost economics. His arguments and examples provided a particularly cogent criticism of contentions that governments should always intervene when high transaction costs hinder efficiency.

Coase's writings provide a comparative analysis of the difficulties of private and government actions. The principles give the theoretic basis of the optimum scope of the public sector and the optimal organization of both the public and private sectors. His exposition was sufficiently compelling to attract wide attention among economists despite his informal approach. Coase avoided elaborate mathematical formulations and sketched his basic argument.

Coase's 1988 book provided a collection of previous articles and an updated commentary on his 1960 article on social costs. The collection provides a better view of Coase's full analysis of the virtues of and the gaps in standard economic theory. The newly prepared essay also makes clear that the earlier Coase articles treat various aspects of a general problem--excessive faith in government intervention. The inclusion of less widely anthologized essays such as his 1946 study of public utility regulation and his 1974 history of lighthouses in Britain gives further illustrations of the implications of his concerns about the limits to government action.

Two articles are central. In 1937, Coase analyzed the optimal organization of firms and their dealing with each other. In 1960, he presented his controversial but influential analysis of the defects of theories of "externalities" such as pollution. The gist of the latter was stated in chapter 3 and is more fully discussed in chapter 10. Here focus in on the 1937 article.

His 1937 article concentrated on analyzing what caused firms to form and why they chose to limit their scope. This theory of the ability of firms to adapt to different circumstances is a key component of the modern extended rationale for reliance on market solutions. While greater scope can involve doing more things of similar types, the extensions critical to Coase were in the area of vertical integration, i.e., producing goods used in other parts of the firm.

Coase's analysis also implies that a combination of procurement approaches might be used. He recognized that a further question was the choice of optimum techniques for conducting transactions with others. He noted that contracts can facilitate dealings by lowering transaction costs. In contracting, the key transaction costs were negotiating and monitoring the contracts. No contract would be a perfect substitute for integration because of these transaction costs (see chapter 7 for an extension of that argument).

Coase argued that optimum organization was based upon a trade-off between transaction costs and problems of managing larger firms (or what Baumol, Panzar, and Willig termed in 1982 "diseconomies of scope"). In principle, the owners of different inputs could transact as frequently as the start of each work period to cooperate in production. Firms are mechanisms for assuring that certain inputs are unambiguously committed to the firm over long time periods. In particular, the firm arranges directly to hire inputs on a longer term basis.

Saving on transaction costs most obviously justifies securing the basic labor, raw material, and machinery inputs needed to produce a particular good. Under some circumstances, it may be more profitable to integrate vertically than to purchase a commodity. A theory must be flexible enough to explain why integration is extensive but not complete. Firms differ radically in how they secure key inputs. Firms stop extending activities when marginal transaction costs equal the marginal cost of increased difficulty of management. Review of the issues indicates the wisdom of Coase's care in limiting his argument. He only argues that vertical integration is justified in some circumstances. He avoids exaggerating the desirability.

Most discussions leave tacit many complications. Vertical integration changes the nature of transactions without necessarily decreasing their number. Inputs to a process are bought instead of the outputs. These inputs can be the outputs of other firms or labor and other resources provided by households. A single transaction with a specialist may be replaced by many transactions with owners of less specialized resources. Vertical integration, therefore, could lead to more transactions and possibly also higher transaction costs.

Implicit in Coase's analysis is that situations *may* occur in which the expense of transactions with specialized suppliers of a good may be substantially greater than those with the less specialized suppliers of the inputs to make that good. Thus, in these cases, transaction costs savings will accrue to integration. As discussed below, views on how much integration is likely greatly influence outlooks on the vigor of competition and the need for government controls.

Demsetz (in Williamson and Winter 1991) suggests a useful alternative view. He argues that the management and transaction costs about which Coase was concerned are better thought of as shifted rather than avoided under different organizational structures. Demsetz adds that differences among firms in costs of production should be added to the analysis. Cost advantages of one producer may be a major influence on choice. Demsetz also warns that, in practice, ambiguity is always present in determining whether costs are for production, management, or transaction. Demsetz suggests the proper interpretation is that a total cost minimizing structure is sought. In short, firms form to lessen the total costs of combining inputs. Exactly how large and vertically integrated the firm should become depends on the circumstances. (See also Baumol 1986.)

Coase and other authors suggest that integration or contracting is most likely when buyer, seller, or both cannot readily change trading partners. The nonexistence of futures markets would encourage adopting integration or a contract as the best available way to smooth out the effects of market fluctuations.

An optimistic view of the ability to effect transactions cheaply also leads to expectations of decentralized firms and many, highly competitive markets. A theory that stresses high transaction costs leads to anticipations that firms will be large, centralized, and self-produce rather than buy (or sell) many goods used (or produced).

Among economists, those stressing high costs for private transactions and low costs of government controls will advocate government controls. The more widespread the perceived advantage of government, the broader the controls proposed. The contrary arguments are symmetric. The greater the perceived advantage of markets over government, the less the enthusiasm about regulation. The critics of regulation add that, in practice, action depends more on the power of pressure groups than on a rational analysis of whether regulation will improve efficiency.

Coase has described situations in which the market solution is likely to be preferable because governments will be less likely to produce economically desirable actions than affected private parties. He illustrates this point by the public-utility example ([1946] 1988), by the small-scale externalities solved by private negotiation or litigation (1960), and by a demonstration that markets in Britain provided lighthouses ([1974] 1988)--commodities that economists (still) often argue cannot be efficiently supplied by markets.

Viner ([1959] 1991) similarly indicates an eighteenth century tendency for "...services which elsewhere were governmental were in England partially or completely left in the hands of franchised businessmen operating for profit...(51-2)." Lighthouses are Viner's first example.[2]

In his first case, Coase contended that the private solution to financing public utilities discussed below was far more feasible than the government subsidies proposed by many theorists. He argued for all the cases that, contrary to the fears of Samuelson (1954), the problem termed "free riding," i.e., incomplete participation by beneficiaries, may cause less inefficiency than the difficulties of getting adequate attention from a busy government.

He thus provided advice on ways the theory can be fruitfully extended and on the limits of many widely used approaches to economic analysis. Coase concluded that traditional theory is marred by asymmetries and chastised theorists for simultaneously fretting over market failures and neglecting the essential problem that causes such failures. The market-failure concept, therefore, should be applied with recognition of the transaction cost barriers to public and private solutions.

With inadequate appreciation of this point, theorists evaluate problems that persist only because of transaction costs and proposed solutions that ignore the existence of these costs. Worse, only the private sector side of the solution problem is considered, and writers on the subject often come dangerously close to postulating that barriers are absent in the design of government solution. Government defects are ignored.

Coase thus deduced that government intervention is too quickly proposed even in the economics literature. His analysis of the consequences of transactions costs created problems caused him to argue that the barriers to private dealing similarly hinder government identification of a satisfactory solution. He urged caution about intervention and used case studies to illustrate this conclusion.

The transaction-cost approach is a valuable corrective to the traditional one-sided "market failure" approach. For the individual firm, the individual industry, and the economy, the critical policy issues thus relate to transaction cost problems. The key determinant is the comparative cost of private and public solutions.

A vital special case of transaction cost economics can be found in Hayek's argument about the superiority of a market economy over a planned economy

---

[2]The 1991 book is a collection of Viner's writings, some previously unpublished. The citation is from an unpublished paper written in 1959 contained in the collection. The book also contains a reprint of a 1968 publication making similar arguments (278).

(discussed below). However, Coase, who is generally treated as an analytic economist, is more critical of the public-good argument than Hayek. The latter's fullest discussion (1960, 223-4) accepts a Samuelson-type public-good argument and its application to provision of parklands. Hayek adopted the traditional assumption that such land is so lightly utilized that charges inefficiently exclude people. The inappropriateness of applying this assumption to congested actual national parks has long been recognized (see chapters 10 and 11).

As noted above, controversy remains about how many allegations of inefficiency would prove invalid if their transaction costs aspects were better appraised. A key example in which the transaction cost explanation seems better is that the affection of theorists for organized markets is excessive. This would be true even if the theorists wanted such markets only for all goods that are regularly traded. The most abstract theorists argue that extensive inefficiency will prevail unless formal markets exist for a far wider variety of goods than are presently traded. It is contended that markets should exist to hedge against any possible future development. With transaction costs, it is less clear that either centralized markets are desirable for all goods or that the list of traded commodities should be greatly extended.

Similarly, it is efficient to limit the number of options explored. Wise shoppers do not regularly collect price data from every store in town on every commodity they wish to buy. The savings produced often would not recover the cost of the extra travel to make the purchases and certainty would not compensate for the time spent. Thus, many failures to seek minimum available prices, maximum quality, or other advantages arise from similar transaction cost considerations. In chapter 7, a review of debates about the implications of different forms of market organization is provided.

Coase, as noted, is concerned about the tendency to propose too much intervention in the presence of transaction costs. In contrast, Samuelson's (1954) analysis of public goods discussed above reflects greater belief that government funding is often the superior way to finance goods with high transaction costs. Coase, therefore, has often used Samuelson as an example of the tendency to overstate the desirability of intervention. (Examples include Coase's articles on marginal cost pricing for natural monopolies and on lighthouses.)

Extensions of Transaction Cost Analysis: Stigler, Williamson, and Others

Discussions of transaction costs by other economists (and lawyers) associated with the University of Chicago (notably Stigler, Demsetz, McGee, and Cheung) have developed arguments that follow Coase in stressing the efficacy of markets. A simple tentative discussion by Stigler is particularly critical. Many more controversial Chicago arguments are expressions of faith in the ability to transact. In contrast, Oliver Williamson (1975, 1985b) developed an enormously influential view of transaction costs that began with stress on the limitations of markets but ultimately added recognition of how markets can adapt.

Stigler ([1951] reprint 1968 and 1986) developed the argument that the selection of the organizational pattern depends profoundly upon the nature, particularly the size and competitiveness, of the markets in which the firm operates. He added the critical observation that as an industry expands and matures the optimum structure changes.

Stigler stressed a trend toward more disintegrated firms and greater reliance on the spot market as demand growth and increased linkages of previously separate markets reduce the risks of open market transactions. Therefore, expansion is likely to make the markets more closely resemble simple textbook models of competition. The scope of the firm will shrink and lesser reliance will be placed on contracts.

Stigler's analysis removes a hiatus in the traditional analysis of the relationship between the firm and the industry. The focus is usually on the effect of firm characteristics on the market. Stigler has shown that market characteristics have implications for the firm (see chapter 7 for further discussion). Later work by Stigler and others has supported this argument (see Levy 1984, Stigler and Sherwin 1985.)

Particularly strong views on the ability of markets to overcome transaction cost barriers to efficient solutions were developed by McGee (1980) and Demsetz (1968). Chapter 4 reviews McGee's argument that the ability to contract allows new firms to enter previously monopolistic industries. In chapter 7 Demsetz's suggestion that competitive bidding for the right to serve could produce efficient behavior by those operating a natural monopoly is examined.

In analyzing firms (and industries), Williamson (1975) initially concentrated on the market implications of high transaction costs that hinder private transactions and raise the risks of using markets and the advantages for highly centralized firms. He (1975 and 1985b) also emphasizes the problems of what he terms "opportunism," heavy dependence on a few suppliers. While the number of potential competitors before the deal is made may be large, dependence on a few suppliers often occurs once arrangements have been completed. These deals, even if made in a competitive market, will establish long lasting and expensive to alter arrangements. To avoid the expense of designing a new arrangement, one of the trading partners may be willing to grant more favorable terms to the other. Opportunism then is taking advantage of this willingness.

Others use the term "agency problem" to describe the difficulties of control. In the theory, a distinction is made between principals who are the beneficiaries of actions and agents to whom implementation is delegated. Whether or not to integrate would depend on which alternative created greater incentives for efficient supply. Williamsonian opportunism arises when the lack of competition makes the supplier a poor agent. Conversely, Coase's concept that at some point difficulties of administration limit firm size can be restated to indicate that at large size, the division managers become poorer agents than outside suppliers.

The difficulties are compounded by the incomplete information available to each firm. To describe this problem, Williamson favors the term "bounded rationality," which he attributes to Herbert Simon. The idea seems similar to the point of Hayek (discussed further below) that since knowledge is expensive to acquire, rational actors limit the information they obtain.

Williamson's 1975 conclusion was that high degrees of vertical integration often arise. His 1975 exposition also implied that barriers to negotiating competitive solutions tended to produce uncompetitive markets. Williamson's initial approach proved highly influential, and many articles have been written on the deleterious effects on competition of transaction costs. For example, Joskow and Schmalensee (1983) use Williamson's analysis as the basis of their conclusion that integration of electric utilities is so desirable that proposals for reorganization should be rejected.

As Williamson (1985b) indicates, he also is heavily influenced by writers, such as Chandler, who show interest in the prevalence of multidivision firms. Chandler is the author of several well-researched studies of the history of large corporations and is most interested in the contributions to economic progress. These studies show how firms succeeded by adopting appropriate organizational forms. Chandler (1962, 1977, 1990) started with recognition of the technologies that created opportunities for large new firms. He centered on the role of transportation and communications in allowing firms to operate over much wider regions. The one town firm gave way to the international firm. These firms generally took advantage of new technologies that produced new commodities and more effective means of production.

Chandler is more a historian than an economist but uses economics concepts relevant to his special concerns. His Austrian inspirations come from Schumpeter. Chandler's latest work (1990) returns Williamson's compliment by explicitly using the latter's concepts. Chandler also does not share the classic concerns with monopolies. He regularly describes the industries studied as oligopolies without demonstrating any of the standard alarms about the fewness of sellers that he observes.

Williamson's 1975 book was the first effort extensively to expand on the Coase analysis. By incorporating other analyses with that of Coase, the result was a view of the working of firms and markets much different from Coase's. In later writings, Williamson moved closer to the original Coase position by adding discussions of the limits to centralization. Williamson originally tended to underestimate the harm to future dealings caused by mistreating customers or suppliers. Another concern is whether opportunism is possible unless the participants posses monopoly or monopsony power. In the absence of such power, many devices are available to design transactions in which opportunism is precluded (see chapter 7). Universally, both sides have interests in preserving the agreement and in protecting their reputations.

The Williamson argument also neglected the implications of the existence of multiplant firms. Where the producers or the users of an input to production have additional plants, they can shift operations. When the buyer or seller had monopoly power before the deal was made, the danger of opportunism is at least greater. It is possible that only firms with long-run monopoly power can engage in opportunistic behavior. (The arguments made in chapter 4 suggest that monopoly power rarely, if ever, persists without government intervention.)

Williamson's (1985b) extensions of the analysis produced a more balanced case. Greater attention was given to both the limits to integration and the different market institutions available to reduce transaction costs. He and others, for example, have written many articles on the theory of contracts. Williamson (1975) initially feared that alternatives to vertical integration, such as contracts, that can lessen the dangers of using the market are also difficult to design and implement efficiently. As the discussion advanced, a more balanced, more optimistic view of contracting has developed (see chapter 7). The contributions to efficiency of mechanisms such as renegotiating and damage liability provisions have been more widely recognized.

At a more popular level, Williamson's early work corresponds nicely with the 1970s efforts to construct ever larger companies. His revisions similarly reflected the growing disenchantment with indiscriminate expansion of corporate activities. (See chapter 7 for examples from the minerals field.)

However, it required further effort on Coase's part to make clear how much his views differed from Williamson's. In addition to the points noted above, Coase's reflections on his analysis indicate two deliberate decisions not to treat issues others have stressed. First, he accepted the view of his teacher Arnold Plant "that monopoly tended to be transitory and generally unimportant except when promoted and supported by the state (Williamson and Winter, 1991, 54)." Thus, while aware of contrary views, Coase chose not to make monopoly avoidance a major element in firm organization.

Another decision was not to stress the dangers of opportunism. Coase's observation of American practice caused him to doubt that vertical integration was essential to prevent opportunism. He noted that General Motors obtained at least one critical part, frames, from an independent supplier (Williamson and Winter 1991, 69-72). The Coase explanation relied on this example probably because a widely cited study of how opportunism promotes integration (Klein, Crawford, and Alchian 1979) used General Motors' purchase of Fisher Body as the main evidence. (Williamson and Winter 1991, 213-16, contains Klein's rejoinder.)

The Problem of Central Planning

A broader, more controversial attack on intervention appears in the numerous writings of Mises (esp. 1981) and Hayek (esp. 1945). These writings are often and somewhat narrowly called a contribution to the socialist calculation debate. Mises frequently asserted that socialism could not work because it could not provide a substitute for the price system. Oscar Lange (1936-7), a Polish socialist, countered that the problem could be solved by creating a planning board that calculated efficient prices. (Lange was a refugee in Britain when he wrote the essays; to the delight of his critics, when he returned to Poland to direct planning, he did not implement his famous proposals.) Hayek (1945) rejoined that this was no answer because the economics of information precluded calculating efficient prices. Hayek's argument is often watered down to asserting only the superior efficiency of markets over planning boards. However, Hayek reiterates Mises's conclusion that the barriers to planning are impossible to overcome. In effect, the market is infinitely superior to planning.

Throughout this section, stress is on Lange and Hayek. A few comments about Mises are desirable. Mises was an opponent of socialism from the 1920s until his death in 1973. His key works are *Socialism: an Economic and Sociological Analysis* (1981), *Liberalism: In the Classical Tradition* (1985), and *Human Action: A Treatise on Economics* (1966). The first book was a sweeping denunciation of socialist tendencies. Such leanings were so broadly defined that they encompassed almost all forms of etatism. The last two books are expositions of the virtues of markets. *Liberalism* is terser and more judiciously phrased than *Human Action*. However, *Human Action* adds a stress, adopted from Schumpeter, on innovation that later disciples of Mises consider the core of his analysis. His elevation of a Schumpeterian theory occurred when Schumpeter was pessimistic on the future of capitalism and accepting of Lange's argument. Mises, as noted, criticized socialism because it had no way of computing prices. His critics consider this an incomplete argument; his defenders claim Mises understood the rationale. What is clear is that Hayek (1945) provided a clearer argument than any given by Mises. However, Mises is more effective than Hayek in warning about the impossibility of forecasts. He correctly warns that the future depends on knowledge that does not yet exist.

As many have noted, Lange "vindicated" socialism by redefining it to mean central control of the economy. He argued that a planning agency that gave efficient price signals could make socialism work. He claimed that he was following Mises's hints and suggested that "a statue of Professor Mises ought to occupy an honorable place in the great hall of the Ministry of Socialization (1936-7)." This statement became particularly ironic in 1989. Mises may rate a statue for a reason opposite to that Lange expected. The successors to Ministries of Socialization were forced to consider how right Mises was. Those calling for the creation of free markets in communist countries are often quoted as being inspired by writers such as Mises and Hayek. (After presenting a seminar in Moscow on free markets, the Cato Institute donated a bust of Hayek.)

Lange implicitly accepted arguments stated below that nationalization by itself has mostly undesirable effects. He saved socialism by redefinition. He evaded the basic Mises challenge of explaining how the proper prices would be determined. What his admirers accept as proof is only an undocumented assertion.

Hayek countered that difficulties in securing and absorbing information limit what governments can successfully undertake. Specialization in knowledge is a particularly useful form of division of labor. This proposition is accepted in economics as is its minimum implication that regulation is usually badly designed because of information collection problems.

Since this argument draws upon familiar facts about the vastness of existing knowledge, it might seem that little elaboration was needed. In the 1940s Hayek published two articles that epitomized his critical contribution, the explanation of the superiority of markets over central planning as ways of transmitting knowledge relevant to decision making. Hayek found, however, that greater explanation was needed to convince people. The failure of the articles to persuade enough readers inspired Hayek to produce several books expanding on the drawbacks of a centralized economy at great length. Four treatises (1944, 1960, 1973-9, 1989) and numerous essays develop more fully his evolving views.

Hayek (1945) suggested that a key, frequently overlooked contribution of division of labor in a market economy is economizing on information. Knowledge is one of the scarcest resources. Available information is less than needed to predict accurately the consequences of human activity. More critically, no one person or group can absorb all the extant information about technology and other forces that affect the performance of an economy. Part of specialization is that the profit motive inspires different people to learn the skills needed to produce different goods and services. The market proves the lowest-cost, feasible transmitter of information about the potential for profitable dealing. This argument is that transaction costs are much higher for governments. Hayek and Mises, as noted, argue that governments cannot learn all that is needed for efficient, long-run planning at any cost.

Hayek's (1945) criticism of socialism charitably ignores the more obvious problem that the Lange "defense" is advocacy of something unlike the standard practice of socialism as government ownership. Such government ownership becomes an irrelevance. Hayek chose to accept the redefinition and analyze whether the planning board could operate efficiently. Hayek, as noted, suggested that it would be highly inefficient to centralize information in this fashion; the market would do better. Lange-type planning resembles the typical vision of democratic planning, and this type of planning is not actually performed in socialist countries.

Since so many government programs involve creating regulatory agencies that are small-scale versions of Lange's planning board, the Hayek argument is applicable to intervention short of comprehensive planning. In effect, Lange argued the public-utility commission technique would be applied to all industry. The shortcomings of actual public utility regulation suggest that its massive extension would be ill-advised. Since these flaws long were known, it is curious that the relationship between Lange's ideas and those about regulating individual industries and the implications of the similarity were neglected by Hayek and later commentators. Hayek had the excuse of unfamiliarity with regulatory practice. Many others were specialists on the subject.

The defects of nationalization also require note because of the prevalence of government ventures even in primarily market-oriented economies. Standard criticisms of nationalization indicate that it tends to harm the attainment of efficiency. Nationalization by its government sanction creates a more solid, less regulated monopoly than private firms possess. The government will be more protective in every sense of the word. Greater insulation from competition will be given the firm. The nationalized firm will be sheltered from the takeover threats and bankruptcy that constrain private firms. The ability to attract, discipline, and fire workers may be restricted.

Price levels and structures will be established to subsidize influential consumer blocs. The government may lend money at below-market rates, be lax about ensuring repayment, and be lenient about regulating government owned ventures as stringently as private ones. The 1991 scandals caused by members of the U.S. House of Representatives who frequently cashed bad checks at a special facility created for them and who rarely paid their bills at the House dining rooms illustrate the problem on a small understandable scale.

The experience with large scale nationalizations provides many more examples of error. The 1948 British coal nationalization was supposed to institute an era of enlightened industry performance including eliminating tumult in labor relations. Instead, it was not until the middle 1980s that the British government was willing to resist the militant demands of the coal miners union for preservation of unproductive mines and the jobs they generated. Through 1994, the resistance was vigorous enough to ensure maintenance of inefficient mines. However, the call under the slogan of privatization for reversal of these changes had its greatest effect in Britain. Steel, gas distribution, telephone service, and electricity have been returned to private ownership; coal is supposed to follow. Its survival in any case was undermined by privatization of steel and electricity, the main customers. As private firms, they could no longer tolerate above-market prices for coal.

The United States, in contrast to its reputation as the bastion of free markets, has strongly resisted privatization although the record of public management is widely criticized by all aware of it. During the U.S. New Deal of the 1930s, advocates of intervention stressed creating U.S. government owned electric-power generating facilities as "yardsticks" against which private performance could be compared. Two major comprehensive efforts, the Tennessee Valley Authority (TVA) in the Southeast and the Bonneville Power Authority (BPA) in the Northwest, were created. While TVA has a wide range of activities, owning and operating numerous hydroelectric and thermal power plants as well as engaging in nonenergy ventures, Bonneville only markets power from hydroelectric projects managed by other federal agencies.

TVA was probably the more familiar example because of its location, broader scope, greater cohesion, and more controversy-filled history. The last involved publicity about its contribution including a book by its chairman extolling its virtues and a dispute in the Eisenhower administration about whether private power should be allowed into the area to build steam fired plants (see Wildavsky 1962). TVA was allowed to build coal-fired and later nuclear plants. This proved the last great successful federal battle for expanded public electric power.

The validity of the yardstick was always undermined by the major differences between public and private power--initially consisting of access to both financing at below market rates and access to sources of cheap hydroelectric power. The latter advantage has gone, and the moves into fuel-based generation have led to tarnished images even among interventionists.

By the 1970s, etatists were regularly complaining that TVA had lost its missionary role and become "just another electric company." It and similar organizations were viewed as at least as devoted to increased generating capacity using nuclear power as any other private company. This change perhaps should be viewed as faulting TVA for maintaining its original goals that the critics felt were outmoded. TVA, moreover, was considered more careless about nuclear safety and coal pollution than private companies.

Bonneville inspired and developed a subsidization program for a massive coal and nuclear plant expansion plan. A major part of the effort was entrusted to a newly created Washington Public Power Supply System (WPPSS, often pronounced Whoops). WPPSS proved a costly failure due to a combination of slower than expected demand growth and deficiencies in construction management resulting from inexperience. Similarly, TVA had to undertake an extended shutdown of all its nuclear plants to correct their deficiencies.

Thus, public firms have not provided the promised yardstick. They have operated defectively, presumably because of the intrinsic drawbacks of government ownership. The yardsticks to which more recent writers refer are generally successful rival private firms. (Such writers, in turn, are cavalier about how to adjust comparisons for the substantial differences among utilities.)

Concern with socialism is not the only reason to take Mises and Hayek seriously. At least by 1960, Hayek began to recognize that socialism had waned as an influence but that pressures for unwise intervention remained intense. His writings turned into more general attacks in the spirit of Adam Smith on self-serving searches for government aid. The present problem is the ancient evil of excessive government intervention. As Hayek does not stress, the socialists and other modern interventionists proved to be the descendants of what Adam Smith and his contemporaries called mercantilists. Socialism has degenerated back to the belief that protectionism is a useful force that can be redirected to nobler aims instead of the evil that classical liberals showed it to be.

In addition to the preference of markets over governments, decentralized decision making is also favored in developing rules of law. Following warnings in Hume's "On the Original Contract," Hayek distrusted the social-contract argument because it exaggerates the ability to develop a priori principles of law. He believed that human ignorance precludes such actions. The best choice must be determined by the competition of institutions in practice. Preference is for a spontaneous order of evolutionary development adopting principles whose efficacy had been established through experience. This viewpoint is made incessantly by Hayek (see esp. 1976, 1989). Where knowledge is lacking, no basis for action prevails. Market processes are preferable to government decree in determining prices of commodities. Governments should not act when they cannot determine what they will accomplish.

He particularly objects to those who postulate the ability consciously to reorganize massively. However, he, like Mises, recognized that other forces such as envy influence the attacks on the spontaneous order (see chapter 13).

Hayek's attacks on the ability consciously to design societies are among the most problematic aspects of his analyses. If taken too literally, his arguments rule out the appraisals of actual societies that Hayek freely makes (see Kukathas 1989). Rothbard (1988) is concerned that the theory rules out conscious innovation and thus slights the stress on innovation Rothbard credits to Mises.

The latter charge is easier to refute. Mises's innovator is searching for what is hoped to be a successful decision but, as Mises incessantly argued, must await the market outcome. Such market testing seems to be precisely what Hayek is stressing. The problem of reconciling attacks on conscious design with policy proposals has not been resolved precisely because the dilemma is a major component of the fallibility of knowledge. Pressing problems force making proposals.

Hayek contends that centralized management cannot be effective unless it becomes sufficiently coercive that it produces what everyone would recognize as tyranny. He asserts, see below, that limited democratic indicative planning would be ineffective. (We often actually get ineffective planning that lessens freedom, albeit more moderately than in a totally planned economy.)

Hayek's later work discusses at great length, but less convincingly, limits that should be imposed on what may be legislated. He advocates (1979) a separate legislative body designed only to define what is legitimate.

Hayek's basic proposition about the advantage of decentralizing knowledge is a critical, widely-accepted proposition of modern economics, but the inferences drawn by Mises and Hayek are often considered extremism. The rhetorical excesses of which both are guilty (Mises more than Hayek) has contributed to this impression, but so has reluctance to recognize that valid points are made. A further difficulty with Hayek is that he dares to grapple with problems that no one has managed to solve.

Other writers have epitomized the intervention problem as a need to recognize government failure, the tendency of governments to perform more poorly than is assumed in abstract theory. Some insist that government failure is a more serious problem than market failure. They are probably correct, but the Hayek principle also warns that this is an informed judgment that may be wrong.

The Drawbacks of Government--Economic Theories of Political Behavior

Economists were not content merely to show how often governments erred. Economic principles were employed to explain government behavior. The starting point of the analysis was to identify exactly what political institutions maximized. In their simplest forms, the theories lead directly to predictions of invariably inefficient behavior. These primitive models proved too simple. Modification produces more complex behavior. In this extended analysis, both additional ways to be inefficient and the possibility to be efficient arise. These qualifications thus limit, but do not eliminate, the contribution of the theory to indicating the prevalence of incentives to governmental inefficiency.

Three main economic theories of political behavior were developed. The first explanation suggested by Schumpeter (1950) and more fully developed by Downs (1957) is that the process of competing for votes may lead to inefficient results. The theory is related to but more sophisticated than the single-issue voter concept used by journalists. The starting point is that typically, a protectionist policy produces significant benefits to a few and scattered, small losses to many. Since protectionism thwarts completion of mutually beneficial trades, the losses exceed the gains. However, the gains from protection are more visible. The beneficiaries are much more likely to vote for advocates of protection than losers are prone to vote against those supporting intervention. It is thus easier to attract votes by responding to the strong feelings of those seeking protection than to rally the victims. Thus, much protectionist legislation arises. (Also see Becker 1983.)

Subsequent writers such as Peltzman (1980) have further extended the analyses of behavior of elected officials to allow for the supplemental effect of ideology. In particular, studies of voting records indicate that popular politicians dealing with issues in which no strong constituent views exist may decide by ideology. Discussions of energy policy, for example, have suggested that many supporters of the dirigisme of the 1970s were intervention-minded Democrats from states on which the impacts of policy choice were small and probably negative on balance. Lacking strong political pressures, these legislators felt free to vote their ideology. For example, many investigations of federal mineral leasing policy were advocated by a Senator from Arkansas, a state that heavily depends on minerals produced in federal lands in other states. He feels free to advocate policies that can only raise the cost of minerals to his constituents because the impacts are so small.

The second argument is that those regulated by government have by far the greatest interest in and influence on the process. The companies can and do offer attractive post-government career options to retiring regulators and become enthusiastic supporters of efforts to move from regulatory commissions to higher offices. This capture theory stresses that regulators' motivation by the long-term monetary consequences to the regulators of their decisions. Thus, regulation may be created to protect the industry, and even if this was not the initial intent, regulators get captured by those they regulate. This has often been suggested in the literature, but an article by Stigler (1971) is widely cited as the clearest statement.

In a contribution antedating his modification discussed above of the analysis of legislative behavior, Peltzman (1976) added to the analysis of regulatory agency behavior by developing a more formal model that took into account the existence of opposition to assisting the industry. As would be expected, the need to consider such antagonism prevents the regulators from allowing the regulated industry to earn maximum monopoly profits. Displeasure increases with price levels and as regulators move away from prices that only repay costs, the intensity of objection increases. The cost of this increased aversion can mount so that regulators may stop short of allowing monopoly rates. This theory is another example of how full analysis shows that many outcomes are possible. Depending on the exact shape of the benefit and cost functions, anything from resistance so strong as to keep rates below costs to opposition so weak that monopoly profits arise might occur.

Another concern, discussed in Niskanen's (1971) analysis of bureaucracy, is that the civil servants who implement the laws are interested in advancing their status inside government. Government salaries are less attractive than in the private sector, but considerable power can be attained. More people within and outside the bureaucracy can be controlled. This causes bureaucrats to seek expansion of activity for its own sake. This theory is even more ambiguous in its implications than the voting competition and capture theories. Expanding power is not undesirable a priori, but the prior discussion here suggests that, in practice, intervention is highly undesirable.

These theories all reflect the central principle proposition of monopoly theory. In politics as in private monopoly, the politician receives gains that exceed the costs inflicted on the victims. The analogy is nearly perfect when the inefficient policy is imposing a monopoly. The principal differences are in the transaction costs of creating and enforcing monopoly by private action or by government support. Enlisting government may be a more expensive way to *establish* the monopoly than a private accord. However, the government can more cheaply *enforce* the maintenance of the monopoly. Some argue, however, that the gains are spent in efforts to attract political favors.

Monopoly, in turn, is but one type of policy in which one group gains from transfers from another group. In all these policies, a net loss occurs because those who make the transfers endure the additional loss of having a useful activity eliminated.

These positive theories of economic motivations to regulate then are less clearly demonstrative of the drawbacks of interference than the attacks on regulatory practice. Nevertheless, the overall impact is reinforcement of doubts about statism. The theories suggests that only if the advocates of efficiency become the dominant influence on policy makers will desirable outcomes occur. Experience suggests that this ideal situation does not prevail.

The effort to explain government action was extended by statistical analysis of political behavior. Appraisals of votes in the U.S. Congress are the most widely performed studies. Votes and the characteristics of those casting them generate data far more readily evaluated than on other political decisions. The results seem to confirm the more complex explanations of behavior. (See Cohen and Noll, 1991 for review of prior work and six original analyses.)

As I write, the U.S. government is trying to grapple with two difficult issues. The simpler case is that of the North American Free Trade Agreement, a modest extension of long-standing U.S. efforts to reduce trade barriers. For reasons that are unclear, trade unions and some environmental groups exaggerated the negative impacts of the treaty and imperiled its ratification. However, the effort to stop NAFTA failed.

An even worse case is health care reform. It is unclear what would be efficient, and thus whether efficiency will increase under the proposed plans. The U.S. health care system already is heavily affected by numerous, often undesirable government actions. These include protection of physicians from competition by grants of monopoly in such areas as prescribing medicines and aids to medical education. The treatment of "employer" contributions to medical insurance as nontaxable income to employees creates an employee bias toward preferring compensation through increased insurance rather through taxable money income. Two major (and at least three others for special groups such as the military, civilian government employees, and veterans) federally-directed health care programs exist, and perennial efforts to limit their costs prevail. Each policy has created beneficiaries who feel strongly about preserving their positions. In this complex environment, no one can know what constitutes the efficient solution. Good reason exists to fear that those benefiting from the inefficiencies will continue to scare politicians into undertaking the inefficient solution.

In sum, what is efficient to political organizations often has inefficient overall impacts. In principle, forces can operate to stimulate more efficient policies. Formidable barriers exist to ensuring that such incentives to efficiency influence decisions. The illustrations provided here and elsewhere in this book are only a few examples of how often inefficiency arises. Even when qualified, the positive theories of intervention still suggest that, despite the known drawbacks of intervention, political processes create great pressures to regulate unwisely.

Summary and Conclusions

Economic theory increasingly emphasizes the critical role of property rights in ensuring efficient transactions. Efforts have been made to deal with the implications of the costs of using markets. Ronald Coase and others particularly those associated with the University of Chicago, stress the ways markets can adapt to these problems and note the lack of clear evidence that government solutions are preferable. Others stimulated by Oliver Williamson's earlier work have emphasized the difficulties of using markets.

A further criticism of government intervention is that decision making is often distorted because such goals as seeking votes, responding to lobbying, and bureaucratic pressures encourage inefficient policies.

Chapter 7

Optimum Economic Organization: The Efficiency of Firms and Its Implications for Public Policy

This chapter shows how the private sector responds to complexity. First, firms and industries select the organizational structure most conducive to efficiency. Similarly, the most efficient of the available methods of transacting are employed. The textbook auction market is often replaced by direct dealing with customers. Better methods of financing are sought. Contracts are used to stabilize relations. When a product cannot be satisfactorily secured from outsiders, the firm may decide to integrate vertically.

These techniques lessen the impacts of sudden changes in market conditions. The most critical organizational steps for easing response are holding inventories and installing plants that increase the firms' flexibility. In large markets with many experienced, sophisticated participants, opportunities to engage in arbitrage are likely to be recognized and taken.

Firms and markets adapt well to complexity. Too many theorists fret excessively about the perils of departing from idealized pure competition. The scattered, often highly technical nature of the relevant literature justifies review. The discussion reinforces the prior arguments about the benefits of reliance on markets by indicating how complex markets can function efficiently.

Government programs to offset instability in individual markets, thus, seem less desirable. This conclusion, for example, undermines the long-standing willingness of economists uncritically to accept claims that protectionist policies would advance national defense, security of supply, or other "non-market" objectives. (See the often quoted words on the priority of defense over opulence of Adam Smith 1979a, sec. IV, 2-16, 464-5; and Corden 1974, 16-7.) The growing recognition that an implicit price exists for many unmarketed goods implies that their supply can be and should be treated by conventional economic principles. This is attempted here, and the conclusion is that again intervention should be viewed skeptically. Calls for government price stabilization are overdone. The contentions too often are another effort to gain respectability for protectionist pleadings.

The discussion begins with a more detailed treatment of efficient organization of firms, markets, and transactions. The theorists' affection for formal markets reflects the advantages arising when it is possible to create such markets. The possibilities for organizing such markets, therefore, are an appropriate part of the review. Alternative approaches are explained. Illustrations are provided, and policy implications are examined.

Experiences in the world oil, natural gas, coal, uranium, metals, and electric-utility markets are surveyed. These are areas in which a particularly extensive, well-documented history exists of efforts to deal with optimum organization in an era of radical changes.

Two policy issues, public-utility regulation and efforts to prevent or lessen the harm from market crises, are viewed. Oil-supply shocks are used as the prime example because so much attention has been given to them. The examinations are no longer relegated to specialized publications; oil is now often reviewed in industrial-organization texts.[1] The undesirability of intervention to lessen fluctuations in other commodity prices is also noted.

The analysis of options is an elaboration of the proposition, implied in Coase's 1937 article, that organizations, transactions, storage, and similar actions are commodities. Decisions should employ the maximizing principles applicable to all commodities. As often occurs in economics, much follows from this basic point. A vast literature arose on which this discussion draws.

The extent to which topics are treated here is based more on their complexity than on their role in making markets perform better. The simpler-to-treat techniques of inventory holding and building facilities and organizations that can adjust quickly may be the most important. However, contracting receives more extensive analysis. The subject is more complex and the extensive but still incomplete and scattered literature on the subject has a critical flaw. The basic concepts are left tacit, and analysis immediately starts examining special problems. The analysis here seeks to fill this gap and suggest that markets in which contracting prevail attain efficiency, albeit by a slower, more complex method that in markets using organized exchanges.

Preview: Defining Products and Markets

Economic theory is deliberately vague about the definitions of commodities, markets, firms, and consumers (in the sense of a household). (See chapter 2.) A product implicitly is anything that has properties that could cause a price difference. An economic market is whatever framework in which this price is determined.

Markets may have components around the world. No terminology has emerged to distinguish clearly between the full market and its parts. Both are simply called markets. Precision only becomes important when the nature of competition is the issue. In such cases, the problems of defining economic markets examined in chapter 4 arise.

The relationships are often complex. Linkages of varying degrees exist among regional demands for different commodities, such as types of coal at different locations. Given the ability to use other fuels, the coal market is, in turn, tied to oil, natural gas, and uranium markets. Depending upon market conditions, different price relationships might prevail. This is illustrated below in the review of the classic case of oil-natural gas competition.

Location is a key component of interrelationships. Given transportation costs, the buyer looks at delivered prices, i.e., those including shipping costs. High transportation costs lessen, but do not necessarily eliminate, connections among suppliers and buyers at different locations. Markets thus range considerably in geographic scope, from world-wide to neighborhood-wide. A very small business in a small market often has less competition than giant firms facing many other giants

---

[1]Several books on broad economic issues appearing in late 1980s and into 1990 paid considerable attention to oil. McGee (1988), Scherer and Ross (1990), and Carlton and Perloff (1990) all refer to it. Blanchard and Fischer (1989) pay limited attention in their survey of macroeconomics, but cite articles on the macroeconomics of oil shocks.

in a world-wide market. The only retailer of any given type in an isolated town has greater monopoly power than the large oil, steel, or automobile companies often used as examples of imperfect competition. Determining the geographic extent of a market also involves the difficulties of appraisal discussed in chapter 4.

One way to increase substitutability is to agree on product standards. Thus, standard grades and types exist for many agricultural products, metals, and petroleum products. When standardization is to costly to establish, it still may be possible to identify critical influences on quality and establish ways to vary price with quality. Coal, for example, is an aggregation of many economically distinct, interrelated commodities. Wide variations prevail within and among coal seams in the quality of the coal in terms of heat, ash, water, and contaminant content. Coal transactions deal with quality variations by basing the price on attainment of various heat, ash, and sulfur content criteria and providing for price adjustments.[2] Similar systems prevail for crude oils and some petroleum products with variable qualities.

The Interactions between Firms and Markets: An Overview

The questions raised by Coase (1937) concern how many activities a firm should undertake and the classic economic issue of the optimum size of each activity. Further issues include deciding which methods to use in undertaking the activities and in organizing and coordinating institutions, such as commodity exchanges and brokerage firms. Stigler's (1951) point about the relationship between the nature of the market and the firms within it provides another critical component of an appraisal of an optimal organization. The efficient resolution of these issues by definition produces a profit-maximizing organizational structure.

Chapter 6 argued that views about markets and the role of firms in them vary with perceptions of the strength of different influences on the ability to perform. The analyses of Demsetz (1968) and McGee (1980) and the criticisms levied against them illustrate this proposition. Firms will trade extensively with each other when entry is free, reputations are discernible, and satisfactory safeguards can be built into contractual arrangements. Where the opportunism about which Williamson (1975) is concerned or imperfect information make contracts hard to design and administer, integration is more likely.

Four main forms of procurement are employed. They are spot buying through exchanges and brokers, spot buying from the producer or a specialized reseller, contract buying, and vertical integration. As shown below, contracts can differ widely in form, and, however structured, must shift with economic realities. Degrees of integration exist. Organized commodity exchanges are the standard textbook starting point for describing spot markets. Less attention is given to the existence of brokers who trade commodities outside and possibly also within organized exchanges. Such brokers play a major role in markets for commodities including

---

[2]These practices are familiar to all who have examined actual practices, but the most accessible information relates to Japan. Japanese coal buyers chose to disclose unusually extensive information to a private publisher of newsletters and yearbooks (all in English). The relevant yearbook, the *Tex Coal Manual*, contains extensive discussion of the mines supplying Japan and the supply contract terms including quality variance penalties. The Manual was used here as a source of much information about how contracting operates, and those interested in a similar detailed view will also find it useful.

minerals such as coal not traded on commodity exchanges. With computers and telephone lines, a network of brokers can function very similarly to an organized market. The efficiency of such methods encourages a substantial amount of off-the-floor trading even in those securities such as stocks and bonds of leading corporations thought of as typically traded on an exchange.

Organized exchanges are suitable for standardized commodities sold in bulk to sophisticated purchasers. Households, of course, generally engage in spot dealing with retail merchants at their stores or increasingly by mail, facsimile machines, or phone. Where special needs are involved, input buying firms may buy spot from the producer or a specialized wholesaler.

Contracts and integration are means to reduce transaction costs including risks of using a spot market. The approaches are most applicable to large-scale transactions. Broad reliance on contracts and integration occurs principally in industry. Housing is the only service in which integration and contracting dominate in the household sector. The owner-occupant is an integrated supplier of housing and its maintenance; a renter uses contracts, albeit ones that often are very loose. Another exception is the prevalence of service contracts for automobiles and appliances.

Several types of transaction costs arise. Immutable expenses occur in securing market intelligence, dealing, and monitoring performance. Possible further problems involve opportunism when the supplier and customer make commitments that make it expensive for either or both to deal with others. Monopoly costs may exist. Integration and contracting are most likely when the transactions costs of spot buying are numerous and high. The extent of the firm and its reliance on more formal arrangements such as contracts with suppliers would increase as the possibilities for opportunism or monopolization became greater. Finally, government regulations may impede the creation of independent suppliers or the ability to buy from them on an efficient basis. For example, imposition of price controls on German coal sales stimulated tendencies of steel mills and electric utilities to purchase coal mines and mines to build powerplants.

As suggested in chapters 4 and 6, many unanswered empirical questions arise about both monopolization and opportunism. The extent of monopoly and the ability to undermine it with contracts or vertical integration are key controversies. Similarly, the importance of opportunism and monopoly is unclear. Finally, if either problem produces inefficiencies, questions remain about the feasibility of effective ameliorative public policies.

Coase's (1937) original analysis sought a theory of the existence and organization of firms and of why firms differed from each other. The owner of each input could operate as a separate firm. Firms arise because it is rarely efficient to engage in frequent negotiations to recombine numerous inputs. The output of these inputs feeds so intimately into production of another output that concentrating these activities into a firm is efficient.

The many simple firms that serve households illustrate natural combinations. The critical inputs to a typical retailing operation include the business facility (often rented at least until the firm becomes well established), the stocks, purchasing agents, clerks to receive, stock, and move the inventories, and salesclerks. At a minimum, a restaurant needs both a kitchen staff and a serving staff. Any form of entertainment requires the performers, the house maintenance staff, ticket sellers, and ushers. However, entertainment ventures, particularly if sporting events are included, are so diverse and so heavily influenced by government intervention that wide differences prevail in organizational forms. Analysis of these widely-known differences probably could improve understanding of the complexities of optimizing transactions. Combination of most these activities in a firm seems the most efficient approach.

Some ties may be looser. Some sections of department stores such as for books, shoes, jewelry, rugs, and postage stamps for collectors are sometimes run by concessionaires. Restaurants differ in how much they rely on foods prepared outside their own kitchens. Automobile dealers compete with independents in providing maintenance services, including some unrelated to meeting warranty responsibilities to car buyers, such as body repairs.

Further adaptation is provided by making the firm more flexible and by holding inventories. One often stressed role of inventories is in offsetting all types of unanticipated shifts in market conditions. Surges in demand or drop-offs in supply can be offset. Stockpiling, in general, can take many forms. Producing facilities, the material itself, or the finished products might be held in inventory.

Another basic role, delineated in the Allais-Baumol-Tobin analysis of money holdings, is in reducing the frequency of transaction.[3] It is simple arithmetic that for any given level of input consumption or output production, the fewer the number of shipments, the higher the volume of each shipment, and the higher the average inventory.

Flexibility involves greater substitutability of all types. The costs of altering the total scale of activity, the mix of outputs, and the mix of inputs can be reduced. Basic analyses of cost patterns (esp. Viner 1931) ignore such complications as the existence of technological progress, price variation, multiple product output, and variation in the level of product output. Again, this is done to eliminate complications. Consideration of the complications will certainly imply different optimal plant designs, plant numbers, and product mixes than in simpler cases. A firm that can better accumulate inventories of outputs and inputs and more cheaply alter its input and output pattern is better able to respond to changes in customer and supplier performance. This can reduce the need to integrate and contract.

In practice, a continuum of procurement methods exists, and many variants occur to each basic form. Many intermediate cases arise between using commodity exchanges and full vertical integration, and, as usual with economic distinctions, the dividing lines are not precise. The consumers may chose various combinations of procurement methods. As Coase (in Williamson and Winter 1991) pointed out, vertical integration may be limited to selected areas. Experience also shows that many forms of lesser participation can prevail.

For example, the search for alternative ways to secure coal led to many different types of participation. Buyers of coal have owned the coal but not the mining capital or the mining capital but not the coal. Equal partnerships with mining firms that were undertaken. Many Japanese and European coal users (and producers) have become stockholders in coal mines in the United States, Canada, and Australia.

Another issue is how market clearing works in markets without formal exchanges. The transaction costs of price changes may make it desirable to limit the

---

[3] Articles by Baumol (1952) and Tobin (1956) on optimizing cash holdings that present the basic principles are widely cited. After the French economist Maurice Allais received the Nobel prize in 1988, Baumol and Tobin (1989) published an article noting that Allais had anticipated their work.

frequency of changes (see Barro 1972). This subject has inspired a scattered literature of which the more important items are the writings of Means, Carlton (1986, 1989), and several papers in Mankiw and Romer (1991).

Alternative Marketing Arrangements Further Considered

Actual centralized markets such as securities and commodity exchanges usually are highly competitive. They also are efficient at collecting, assimilating, and responding to information on the participants' individual supplies and demands. These centralized markets are capable of providing futures markets to meet intermediate-term needs for price and quantity assurance. Information on the outcomes is easily obtainable from brokers and in newspapers. (See the classic studies of Houthakker 1957, 1959 and such later studies as Williams 1986 and Carlton 1984.)

The existence of many buyers and sellers was traditionally considered a critical influence on whether it is feasible and desirable to have an organized market. The absence of requirements of presale or postsale aid from the seller is another key requirement for allowing use of commodity markets. The inability to use commodity exchanges arises from a low volume of transactions and product characteristics that make desirable direct dealing with a supplier, a specialized retailer, or both.

Direct dealing on a large scale involves higher transaction costs than buying on commodity exchanges. These costs are incurred because of the value of the extra services secured in direct dealing. Where the good can be tailored in many different ways such as an automobile or a steel shape, direct contact with the producer or its representative may be desirable. Even here, issues arise about whether the benefits of customization are worth the cost. Established Japanese steelmakers pride themselves on their ability to vary product quality. Competitive challenges are being provided around the world by firms concentrating on cheaply producing standard grades of steel. Questions then arise about the extent to which the benefits of higher quality exceed the costs, and whether steel might follow other metals into commodity exchanges. Where follow-up or service is needed, a seller equipped to provide such aid may be desirable. In these and similar cases, a commodity exchange is not an economical place in which to deal.

Both vigorous competition without commodity exchanges and exchange trading in at least partially monopolized commodities are possible. As discussed below, it is widely argued that at least some members of the Organization of Petroleum Exporting Countries (OPEC) exercise monopoly power over oil. Nevertheless, active trading in oil has arisen on commodity exchanges. If oil is monopolized, the existence of trading in it implies that under some circumstances use of commodity exchanges may be appropriate for oligopolistic markets. The usefulness of commodity exchanges probably varies inversely with the degree of monopoly power.

The pure monopolist, by textbook definition, has total control of the market and does not need or desire to deal on a commodity exchange. A cohesive oligopoly probably would feel similarly. The need for a more open, formal market is probably greatest when cooperation among the oligopolists is weak and a large competitive fringe exists. The exchanges are the medium through which skilled observers of cartel coherence can inform buyers and other producers of prevailing conditions. Thus, imperfectly competitive markets in which commodity exchange trading is most feasible are probably those in which the monopoly power is limited.

Commodity exchanges, as noted, often coexist with direct dealing between buyers and sellers. Some, possibly a minority, of the participants fill their needs in the commodity exchange. Other customers deal directly with producers or producer representatives. This prevails even in areas, such as securities trading, in which exchange activity is heavily stressed. Off-floor trading is extensive for stocks traded on formal exchanges, and stocks not listed on the exchange are traded in a computerized network.

Economic analysis, particularly the arbitrage principle, implies that whatever their share in transactions may be, commodity exchanges accurately measure market conditions so the exchange price is *the* market price. Commodities that are traded on exchanges are produced, bought, and sold by sophisticated firms with strong motivation to be well informed about market conditions; these attributes are precisely those necessary to ensure that arbitrage is efficient. Many attacks on spot markets amount to complaints that bad economic news is accurately reflected in the spot price. Thus, the markets were criticized for the 1987 stock-market declines (or as journalists like to say, plummet or plunge) or the 1990 oil price increases.

The conditions that permit the existence of commodities market trading also tend to lessen the dangers of sudden movements in prices. Where many independent buyers and sellers operate, surges and drops in supply are less likely than when few participate.

Fluctuations cannot be avoided entirely. The market may be shaken by events that affect many buyers and sellers. Commodity exchanges also allow hedging against such contingencies. Futures markets are available for, among other things, locking in transaction prices and providing guidance about expectations. In a futures contract, the parties agree on the price that will be paid on a delivery of a specified amount of a particular good on a given future date. Such information guides the profitability of stockpiling for crises. Williams (1986) notes that futures markets also ease financing of stockpiling. Those wishing to stockpile temporarily buy spot (i.e., a conventional purchase with immediate payment on delivery of the goods) and immediately undertake a futures contract to arrange for disposal when the need is expected to end. Thus, the cost of inventory holding is fixed at the difference between the futures and spot prices. Critics complain that the durations of futures contracts are too short to provide full protection (recall chapter 3). Other views are that instability is transitory and only short term risks are worth hedging. Williams further argues that the primary use of futures markets is to facilitate short-run stockholding and the number of available contracts is sufficient for that purpose.

Commodity exchange prices, however, are viewed suspiciously by practitioners. Some suppliers, most notoriously of copper, long denied the relevance of the commodity market and tried to maintain different prices. In the copper case, producers ultimately recognized that the commodity market was correctly recording prevailing conditions. Direct sales began to be made at the commodity market price.

Similarly, as the markets broadened, commodity exchange trading arose for other minerals such as crude oil and aluminum. These developments are examples of verification of Stigler's predictions about market extent. The tendency to more impersonal dealings has been dubbed commoditization, meaning the loss of characteristics that preclude use of exchanges (see, e.g., Verleger 1987).

Price reporting services such as those for oil, coal, and uranium arise to record what occurs in these less formal markets. While such estimates are regarded even more warily than exchange prices, accurate estimates can be made for well-functioning markets. Conversely, the nonexistence of commodity markets need not produce problems of opportunism and supply disruption or even of significant inefficiencies. Again if the (actual or potential) participants are numerous, prices will move to a market clearing level. Thus, the market will normally function much like one in which a commodity exchange exists. In particular, disruption is unlikely.

In large markets such as the United States with its well developed communications and transportation systems, highly competitive markets can prevail involving direct purchases from individual retailers. A wide variety of products such as clothing, consumer durables, business and electronic equipment, and many electric appliances are sold by different types of retailers. These range from low priced phone-order discount houses to expensive "full-service" dealers. The key tools of national marketing are massive mailing of catalogs, advertisements in strategic publications, and provision of toll-free numbers to customers. (Much writing exists on how well the retail system works and what institutional reforms might be desirable. For example, several Chicago school writers, notably Telser (1960) and Bork (1965, 1966b), have explored the circumstances under which it is desirable for manufacturers to restrict the selling practices of retail dealers. Review is unnecessary here; Bork's (1965, 1966b) full discussion of the complexities is much preferable to later, less extensive treatments he and his critics have presented.)

However markets are organized, their adjustment mechanisms lessen, but do not eliminate, the impacts of radical changes in market conditions. Futures trading, speculation, and holding inventories can provide the efficient degree of stabilization, which is not maintaining rigidity. Under most circumstances, inventory holding can and should only ensure a slower rise in prices.

Without the benefits of a price rise, it would not pay to hold inventories. The nature of optimal holdings for crises is best seen by considering the behavior appropriate for predictable changes. Such predictable changes in market conditions as those associated with seasonal variations in supply or demand will lead to a systematic gradual rise in prices. The amount of the price rise is determined by the costs including interest charges of owning inventories. The low point is reached when the supply demand balance least favorable to producers prevails, e.g., crops at harvest time or heating oil in summer; the high, when the supply demand balance most favorable to producers occurs, e.g., heating oil in the coldest part of winter (see Samuelson 1957).

A supply shock, by definition, involves infrequent disruptions of unknown size at an unknown date. The long wait and the higher cumulative carrying costs associated with it discourage stockpiling for predictable but infrequent disruptions. Stockpiling is even less attractive if the disturbance has a low probability of occurrence, is unpredictable, and is unlikely to cause much damage. Thus, efficient stockpiling for a crisis will lessen but not eliminate price increases.

The Economics of Contracting

Issues about contracting include what comprises an efficient contract, the logically possible ways actual contracts could ensure that efficiency is attained, and the performance of actual contracting. Economic analysis of contracting started with asides made in discussions of the organization of firms such as the Coase's 1937 article reviewed above, but most of the work occurred after the middle 1970s.

Coase's analysis indicates that contracts seek to specify means of adjusting to changing circumstances.[4] He also noted that contracts reduce, but do not eliminate, the direct transaction costs that disappear with integration. Contracts also cause lesser increases in the costs of managing the firm. The net effect can be to make contracting profitable where integration would not be.

Contracting provides the buyer of the product less control over and less responsibility for the outcomes than does vertical integration. With integration, the integrated firm assumes all the risks of changing market conditions. Risk bearing involves both receiving the benefits of better than expected performance and enduring the costs of worse than anticipated performance. Many integrated firms were established to ensure energy supplies during the height of panic about an oil crisis but endured losses when the fears were not realized. Contract suppliers who insisted on tying prices to market conditions also experienced losses.

Subsequent work has done much to amplify the analysis. Both the theoretic implications of different problems of contracting and the connotations of the practices in actual contracts are now better understood. The literature has identified several devices that promote efficient contracting and analyzed their operation under various cases. Contract efficiency can be produced by such methods as built-in renegotiation clauses, action motivated by fears of damage to reputation, and provision of damage payments. Williamson (1983, 1985b) suggests that a network of deals could reduce opportunism. If a pair of companies frequently bought and sold with each other, one could retaliate if the other tried to raise prices in any area. The central consideration about contracting is that a contract is based on initial perceptions of future developments and cannot be maintained unless the prices paid on average track actual market conditions. Thus any contract whose initial terms fail to ensure prices corresponding to market conditions will be adjusted. The terms of the contract influence but do not necessarily fully determine how this adjustment is shared. Associated with any such price adjustment is reappraisal by buyer and seller of the volume of transaction.

A central premise about a market economy is that participants freely enter contracts based on their expectations of market prospects. Prudent business executives should be aware of the motives and biases of competitors, customers, and government agencies. Contracts are made because buyer, seller, or both expect that arrangement will be more profitable than more frequent dealing. As noted, no price benefit from deviations between contract and spot prices can persist; the gains from contracts are due to lower transaction costs.

---

[4]The literature on contracting is enormous. Williamson's writings, part I of Schmalensee and Willig (1989), and the Williamson-Winter (1991) symposium on the Coase article are obvious starting points. See G. Walker and Weber (1984), Lowry (1976), and Dye (1985) for broad surveys of contracting. The bibliographies here and in the cited material list many more useful sources. Those at the theoretic level include Goldberg (1976), Posner and Rosenfield (1977), Diamond and Maskin (1979), Telser (1980), B. Klein (1980), Riordan (1984), Rogerson (1984), Tirole (1986), Bull (1987), and Hart and Moore (1988). Case studies of contracting include: Gordon (1974b, 1975), Joskow (1977, 1985, 1987, 1988, 1990), Goldberg and Erickson (1987), Masten and Crocker (1983), Kornhauser (1983), Crocker and Masten (1988), Mulherin (1986), and Broadman and Toman (1986). The present discussion also relies on information about contracting gleaned from research and acting as a consultant and, in one case, as an arbitrator in contract cases.

The terms of the initial contract will vary with market conditions. If expectations are for high cost and unstable supplies, consumers will undertake arrangements to pay high prices for supplies and agree to strong guarantees of compliance. Anticipations of lower prices and greater availability of options produce contracts giving few assurances to sellers and more to buyers.

Sellers will not sign a contract unless the price ensures profitability over the contract life. The required price depends on how far the supplier has committed itself to the venture. A contract to secure the output of a not-yet-existent facility must repay all the necessary investments. If a firm has already undertaken substantial outlays, less than full compensation for past outlays may be accepted. The partial recovery possible from sales is preferable to the total loss from a shut-down.

The seller under a new contract, however, will not settle for cost recovery but will demand a price equal to the going market price. The correct market price is the amount that would be paid on a transaction similar to the ones between the contracting parties; namely, comparable contracts signed at that time. This price reflects the interaction of supply and demand. Thus it is determined by the relationship between the ability of buyers to pay and the ability of sellers to produce. By definition, buyers will be forced to pay the prevailing prices. Also by definition, supplies at these prices have marginal costs at or below the price. Thus, incentives arise for such sellers to displace other sellers with higher marginal costs temporarily staying in business because of old contracts allowing recovery of these higher costs.

Valuation of contracts must take account of the need to earn returns on investment. In economics, finance, and law, present value is the usual measure of the time weighted value (see I. Fisher 1930). The present value calculation reduces the amount of future receipts or payments by the interest lost or avoided by waiting. Thus, the technically correct description of a satisfactory contract is that it provides the agreed volume of transactions at a present value no greater than the present value that would be paid other suppliers.

The effect of contracting on the level and structure of prices seems indeterminate. Ease of contracting raises demand and supply. The relationship between spot and contract prices is also unclear since both sides benefit from the assurance from a contract.

Prices determined through strict adherence to old contracts are artifacts of past decisions and often may not accurately reflect current market conditions. However, if this is true, efforts are made to change the contract. The more unrealistic are contract prices, the more likely are efforts to alter the terms. Price and quantity levels due to contracts that incorrectly reflect market conditions then are likely to vanish. Ultimately, all prices will be based on current market conditions. The adjustment process will be slower and more complex than on a commodity exchange, but it will arise. The extent of disputes is a good indicator of the unrealism of existing contracts. Contract prices, thus, are accurate measures only when they are unchallenged.

Given the likelihood and consequences of unanticipated developments, both buyers and sellers, therefore, need provisions allowing adjustment to changing circumstances. The logical possibilities are for market conditions to be weaker or stronger than anticipated when the contract was signed. With strong markets, the problem is how to share the profits from the unanticipated bonanza. Lower than anticipated supply or higher than expected demand puts upward pressures on prices.

Sellers will seek rises in prices under existing contracts as market conditions cause higher prices on current deals.

With weaker than anticipated markets, the issue is loss sharing. Higher than expected supply or weaker than expected demand puts downward pressures on prices. By settling for lower than expected profits, suppliers can lessen the decline of output from the anticipated level. Buyers will seek reductions in prices under existing contracts as market conditions cause lower prices on current deals.

In another variant of the Coase theorem on social costs, the burdens of adjustment can be shared between buyer and seller in widely different fashions. The apportionment is determined by the interaction between contract terms and economic realities. Many contracts explicitly include provisions requiring adjustments if the basic contract terms produce a price significantly different from that prevailing on other sales. If no adjustment procedures are included in the contracts, efforts will still be made to readjust the price. This may be by renegotiation, arbitration, or litigation. Following standard legal principles, a direct agreement is preferred. Litigation or arbitration of contract disputes is initiated only when direct dealing breaks down. The proceedings are not inevitably carried to completion. At any point before the court or arbitrator decides, the parties can conclude that accord becomes preferable to continued contest.

Posner's (1986) argument that the common law seeks to promote economic efficiency indicates that sanctity of contract does not imply that inappropriate arrangements are perpetuated. Since common law is the compilation of decisions of many separate judges over many centuries, the view that the common law reflects a consistent viewpoint naturally is controversial. The weaker point that efficiency is the most practical guide to decision making seems sufficient for guidance. Adjustments still must be made. Sanctity means that the terms of the contract affect how the costs of adjustment are shared. However contract disputes are structured, the issues are reaching an appropriate price and assigning the burden of modification. The parties must cut through the formalities and respond to prevailing conditions. The resolution of disputes over contract terms determines what changes are made and particularly who pays whom for instituting changes.

The critical considerations are what commitments were made and the economic desirability of enforcing them. Agreements by buyer or producer to make payments only set upper limits on what can be obtained. The appropriateness of compensation for past investments depends both on the existence of a legal commitment and the ability of the buyer to make payments. The seller cannot pay premiums above market price that exceed the funds available to it. If the theoretic presumption that competition eliminates excess profits is correct, no premiums can be paid. Insistence on contractual rights is futile. The resulting bankruptcy will preclude the payments. This is why sellers often agree to accept no more than market price. Similar adjustment principles apply to seller commitments to lenders and its other suppliers.

If adjustment remains incomplete, existing contracts with high-cost producers can affect total production and the prices paid other producers.[5] Contracts reserve

---

[5]The problem can be analyzed more fully using a variant of a technique for analyzing price controls suggested to me by Robert L. Bishop for use in my 1960 Ph.D. thesis. Both my 1970 book on European energy (a radical revision of my thesis) and my 1981 book on energy economics present the analysis. Modification for the case in which buyers adjust to their

some demand for particular suppliers. This only matters if capacity that would have otherwise shut down is preserved. This maintenance of supply lowers prices. Those lacking contracts face lower demands and prices because of their loss of markets to high cost producers. In the longer run, such price and quantity effects due to contracts that incorrectly reflect market conditions vanish as unrealistic contracts are adjusted. The compensation issue is different from the question of whether the contract continues. The latter question depends solely on whether the supplier can produce at costs at or below prevailing market prices.

The existence of monopoly or monopsony does not invalidate these arguments. Monopoly or monopsony has the same role in contract prices as in spot markets. Unless devices such as vertical integration or giving a contract to a new firm are available, as they often are, to undermine or bypass the monopoly, participants must accept the monopoly or monopsony price. Such monopolistic manipulation of prices is a foreseeable risk of contracting and, therefore, does not intrinsically justify compensation for its effects. Prevailing antimonopoly principles of statutory and common law may make the *monopolist* liable for the effects of its price manipulation.

Types of Contracts

The principles of the prior section govern why clauses known to exist in contracts are adopted. Three basic contract provision types can be distinguished. The first deals with the quantities purchased, their quality specifications, and possibilities of altering the quantity supplied. Guarantees of quality are normal features of contracts and industrial spot sales agreements (see Klein and Leffler 1981 for a rigorous but indirect proof of the desirability of such guarantees). The second type of contract provision treats basic price setting rules. The third specifies under what conditions the basic price and quantity setting rules can be altered. Such provisions are the practical solution to the theoretic problem of the prohibitive costs of explicitly hedging against every possible development.

Contracts generally set a base quantity the buyer will take from the seller and allow for at least a limited deviation from that level at the discretion of the buyer, seller, or both. Clauses granting more latitude are possible. The buyer might secure the right to lower shipments in the face of decreased total use of the product. The customer customarily has the right to reject deliveries that do not meet product quality specifications. Contracts also apply the principle of *force majeure*--that neither side can be held to a contract if circumstances beyond the contracting parties' control prevent compliance. The list of circumstances constituting *force majeure* differs from contract to contract but typically includes "acts of God," wars, government intervention, and strikes.

At least three main pricing principles exist: cost recovery, escalated-base price, and market price. Considerable differences in detail exist within each category, and again the dividing lines are not precise. Moreover, as noted above, terms that lead to deviations from market prices cannot persist. Guarantees of cost recovery can be and have been provided by cost-plus contracts. The cost-recovery contract concept is

---

commitments to buy from uneconomic suppliers is straight-forward but more elaborate than seems appropriate here. The intuitive argument presented seems sufficient.

virtually self-explanatory. Such contracts state that the price paid will be the actual costs, measured by rules specified in the contract.

The disadvantages are that too lenient a cost recovery clause can discourage supplier efficiency, that verification of costs is expensive, and that the cost plus contract fails to adjust for divergences between costs and prices. Differences can arise in cost definition and determination and more critically in what provisions, if any, are included to give incentives to cost control. Difficulties in designing such incentives are barriers to using purely cost-based provision. Another critical problem is that no valid way exists to allocate the supplier's firm-wide administrative costs.

The escalation-clause approach typically sets a base price, divides it into components related to cost elements such as labor, supplies, and equipment, and defines a basis for escalating each component. The changes are in proportion to the alteration in a specified measure of trends in each cost realm. The principal variations involve methods of selecting escalators and particularly how closely they are related to actual firm experience. The objective of escalation clauses is to provide a simple way to adjust for cost-based changes. Use of escalation clauses involves expectation that prices follow costs.

Efforts are made to find measures of escalation that are correlated with the supplier's costs but are not affected by the supplier's actions. Consider the labor component of cost. Possible measures include change in wages and fringes paid under an industry-wide contract with a union, a government index of wages in the industry to which the supplier belongs, a government index of wages in the broader sector of the economy to which the industry belongs, or a government index of general wages.

Thus, at one time, coal mine labor costs were determined by the national contract signed by the United Mine Workers of America (UMW). Actual wages and fringes paid as determined by the contract could be used as the basis for labor cost escalation in coal contracts. UMW wages and fringes became less representative as the proportion of coal produced by mines with UMW contacts decreased. Alternatives such as government wage indexes for coal or for all mining might become preferable bases for escalation. A component of a government producer price index is often presumed to measure satisfactorily changes in the cost of purchased goods.

Escalation provides unambiguous rules for price determination. Unlike a contract that guarantees cost recovery, an escalated price contract makes a seller more liable for the consequences of mismanagement. The buyer still shares the risks of deviations between supplier costs and market prices. The escalated price approach introduces problems that could not exist with spot buying, integration, or other forms of contracts. While cost recovery may be the goal, the extent to which cost recovery is ensured is unclear. To attain perfect cost recovery, the bases of escalation must change exactly as do costs. Difficulties arise because escalation is often related to *indicators* of *per-unit-of-output* costs of resources used. The actual unit cost may change at a faster or slower rate than the chosen indicator. The number of units of the resource used per unit of output also might change. More or less labor, for example, might subsequently be needed to produce a ton of coal than was anticipated when the base price was set. The escalated base price can be greater or less than costs so both buyer and seller are exposed to the risk that actual costs deviate from the escalated base price.

Contracts can be and are tied to market prices. A market price clause is included because of fears that the expectations upon which the contract was based may prove incorrect. The clause is designed to ease adjustment to new perceptions of market prospects as reflected in currently determined prices. A market price contract involves the buyer and seller accepting the same price-risk exposure that would prevail if no contracts exist. Such contracts eliminate the need for further price adjustment clauses. By the definition of market prices, they represent what is attainable under present conditions. Thus, a market price contract adjusts terms to those that reflect current realities.

The principal difference among market price contracts is how explicit they are about defining the market price. The problems of finding acceptable market price indicators cause variations in practice. If something clear-cut such as a price on a particular commodity exchange is available, it probably will be used. Otherwise vaguer concepts must be employed. The contract may refer to "prices in similar transactions" or provide no definition. The most complex specific formula of which I am aware involves a contract between a U.S. coal mine and the Japanese steel industry. The price depends on the prices paid by the Japanese steel industry to five other specified mines (two U.S. and three Australian), the average price of U.S. coking coal exported to countries other than Japan, and the average price of underground-mined coal sold to U.S. electric utilities (Tex 1993, 138).

Where meanings are unspecified or vague, the definitions have to be determined when a dispute arises. Much effort then is devoted to defining and measuring appropriate prices. Many contracts include provisions requiring further price adjustments if the price adjustment formulas produce a price significantly different from that prevailing on other transactions. Other supplementary provisions can be employed to effect alterations in the basic procedures.

One possibility is specifying times during the life of the contract at which either party can be granted a price review. Clauses might allow price review if any significant change in the market takes place at any time during the term of the contract. Reliance might be on a general clause involving agreement to solve any hardships arising from any unforeseen circumstances.

Another complexity is that the provisions may be asymmetric. Allowable price changes could be one-way--rises but not falls or falls but not rises. In the late 1960s, residual fuel oil could be bought under contracts that provided only for decreases when market prices fell. Conversely, many natural gas contracts signed in the 1970s with U.S. producers only allowed price increases. A few contracts granted a preset rate of annual increase. Others tied prices to measures such as federal-government set ceilings that were likely only to rise. Clauses setting floors on prices were more common than those with ceilings (see the survey of gas contracts prepared in the U.S. Department of Energy by O'Neill, Heinkel, and Stokes 1981).

Another approach used in various contracts in such areas as the U.S. coal and natural gas markets is the "take or pay" contract. Such contracts guarantee continuing payments, usually an amount sufficient cover the investment costs including a reasonable rate of return, whether or not shipments are made. Such clauses are clearly more favorable to sellers and are most likely to occur when expectations of price rises prevail.

If only the basic provisions are considered, all arrangements except a market price contract attempt to shift risks to the buyer. An escalated base price contract is the least effective approach because of the imperfect relationship between the movements of the determinants of escalation and actual costs. A take or pay approach reinforces the assumption of risks by buyers.

A standard rule of risk bearing is that the party best able to assume a risk should do so. Buyers are not always the better risk bearer. This undesirability to both buyer and seller of complete assumption of risks by buyers is what causes introduction of subsidiary clauses and the eventual adjustment of contracts that fail to correspond to market prices.

Clauses based on market conditions shift risks back to the supplier. The supplier will invoke the clause to benefit from higher than expected prices; the buyer, to secure redress when market prices are lower than was postulated when the contract was signed. This is appropriate because sellers as specialists in the market for the commodity sold are better able to evaluate prospects and assume the risks.

Experience shows that whatever the clauses, the principle of adjustment to reality prevails. The cheap oil and coal contracts were broken; expensive fuel contracts in oil, gas, coal, and uranium were renegotiated.

The Lessons of Energy and Mineral Procurement Experiences

A. Contracting

The world energy markets are ones in which many different arrangements prevail, and radical change has occurred. The evolution of fuel buying practices illustrates both the variety of possible practices and how they have altered with shifting market conditions. Major metamorphoses occurred in oil (see below), natural gas (see Carpenter, Wright, and Jacoby 1987, Tussing and Barlow 1984, and Stern 1982, 1884, 1985), uranium (see Neff 1984 and Gordon 1981c), and coal (see Zimmerman 1981 and Gordon 1987c). The principal reversals were retreats from vertical integration, insistence on more flexible new contracts, and efforts to rearrange existing contracts to produce greater flexibility. Oil companies also became less enthusiastic about diversification.

The oil industry shifted from one in which "integrated" oil companies dominated the production and marketing of crude oil from the countries such as the members of OPEC. The old system never truly involved producing only for one's own refineries and meeting all their needs. Historically, some companies such as Gulf and BP were large net sellers while others, particularly Royal Dutch/Shell, were large net buyers.

Verleger (1987) has discussed the end of vertical integration in oil, the resulting commoditization of trade, and how the analysis of his teacher (and mine) M. A. Adelman facilitates understanding of these trends. Starting in the 1970s, the governments of countries such as Saudi Arabia that produced large amounts of oil, predominantly for export, greatly increased their control over the oil industry. Initially, these governments imposed substantial taxes on oil production that produced the usual price raising/output lowering impacts of such taxes. Adelman (1973) described this process as using the oil companies as tax collectors. The critical point is that high taxes are more effective than is a cartel in pushing up prices. Adelman also correctly foresaw that the process had self-destructing features. The search for control produced pressures directly to market oil and face the difficulties of maintaining sufficient discipline over output to keep prices up. The advantages to the oil companies of "owning" concessions was eroded by the tax schemes.

Rearrangement of natural-gas contracts has been widespread. The focal issues were the probable future price of oil and the scarcity of gas relative to oil. The oil price issue is the more straight-forward. An increase in oil prices encourages a shift to gas and other substitute fuels and raises the prices of these substitutes. Exactly what price relationships result can differ radically depending upon circumstances. Two basic types of oil are used in boilers. Smaller scale users such as households use the more fluid, lighter (in weight) fuel oils; only large scale users such as electric power plants, factories, and large buildings can readily handle the more tarry, heavy or residual oils. Premiums are paid for lighter oil.

Gas has radically different values depending on its uses. The most valuable uses are for home heating at the height of the winter; the lowest value uses are to replace heavy fuel oil. When gas supplies are ample, gas competes with light and heavy fuel oils and sells at a price (per unit of heat supplied) equal to that of heavy fuel oil. (This discussion abstracts from the complications produced by the substantial differences in the costs of serving different customers.)

Long-held but still unrealized expectations are that market conditions will alter. With limited gas supplies, use might be confined to the high value uses and gas at the point of delivery would sell at the price of the higher priced fuel oils used in such markets. The traditional ability to supply industrial markets at a price competitive with that of heavy oil might persist.

During the energy panics between 1973 and 1980, gas buyers signed many contracts that presumed continued oil price rises and gas scarcity would push gas to light fuel oil parity at a high price. These contracts became burdens when prices weakened in the 1980s. Problems arose of adjusting. Heavy regulation of U.S. natural gas production and distribution limited the options available to effect changes. The industry and its regulators moved to alleviate these difficulties. Existing contracts were adjusted, and the practice of reliance on extensive contracting by pipeline companies to ensure supplies eroded.

In both uranium and coal, major changes occurred with only the specialists taking notice. With uranium, most of the U.S. industry was dismantled without much fuss or litigation. The U.S. uranium industry was created to meet the needs of the U.S. atomic weapon program and expanded to serve the nuclear power sector. At different times, government buying programs and import prohibitions provided stimulus.

The participants included a mixture of traditional mining companies such as Anaconda, Phelps Dodge, and Union Carbide (before restructuring), oil companies (particularly Kerr-McGee and Exxon) and various newcomers (such as Utah International and United Nuclear). Utilities such as Commonwealth Edison, Southern California Edison, the Tennessee Valley Authority, and Long Island Lighting invested in the industry.

Most of this has vanished. The end of import controls and expansion of world uranium supplies encouraged a shift to imports. The only concession to protectionism is a requirement that the U.S. Energy Information Administration annually survey the dangers of imports. The reports have refrained from urging renewed protection. (These reports comprise the most accessible source of information on the changes noted here, but see Gordon 1981c for the earlier history.)

This illustrates the proposition that studies are a substitute for action. The reviews employ a set format and stress a sober factual review. The tone differs little from the other uranium reports of the U.S. Energy Information Administration. The assignment to that part of the DOE rather than to a policy group suggests that vigorous advocacy was unwanted.

Such U.S. uranium producers as United Nuclear, Pathfinder (the separate uranium company created out of Utah International when it was acquired by General Electric, which subsequently resold Utah to Broken Hill Proprietary, a large Australian minerals company), and Exxon simply faded away. Imported uranium was substituted for domestic. Some contracts did not specify the source, and the change needed no approval. Approval was given if needed.

The changes in coal were less profound but harder fought. Again, the basic situation was the development of extensive reliance on contracts and some vertical integration and a later tendency to contract somewhat less, renegotiate contracts, and sell integrated facilities.

While the history of reliance on contracts is fragmentary, the present situation is well-documented. Patterns correspond well with what those familiar with the markets would predict. For example, use of very long-term contracts is universal for independent supplies to mine mouth plants--one next to a coal mine or, to stretch the definition a bit, connected to the mine by a special transportation facility such as a private rail line or a slurry pipeline. When long distances separate customers from suppliers, contracts are likely. Conversely, spot buying is more likely when the buyer has ready access to many nearby coal suppliers. Large U.S. utilities, even in regions where numerous suppliers are nearby, tend to contract for the bulk of their supplies although the dependence on contracts is less than when proximity is lower.

Contracts with U.S. utilities apparently provide strong enough protective clauses to sellers that courts tend to require utilities to pay their suppliers for contract adjustments. Some have sought ways to escape by invalidating the contracts. Such attacks can at least lessen the adjustment costs. Claims of nonperformance are typical. In one case (between Texas Utilities and the coal subsidiary of the Santa Fe Railroad), a conspiracy in restraint of trade by Santa Fe contrary to the Sherman Antitrust Act was alleged. In this case and in at least one main nonperformance dispute, payments were reduced below those required in the contract in out of court settlements. (The formal literature seems to consist of Gordon (1974b, 1975) and Joskow (1985, 1987, 1988, 1990); the discussion here was augmented by examination of material in the trade press.)

Internationally, the transactions are less well reported. Other countries appear to play the market to a greater extent. They can choose among U.S., Australian, South African, Colombian, and Canadian supplies and seem to want to take advantage of the swings resulting from both coal market and foreign exchange developments.

In metallurgical coal procurement by the Japanese steel industry, formal arrangements were typically made, but the framework ranged from 10-15 year contracts to annual renegotiation. At least in the case of New South Wales in Australia annual renewals are routinely negotiated. In the late 1970s, several then extant contracts for Canadian and Australian coal were converted to an annually negotiated basis. The impetus came from producers expecting rising prices. The surge in coal imports around 1980 stimulated signing contracts with new mines using an escalated price method. When the tightness of the market vanished, the Japanese moved toward employment of annual negotiation with these new contracts. The few major old Australian contracts that had not shifted to annual renegotiations were converted when they expired.

The mining companies and the Japanese agree on what constitutes an appropriate price and how the quantity purchased should be adjusted to reflect current market conditions. Three mines in Canada held out, and the Japanese moved to secure a changed arrangement. In the most troublesome case, arbitration was necessary. The sellers resisted buyer claims that the adjustment clauses necessitate lowering prices to parity with those on other contracts. (The arbitration panel reached a compromise position. The demand to lower the price to world levels was refused. Instead, a phased reduction was set in the portion of the base price that was not subject to escalation. This forced a reorganization of the venture.)

These deals were characterized by coal executives interviewed in Australia and elsewhere as clever devices to break the market. This argument dubiously assumes limited interaction between coking coal sales in Asia and purchases of coal and rival fuels. Moreover, to protect their contractual rights, the Japanese had to continue buying from these high cost mines the contractually set volumes at the contract price. With the failure of coal use to rise to absorb the additional amounts contracted for all these new mines, old and new mines that moved to lower prices supplied less than before. The probable net effect was higher costs to the Japanese.

The Lessons of Energy and Mineral Procurement Experiences

B. Vertical Integration in Coal

In the coal industry, full vertical integration occurs predominantly when the mine is near the customer. Thus, the classic examples of vertical integration have been ownership of mines by steel companies in the United States and Germany. Historically, in the few cases of vertical integration by U.S. electric utilities, the acquired mines were near power plants. Electric-utility involvement with mines in more distant locations emerged in the 1970s and was one of the first areas in which withdrawal occurred. In contrast, investment by smelters and refiners in foreign metals mines long has been common.

The patterns undoubtedly reflect differences among industries in the transaction and management costs involved in alternative arrangements. Many coal mine operators are experienced with both mining of other minerals and some types of construction such as road building that involve materials handling problems similar to those occurring in surface coal mining. Many important coal using companies lacked similar expertise and probably found it preferable on balance to rely on contracts with others.

Integration seems to have been begun by a few eastern utilities--American Electric Power, the Southern Company, Ohio Edison, and Duquesne Light. Others integrated later. No obvious pattern explains why these utilities integrated while similar companies did not.

Subsequently, several companies building coal fired plants west of the Mississippi decided to construct and operate their own mines. The mines involved creating new ventures in areas where only a few, if any, established producers existed and where the strip mining technologies involved were easy to learn. This produced the operations of Texas Utilities and Washington Irrigation and Development entirely for their use and those of what initially was PacifiCorp's Nerco, Montana Power's Western Energy, and Montana Dakota Utilities's Knife River, which also engage in substantial sales to coal users other than the affiliated utilities. (Washington Irrigation serves a jointly owned plant in that state and is owned by the owners of the plant; PacifiCorp has the largest ownership. Nerco was sold in 1993 to Kennecott, now a subsidiary of RTZ. Texas Utilities and Washington Irrigation are cases in which no other mining ventures existed in the state when utility entry arose.)

Other western plants are supplied by independent mining companies. In one case, Utah International, the operator of the mine supplying the Four Corners power plant in New Mexico, took over the previously utility-owned mine serving the nearby San Juan plant. The decision probably was influenced by the financial problems of the two partners in the power plant and mine. One of these partners took the unusual step of creating a separately incorporated company to own another generating unit it constructed and spinning off the corporation.

Vertical integration in the eastern U.S. has greatly diminished. Many changes have occurred. Companies such as Duke Power and Virginia Electric and Power have withdrawn completely; others, notably American Electric Power, have sold substantial portions of their coal mines. Coal mining has not proved advantageous to such companies. The western strip miners largely endure. In some cases, those selling on the open market produce more profits than the electric utility that created them.

The difference between eastern and western experience was greatly influenced by radical differences in the market climates. Utilities in the East and West expected rising output in the regions supplying them with coal and invested in mines to meet these needs. In the West, substantial production rises occurred. In the East, output was flat or falling. Thus, new capacity was more usable in the West than in the East.

The experience in other coal producing countries is also diverse. The electricity boards of New South Wales and Victoria in Australia engage in coal mining (lignite in the latter case); their Queensland and South African counterparts do not. The New South Wales board is seeking to sell its mines, but unfavorable economics have hindered the disposal.

German coal industry organization is particularly complex. The evolution of that structure is part of the response to the coal crisis that emerged in 1958 and still persists. The German government apparently thought that mergers would alleviate the crisis. As this belief proved unfounded, the merger movement, nevertheless, was extended. The merged company served as the organization through which state aid could best be channeled.

The merger was initially confined to the dominant producing area, the Ruhr, and thus named Ruhrkohle. The merged company was structured as a joint venture of the prior owners. Steel companies held the majority of the stock. Subsequently, in Germany as in other industrial countries, steel industry coal use declined, and electric power coal consumption rose. Ownership of Ruhrkohle was altered in the early 1980s to reflect this. A diversified energy company with large electric utility interests (VEBA) and an electric utility (Vereinigte Elektrizitätswerke Westfalen) then became the largest stockholders. Subsequently Ruhrkohle also acquired the remaining separate mines in the Ruhr and the mines in the Aachen region. The German lignite industry is dominated by subsidiaries of two electric utilities (RWE, the former Rheinisch-Westfälisches Elektrizitätswerk, and VEBA). In Europe, particularly Germany and France, the opposite form of vertical integration also prevails; the coal industry owns power plants that sell electricity to the utilities.

The Lessons of Energy and Mineral Procurement Experiences

C. U.S. Electric Utility Horizontal and Vertical Structure

U. S. electric public utilities represent an older example of the problems of how to structure an industry. Questions of optimum scale and scope and how to attain them are continually raised. Among the issues are minimum efficient size for each phase of operations and the extent to which different phases should be combined. The latter involves both the range of activities with a given commodity and whether the same company should supply more than one commodity.

Secondary aspects of the activity range issue, such as integration into fuel production and plant construction design and implementation, were noted above. The concern that is more closely scrutinized is the need for vertical integration of electricity generation, long-distance transmission, and local distribution (see below). Such integration is the dominant mode. The principal now prevalent form of multicommodity involvement is gas distribution by a company that is also an integrated electric company. Many examples prevail with by far the largest being Pacific Gas and Electric (in California), Consumers Power (in Michigan), and Public Service Electric and Gas (in New Jersey).

A long-term tendency prevails towards larger utilities in a given field. The situation is complicated by the holding company movement of the 1920s and federal legislation in 1935 to restrict holding company activities.[6] The holding companies created in the 1920s attained a size and complexity that seemed excessive to the politicians of the time, particularly after the collapses with the great depression. The companies acquired companies in many different fields--gas, electricity, urban transportation (then predominately electric powered), and water supply. The operations often were in widely separated areas.

The 1935 legislation restricted involvement of holding companies to one activity in a contiguous service area. Combination companies survived largely because they were not holding companies; in a few cases difficulties in arranging sales led to continued small gas distribution activities by holding companies. Similarly, wide differences prevailed in what was viewed as an integrated operation involving contiguous areas. The surviving holding companies contracted to single regions. For

---

[6]The present discussion is based on the research for Gordon (1992c), a contribution to a symposium on the electric-utility regulation reforms proposed (and enacted) in 1992. Prior work and long observation of the industry suggested the existing structure probably was defective. To expand my impressions, I arranged to secure data from Moody's manuals on the holding companies extant in the 1920s, their breakup, and the present state of the industry; this uncovered evidence that reinforced my concerns. A literature review made clear that most treatments of holding companies derive, at least indirectly, from the summary volumes of a massive Federal Trade Commission study lasting from 1929 to 1935. Examination of these studies suggested their uncritical acceptance was unwarranted. The reports merely view with alarm various bookkeeping practices without any consideration of their true economic implications. The FTC's suggestion was that the primary goal was to mislead investors. However, the manipulations were not ones that would have misled analysts. It may be true that the companies were trying to evade regulation, but this conclusion can only be reached with a clearer understanding of the subject than the writers of the FTC report displayed. The restructuring proved a case of defective regulation that still has not been adequately appraised. The text here provides an tentative effort at such an assessment.

example, American Electric Power now operates in parts of Virginia, West Virginia, Ohio, Indiana, Michigan, and Kentucky; the Southern Company in most of Georgia and parts of Alabama, Florida, and Mississippi.

Whatever the best structure might be, it certainly is not the one prevailing in 1994. Many readily altered differences in size prevail. To cite the extremes, until the early 1990s, six companies served Iowa while the largest supplier by far in Georgia was allowed to buy the only other private electric utility in the state. This cannot be explained by differences in scale of operation; electricity sales in Georgia are more than two and a half times those in Iowa. If either the view of many in the industry in the twenties that very large companies are desirable or the more moderate view that many companies were inefficiently small is correct, many opportunities for consolidation were lost. If much smaller companies are appropriate, too much integration was allowed.

The reorganizations did not destroy the physically integrated operations that had emerged. Closer scrutiny, however, suggests that the reorganizations were unimaginatively implemented and that the 1935 law and state regulation hindered optimum organization. The record shows many lost opportunities to combine units of a given holding companies into integrated firms of larger size. Many of these companies that were kept separate incurred difficulties aggravated by their small size. Thus, once again, a widely praised intervention may have been worse than doing nothing.

Application to Natural Monopoly

The extent of natural monopoly problems and how to cure them are also the subjects of extensive and heated yet still inconclusive debates. An enormous literature exists on the theory and practice of public utility regulation. As in industrial organization, a move has occurred from texts blending assorted theories with detailed descriptions to books that are predominantly theoretical. (See, e.g., for the first type, Kahn 1970, Phillips 1984, and Bonbright, Danielson, and Kamerschen 1988, for the second, Sharkey 1982, Brown and Sibley 1986, Berg and Tschirhart 1988, Train 1991, Sherman 1989, and Spulber 1989. Schmalensee 1979 is an excellent survey of the general issues about regulation. Joskow and Schmalensee 1983 is a thoughtful examination of the electric utility situation with a preference to reforming regulation. A good but dated overview is Breyer 1982. Laffont and Tirole 1993 present an abstruse development of more sophisticated approaches to regulation.) As suggested above, public-utility regulation is Lange's (1936-7) planning board on a small scale. Lange and his critics then contribute to understanding natural monopoly regulation. Conversely, the literature on natural monopoly demonstrates the problems of planning.

Government regulation theoretically could control natural monopoly by forcing the industry to perform better. Regulation works so badly and so often fosters monopoly that its defenders are lukewarm at best. Regulation of industry is considered, at best, a last resort when dire problems exist. Specialists on regulation only argue that it is more feasible or slightly better than doing nothing.

Regulation is overdone. Economic analyses naturally disapprove of controls on competitive firms. Price controls whether imposed on wages, oil, natural gas, or apartment houses have proven unsatisfactory. Direction imposed on areas such as most of the transportation industry in which competition is strong is similarly unjustified. Even regulation of the allegedly oligopolistic steel industry seems to have been harmful. To protect vested interests, the industries' operations are distorted, and complex regulations must be devised.

Even where competition seems weak, questions remain about the extent to which the industries are monopolistic and about whether regulation or government ownership really improves things. For example, the literature on public utilities suggests that perhaps the retail distribution of electricity, gas, and water is so monopolistic that regulation could be beneficial. The United States relies predominantly on regulation to control public utilities. Government ownership of many public utilities--waterworks, gas distribution companies, and electric companies--was the preferred alternative in much of the rest of the world, but privatization is increasingly being attempted.

The extent of the monopoly may be exaggerated. Therefore, regulation often may be redundant. For example, Baumol, Panzar, and Willig (1982) related their contestability concept to the natural monopoly debate. Skeptics suggest this analysis overstates the prospects for entry. Considering the care with which the analysis is stated and qualified, this reaction seems excessive. It is tempting to conclude that devotees of the natural monopoly concept are unwilling to consider the possibility that they are wrong about some cases.

Demsetz's (1968) proposal to substitute competition to serve for regulation reflects yet another form of market solution to transaction cost problems. Demsetz made the controversial argument that transaction costs were low enough that it would be possible to secure competitive behavior by bidding for the contract to operate a natural monopoly. He suggested that the feasibility would be greatest if the contract was to operate an existing publicly owned facility.

The argument was attacked because the monitoring problems that plagued regulation would plague bidding and an inadequate number of bidders would emerge. The latter problem seems the more critical. If numerous bidders arise and bidding takes place often, the process would be self-monitoring. Any successful bidder that failed to behave competitively would lose to another bidder. The Demsetz analysis pushes optimism about competition to its limits. This does not mean that the argument is as dubious as critics have contended. Demsetz is responding to a widely perceived need to find replacements for traditional techniques. His critics display the standard conservatism about new ideas, particularly those with a Chicago label.

Demsetz is challenging the automatic assumption that transaction costs in franchise bidding are so high that satisfactory results are impossible. This is an empirical question that deserves more than casual testing by observers with obvious preconceptions. (Spulber 1989, gives a good introduction to this debate. The chief critic is Williamson 1985b, who believes cable television experience refutes Demsetz. Zupan 1989, however, suggests that bidding works better than Williamson believed. Zupan found the worst problem was a government failure. Inefficient requirements about what stations must be supplied were a usual demand of licensing agencies upon bidders.) Demsetz may concede too much to the advocates of regulation. Natural monopoly may not be as serious a problem as he is willing to assume. The government failures that plague regulation will arise in franchise bidding. Inaction may be better.

The growth of markets can mean that whatever justification regulation may have can disappear. The economics literature on public utility regulation displays the standard pattern of nearly total disapproval of practices. Many observers have recognized that the most effective reform may be deregulation, but support is generally qualified even among those accused of extremism. For example, Milton Friedman argues, "I reluctantly conclude that, if tolerable, private monopoly may be the least of the evils (1962, 28)."

This restraint is typical of discussions in the writings of the leading defenders of the market economy. Hayek, for example, is even more equivocal. *The Road to Serfdom* is more moderate in criticism of intervention than his later writings and contains a qualified acceptance of public utility regulation (1944, 198). Hayek's later treatises (1960, 1973, 1976, 1979, 1989) on economic policy lack a clear treatment of the issue. The reviews of government price fixing suggest skepticism about public utility regulation (see esp. 1960, 265-6 on the regulation of monopoly).

Posner (1969, 549) developed a stronger criticism of public utility regulation. He argued the prospects for monopoly profits may be limited and that the ability, widely discussed in the literature on public utilities, to engage in price discrimination would lessen the inefficiency of any monopolizing. He recognized distributional effects but considered them too small to matter much.

Public utility specialists tend either to accept the need for regulation or at least to consider radical suggestions impractical. The modest proposals since the early 1970s proved ineffective. Rethinking seems critical.

A more general argument implied by Coase's (1988) writings on optimum policy with transaction costs also can justify full deregulation. Coase has repeatedly argued that the difficulties of determining and attaining an optimum hinder public and private solutions. The choice of solutions, therefore, is unclear and includes the possibility of inaction (recall chapter 6).

Key rationales for skepticism about regulation are provided by Stigler in two classic articles. The first with Friedland (1961) concluded regulation was ineffective. Their statistical study suggested that regulation has no measurable effects. Stigler (1971) added the argument, noted in chapter 6, that regulation is often designed to protect regulated firms from competition. An important supplement to Stigler is Peltzman's (1976) formal model of regulation (also noted in chapter 6). Peltzman introduces the limits to full capture by those regulated imposed by the need of regulators to consider the reactions of other interested parties. Regulators must reconcile the conflicting political forces concerned about the outcome. As a result, maximum monopoly profits will not be allowed. (The two articles and that of Demsetz all are available in Stigler's 1989 anthology of "Chicago" contributions to economics.)

Some specialists think the evils of natural monopoly are so great that we should continue seeking to reform the process. Others resort to a timid "realism" that holds reform is the only politically acceptable approach. Therefore, bolder proposals are unrealistic and fruitless to consider. Both these claims *and* their rejection remain inadequately proven statements of faith.

Joskow and Schmalensee (1983), for example, recognize that it is unclear whether unregulated prices are less efficient than actual regulated prices. They believe, "...regulatory commissions can structure retail rates that are more efficient than those we now observe or those that would be charged by an unregulated monopoly (1983, 155)." This follows the tradition that regulation is so desirable and reform is so feasible that changing the existing system is clearly the best approach. Given the defects, the presumptions that actual regulation of even the less vigorously competitive markets does good and is capable of reform should be challenged more often by public utility specialists.

We are far from knowing whether feasible regulatory improvement is preferable to feasible deregulation. Modest reform proved infeasible. Although the breakdown of regulation became evident by the middle 1970s, reforms that will lead to improvements are not in sight. The changes that have occurred preserve many distortions and in some cases introduced new ones. The optimum approach to natural monopoly then is far less certain than the advocates of regulation or deregulation assert. If we accept Director's (1964) principle that the burden of proof is on the interveners, we would prefer deregulation.

It is agreed that no fully satisfactory cures exist. Government performance is so often maladroit that fears exist that intervention may be worse than nothing even when actual monopoly power exists. The most obvious implication of the principles stated here is that it is unwise to regulate markets that seem highly competitive. As argued above, eliminating such regulations is a formidable task.

Again, the information does not suffice to indicate the best feasible solution. Experience suggests that radical change is essential. The resistance to consideration of even moderate reform is excessive. Calls for reform have languished since the early 1970s. Reforms might include removing public utility regulation at the federal, state, and local levels, fully repealing of the 1935 law that gave the Securities and Exchange Commission control over mergers between electric utilities in different states, letting normal liability law replace nuclear regulation (see chapter 10 for theories that justify this position), eliminating the tendency, mostly in California, to develop energy plans, reforming environmental regulation, and selling public and cooperative power to the private sector. (See Gordon 1982, 1984a for arguments in favor of all but the last policy. Gordon 1982 notes the deficiencies of public and cooperative ownership but fails to call for its end.)

Others have made proposals for partial deregulation. Two such proposals were presented in the 1975 publication of papers presented at a 1971 Brookings Institution Conference. In one paper, Leonard W. Weiss contended that electricity generation had at least matured to a state in which competition was possible. Since this was allegedly not true for long-distance transmission or local distribution, Weiss proposed separating generation from the other two sectors. Unregulated generating companies would sell to regulated distribution companies. Transmission lines would be required to allow these flows to occur. In the other paper, Walter J. Primeaux Jr. (1975) presented the assertion that multiple distribution companies lowered prices. He more fully developed this point in a 1986 book. Weiss's proposals attracted much approval, but some dissents, most notably from Joskow and Schmalensee (1983). Primeaux's assertions were viewed much more skeptically.

One key question about the Weiss proposals is whether the time for dismembering the integrated structure of the industry has emerged. A basic part of the debate has centered on what sort of power market would prevail. Industry critics of deregulated generation, strongly echoed by Joskow and Schmalensee, emphasize the need to rely on long-term contracts with strong cost recovery clauses. They convincingly conclude that such an arrangement would have the same economic consequences as integration.

A group of engineers and economists all originally at MIT (Schweppe, Caramanis, Tabors, and Bohn 1988) suggested spot market pricing was feasible and the barrier to independent plant construction was more regulatory than market uncertainty.[7] They argued that existing computer technology allowed short-term coordination without contracts. They also noted that in unregulated markets large plants get built without contracts. Deregulation could lessen financing problems. They implicitly were using Stigler's (1951) further point that less formal arrangements are possible in larger markets. Since the group had participants who were knowledgeable about electric power, their concept of feasibility incorporated the preservation of such vital industry characteristics as maintenance of reliable service.

An intermediate position is that contracts with more flexibility could be arranged. One possibility is that a consortium contracts to guarantee to cover any deficiency of revenues relative to costs. Sales could be made and priced, if not in a true spot market, at least daily.

A critical issue is the extent to which the electric utility markets have evolved. Contracts that do not link prices to spot prices are appropriate only when spot prices are difficult to determine (see above). Vigorous spot markets already exist in wholesale electric power. Too much of the economics literature on contracts, including the Joskow and Schmalensee (1983) book, emphasizes Williamson's earlier analyses of the drawbacks of transactions when open markets do not exist.

Joskow and Schmalensee fear that the conditions for competitive generation do not exist. Their need-for-contract argument reflects belief in inadequate competition. Their negativism seems overly grounded in traditional proregulation arguments, inadequately appreciative of counterproposals, and thus premature. Fuller analysis is needed.

My reservations about deregulating *only* generation remain hard to resolve (1982, 27-59). One objection, echoed by Joskow and Schmalensee, relates to the short and long-run costs of disintegration. The short-run costs are the transaction costs of reorganization; the long-run impacts are possible losses of economies of coordinating activities. The latter would be small if a flexible spot market is feasible. Partial deregulation may be a chimera. Regulation has extended to all the decisions of the regulated firms including the prudence of its purchases. The deregulated generators might find regulations restricting what could be paid. Peter Fox-Penner astutely pointed out in a letter to me that the change makes the cost of regulation more explicit. Setting such prices on regulatory burdens may improve understanding of the problem and lead to reform. The skepticism expressed here about the prospects for moderate reform applies to the hope that increased visibility will help. A more germane concern is whether a truly deregulated generation industry can arise with tightly regulated transmission and distribution. The regulators may control buying from generators as tightly as they now control such purchases as interutility dealing, prudence of construction, and fuel buying.

Deregulation is justified (see Gordon 1982) if interfuel competition produces a more efficient outcome than feasible regulation. Such an argument rests as much on distrust of the regulatory process as on trust of the strength of interfuel competition. Implementation of Weiss's secondary proposal to increase competition by breaking-up combination electric and gas companies would be desirable.

---

[7]The order in which the names were listed differed among publications. Bohn (1983, 1984) was listed first twice and another collaborator, Golub (1983), was the first named in one of the contributions to Plummer et al.

Weiss's (1975) analysis is probably valid in its conclusion that electric utilities have exhausted their economies of scale and scope and the natural-monopoly break-even problem does not exist. Efficient prices would produce revenues equal to or above costs and all the conundrums that fascinate the theorists would not arise. Regulation could more readily impose efficient prices. In any case, independent power producers were providing the majority of new electricity-generating capacity in the early 1990s.

Primeaux (1975) concludes from statistical study of the effects of multiple distribution utilities in the same community that competition is possible in retail distribution of electricity. His critics, such as Joskow and Schmalensee (1983), rightfully question whether his sample, which is heavily weighted with municipally-owned utilities, is representative. Thus, the Primeaux argument is harder to support than the case for deregulation of generation or of all the electric power industry. At best, the present evidence is consistent with many different views of what comprises the best approach to electric power.

Political Supply Insecurity

Still another separate literature treats "political" disruptions of markets. This literature tends to be isolated from all the other literatures cited and suffers greatly from this failure. The arguments, advanced throughout this book, that market responses to crises exist constitute a challenge to any case for government aid including that applied to political supply crises.

The origins of crisis are irrelevant to what responses are optimal. If private parties are at least as competent as governments in anticipating a crisis, the usual private hedges such as stockpiles and spare capacity will provide the most efficient level of stabilization. Moreover, the difference between political and other forms of market disruption is often exaggerated. In practice, much of what is termed political is indistinguishable, in cause as well as in effect, from other disruptions. It is no coincidence that lawyers lump under *force majeure* both acts of God and political upheaval. Economically, the two are quite similar. In addition, some of the most severe "political" interventions are conscious public impositions of monopoly. Conversely, supply disturbances for other reasons can trigger a move to monopoly prices that persists after the original stimulus is removed.

The oil price rises of the 1970s were widely viewed as proof of the seriousness of the supply insecurity problem in oil and the need for a political response. Granting a connection between oil crises and oil cartelization still does not lead to acceptance of intervention to offset crises. The extension of the cartel risk argument to justify regulation involves concentration on too small a sample of cases and may involve misinterpretation of the oil cases. Most critically, a public origin of difficulties does not imply that the optimum response is also public. The private response possibilities discussed above, particularly inventory holding, are applicable to these government induced crises and could obviate public actions. Before examining this issue, the oil case should be examined more closely.

Until the 1970s, few expected rising oil prices; most warnings were subterfuges to justify protectionism. The oil price record of the 1960s suggests that the snapback of supplies in 1958 radically transformed views of oil supply conditions. Customers became more aware of the ability to sustain low cost supplies. Nominal dollar prices drifted downward even as world inflation became virulent.

For reasons that remain controversial, this situation changed in the 1970s. Adelman, (1973, 1993a) the most plausible analyst of the situation, has long argued that oil crises were important because they facilitate collusion to raise world oil prices. He has proposed a model in which the oil producers are uncertain about market conditions and unable to agree initially on a monopoly-profit-maximizing output level and its apportionment among themselves. A sudden disruption in the market provides an indication of what supply restriction can accomplish and efforts are made to maintain output at close to the disruption period level so the high price that arose can be maintained. The problem is a new-found (imperfect) ability of Middle Eastern countries to engage in monopolistic restriction of supply.

The process is unsystematic, complex, and imperfectly understood by all, including probably the OPEC countries themselves. Considerable discussion has arisen over which countries practice output restriction. It is suggested that only the core of OPEC members with low costs, low populations, and substantial influence on world oil prices finds supply restriction profitable. Views on the extent differ. Some feel that Saudi Arabia alone controls supply. Others believe that at least Kuwait and the United Arab Emirates also were involved. The extensive output cuts in these last countries suggests that they were at least some part of the core.

Absence of cohesion prevents maintenance of the price. Others nibble away at the market share of those most dedicated to maintaining the monopoly prices. Adelman (1972, 1973) argued in the early 1970s that these weaknesses could be exploited to break up the collusion. His writings of the late 1980s (Adelman 1993a) argue that the benefits of success encourage the continued reconstitution by the OPEC countries of reductions in their outputs. He also still seems to believe that the efforts can be undermined.

Verleger's work (1982, 1987, 1993), by providing an explanation of how the cartelization proceeds, fills a gap in Adelman's analysis. Verleger notes the critical and growing role of (increasingly more formalized) spot markets in price formation. He shows that prices set by OPEC countries on direct sales have followed spot market prices. The Adelman model and the Verleger analysis combine to indicate that the uncertainties of impact necessitate waiting to learn from the marketplace what price can be charged. Thus, the output restricting members of OPEC lower production, wait for the spot market to determine the price at which the output can be sold, and charge it.

If anything, Verleger's analysis overstates the role of the spot market. He believes traders overreacted in panic. Another view is that the traders correctly foresaw the dangers of government interference with the adjustment process. More critically, the spot market has expanded and built up considerable experience since 1974 and thus performed more satisfactorily in the 1990-91 crisis (as Verleger 1993 recognizes).

The imperfect cartel explanation has been challenged by other explanations, but these seem much less able to fit the facts. Some observers insist that world oil price movements reflect a change in perceptions of long-run competitive supply-demand relationships. Assertions of oil shortages arise from a misunderstanding of oil economics. Failures to develop new *proved* reserves in the Middle East are the effect, not the cause, of the price rise process. Proved reserves consist only of the oil in fields being developed for production. Countries seeking to limit output to keep up prices have no desire to develop additional capacity and thus increase proved reserves. Even so, they have not been able to avoid substantial reserve increases.

While many suggestions were made that oil price shocks caused inflation, the contrary view that inflation inspired the effort to raise prices has been expressed.

Similarly, examination of the (overelaborate) economic theory of exhaustible resources fails to disclose any plausible way to relate OPEC behavior to impending exhaustion. (See Gordon 1981a for further analysis of OPEC and exhaustible-resource economics and fuller citations of the key writings.) Exhaustion, per se, would produce some form of gradual relentless rises in prices, not the sharp rises followed by erosion that occurred. (Relentless price rises are quite different from following some simple price-raising rule. The rate of price rise in a general case would not be at a constant rate or amount for reasons explained in detail in Gordon 1981a.) More complex models can be developed to explain anything. However, even if OPEC were a cartel concerned with exhaustion, only bizarre instabilities in market demand could produce the actual behavior. Massive erratic year to year changes in the demand for petroleum and in its costs of production would have to arise. Experience suggests the observed price instabilities are more likely to occur from cartel breakdown and reconstruction than from the demand or cost fluctuations that prevail.

The suddenness of the price rises and the tendency to collapses are more consistent with the monopolization than with the scarcity view. Perception of long-term changes would build up gradually and produce a slow, steady, uninterrupted process of restricting current output and forcing up price. The theoretical and applied analyses of oligopoly better identify characteristics that explain world price movements. The critical problems are uncertainty about the short and long-run degree of monopoly power and difficulties in creating and maintaining collusion.

The Iran-Iraq war did not prevent another era of falling oil prices. With the end of that war, the downward pressure on prices increased. Of course, Iraq decided it would start a war it could win and precipitated what proved a short-lived crisis. Moreover, the oil-market effects were mild. Given the output cutbacks of the 1980s, others, primarily Saudi Arabia, could and largely did offset the loss of Iraqi and Kuwaiti oil. The way is taken as evidence that the United States incurs costs to protect oil supplies. However, critics of U.S. policy suggest that the war was yet another example of the disasters that arise from politicizing oil. Had the U.S. not sought special relations with oil states, the war could have been avoided. A depolitization of oil and insistence on observation of the rules of international law could have discouraged Iraq far more cheaply than the money spent first aiding and then fighting Iraq.

The events have the potential for leading to sharp price declines. Restoration of Kuwaiti production further strained OPEC's ability to maintain prices; the return of Iraq certainly will aggravate the difficulties. The tendency could be spurred even more by the collapse of communism. Inefficient pricing certainly overstimulated energy consumption. Bad planning may on balance have made energy output too low. Reform then could raise exports by increasing output and lowering consumption. Private operations will prevent oil boycotts in times of crises or of spite. We know that the problems of 73-74 were the production cuts, not the boycotts. The latter failed. Misery was shared in proportion to import use. Most trade boycotts break down. We are left with only two cases in which a supply crisis led to price rises that persisted after the disruption--the 1973-1974 and 1979-1980 oil cases. Even such crises may be unavoidable except at inordinate cost. It is probably more feasible to create a climate in which such crises are not so supportive of cartel formation. Policies that maximize competition and flexibility would promote the desired atmosphere.

Supply crises have a long history outside OPEC oil. Agricultural regions have faced many drought, flood, and storm damages to crops. Coal strikes have been common in the United States, Britain, and Australia. Cobalt supplies were disrupted by civil war in Zaire. Moreover, the experience in oil itself involves many countries with such diverse crises that a universal cause or cure does not exist. Nationalizations in Mexico and Iran, the 1956 Suez Canal closing, revolutions in Iraq and Libya, the 1980s Iran-Iraq war, and the civil war in Lebanon (through which oil flows to the Mediterranean) are among the diverse shocks that actually arose in oil. In many of these cases, world supply was not significantly affected. In the others, only temporary rises in prices occurred. Political disruption rarely has long-run effects. Even short-run damages can be small. The concerns produced by the disruption may unleash consumer responses that cause post-crisis prices to be lower than they otherwise would have been. Conjectures of this sort have appeared about the disruption of Zaire cobalt supplies.

Given all this experience, the idea that crises have severe impacts that predictably originate in specific industries becomes questionable. Both the probability of future crises that will produce persistent price increases and how optimally to react to the dangers are uncertain. Caution should be exercised in reacting to the insecurity problem. Many instances may prevail in which no problems exist. Even if threats prevail, the ability of private parties to anticipate and prudently hedge against these crises probably is superior to public ones.

The Hayek principle and Coase's warnings about government intervention particularly apply to responses to any crises. Profit-seeking experts in areas such as oil trade are better able than governments to conduct the speculation and inventory holding that will efficiently cushion the response to shocks. It can be argued that the absence of a well organized spot markets and government produced uncertainties were the key problems during oil crises.

Government, as noted, more often acts as the creator, not the controller, of monopoly. Such action is usually justified as protecting the unfortunate from the excesses of competition. Such policies are common in oil. The U.S. reliance on domestic production controls sustained by import quotas provided a model for OPEC. However, the most pervasive and clear-cut example is agriculture. Throughout the industrialized western world, governments have acted for at least a half century to protect farmers from competition. In less developed and communist countries, governments turn their monopoly power against farmers and force prices down below competitive levels. Just as textbook economics predicts, the result is perennial excesses of output over consumption (gluts) in developed countries and less output than desired consumption (shortages) elsewhere.

Public Stockpiles and the Problem of Supply Insecurity

Despite the cautions just expressed, proposals for government owned oil stockpiling and oil import taxes have been widely advocated in the United States. (See, for example, the anthologies edited by Plummer 1982 and Deese and Nye 1981, and the surveys by Horwich and Weimer 1984 and Bohi and Montgomery 1982.) The supporting arguments are dubious.

Publicness is one justification for both stockpiling and import tariffs. Oil crises are supposed to cause widespread effects such as increased inflation that go beyond the direct impacts of price increases on energy markets. Correction of these effects is a public good. The import tax is supposed, in part, to charge for these public-good effects. Similarly, stockpiles help offset the effects. Another buffer is provided by building plants capable of burning substitute fuels. Two controversial contentions are then involved--that publicness is involved in oil disruptions and that the cure lies in controlling oil instead of using traditional stabilization measures. Resolution requires settling some of the thorniest empirical issues in applied economics, those about economic stability. These issues are sufficiently complex that they are discussed separately in chapter 8.

Stockpiles and imports taxes each have a different additional justification. The second rationale for stockpiling relates to the efficient organization argument of this chapter. The case for import taxes, based on exercise of *national* monopoly buying power, is treated here in chapter 5. The efficiency rationale for stockpiles is that private stockpiling is discouraged by the tendency to impose windfall profits taxes on price controls and thus prevent the price rise needed to allow those who inventory to recover their investment. Public stockpiling is needed to offset the prevention of private stockpiling (a point made in the too little noted work of Newlon and Breckner 1975). This argument implies public stockpiling is only an effort to correct for government failure. It is questionable, moreover, whether this is preferable in any sense to private stockpiling. The shift to public stockpiles treats the symptoms rather than the disease. The literature on stockpiling suggests that the same fears of windfalls that lead to private controls are likely to hinder efficient use of public stockpiles. Discussions of stockpiling (e.g., Plummer 1982 and Deese and Nye 1981) are full of complaints about problems of prompt release of stockpiles in crises.

The writers fail to recognize that, in fact, such stockpiles are plagued by the same government failure that hindered private stockpiling--inordinate fear of excess profits. It is unclear whether the resistance to windfalls is based on strong public feelings or upon the self-generated convictions of politicians. Until this fear is eliminated, no efficient stockpile policy is possible. Once it is rooted out, no public stockpile against market instability is needed. Such a change of attitude will be hard to effect, but it must occur if stabilization is to succeed.

The reluctance in 1990 to use oil stockpiles confirms these concerns. The nonsense excuse was given that no shortages had arisen. As the analysis of chapter 2 indicated, no shortages will arise as long as prices are uncontrolled. The question is the price needed to eliminate the shortage. The stockpile is supposed to lessen the price rise. The suggestions that the cure is higher stockpiles reflect the persistent unwillingness adequately to challenge intervention.

Another often raised proposal is for intervention to reduce the fluctuations (and often to raise the level) of commodity prices. This argument suffers from the standard defects of many intervention proposals. It is not apparent what market failure makes the price fluctuations inefficient or that a stabilization scheme will improve things. The substantial literature on the theory and practice of stabilization has greatly undermined the case for such schemes. Among the considerations are that price fluctuations are neither universal to nor confined to poor countries. Not all poor countries are heavy exporters of commodities with volatile prices, but many rich countries do export such goods. (Macbean 1966 is the classic presentation of this argument; Newbery and Stiglitz 1981 provide a formal review that takes market failure problems more seriously but still is skeptical about the value of stabilization schemes.)

The present discussion has tried to demonstrate that market institutions have great ability to adapt to changing conditions. All that might be added is that the record of stabilization schemes follows the pattern of unsatisfactory implementation.

Conclusions

This chapter attempted to show that a general question of the benefits and costs of different organization forms applies to a range of issues in private and public policy. Much remains to be resolved about the magnitudes of benefits and costs in specific cases. The main points are:

(1) that the optimal organization depends on the nature of both the firm and the markets in which it participates,

(2) that attaining efficiency with spot markets and contracts is more feasible than many believe, and

(3) that many arguments for intervention overstate the problems of efficient private organization and understate the drawbacks of government.

Chapter 8

Market Regulation and Macroeconomics Problems

At least since the 1930s, some economists have argued that imperfections of competition caused economic instability from unemployment and inflation. A few added that policies to reduce these imperfections were the most satisfactory cure. The first part of the argument became widely accepted, but the policy conclusions have commanded little acceptance among specialists in economic instability.

Discussion of impacts on employment of monopolies possessed by firms is most often found at the fringes of the industrial organization literature. Another monopoly theory, that of trade unions, was widely held by older anti-intervention economists (see, e.g., Mises 1966, 538-634, 758-79, esp. 770ff.). A newer argument is that rigidities introduced by transaction costs cause the problems. The commitments made under union contracts are often used as an example. (Mankiw and Romer 1991 contains the critical contributions to the last argument.)

Market intervention has limited acceptance as a stabilization tool. Thus, one leading textbook writer Robert J. Gordon (1990, 294-5) considers market regulation unwise; major rivals, Dornbusch and Fischer (1987, 527-30), suggest that temporary controls might ease the way for vigorous application of traditional measures. Periodically, this advice is avoided, particularly among industrial organization economists. Thus, many energy specialists supported intervention in the oil market to promote economic stabilization.

This chapter surveys the issues involved in evaluating the wisdom of regulating individual markets to stabilize the economy. First, macroeconomics is defined, and an effort is made to epitomize the debates in the field. Then, the possible role of different policies is examined. With this background, the case of oil import control is treated. The basic conclusion is that the long chain of reasoning required to implement regulation of oil markets is composed of nothing but weak links.

Given the intrinsic intractability of the issues and the usual tendency to cloud the discussion with debates over form, no pretense can be made of providing the answers that have eluded the specialists. The goal is to identify the critical issues. For present purposes, summary views based on a selective survey of the literature suffice. The conclusion again is that the criticisms of intervention to stabilize the economy are more valid and more accepted than the defenders of "activism" are willing to admit. The defenders of active stabilization policy have conceded a great deal to those warning about the limits of intervention.

To provide perspective, attention is given to the state of the field before the 1930s and the changes in the thirties. The latter created an outlook that greatly contributed to reluctance to admit the extent to which economic analysis produces distrust of government. Finally, an effort is made to identify critical significant differences among views of macroeconomics.

An Overview of Macroeconomics

To understand this debate, it is essential to examine the underlying questions. Given the difficulties of establishing precision in economics, the border between macro- and microeconomics is unclear, and the macro-micro distinction can be misleading. The difference between the two branches is not whether the whole economy is studied. Neither area covers everything, but both in their way try to deal with global issues. Microeconomics stresses the aspects of an economy involving the actions and interactions of the many individual parts. The general equilibrium model, which has become the heart of microeconomics, is by definition an economy-wide analysis.

Macroeconomics is the term adopted after World War II for studies of the economic instabilities. The focus is primarily unemployment but with increased concern with inflation and balance of payments equilibrium, issues microeconomics traditionally assumes away. For reasons discussed below, such instability is critically related to the role of money in the economy. Thus, another terminology, namely, of price theory and monetary economics, might be more satisfactory. Practice is too well established to change.

One peculiarity is the treatment of growth. Microeconomic tools are used, but the concept of growth is taught in macroeconomics. This situation is attributable to historical accident. The pioneering work in growth analysis was inspired by recognition that early macroeconomic analysis considered investment but not the growth it produced. Even after growth theory became more obviously microeconomic, the relationship to macroeconomic issues was sufficient to keep discussions in the macroeconomic textbooks.

Views on the field of macroeconomics differ widely. At one extreme, the questions discussed are viewed as far more exciting than the mundane ones of how markets operate. The answers provided are thought sufficient to guide public policies to lessen the problem. At the other extreme, the subject is viewed as a mass of ill-developed ideas unfit to coexist with the time-tested, clearer principles of market analysis. The intermediate view that seems increasingly influential is that the rise of macroeconomics greatly improved the discussion of economic instability but the field still lacks the coherence attained by macroeconomics.

In particular, much macroeconomics postulates behavior that cannot be readily related to what microeconomics predicts. Given this situation, much effort has been devoted to linking macroeconomic theory with microeconomic theory. The critical problem is the greater intractability. Mathematical analysis in microeconomics is feasible because no matter how may different goods, consumers, and producers are considered, a few basic equilibrium conditions describe the situation. In fact, all these conditions are variants of one basic rule that optimums occur when marginal costs equal marginal benefits.

Extensive theorizing, practicing, and observing has shown that no comparable unifying principle exists for the basic issues of economic stabilization. Each problem raises questions that require special models. Typically, the analysis of any one issue proves overwhelming. The models become unmanageable long before they can include enough detail to meet minimal policy needs. This proved true with both business cycle and growth models. The business-cycle modelers (e.g., Baumol 1959, Goodwin 1955, and Samuelson 1939) never succeeded in developing a model that could simultaneously handle monetary and nonmonetary forces. Similarly, the most elaborate growth models (see Solow 1956 and Stiglitz and Uzawa 1969) developed could not deal with large numbers of inputs and outputs in a technically progressive world.

A critical aspect of the debate over macroeconomics is public policy. Keynes's 1936 exposition was welcomed by many as showing how actively to cure the great depression. The support was stronger among younger economists; many distinguished, older economists were skeptical. Advocacy of active stabilization policy emerged and became increasingly influential, initially in economics and then in the 1960s in public policy. The successes apparently attained in the early 1960s seemed ample vindication of the faith. Hubris developed with claims the policy could be greatly refined. The subsequent Viet Nam war inflation and the difficulties in restoring satisfactory economic performance shattered this confidence. Increasingly, economists began accepting and extending the criticisms levied at Keynes in the thirties.

Critical Issues in Macroeconomics

Before the 1930s, economic analysis emphasized the resource allocation issues treated here in chapters 2, 3, 4, and 5. Discussion of aggregative disturbances was limited, scattered, and apparently not widely stressed at least in the introductory texts. However, it is an exaggeration to state that the issues were not considered. Inflation and the balance of payments problems have been well understood for over two centuries. Unemployment has also been long discussed, but before the thirties (and many would add, to this day), the causes and cures were imperfectly known.

Inflation is largely explicable by the long-extant quantity theory of money. (Hume provided a reasonably clear statement in his essay "Of Money," 281-295, esp. 290.) That theory stresses the role of monetary supply expansion in sustaining inflation. The only major modern modification involves consideration of separate private wage and price decisions that collectively imply an increase in price levels. Discussions in the 1950s established that such efforts could not succeed unless the money supply sufficiently expands to sustain the private decisions. If the monetary authorities refuse to undertake the expansion *and* the wage and price decisions are not rapidly reversed, unemployment will occur.

One major controversy about such arguments relates to the causes of such wage and price decisions. Some suggest such actions only occur in the later stages of inflation, generated by the monetary authorities to support government policies. Ultimately, private parties attempt preemptive action. This theory implies private-action problems are best avoided by not initiating inflations. Conversely, only the occurrence of autonomously generated actions that are difficult to reverse would necessitate going beyond conventional measures to limit money-supply expansion. As suggested above, assertions are regularly made about the widespread occurrence of these unwise hard to reverse private decisions.

Balance of payments theory is more complex. Domestic inflation and changing competitiveness are among the causes of changing balance of payments conditions. Whatever the causes, the cures are clear-cut. In principle, a country can choose between adjusting exchange rates or seeking to adjust domestic price levels. Since World War I, exchange rate adjustment has been the option chosen. This contrasts with the prior century in which British leadership helped stabilize exchange rates. One aspect of the change was that post-World War I Britain was too weak economically and politically to continue its prior role. Another influence was that the credibility of anti-inflationary policies universally declined.

Studies of the gold standard indicate that British behavior and the general climate allowed stabilization without total conformance to the rigorous rules that economic textbooks show would guarantee the desired results. These rules call for gold holdings in all countries, a rigid tie between these gold holdings and the money supply, willingness to buy and sell gold at a fixed price, and free trade in gold. Under these rules, any balance of payments problems produce self-correcting reactions. If a country faces a balance of payments deficit, arbitrageurs buy gold and resell it abroad. This action not only covers the immediate deficit, but it also institutes actions that eliminate the deficit. The gold losing country responds by reducing the money supply and this produces price declines that bring make the country's exports more attractive. The gold gaining country responds by increasing the money supply and this produces price rises that bring make the country's exports less attractive.

Money supply expansion by gold gainers was more prevalent in practice than money supply contraction by gold losers. Britain, moreover, assumed a large part of the adjustment burden. The system prevailed in and contributed to a long period of peace, British prosperity, and slowly declining prices. World War I shattered the systems and Britain's ability to maintain leadership.

The nature of the contribution of Keynes's (1936) *General Theory* to understanding the economics of unemployment inspired controversies that still influence discussions. Haberler's ([1938] 1958) survey reported that numerous alternative explanations had previously been provided. Many agree that, nevertheless, Keynes's work filled a serious void. What is unclear is exactly what the contribution was. (Among the main critiques are L. R. Klein 1947, Leijonhufvud 1968, and Patinkin 1965. A good survey of later developments is Goodhart 1989.)

Samuelson's (1948) introductory textbook revolutionized the teaching of economics by incorporating aspects of Keynesian concepts. In later writings (e.g., Samuelson 1977, 881-97; Samuelson 1986, 283-90), Samuelson contends that he received no useful guidance about unemployment until he read Keynes. However, Samuelson does not make clear whether this deficiency arose because the prior work seemed so poor or merely because his teachers did not consider it important enough to teach.

One contribution of Keynes was a new model of unemployment that was used as the basis of many alternative views of unemployment problems. Another influence was his argument that the nature of the difficulties was such that governments could and should intervene to effect a correction. It is possible to approve of only one of the two elements of Keynes's work, neither, or both, and cases arose of adoptions of all possible positions.

For reasons already stated, the resolution of these debates is not critical to the question of the wisdom of regulating markets to stabilize the economy. It was shown above that believers in active stabilization do not consider control of individual industries the most effective policy. The case against active stabilization, however, is worth examining because of its increased influence and implications. Lesser certainty about any form of stabilization reinforces the basic objections to market intervention on macroeconomic grounds.

As with debates over market-level issues, the central concern about the feasibility of active stabilization policy is over the adjustive powers of the economy. The view that these adjustive powers were so poor that governments should intervene to eliminate unemployment became popular and was reinforced by Keynes's analysis.

The most devastating criticism of intervention holds that when automatic corrective processes occur rapidly enough, intervention may be harmful or at best ineffective. Milton Friedman is the dominant contributor. His major policy statements appear in a series of essays, most of which are available in various anthologies on either the issues or Friedman's work. He collaborated with Anna Schwartz (1963) in a massive review of U.S. experience.

Rapidity is comparative. As discussed in the macroeconomics texts consulted, delays are inherent in intervention. Determining that a downturn has occurred may not be possible until automatic recovery forces become operative. As careful observation of business news makes clear, preliminary data about what happened in a given month may not become available until more than a month afterwards and are often revised in later months. Until declines have persisted for several months, it is unclear whether more than a random disturbance has occurred. Additional time is required to design and implement a policy. That policy's impact may occur slowly. Therefore, the stimulus will take effect when recovery is already underway and create inflationary pressures.

The attack on intervention changed drastically in the 1970s. The contention that controls worked badly was replaced by claims that action could succeed only temporarily. At least under some economic circumstances, stimulatory policy will work only if private decision makers are unaware of what the government is doing. Once awareness of policy actions arises, private entities will take measures to counteract the government efforts. The core of the case is the economic theory of rational expectation. That concept was developed by Muth in 1971 as a way to treat microeconomic issues. It was applied to macroeconomics by a group led by Lucas and Sargent. Rational expectations are ones in which efficient use is made of available information. Private and public decision makers do not, as was widely assumed in prior work, simply expect past trends to persist. Whatever is available about future plans is used.

The concept of rational expectations simply says that decision making employs all information the decision makers find worth acquiring. Any valuable evidence that the past will differ from the future will be recognized. This was not a new, radical theoretic principle; it is implicit in a careful definition of rational behavior. What was fresh in the later work was criticizing the widespread neglect of the principle in statistical analyses of macroeconomic behavior and suggesting ways to remedy the defects. The controversies about rational expectations relate to appropriate ways to represent expectations.

Rational expectation models are best justified by the price-theory principle that the markets are dominated by people who on average correctly anticipate the future. This can be distorted as implying everyone has perfect knowledge and thus criticized as wildly optimistic. It suffices that well informed speculators exist to push prices to ones more accurately predicting the future. Such people cannot be fooled by policy makers. This concept, adapted from Houthakker's 1957 analysis of speculators in commodity markets, is one that is often neglected in discussions of rational expectations.

The pioneers of application of rational expectations to macroeconomics argued that their analysis reinforced Friedman's criticism of active stabilization policy. (See Lucas and Sargent 1981, a collection of largely technical papers by numerous authors and Lucas 1981, consisting entirely of articles authored or coauthored by Lucas including several that noneconomists can comprehend.)

Two major components of the analysis are insistence on concentrating on the natural rate of unemployment and assuming continual market clearing. The natural rate argument is that even in a well-functioning economy some people will always be temporarily unemployed as they make desirable job changes. Feasible reductions in unemployment are limited by the effects of these shifts.

As Lucas (1981, 288) makes clear, market clearing is a technical device to eliminate what he terms an excess of "free parameters" available in a disequilibrium model. Too few restrictions are placed on possible behavior. Lucas finds it preferable to redefine unemployment as a preference to continue job search rather than accepting available jobs. He explicitly reminds his readers that equilibrium does not invariably mean a desirable outcome. He writes, "One doesn't want to suggest people *like* depressions (126, emphasis and punctuation in the original)!" Moreover, the full rational expectations analysis implies that supply and demand shifts continuously occur so that the equilibrium outcomes change. In short, Lucas is only arguing that adjustment is best treated as movements from worse to better equilibriums. The policy-ineffectiveness conclusion then indicates governments cannot alter these progressions.

The original Friedman (1948, 1968a) analysis and its extension by rational-expectations macroeconomists at least implicitly share with many others concern with the absence of satisfactory explanations of the causes of recessions. Despite extensive studies, the causes of the short, shallow recessions that normally prevail remain unclear. Analysts are unable to explain why and when they occur and what their depth and duration would be under alternative policy choices.

Such uncertainties imply that the ability to stabilize is imperfect. What remains unclear is the exact extent of the imperfection and how best to respond. Those believing in policy ineffectiveness note that at least three ways exist to remove discretion. One method proposed to eliminate discretionary monetary policy is total adherence to a gold standard following the rules that guarantee maintenance of balance of payments equilibrium. Friedman (1948, 1968a) long advocated the alternative of imposing a "monetary rule" under which the monetary authorities would allow the money supply to grow at a steady rate. Hayek (1978, 207-8), in turn, raised doubts about the workability of the rule approach. Part of the concern relates to problems in defining money with the proliferation of alternative forms of liquid assets. The more fundamental point is that central banks are monopolies and thus difficult to control.

Hayek (see, e.g., 1978, 218-31), therefore, proposed free market banking. Hayek would supplement government currency with that from competing private banks. Hayek argued that the competition to secure acceptance would produce more stable money than central banks have done. Experience in the U.S. and Scotland is interpreted to support this view.

The Case of An Oil Import Fee

The oil price shocks of the 1970s and to a lesser extent the run-up of mineral prices in the early seventies produced concerns over the effects of such instability on the economy. (See, e.g., Mork and Hall 1980a, 1980b, Darby 1982, Svensson 1984, Hamilton 1983, and Bohi 1990.) These proposals are a distant descendant of 1930s and 1950s advice to use market policies to deal with economic instability and are viewed here as both an interesting special case and as an example of a more general argument.

Hamilton (1983) presented the result that all but one postwar recession was associated with oil price rises. He employed statistical tests in an attempt to determine whether the oil shocks were a cause or an effect. Establishing causation is widely and properly viewed as impossible. Available methodologies can only show whether a causal influence *might* be at work. The tests used rely on the indirect indicator that causes are likely to occur before their effects. The main problem is that other events also may occur previously. Theory can reduce, but not eliminate, the number of prior events that could be causal. Hamilton's results were consistent with the hypothesis that oil prices caused recessions. While Hamilton recognized that no statistical test is conclusive, he could not identify a third force that might have caused both oil price moves and recessions.

Hamilton's conclusions seem too strong and have been challenged by subsequent writers. Oil price changes before 1973 were generally small, and the oil price drops of 1986 had modest impact. Hamilton's critics observe other causes for recession including inept public policy. Hamilton may not have considered enough alternative explanations. Despite these reservations about the Hamilton analysis, it has been widely cited by advocates of both market-clearing real business cycles and of "new Keynesian" market rigidity models.

In contrast, Bohi (1990), previously a supporter of an oil import tax, found that he could not construct a satisfactory proof of the validity of the stabilization argument for such a tax. It seemed more likely to him that defective monetary policy was the problem. He, therefore, concluded import taxes could be justified only on the optimal tariff grounds criticized here in chapter 5.

Well before Hamilton provided his evidence, energy economists had responded to the 1973-74 oil price rises by proposing both oil import taxes to lessen and pay for the aggregative impacts and government purchase, ownership, and management of inventories to alleviate the pressures. For specialists in macroeconomics, the experience was yet another problem in the continuing effort to grapple with the complexities of the field.

This devotion to oil tax proposals involves excessive faith in the state of macroeconomic knowledge. Awareness of the disarray in macroeconomics is absent. The prior discussion indicated the barriers to agreeing on any policy. These difficulties apply to oil taxes. An oil tax is justified in principle only if consensus on the causes and cures of instability prevails. The effects of oil shocks on the economy must be better demonstrated than they have been. It must be proved that some tax would stabilize the markets better than conventional monetary and fiscal policy. None of these tests have been met.

Precise ability to measure the macroeconomic impacts of policies is required before the vague idea that some tax is needed can be turned into an operational tax recommendation. The influence of oil shocks and of the oil tax must be quantifiable with sufficient accuracy that assurance is given that the tax can be expected to do more good than harm. If higher oil prices have unfavorable macroeconomic consequences, we must recognize that the price-raising effect of oil taxes will itself have such undesirable impacts. The tax imposes clear efficiency losses and possibly a persistent drag on the economy. We must be able to estimate the frequency and impacts of supply shocks and the effects of the tax when supplies are normal. Again the Hayek principle applies.

All this may take the proposal too seriously. LaCasse and Plourde (1992b) pointed out that the only way adequately to insulate an economy from shocks is for it and every other country with which it trades to cease trading with OPEC. The proposition is presented as a demonstration of the untenability of macroeconomic stabilization by limiting oil imports.

The economic theory of politics is also critical. The political pressures that distort implementation mean that even if we knew the optimum price, it is unlikely that the regulators would ensure its attainment. Energy industries and their political allies predictably found the import tax appealing. Thus, a classic danger arises. As often occurs, a policy that might be beneficial if properly implemented probably would be inefficiently applied. The theory of optimum stabilization would be perverted into an excuse for undesirable protectionism.

Conclusions

Macroeconomics has clarified but not resolved the issues in stabilizing the economy. We have excellent theories of inflation and balance of payments adjustment. After more than a half century of debate, we still, however, lack a satisfactory analysis of the causes and cures of unemployment. Whatever possibilities for stabilization exist are more likely to emerge from traditional monetary and fiscal policies than from regulating markets. Support in the economics literature for use of wage and price controls is limited. The advocates of such controls tend to prefer applying them to the whole economy. The already insuperable barriers to success of wage and price controls increase if attempts are made to identify the industries in which controls are most effective. Proposals to stabilize by targeting specific industries most often come from specialists in these industries with limited knowledge of macroeconomics. The case for intervening in a particular market suffers from all the defects of the case for any activist macroeconomic policies plus the added doubts that broad or narrow industry-controlling policies are good stabilizing measures. In short, support of regulating individual markets to attain macroeconomic goals is weak.

Chapter 9

Notes on Fairness and the Market Economy

The discussion begins with examination of why the problem of defining and attaining a fair outcome is intractable. Then it is argued that whatever income redistribution goals may be adopted, regulation of markets is a poor way to attain them. Since this book stresses regulation of markets, the second point is more critical here. The argument starts by recognizing the absence of clear rules of fairness. Ethical issues that have remained unresolved though millennia of effort are involved. The facts about prevailing conditions and the impacts of alternative policies are difficult and perhaps impossible to determine. Throughout, it is presumed that this view of income distribution dominates the economic literature.

One chronic effect of the uncertainties is a tendency of too many dissatisfied groups to claim they deserve favoritism on equity grounds. Aid often goes to those with strong political influence. They may be at least sufficiently affluent and adaptable that their need for assistance is questionable. They may even be people others would consider rich.

Market policy should concentrate on increasing efficiency. Redistribution by regulation of markets is undesirable for at least two reasons. First, market regulation is more likely than other kinds of assistance to benefit the unworthy. Second, even if the beneficiaries are largely deserving, regulation is likely to be more inefficient than other feasible methods of aid. In principle, direct aid should involve fewer distortions and transaction costs than regulating markets. The perennial attacks on the practices of the welfare state arise because it proves to cause its own substantial distortions and transaction costs.

These views should be distinguished from a failed effort to replace explicit concern with equity with limiting policy to efficiency increasing measures. While such proposals lost favor long ago, they are still used as easy targets for those wishing to demonstrate shortcomings of economics. I forgot about this older position until encountering an attack upon it in a chance reading of a book on my shelf of unread material. No further comment or references seem necessary here. This chapter differs from the rest of the book in its referencing. Where other chapters include citations of supplemental material some of which was only skimmed, this chapter only cites material actually used and omits much that was fully read. No other satisfactory stopping place was apparent.

Intervention in Perspective: The Problem of Income Distribution

Many questions arise about income distribution, and, as noted, most are impossible to resolve. Among the key issues are: the goals, how best to finance them, how best to use these funds, and how to distinguish between legitimate aid and protection of powerful but undeserving groups. We have neither widely accepted, readily implemented criteria for judging what constitutes neediness nor adequate knowledge about the actual problems of the less fortunate. Even worse, the evidence suggests that no one knows how to design even a hypothetical research program that would significantly reduce the uncertainties.

A major element in late nineteenth century economics was the incorporation of these insights about equity. The prior notion was that well-being was a measurable phenomenon and should be maximized. This contention was repudiated. Measurability was shown infeasible and of dubious relevance. Once the implicit value judgment that rewards should be proportional to the ability to enjoy was discerned, its dubious merits became apparent.

Despite these changes, economics remains the critical field for clarification of income distribution issues. No one is able satisfactorily to resolve what income distribution rules should be. Economics well analyzes the consequences of different ways to attain any goal. The issues that particularly concern economists such as preservation of incentives and freedom of exchange are critical ones in the debate over fairness. Both the recipients of aid and those taxed to provide it may become less productive if aided and taxed inefficiently.

In contrast, the evidence is overwhelming that established religious and secular moral principles are too general to resolve equity and other policy debates. It is notorious that different branches of at least Christianity and Judaism reach opposite views in policy debates. Interdisciplinary discussions of equity only disclose these discords (see Block, Brennan, and Elzinga 1985, Block and Hexham 1986).

Traditional Christian and Jewish ethics, for example, stressed voluntary private efforts and aid to help people become self-sufficient. Viner ([1960] 1991, 208) points to contentions by medieval Christian moral philosophers that charity should be voluntary. Tamari (1987) indicates that similar views were in practice modified by pressures to participate exerted by local, self-governing Jewish communities. The great religious debates of at least the 1980s and 1990s involve criticisms by the more traditionally minded of the enthusiasm for government aid held by many Christian ministers and Jewish rabbis.

Another way to make the point is to examine various efforts to establish principles of fairness. Not surprisingly, discord is rampant. Following a pattern often noted here, the arguments prove more imprecise that the authors admit. The fundamental problem is that any full discussion must recognize counterarguments. Once this is done, the position becomes fuzzy.

The efforts of Harvard philosopher John Rawls (1971) to state rules for an approach providing for greater equality proved a tempting target for those stressing the problems of establishing clear rules. Rawls produced an exhaustive (600 page), thoughtful survey that showed unusual depth and breadth of knowledge. Ample commentary is available, including several books. Rawls calls for the maximum individual liberty consistent with other people's liberty and that inequalities are allowed if they are to "everyone's advantage" and "attached to positions and offices open to all (60)." Distributions are to be judged by their effects on "the least advantaged members of society (75)." He termed this last concept the "difference principle." As is typical with Rawls, these principles prove, under scrutiny, too vague to implement.

Rawls's exposition generally displayed confidence in the arguments inadequately supported by the exposition. A tension prevailed between zeal for results and knowledge of the problems of resolving the issues. Rawls was too honest to ignore arguments that undermine his case. He failed adequately to consider the implications of his caveats. Despite ample warning of the problems of consensus, he implied that he had provided an unambiguous, universally acceptable criterion of fairness. It was an invitation to criticism, and many responded. The existence of so massive a reaction is simultaneously proof of how interesting the work was and how it could not settle the debate. In short, while he failed to provide a widely accepted answer, he identified the right questions and provided interesting but widely disputed discussions.

Posner (1986, 438), for example, argues," ...Rawls's theory of distributive justice has almost no empirical content." Posner sees the analysis as compatible with attitudes ranging from "out-and-out socialism" to "laissez-faire capitalism." Hayek (1976, 100, esp. 183) believes that Rawls's critics have misread him and exaggerated his egalitarianism. Rawls's (1971, 62-75, 546) admissions that recognition must be made of the inefficiencies associated with any redistribution policy seem sufficient to justify Posner's conclusion. If tradeoffs must be considered, the rules become inoperative. No criteria are provided to determine the proper balance. This admission seems *the* fatal flaw.

Rawls (1971, 118-92) further strains credulity with the construct used to justify his rules of distribution. He asks us to imagine what distribution would be chosen by deliberative body whose members have full knowledge of every critical influence except what their role in society would be. This leaves much too much room for speculation. Given that Rawls designed the group, it is not surprising that he expects the appraisers to reach his conclusions. This device, thus, is too artificial to increase acceptance of Rawls's views. The assumption of a consensus by an imaginary group is at least as hard and probably harder to accept than Rawls's direct defense of his rules.

Posner (1986) tacitly accepts the principle of a Rawlsian conclave and bases his complaints on the difficulties in defining this imaginary consensus. Posner suggests that the degree of risk aversion, how broad a definition of the worst-off group is adopted, and relative faith in government and markets would affect the choice. More broadly, Rawls's principles tend to define away the difficulties. The reconciliation of liberties, for example, regularly produces vigorous debates and a consensus on who are legitimately the least advantaged would be hard to attain.

The inability precisely to define an acceptable balance also plagues critics of egalitarian policies. Those who criticize egalitarian policies because of belief that private property rights are sacrosanct or of concerns over inefficiency still admit the desirability of helping the needy. These critics are concerned with such drawbacks of income redistribution as the resulting alienation of property rights, the inefficiencies, and the enormous problems of administration. Since no satisfactory definition of neediness is available, it is impossible to identify the number of people needing assistance, let alone the amount of money required to assist them. A broad definition of worthiness could lead to considerable redistribution.

A further complication is introduced by consideration of the appropriate way to finance aid. It can be argued, as Nozick (1974) does, that principles of noncoercion make it inappropriate to finance aid to the poor through taxes. Charity must be private. In principle, this position could be independent of views about the amount of redistribution wanted. Even a believer in extensive transfers might have both enough faith in private ventures and enough belief in avoiding coercion to advocate purely private programs.

Advocates of vigorous redistribution also tend to support government programs to effect the transfers. Critics of redistribution are more divided on the subject.

Mises's views on poverty in *Human Action* (1966, 603, 835-40) suggest that private charity may be preferable to direct public aid (838). The discussion also includes an extensive general examination of the subjectivity of prevailing views of minimum acceptable levels of income (602-11). Hayek notes, "There is little reason why the government should not also play some role, or even take the initiative, in such areas as social insurance and education....(1960, 257-8)."

With these principles in mind, some difficulties in developing and appraising policies can be explored. The first point that needs further consideration is what economic analysis can contribute to the debate. Discussions of income distribution regularly focus on conflicts between economic efficiency and policies to redistribute income. In particular, such programs may cause disincentives to undertake productive activities. Those aided may find it unprofitable to work. The taxes used to provide the funds may discourage efforts by taxpayers. Moreover, we lack the knowledge of the magnitude of redistribution benefits and the efficiency losses produced by redistributive policies.

A key point made by many observers, including Mises and Hayek, is that complete equality is difficult to define and attain. No readily-computed measure of well-being exists. Equality of money incomes may not produce equality of benefits. At a minimum, non-monetary benefits are obtained, but, many of them are hard to identify and value. Further problems arise from possible differences in the ability to benefit from wealth.

As Hayek often warns (see esp. 1976, 80-4), the natural tendency of inequalities to arise means that only excessively oppressive governments could enforce complete equality, however defined. Regulators would have to monitor individual well-being and intrude to eliminate inequalities. Since it involves doing nothing, it is simple and feasible to preserve existing income distributions (or, more correctly, to limit changes to those initiated by voluntary private actions). Many barriers arise in trying to reach the opposite pole of full equality. More critically, since the extent of the impediments is unclear, the tolerable degree of inequality reduction remains unknown.

Further questions arise over what should be done and how. Directing aid at promoting self-sufficiency seems accepted as preferable, but again with a debilitating caveat that some compensation be given for insuperable barriers to achievement, another impossible to define concept.

As far as methods of aid, poverty debates are dominated by consideration of the merits of direct, unrestricted monetary aid versus more restricted grants. The latter range from restrictions on the use of monetary grants to providing specific services. The economics literature on poverty issues stresses less restrictive policies. Providing grants for specific services or even imposing extensive supervision of general aid may benefit the provider more than the beneficiary. Subsidies of some services may benefit affluent users. Critics of legal aid frequently make this charge (see, e.g., William Tucker 1990, 302, 305-6). Health care reform is another example. (It is also an illustration of the tendency to cure bad regulation by more regulation.)

Other redistribution arguments stress that certain incomes are unearned, undeserved, and thus should be taxed away. The previously presented arguments stress the existence of the impoverished who deserve aid. The unearned income argument focuses on people deemed so improperly wealthy that they merit penalties. While quite fashionable among politicians and at least some economists, the argument has severe defects.

Economic theorists long noted the possibility that actual compensation exceeds the reward necessary to produce the sacrifice. This difference is generally termed a rent but is also called an excess or windfall profit. The extra returns earned by a superior resource such as a well located or fertile piece of land are classic examples of such rents. It is popular, or at least politically expedient, to denounce receipt of such windfalls. An impeccable (in fact, tautological) economic theory demonstrates that excess-profits can be taxed painlessly (see chapter 11). The definition of an excess is income greater than needed to elicit the dedication of a resource to its most profitable use. Taxing an excess lowers receipts to the minimum required level and so preserves the allocation to an efficient use.

Implementing the theory is hindered by the difficulties of identifying excesses. Separation of the rent component of compensation from the necessary reward is a formidable and probably impossible-to-effect task. It is often difficult to distinguish the portion of the reward due to the diligence of the individual from that due to innate skill, or talent.

John Locke argued three centuries ago that the value of land is to a large extent created by the efforts of its owners. Erich Zimmermann (1964) had the related view that natural resources are all created. Some of the greatest rents accrue to talented individuals--entertainers, artists, athletes, and business executives. This, of course, is the economic analog of the notorious problem of determining the relative importance of heredity and environment.

Critics of rent taxation delight in pointing out that the advocates arbitrarily choose which rents to tax. Windfalls clearly due to obviously personal achievements such as of popular entertainers are never specially taxed. Less successful participants demand being raised to the same level rather than having the stars penalized. Whenever the gains are associated with land and capital goods, the results become suspect. The prior arguments imply that these profits often are a reward to a different type of individual talent, the ability to develop a profitable business. The tax system is too blunt an instrument to sort out these issues. Actual taxes directed at suspected sources of excesses, moreover, usually take forms that do discourage effort (see chapter 11 for illustrations from land law experience). These problems suggest that enthusiasm for excess-profits taxes is unwise.

Moreover, the broad concept of "fair" taxation proved a disaster in practice. The underlying struggle to correct inequities inspired proliferating complications of the law. No one can possibly know what was the net effect of departing from a simple flat income tax. In particular, neither the revenue nor equity effects of complex taxation is knowable. The high administrative costs are obvious, particularly to those who do their own income tax forms.

Market Regulation and Equity

Both theory and practice indicate that regulation of markets is an undesirable way to redistribute income. As suggested above, even if many participants in the market are worthy of aid, inefficiencies necessarily arise in using market regulations to redistribute income. These tend to be greater distortions than those produced by more direct aid. Additional, particularly critical, objections arise because market regulation is the form of redistributive policy most often used to aid the unworthy.

Many inefficiencies arise. One is that excess benefits are invariably provided. The correlations between need and involvement in a given market are unlikely to be so perfect to ensure that every one in the regulated market needs aid. To make matters worse, the distribution of benefits by regulation is likely to have perverse outcomes. The policies adopted usually make receipts of benefits proportional to the extent of participation in the market. Greater participation is a market is typically associated with greater wealth, which is equivalent to lesser need. Protection similarly preserves existing interests, and those protected are likely to possess initially or eventually greater wealth than those excluded.

Further costs are produced by the impacts on the regulated industries. The inefficiencies differ with the policy. In general, assistance to buyers leads to inefficiently low production; assistance to sellers, to inefficiently high output. Another problem is most frequently associated with aid to buyers. A typical form of buyer protection is price controls, and such controls force reliance on nonprice alternatives such as allocation by a government agency. Such alternatives are both more expensive and less likely to produce efficient allocations than are markets. Another effect that was observed briefly in the U.S. gasoline price controls and was a chronic problem in communist states is that consumers must spend large amounts of time standing in line for goods. These hidden costs also may be borne more heavily by the poor. Indeed, the former Soviet Union maintained special stores to shelter high officials from shopping delays.

Similar problems would arise from decreeing minimum prices to protect producers. Such policies are not prevalent because governments are wisely reluctant to decide which producers of the product to favor. Picking favorites undermined many policies such as U.S. state controls of oil production and U.S. federal controls of oil imports and later of domestic oil and gas prices.

When governments wish to raise prices, programs, such those typical in aid to agriculture, to buy the commodity or restrict the output of the product are preferred. Government may purchase output or pay producers not to produce. In either case, consumer purchases are inefficiently low. With commodity purchases, output is inefficiently high. Payments to limit output make production inefficiently low. Again, government action produces monopoly-like results that the industry could not impose on its own.

Other policies designed to protect sellers impose taxes or sales ceilings on rivals. The inefficiencies are lowering consumption by lessening supplies and placing upward pressures on price. The rivals captured markets by being more efficient than the firms being aided. The policies that shift sales to the protected firms necessarily move output to less efficient producers. Such practices amount to the using governmental power to produce the output restrictions that would have occurred had the industry been monopolized. Thus, private firms unable to cartelize seek government promotion of the desired outcome. The classic examples of misuse of equity arguments are tariffs and quotas on international trade, discussed in chapter 5. International trade theorists long have stressed the monopolistic nature of such trade restrictions. Claims that the rivals lack a cost advantage are noted and attacked in chapters 4 and 5.

Given these inefficiencies and the high administrative costs of these programs, they are unlikely to be superior to direct aid. Regulation of markets and subsidizing specific services are not advocated or initiated by those who have assessed the problems of the disadvantaged and are determined to resolve them. Regulation is the response to lobbying by those who have suffered from developments in markets. The natural suspicion that such lobbying is most often done by the undeserving is amply confirmed by experience. The dominance of lobbying by representatives of the affluent is widely publicized. What are less well recognized are the deficiencies of lobbyists purporting to speak for the less affluent. Such groups are flawed in many ways. Those speaking for the aged fail to recognize that the elderly differ markedly in affluence. Consumer advocates propose their idiosyncratic views of what is appropriate. The representatives of the aged speak for those affluent enough to support the organizations. Those purporting to speak for disadvantaged minorities similarly may adopt agendas that prove harmful.

The problem is complicated by the ability of these interest groups to attract members for reasons other than belief in the policy positions. Benefits are made available to members, and many may join despite unconcern or even disapproval of the political positions. The American Association of Retired People is a case in which this situation is sensed by members. The American Automobile Association provides a more striking example; its benefits are far more obvious than its lobbying. (I belong to both.)

A classic example of discord between economic principles and political practice is implementation of price controls. Politicians claim to be protecting the worthy against the avaricious. Economists contend the politically powerful are preserving their positions. It is also pointed out that price controls restrict supplies and can ultimately cause disastrous long-run consequences.

Rent controls are a favorite example (see William Tucker 1990). They clearly encourage tenants to remain entrenched. Such normal processes as moving to a smaller apartment after the children leave are discouraged. Worse, over time, the stock of housing declines. Economists naturally suspect that the growing number of street people in major cities is affected by rent controls, among other things.

Tucker presents a more complex analysis. He notes that another influence is the release of mentally ill from institutions. Such release does not inevitably lead to homelessness. Prevailing pressures on housing in some municipalities prevent response. First, supply is limited by regulations. Then rent controls are imposed to shelter established tenants from the consequences of supply restriction. He provides examples in which the tenants in rent controlled housing are more affluent than their landlords. The clearest case is Berkeley, California in which college students historically rented apartments in working-class homes. He also confirms that often the controls transfer profits to absentee leaseholders. Requirements that the leasers occupy apartments are unenforceable. The same beliefs that lead to rent controls produce severe barriers to securing landlords' rights. Proving failure to occupy becomes inordinately difficult.

Energy price controls protected the interests of those fortunate enough to have had access to the fuel before its price rose. These beneficiaries were are unlikely to be the poor whom price controls purportedly protect. U.S. oil and gas price controls protected existing, largely middle class users. With price controls, the poor who were newcomers to the market were forced to use oil. This might have been more expensive than bidding natural gas away from protected users.

Another widely used argument, that "small business" should be protected against "big business," is even more dubious. The discussions invalidly use the size of corporations as the measure of bigness. Critical differences among companies in the nature of their stockholders are ignored. The actual situation is unknown because data are not collected about the ultimate owners of much stock. Big companies are widely held by institutional investors--organizations that pool the funds of those insufficiently affluent to invest directly in individual firms. In addition, stocks bought through brokerage accounts are nominally owned by "street names", companies established to act as custodians. The nominal holder usually has little or no information about the actual beneficiaries, and the latter, at best, are incompletely informed about their situation. Pension funds and insurance companies do not automatically provide participants with detailed information on investments; mutual funds report only periodically. It is unclear how closely these reports are examined. Since one reason for investing in such funds is to simplify investing, many may ignore the details.

The owners of big companies are probably on average less wealthy than the owners of those small businesses *eligible for government aid*. The prevailing concept of "small-business" aid is assisting larger, more prosperous owner-managed companies rather than the smallest struggling ventures. A "small" owner-operated government-assisted company often is closely held by a family of greater than average and possibly considerable wealth. Historically, person who can directly buy stocks of publicly held companies was necessarily more affluent than someone who must invest through a financial intermediary. The traditional brokerage firms were unwilling to sell stocks to those with small portfolios; the rise of discount brokers has increased access. Problems remain of adequate diversification with small amounts of direct investment. Neither small businesses nor small investors as usually defined are particularly poor and deserving. Many examples exist. The development of a more efficient U.S. banking system is hindered by legislation protecting small local banks. A major reason why the savings and loan bank crisis arose is that the U.S. Congress was so anxious to preserve these banks. That other local notable, the auto dealer, similarly receives legal protection from pressure by automobile companies.

Similarly, despite its political popularity, the argument that deteriorating market conditions justify intervention is also dubious. Again the deficiencies of intervention in theory and practice apply. Clear criteria for providing adjustment aid cannot readily be stated or implemented. No rules are apparent to define which of the many displacements that occur in an economy are severe enough to justify aid. Presumably, large permanent loss of income must occur. The most critical difficulty is that here too political influence rather than need determines who is aided.

Even if need existed, intervention in markets is still inferior to other forms of aid. The defects noted above about regulation prevail in any industry whether growing, declining, or stagnant. It is often asserted without proof that many workers are so inflexible that preserving the industry is cheaper than providing benefits. This appears questionable. It becomes untenable when the aid persists so long that all the recipients entered after the program was created. Another favorite exercise in this realm is to compute the costs of preserving an unproductive job. The costs often prove to exceed those of a comfortable pension.

Aid is often justified by the allegation that the crisis is temporary and assistance is the optimal response to the difficulties. It is not necessarily true that subsidy is the most efficient way to ensure reestablishment of an industry. If the preservation was obviously efficient, private financing would be obtainable. A more obvious objection is that these claims often have been spectacularly wrong. Aid to preserve jobs endures long after it becomes apparent that the difficulties are not merely temporary. Several new generations are attracted and become trapped. The classic example is agricultural subsidies in the United States, Western Europe, and Japan. The aid has persisted despite a half century of an economic expansion that has obliterated the impacts of the great depression that initially inspired the aid.

An even more long-standing problem is the pernicious effects of the U.S. Jones Act. The act requires among other things that merchant ships used in interstate commerce be built in the U.S., be owned by U.S. companies, operate under U.S. laws, and employ only U.S. crews and thus endure cost disadvantages due to onerous regulations and high labor costs. The harms include barriers to trade among Alaska, Hawaii, and the 48 contiguous states. The burden of the Jones Act may cause a shift to purchase from or sales to another country. Canada, in particular, may gain over Alaska, particularly in lumber trade. Similarly, the use of water shipping within the U.S. will be inefficiently low. The Act combined with a Congressionally-imposed ban on international exports of Alaskan oil produces other important inefficiencies. The persistence of this law in the face of shrinkage in the number of beneficiaries illustrates the problems of removing protection.

In my 1960 Ph.D. thesis, I argued that the Western Europe coal industry was doomed. Western European governments, particularly the German, vigorously resisted this reality and maintained subsidies to the coal industry (see Gordon 1970, 1987c, 1992a). These examples failed to prevent the creation of equally ill-conceived protracted programs in the United States to lessen the decline of jobs in both automobile and steel manufacturing. Western Europe adopted similar policies for steel. In discussions with Germans familiar with the situation, I was told that creation of alternative industry was discouraged to prevent the loss of workers in steel and coal. I encountered arguments for preservation that made American energy lobbyists seem admirers of Adam Smith. The German coal aid program seems to have saved at most 23,000 jobs at the cost of attracting at least 91,000 new workers and 11.5 billion DM in extra costs in 1992. (The doom of German coal became apparent in 1958. The youngest workers in German coal mining are 16 and so those of 1958 would be 50 in 1992, 34 years later. Only 22,700 workers in 1992 were older than 45.) (See Statistik der Kohlenwirschaft 1993, 40, 43 for the basis of employment figures and International Energy Agency 1993, 218 for the estimate of extra costs consisting of subsidies and payments in excess of world prices.) Similarly, Japan is not gracefully adapting to stagnant steel output. As Peltzman's (1976) analysis of regulation suggests, the limits to feasible subsidy cause the efforts to fall short of their goals. Those in long protected industries regularly bemoan their problems. Farmer protests, for example, occur regularly.

Conclusions

While concerns over the defects of existing policies are most vigorously expressed by Hayek and various University of Chicago economists, they are also widely shared in the economics literature. The main difference between Chicago and other economic writers again is that the latter believe that sufficient cajoling will remedy the problem. Economists at Chicago and elsewhere have shown that strong political forces lead to undesirable outcomes and raise severe barriers to reform.

Aaron Director of the University of Chicago is credited with the view that, in practice, twentieth century governments tax the poor and the very rich to aid the middle class. While Director rarely published, Stigler ([1970] 1988) favorably reviewed the argument, the supporting evidence, and theory.

Hayek has responded to the prevalence of protectionist policies by denouncing the *implementation* of the "welfare state" (1960) and "social justice" policies (1976). (The latter case was reiterated in 1989.) Hayek contends that these perversions are so much the essence of the welfare state that we must repudiate the *concepts* of both the welfare state and social justice. An earlier, similar attack was made by Mises (1966, 833-54) but does not develop the misrepresentation charge as clearly as Hayek did (see Butler 1988, 77, 119 for assertions of a clear recognition by Mises of this problem). Hayek implicitly argues that terminology is so critical that reform must include a name change. The concepts have been so contaminated and confused that a satisfactory discussion is possible only using new phrases.

An initial reaction is that the argument elevates form over substance and creates the misimpression that Hayek dismisses worthy arguments for aiding the unfortunate. His exposition seems to harm his case. Viewing Bork's failed effort (1989) to rescue the concept of the original-intent of lawmakers suggests that Hayek may have correctly recognized that the choice of form sometimes is critical to reaching proper conclusions. Clearing away the debris from ancient debates may be the first essential step in a proper rethinking. Moreover, it may not be Hayek's ambiguity, but his care, that angers his critics.

Formal religions, secular ethics, and economics are unable to determine conclusively what is a fairer income distribution. How much equality should increase and how to attain such increases have proved issues impossible to resolve by pure logic. This is not an argument for inaction but provides warning of what is needed to secure satisfactory results--a consensus on goals and the most careful possible appraisals of which policies will best meet these goals. In this realm too, accord will remain difficult.

Even if the problems of seeking inappropriate goals could be eliminated, long experience with appraising fairness suggests that little conclusive evidence can be added to the basic point that subjective moral judgments are involved. Much passion can be generated, but the discords remain. Balance between raising the lowest incomes and allowing people to benefit from their achievements seems preferred over extreme positions. Economists, thus, are not more indifferent to the plight of the poor but more aware than anyone else of the intrinsic problems of devising a solution.

The fairness argument has been sufficiently misused that suspicion of equity bases for intervention in markets is justified. Other tools are better to promote equity among classes and regions. Therefore, regulation of markets to promote fairness is undesirable. Intervention in *markets* is justified only if it leads to a more productive economy. Thus, the part of distributional debates most relevant to this book is the most clear cut.

Chapter 10

Problems of Environmental Impacts and Regulating Business Practices

At least since the widely cited but now hopelessly old-fashioned treatise by Pigou, economists have examined the problem of the unintended side effects or externalities associated with economic activity. Environmental damages were a classic example of side effects. Therefore, economists had a well-developed theory of environmental issues before the burst of concern over the subject started around the 1960s. What was lacking was sufficient interest to inspire elaboration and application, a deficiency that rapidly was overcome during the 1970s.

Concerns over the environment prevailed for at least four centuries. Attacks on coal burning starting with the rise of substantial use in seventeenth century Britain are a standard example of early concerns. The new enthusiasm involved powerful pressures to treat far more problems. A vigorous movement arose throughout the industrialized world to promote policies to prevent the degradation of environmental conditions.

This chapter explores issues associated with such environmental policies. First, review is provided of the basic efficiency conditions for reaction to externalities. Then, Coase's analysis of externalities is examined. Coase provided several distinct insights into environmental problems and failure to understand them all undermines appreciation of the problems of environmental policy. In particular, few of the many commentators on Coase mention his skepticism over intervention. Coase's warning against Pigou's faith in government is treated as a refinement of Pigou's argument for government action.

Then alternative techniques for regulating pollution are evaluated. Classic economic theories of externalities call for charging polluters for the damages created. Actual regulations tend to specify in great detail how much individual polluters may emit and often also restrict the choice of control techniques. Analyses of the implications of difficulties in estimating an efficient tax have shown that the use of such taxes may not always be the ideal approach. However, alternative financial incentives have been proposed as a way to overcome the drawbacks of regulation and taxes. Another approach, tradable permits, has received considerable theoretic and practical support. Regulators would set total emission limits, divide the rights among sources, and allow free trade of these rights.

Next, Spulber's (1989) analysis of what he terms internalities, imperfections in private dealing that allegedly justify government regulation, is examined. Spulber (1989, 68-9) uses the term to bring out the symmetry of the analyses with those of the impact of externalities. Rather than claiming originality, he notes an inability to find prior use of the term, wisely recognizing the ability of diligent scholars to uncover earlier use. Many interesting examples exist of controls on internalities. These include the regulation of occupational and product-use health and safety. Control of financial transactions is another major area. A further example is how the case for public land ownership indiscriminately mixes together true externality problems with a dubious recreational internality case.

The chapter turns to an overview of environmental problems, the difficulties of assessing them, and the practice of environmental policy. As usual, the coverage is limited to interesting cases familiar to me. Stress is on energy in the U.S. The evidence suggests that these are the most pressing issues. Finally, attention is given to concerns some have expressed that many environmentalists are pursuing an elitist exclusionary policy. An effort is made to present as balanced a view of this debate as is possible, given my belief that such defects are widespread.

Prelude on the Optimality Conditions with Externalities

The marginal principle applies to externalities as well as to ordinary goods. Limiting abatement by cost considerations, while often attacked as immoral, is unavoidable. Creating pollution is intrinsic. Useful activities produce wastes, and the laws of physics and chemistry imply these wastes must go somewhere. Zero tolerance (i.e., elimination) is impossible. Full control of noxious effects can only occur by removing many other amenities. Only the most severe problems can be tolerably reduced.

Abatement costs rise sharply as restrictions are tightened. Intolerably high costs would be required to attain most of the purported goals of environmentalists. So many inconsistent goals are proposed that full attainment is impossible. Aspirations must be limited to a finite amount of control. These controls have definite limited costs, and thus tacitly a limit is imposed on the expenditures worth taking. Pricing pollution is simply a recognition that valuation is always made at least implicitly and that explicit valuation is preferable.

Reaction to externalities is optimized in the standard economic fashion of equating marginal costs to marginal benefits. A few complications arise in expressing the rule. The most substantial is that externalities, in principle, may be beneficial or harmful. Benefits could consist of inadvertent aid to bystanders. Bees may pollinate apple orchards. Beneficial externalities are rare and apparently easy to internalize. They are mentioned only for completeness.

At a technical level, two equivalent ways exist to treat both detrimental and beneficial externalities, and the approach chosen, particularly for detrimental externalities, depends on what seems more convenient. The perspective of either the creator of the externality or the recipient of the effects can be taken. The nature of these viewpoints naturally reverses when the externality becomes beneficial rather than detrimental. With detrimental externalities for which no penalties are imposed, their generators increase their profitability by imposing costs on others. The social objective is to induce lesser damage. With beneficial externalities for which no compensation is provided, the generators maximize their profitability by not recognizing the benefits they bestow on others.

A generator-oriented analysis of a detrimental uncontrolled externality calculates the optimum amount of damage by comparing the marginal benefits to the source to the marginal damage costs to others. A victim-oriented approach optimizes abatement by equating the marginal benefits of externality reduction to the marginal cost to the source making the reduction. A generator-oriented optimum-creation view of an unrewarded beneficial externality relates the marginal benefits to others of increased externality creation to the marginal costs incurred. Taking a recipient oriented optimal-increase approach, the benefits to generators of not producing externalities would be related to the losses to potential recipients.

Securing adequate information as stressed by Hayek and Coase and inspiring someone to act vigorously are critical to reaching an optimum. The marginal value at the point of efficient output must be determined. This requires enormous knowledge about the benefit and loss functions of the affected parties and the cost functions of the generators. Therefore, it is not surprising that suggestions that financial incentives be used to stimulate optimal externality levels are heavily qualified. As discussed below, a strong case for financial incentives remains. The arguments are based on prospects for securing better rather than ideal outcomes but leave open whether taxing is preferable to allowing trade in pollution rights. As already suggested the discussions are deficient in stressing Coase's warnings about the pitfalls of any action. Examining this warning then is critical first step.

The Coase Analysis of Social Costs

Coase's 1960 analysis discussed above revolutionized the treatment of side effects by removing the confusion surrounding the economics of the issue. Coase's exposition was more a presentation of basic points than a systematic analysis; Coase (1988, 157-8) credits the formalization to Stigler ([1966] 1987).[1] Before Coase, externalities were considered a separate policy issue. Coase's most widely accepted insight was that this perception was incorrect. Coase's analysis also illuminated most of the critical aspects of externalities. Commentators too often concentrate on narrow, econdary issues.

His main contribution was clarifying the extent to which externalities were a policy problem. He demonstrated by numerous practical examples that control of many externalities such as noisy neighbors was effected by private dealings and nuisance law. Difficulties arose when transaction costs became prohibitively high. This is precisely the type of problems that Samuelson (1954) identified as relating to public goods. Thus, another statement of Coase's views is that it is the publicness of *some* externalities, not the mere existence of externalities, that causes problems. (Coase's discussions make no explicit references to Samuelson's analysis, but the implicit relationship is clear to those familiar with Samuelson's articles and the many commentaries and reiterations in the literature.) Thus, the prior presumptions that externalities were a special problem were no longer sustainable.

One of Coase's conclusions is that when transaction costs are explicitly considered, the full cost of abatement for some externalities would exceed the damages they produce. As discussed in chapters 3 and 6, Coase also argued that the problems that hinder private solutions also impede government solutions. In a later article also appearing in his collected writings (1988), he argues that private ownership of British lighthouses worked efficiently. The nonparticipation of some beneficiaries about which Samuelson was concerned did prevail. However, the system still generated more funds than Parliament was willing to appropriate. (Coase picked this case because lighthouses are often used as an example of a good that cannot be efficiently provided privately. His efforts have not eliminated misuse of the example.) His views are part of the broader criticism of intervention that Coase

---

[1]The argument first appeared in the 1966 edition of Stigler (110-114). Stigler (1987, 117-21) reiterates.

and his associates have conducted. These, in turn, reflect appreciation of Hayek's (1945) analysis of efficient provision of information.

Coase included a remark about the difficulties of policy implementation in his 1960 article, but subsequent writers have tended to ignore the hint. Some of the blame may be due to Coase's cursory discussion of the point. A greater problem is the unpalatability of the advice. Thus, the economics literature tends to dismiss Coase's concerns by ignoring the intrinsic barriers to success. Discussions such as those examined below concentrate upon making environmental policy better.

The widespread discontent with the practice of environmental policy suggests the validity of Coase's warnings about the intrinsic drawbacks of a political approach. Had his caveats been more consciously incorporated into the discussion, environmental economists might have been better prepared to anticipate the problems and more vigorously warn against uncritical enthusiasm for regulatory proposals. This chapter shows many cases in which heeding Coase's warnings would have helped.

In particular, many writers sympathetic to environmental controls present devastating criticisms of the implementation of all policies and of the desirability of some programs. The discussions unwisely neglect Coase's skepticism about intervention. The disparity shown here between confidence in environmental goals and the supporting evidence suggests need for such suspicion.

Instead of dealing with these basic issues, writers have concentrated on Coase's efficiency argument that subsidization of abatement can produce exactly the same results as taxing damages. Coase's casually stated argument has emerged largely unscathed from extensive efforts to refute him. His critics have only succeeded in indicating that the practical relevance of his theory may be limited at least in cases of widespread damages. Even here, Coase's critics should not be so quick to criticize the unrealism of his symmetry argument when they ignore Coase's more critical warning about illusory confidence in a political solution.

Coase's efficiency argument begins with the traditional economic proposition that producing a reaction to detrimental externalities requires that their generator suffer a financial loss as pollution rises. Coase points out that the *marginal* effect of a tax increase or a subsidy decrease of equal magnitude would be identical since both produce losses. Here Coase was developing the previously neglected implications of the basics.

The marginal rules stated above imply that financial pressures must raise the level of abatement to the point at which its marginal cost equals the marginal damage reduction. If the subsidy and tax are equal, the marginal influence of a subsidy withdrawal is the same as that of a tax increase. The marginal effect of a subsidy increase is the same as that of a tax decrease. Thus, if we want to encourage a pollution reduction worth $10 to the victims, a $10 tax saving would induce the change. So would a $10 subsidy increase. That is almost all that is needed to produce identical outcomes.

Where Coase's critics thought they found a fundamental flaw was in neglect of the differential effects of taxes and subsidies on entry. A tax will lessen profits and cause exit. A subsidy will raise profits and encourage entry. Baumol and Oates (1988), for example, show that with these different effects, imposition of optimal *marginal* subsidies that are available to all producers raises pollution by inviting entry.

Baumol and Oates (1988) recognize that the problem lies in the inefficiency of making subsidies available to all. An implicit additional efficiency requirement for all firms is that they provide a total benefit to society at least as great as the total costs of the resources employed. An optimum subsidy (or tax) program must be designed to discourage a socially unprofitable firm from operating. The subsidy for not operating must exceed the maximum that otherwise can be earned in subsides and profits on sales. Baumol and Oates (1988) suggest that such subsidy schedules are hard to design. While this is a valid point, it is a less conclusive response than they seem to believe. As they recognize elsewhere in the book, an efficient marginal tax schedule also can lead to an inefficient number of firms. Too little or too much incentive to exit may be provided.

More critically, the selective criticism of the undue complexity of one aspect of optimal policy is embedded in a discussion that proposes rules that are themselves impossible to apply. Baumol and Oates (1975), particularly in their first edition, tend to miss Coase's warnings about the general problems of attaining efficiency when publicness is involved. They also are fixated by the alleged existence of a Coase argument that taxes on victims are essential to ensure that such victims undertake self-protection measures that are cheaper than reducing emissions. The actual argument is that with the problems of efficient regulation, inadequate incentives to self-protection are likely to arise and a tax on victims may be needed to offset the suboptimal tax.

The Coase analysis follows the widespread practice of neglecting differential distributional effects of taxes compared to subsidies. His discussion says nothing about the widely recognized proposition that profound differences in the tastes of different people could produce profound changes in the composition of output because of the redistribution. Someone attempting a complete appraisal might argue that these effects would be small in most cases. Even if they were not, the problems of redistribution do not become special because externalities are involved. We would be back to grappling with the difficulties reviewed in chapter 9.

Coase did make clear that determining the equitable rule for assignment of liability to enact curative measures was more difficult than often presumed in environmental discussions. As should have been realized, the ambiguities that plague deciding what is fair in other contexts did not disappear if an externality was involved. Understanding of this point was hindered by undue concentration by others on the efficiency side of his argument and by Coase's reliance on examples.

The basic points are that cases exist of people deciding to locate where known externalities occur and that one amenity may harm another. A shade tree might block a view. Where people voluntarily expose themselves to nuisances, they should be liable on moral and practical grounds. Where two virtues conflict, the greater one may be hard to identify. Some have claimed Coase ignores the ethical basis of choice. Coase is recognizing the difficulties of deciding what is fair. His discussion clearly shows that the choices are not simple, clear-cut, and identical in all cases.

The Choice Among Pollution Taxes, Tradable Emissions, and Direct Regulation

The key serious problem of pollution control is in determining the optimum and defining policies that will best attain it. The Coase analysis suggests that some externalities may cause damages that are less than the abatement costs. In this section, the discussion relates to those externalities that can profitably be eliminated.

Economic analysis, as noted, favors use of financial incentives over massive direct controls. The basis of this preference is recognition that the best way to handle regulation of numerous sources is to provide clear, uniform, immutable pressures on every polluter. Financial incentives possess these properties. Such incentives give an unambiguous uniform signal to all polluters that is less subject to distortion than a set of rules.

The distortions that emerged in practice proved to include much more than the Hayek problem of inability accurately to determine the optimum division of abatement responsibilities among sources. Coase-Stigler-Peltzman type problems of distortions by needs to respond to political pressures also arose. Economic advice was ignored. Complex regulations were adopted instead of financial incentives. The outcome is now widely criticized as the command and control approach.

First, interventions were extended to limit the choice of abatement strategies. In some cases such as water pollution and toxic wastes, stress was on approaches that relied on government public-works programs. With air pollution, policies were imposed to discourage switching to less polluting fuels. Control by more cleanly utilizing currently used fuels was stressed. In particular, electric utilities were required to use some form of postcombustion removal technology (usually termed scrubbing) to control sulfur oxide emissions. This was to discourage shifts from high sulfur to low sulfur coal. These policies were consciously imposed to protect existing suppliers and their workers. Second, implementation became bogged down in a complex administrative process and claims by polluters of an inability to comply. Third, a policy that stresses installing specific control facilities may produce inadequate monitoring of results. The operation of the device may be considered sufficient evidence of compliance when, in fact, the promised results are not being attained. (For criticisms of EPA for making this error, see MacAvoy 1987, 127.)

Economic writings on pollution often argue that the best way to limit pollution is to tax its occurrence. The marginal cost of pollution abatement will be equated to the tax. Thus, gross differences in the marginal cost of abatement among polluters would be eliminated. Such disparities plague present regulations. As noted above, with sufficient information, the tax also will produce the optimum level of pollution. With inadequate information, the tax only guarantees attainment of the level of abatement whose marginal benefit equals the tax. That level could be greater or less than the optimum depending on how well the tax was selected.

Attention has turned to another method of providing financial incentives called tradable permits. Regulators would set limits on total pollution. Again, the goal could be excessive or deficient. Shares in the right to pollute would be allocated to individuals. These people could freely trade these rights. Those facing higher control costs would bid the rights away from those with lower costs. This would minimize the cost of attaining the pollution goal. This is an implication of basic market principle that all mutually beneficial trades are undertaken. Every source with high control costs will seek and find a source with lower costs. Equilibrium will occur only when every mutually beneficial transfer occurs. This is when no further disparities in pollution control costs remain.

The best way to reach an optimum is unclear even at a theoretical level. It depends on the nature of the errors made, the adaptability of different systems, the sensitivity of costs and benefits to levels of pollution, the transaction costs of alternatives, and political feasibility. Available analyses are incomplete but still too elaborate for presentation here. The limited appraisals produce the familiar result that the choice depends on circumstances. (Those literate in economic analysis should consult Baumol and Oates 1988, 57-78, 177-89. They analyze only the impacts of imperfect knowledge of either the costs or the benefits of control; these uncertainties alone suffice to create numerous ways in which intervention will more or less than is optimal. The possibility of error and the difficulties of determining what has occurred naturally increase if more uncertainties are considered. The analysis is presented as an extension of that by Weitzman (1974); Weitzman's analysis contrasts taxes to direct controls without the trading option Baumol and Oates introduced to increase feasibility. Other contributions are Carlton and Loury 1980, 1986, and Collinge and Oates 1982.)

However, these uncertainties should not hinder experiments with taxes and tradable permits. Action is needed to lessen the intrusive, inefficient practices of actual policies. Whether this is by taxes or by allowing trade of permits is secondary to the benefits of removing the rigidities of overly specific regulations. Either should improve on the administrative monstrosities used now. The valuations arising from taxes or selling permits will provide cost indicators that may alert policy makers to deficiencies of their decisions. What responses will emerge is another uncertainty.

The Problem of Internalities

As much theoretic work has shown, the Coase explanation of the problems of government involvement in externalities also improves understanding of the numerous government polices that control private transactions allegedly on efficiency grounds. (For a good verbal discussion of the issues and a mathematical review of the theoretical appraisals, see Spulber 1989, 385-459.) This realm is vast and yet another example of policies uncritically accepted by noneconomists and distrusted by economists.

The key concerns are health, safety, and integrity. Examples include the long-extant program of the Food and Drug Administration to regulate the safety and effectiveness of foods and drugs, the Occupational Safety and Health Administration's efforts to control workplace behavior, the Mine Safety and Health Administration's special efforts for coal mining, the Consumer Product Safety Administration's product safety program, the special Department of Transportation program for motor vehicles, the extensive network of controls on the banking, insurance, and securities industries, the programs discussed below of government management of crowded recreation facilities, and the aspects of "environmental" policy that deal with voluntarily assumed risks such as pollution exposure in the home and workplace.

Discussions of the problems of efficient dealing previously have concentrated on the high cost of information. It is further recognized that where markets cannot economically provide information, government intervention might be limited to providing the information. Only when private solutions are more expensive than public ones would it be preferable for government use of the information to effect the efficient result. Discussions such as Spulber's (1989) have extended the understanding.

At least three basic points emerge. The first is the inevitable one that here too considerable evidence exists that the efficiency justification is a rationalization of programs designed to protect a powerful interest group such as a trade union. Union searches for political solutions are particularly thought-provoking. For those who doubt that employers possess monopoly powers, the main justification for trade unions is the ability to negotiate efficient cures for problems arising in the workplace. The Hayek principle suggests that this should be superior to government intervention. The search for intervention is then an admission of either ineptitude or of the classic anti-union assertion that the real motive is to monopolize by all possible means. As employers are increasingly able to resist efforts to monopolize by collective bargaining, unions have turned to securing government aids to monopolization. The second key point, illustrated in Spulber's (1989) examples, is that the Coase analysis carries over intact. High transaction costs again create barriers to private and public solutions for some of these problems. The third point is that because of the purely private nature of these problems, more private alternatives exist, and the danger that a private solution cannot emerge are less.

Many studies have been made of the problems of implementing programs of the types listed. Occupational and product safety rules are a perennial butt of sarcastic observations; financial regulation is seen as protecting powerful local interests from natural pressures to develop the nationwide banking systems prevalent in the rest of the world.

Theorists, particularly Shavell (1980, 1984, 1987), have done much to show the different ways that feasible private solutions can arise in competitive markets. Shavell talks about accidents, but most of the regulations discussed here can be dealt with by his analysis. The critical options are strict liability for damages or an appropriate legal definition of negligence. The latter involves deciding what level of spending on maintaining product quality and work-place safety is sufficient to exempt firms from guilt of negligence. A further requirement when consumers' actions affect performance is that the law make consumers responsible for their negligence.

An efficient legal system would either limit liability to actual damages or define negligence as failure to spend enough on safety to match marginal costs to marginal benefits. Again, transaction costs may preclude achieving efficiency by comprehensive regulation. The critical question is which system does better.

Another problem is the role of insurance in overcoming the limited ability of any one entity to assume full damage liability. Efficient provision of insurance is hindered by the costs of observing behavior of the insured and thus the difficulty in detecting whether the insured exerts the efficient degree of caution. This poses further barriers to private attainment of efficiency, but these barriers also hinder efficient public intervention.

Finally, other private actions may be more efficient than intervention at assuring quality and performance. Possibilities include signals about product quality by pricing, advertising, making the quality more observable, and creating a reputation for reliability.

An Overview of Environmental Goals and Their Implementation

The ample literature on the environment suggests that many objectives are pursued and that possibly a disparity exists between nominal defenses and the best justifications. Threats to human life and to the well being of all individuals are the concerns that make environmentalism so appealing a force. The dangers include direct damages through exposure to dangerous chemicals and indirect damages due to alteration and even destruction of natural environments that contribute to the maintenance of human life. (In reading a draft of this manuscript, Walter Mead argued that harm to animals and plants influences policy more than direct damages to people.) In practice, it is unclear what motivations are dominant. As discussed below, all the nominal rationales may be designed to attract support for the objective of opposing industrialization.

Indisputably, some professional environmentalists propose an agenda to curb everything they define as pollution, alleged overuse of natural resources, overpopulation, and nuclear armaments. Many of these additional ideas are invalid; for example, analysis of mineral markets indicates that fear of overuse is unjustified. (See Barnett and Morse 1963, Adelman 1993a, and Gordon 1966, 1967, 1981a; for a contrary view, see Solow 1992.) Despite this, a frequently used rationale for restricting energy consumption is that even if the pollution threat proves invalid, the prevention of exhaustion still justifies the policy. The proposals often involve conscious preference for pantheism over the Biblical idea that creation was for humanity. More critically, the postures involve a new way to attack capitalism and reinstate acceptance of planning.

Dubious goals are advocated even by the purportedly moderate organizations. They too quickly propose actions on many matters. Too often, as in many of the publicized scares about toxic materials, closer scrutiny shows that dangers were exaggerated and may not have been great enough to justify action. Another often-criticized weak spot of environmental concerns is the desire to protect amenities of the affluent. For example, Frieden (1979) entitled a study of zoning and other growth control policies in California *The Environmental Protection Hustle*. He views the policies as allowing the established to exclude newcomers. Such observers as Neuhaus (1971) and William Tucker (1982) fear that exclusionary tendencies are widespread among environmentalists. The problem is to separate identification of externalities deserving of action from anticapitalist propaganda. (Other critiques include T. L. Anderson and Leal 1991, Bailey 1993, and Ray 1990, 1993. Frankland and Schoonmaker 1992 treat the special case of the Green Party in Germany.)

Two 1990 efforts to evaluate environmental policy suggest several additional problem areas. In one, Landy, Roberts, and Thomas worry among other things about the overemphasis of health effects of environmental policies. They note that "Pollution control is a much less important lever for improving health than the control of smoking, drinking, diet, drug use, highway safety, and crime, which are all beyond EPA's control (292)." They discuss the consequences of integrating pollution control into the overall health policy. They note such an integration "could prove very damaging to environmental programs. Lives saved by environmental protection can cost 10 to 100 times more than saving lives through even the most expensive medical interventions--such as organ transplants (292)." They suggest, "For those whose instincts suggest that a major environmental retreat would be mistaken, a vision of EPA's mandate that encompasses more than health protection is necessary (292)."

Health effects are stressed because of both the political effectiveness of such an approach and the availability of more (albeit far from conclusive) evidence. Other impacts are even harder to appraise. Their discussion indicates that Landy, Roberts, and Thomas favor environmental policies. The writers argue that EPA has the right to consider other issues and advocate a conscious effort to improve awareness of such broader quality of life benefits. The advocates presume without any supporting evidence that this effort will prove that the benefits justify existing programs. Thus, the writers may be guilty of the widely prevalent tendency to believe that a valid and important vision must be behind the vigorous efforts of environmentalists.

The other 1990 study was an anthology edited (and contributed to) by Portney. It reviews the major policies and the data on their benefits and costs. In one of Portney's contributions, he lists four problems of policy: (1) seeking too rapidly to implement complex standards, (2) inadequate compliance because of limited resources for monitoring and enforcing, (3) imposition of unattainably "absolutist" goals, and (4) contamination by other objectives (Portney 1990, 21-3). Except for compliance, these are the concerns most widely expressed by other environmental economists; they are shared, for example, by Landy, Roberts, and Thomas (1990). The compliance point is an unconscious reprise of Coase's criticism of government solutions.

Unfortunately, the clearest conclusion of the surveys of benefits and costs of pollution control is that the information is very uncertain. Portney uses an updating of a 1982 study by Freeman as the foundation for the estimates of the benefits of air pollution control. The benefits on the stationary source side are from $8.6 to $86.7 billion (1984 dollars) with a most likely figure of $36.8 billion. Beneficial health effects--$5.0 to $64.3 billion with a best estimate of $27.2 million--are the main contributors. The mobile source (i.e., automobiles and other motor vehicles) benefits range from $0.2 to $4.9 billion with the most likely figure $0.5 billion (1990, 57).

Portney's (1990) discussion of his tabulations identifies various data revisions and deficiencies that justify a more thorough revision of the numbers. Underestimates arise from new data suggesting higher benefits in such realms as crop damages and aesthetics. Alternatively, Freeman measured all improvements in air quality and some may be due to forces other than federal legislation. His valuation of lives saved may not have adjusted for the tendency for the oldest part of the population to benefit most. The benefits of not dying depend upon how many years of life are added, and the addition is less for older people.

Similarly, costs are subject to uncertainty. One survey quoted set costs at $31.2 billion with $11.6 billion due to mobile source control; another, $23.3 billion with $6.9 due to mobile sources (66-7). Thus, the benefit range for stationary sources overlaps the cost range. The best estimate does exceed the costs. However, the maximum benefit of mobile source controls is less than the lower cost estimate, a standard but badly publicized conclusion about motor vehicle pollution control.

Freeman contributed the water chapter to the Portney survey which is an update of Freeman's earlier work on water. He gets a $5.7-$27.7 billion range and a $14.0 billion best estimate of the benefits of attaining pollution goals and a $33.4 billion cost in 1988 of meeting prevailing rules (1990, 122-7). The chapters on hazardous wastes and toxic substances indicate little is known about the benefits of control. This appears to be a polite way of saying that the risks are poorly proved.

All this suggests that more attention should be paid to the drawbacks of environmentalism. In particular, the apology that the excesses of a few should not obscure the alleged clear dangers identified deserves closer scrutiny. The nature and certainty of the threats are more uncertain than the assertions would indicate.

The environmental movement has secured great credibility as a well informed advocate of environmental values. This probably reflects another aspect of Stigler's (1984) theory of tastes. The environmentalists are excellent at enlivening newspapers, magazines, and television shows.

Experience with economic debates shows that the perceived virtues of a cause are no guarantee that sound arguments are presented. Sincerity, nobility, or ignominy of the goals and the inevitable contamination of the arguments by self-interest do not clearly determine the quality of the argument. Defenders of the noblest causes can overstate. Blatantly self-serving industry advocates with a long record of seeking unwise protection can sometimes be correct. It is ironic that in an era in which people subject to the discipline of elections are increasingly scrutinized, self-appointed private guardians of virtue are so admired.

Every interest group believes that advancing its goals is in the general interest of the public. Self-criticism is not to be expected, and wise outside observers should recognize this about all advocacy groups. The parochialism of environmentalists is admitted by them and by itself need not be a problem. The critical issue is whether the proposals are so uncritically evaluated that serious inefficiencies are introduced. That inefficient means are adopted is well demonstrated. The more difficult question is whether the goals are too ambitious.

The difficulties of appraising environmental problems are formidable. Similarly, trusting environmental cures to governments suffers from the limitations of government as an agency for attaining socially efficient results. The reality of this problem is confirmed by widespread complaints. Academic economists specializing in environmental problems, the environmental groups, and the regulated industries criticize the deficiencies of policy implementation.

Since many environmentalists share the general inability to appreciate basic economic principles, they are culpable of economic errors. The environmentalists are regularly guilty of seeing publicness where it may not exist. Even worse is the effort to silence all dissent. Analyses casting doubt on the arguments are routinely ridiculed. For example, many environmentalists suggest bans on benefit-cost analysis because of an alleged systematic tendency to underestimate the benefits of environmental controls. Some have gone on to suggest that all criticism be ignored. This is hardly only the view of a few extremists; Vice President Gore's (1992) preelection book on environmental issues adopts such a view. It also simultaneously reiterates criticisms of benefit-cost analysis and advocates incorporating environmental damages into national output measures. Such inclusion is impossible without good cost-benefit data. (For more on the problems with Gore's polemic, see Lott 1992.)

The difficulties of appraisal are complicated by the vigorous way in which environmental goals are advocated. The environmental movement has identified a wide range of problems and aggressively seeks action against most of these problems. The case is stated with a confidence that is unjustified by the available data. Environmental opposition seems to be made with equal vigor to options with widely different consequences. For example, a highly successful campaign has been mounted to limit offshore oil and gas drilling in the U.S. The main rationale is to prevent oil spills. Such attacks ignore that oil spills generally have smaller, more transitory effects than the damages produced by alternative supplies. The closest substitute for offshore oil and gas is imported oil, and accidents in transportation of this supply are more frequent and generally more harmful than those with offshore oil and gas. Other substitutes such as coal have even worse effects.

Similarly, the environmentalists have largely been reluctant to admit that their antinuclear power campaign was overblown and might have been unwise if their latest concern over global warming is valid. Nuclear power is a way to shift from fossil fuel. Some admit this. Others continue to suggest conservation as the solution. Conservation, in fact, is proposed as an alternative to all energy supply developments. The advocates probably exaggerate how much this approach can accomplish and certainly ignore that conservation merely lessens the need to develop energy supplies. Energy use cannot be eliminated, and depletion of existing supplies requires development of new ones. It is implausible that every supply option is more expensive than the conservation measures needed to replace all energy production initiatives.

More broadly, the tendency cynically to employ every device available to retard action is a threat to the preservation of democratic government. A long history exists of using both environmental and other laws to object to developing resources for private use. A device widely used in the 1970s was to complain of the inadequacy of the statements federal law required to evaluate the environmental impacts of federal actions needed to allow private development in public land. Claims of harm to endangered species often are made to invoke the provisions of the act intended to protect such species. Small differences in characteristics allegedly often can be found so that every region has an endangered species. Critics assert that many purported differences are biologically insignificant and that candid environmentalists admit they create dubious distinctions as another obstructive ploy. Sometimes the effort creates enough animosity to undermine the effort. Whenever the nonenvironmental side of regulation is complex, it is easy to find failures fully to comply. Such complaints were successfully used against nuclear power plants and mineral leasing (see chapter 11 for a review of examples in the latter area).

The widely used argument that we all live on this planet receives far more credibility than it deserves. This tautology is not helpful. Implicitly, it asks us to accept precisely what is not true, that the claims of danger are undeniably proved. Perhaps much of the overstatement is only political posturing. The net effect still may be undesirable.

Environmentalism is descended from an aristocratic conservation movement that called for wise management of our resources. This implied limiting access by imposing barriers to immigration and economic progress. Further concerns are that environmentalism is unduly influenced by 1960s anti-establishment, anti-industrialist radicalism. Environmental criticisms of nuclear power often get entangled with the nuclear disarmament movement.

Unlike classic radicals, environmentalists propose a restraint that favors amenities for the affluent. The attraction to such rebels of ideas originating in the most entrenched part of the establishment might be justified by changing circumstances. Environmental problems may have changed to an extent that it is the weak who are most damaged. Another view is that the attacks on the establishment are badly muddled. A desire has arisen to thwart businesses indiscriminately. The unsuccessful 1993 push to kill the North American Free Trade Agreement for removing tariff barriers that exist among the U.S., Canada, and Mexico consisted more of blatant protectionist arguments than of careful environmental analysis (see T. L. Anderson, 1993, Globerman and M. Walker 1993, and Hufbauer and Schott 1992, 1993).

The situation is aggravated by sanctimony, and, environmentalists too often engage in excessive personal attacks on opponents. In other debates, the existence of honest differences of opinion is recognized. Environmentalists like to prove their opponents are knaves as well as fools. In short, the apparent nobility is tarnished by precisely the flaws that have undone prior zealots.

The problem is aggravated by the limitations of the political base of the environmental movement. Its successes often could only be earned by undertaking what have been called unholy alliances. Some parochial interest group such as industries or sectors of industries that could benefit or affluent landowners affected by a development is enlisted to ensure passage of legislation. The price of this support is a less efficient form of intervention. Actions with other strong enemies get the greatest attention. Domestic oil and gas are harmed more than oil imports because, despite the frequent rote expressions of concern, no one has passionate fears of imports.

Environmentalism is embraced by many to whom the antiprogress aspects would be repellent. It is not clear that those leading the political battles favor efficient economic development. Too much is based on questionable data or even instinct. That environmentalism is based more on excessive protectionism or envy than on sound science must be considered. In particular, people should be more willing to recognize that environmental zealotry may be as ill-advised as past crusades. History is full of examples of sincere enthusiasts who were disastrously wrong. Why is this experience cast aside for environmentalists?

An Overview of Environmental Problems

Since every activity by a living thing affects the environment, a vast number of impacts could be considered. The basic principle is that activities such as extracting, processing, and using energy and metals and disturb land and produce residuals. These residuals must be placed somewhere and then may migrate elsewhere. During these steps, the material may undergo transformation.

Energy and mineral extraction, processing, transportation, and use disturb land (and the oceans) and create wastes that may be left on the ground or go into the water or air. Environmental impact analysis then must observe these effects and identify those that produce harm. This means developing a sense of what residuals are created, where and in what form they settle, and what effects this settling may have. Much is unknown about all these questions. Action is largely based on feeling that the case is sufficiently well proven to justify policy responses.

The final concern is the problem of assessing the social payoff of environmental policies. The costs to society of environmental damages are difficult to measure. Damages are more difficult to identify than control costs and probably also more difficult to measure. The environmental movement has succeeded in convincing policy makers that "faulty" measurement techniques should not prevent the implementation of environmental policies. However, action was so sweeping that the economic literature suggests that many programs were clearly questionable (see below).

The principal land use problem is internalizing whatever public good amenities are associated with the use of the land. At least three have been discussed--damages to heath and property of people outside the land, visual impacts, and the loss of biological resources stressed by Krutilla (1967).

Review of wastes is a more involved problem since so many different wastes, migration paths, and potential effects are involved. The discharge may be in one medium and the damage in another. Air pollution policies heavily emphasize reducing the effects of the deposition on land or water of pollutants discharged into the atmosphere. The main exceptions are efforts to curb the most obvious visual effects of air pollution such as the celebrated cleanups of the noxious atmospheres of London and Pittsburgh.

Attention is given to the possibility that some pollutants will remain in the atmosphere and harm it. Earlier discussions noted that discharge of carbon dioxide, a product of fossil fuel combustion, might lead to global warming while the fine particles (particulates) released from fossil fuel burning might form a shield that would cool the earth. By the late 1980s, global warming had become by far the greater concern about harm to the atmosphere; analyses proliferate (e.g. on the science, Lindzen 1992 and Michaels, 1992; on the economics, Dornbusch and Poterba 1991, Nordhaus 1991, and Cline 1992.) However, a special form of the particle damage argument has emerged as the nuclear winter concept. The start of U.S. attacks on Iraq in 1991 led to modifying the argument to cover effects that never appeared of burning oil fields. The primary fears about discharge of wastes into waterways or leaving them on land, however, relate to the respective effects on water and land. Concerns with transmission from water to land or land to water tend to be secondary.

Controls can involve combinations of using a less polluting technology, adding devices to alter where the wastes are deposited, or reducing pollution causing activities. Thus, the pollution problems associated with the many boilers used around the world could be reduced by shifting among the naturally available fuels. Pollutant removal techniques might be adopted by fuel suppliers. Technologies exist to alter where the wastes are deposited. Finally, firms can simply decrease output of commodities whose production produces extensive pollution.

The cleanness of fuels can be ranked unambiguously only if we look at one or two pollutants at a time. If the concerns are sulfur oxides, particulates, or a combination of them, a clear hierarchy emerges. Nuclear power is free from these problems. Oil and gas are low in particulates but have highly variable sulfur contents. With gas, sulfur damage to pipelines encouraged development of sulfur removal techniques so that marketed gas is sulfur free.

The situation with oil is more complex. Sulfur removal is much cheaper for the lighter more fluid products such as gasoline and kerosene. A tarry residuum is mixed with a bit of lighter oil and marketed as heavy fuel oil. It suffers from the tendency of sulfur to settle in the residuum during refining and from the high cost of sulfur removal from residuum.

Coal has a substantial but variable particle content. At best, the content is much greater than for oil or gas. Sulfur contents are much more widely variable, and the lowest sulfur coals may have considerably less sulfur than many crude oils.

Available coal washing and sorting technologies can only partially reduce particle and sulfur content. An alternative is to trap the particles and sulfur before discharge into the air and deposit the trapped wastes on nearby lands. The latter approach is widely used. Particle-control techniques are long extant, at least for the larger particles responsible for darkened skies, and have low control costs. Control of the smaller particulates able to lodge in lungs and cause health damages is more difficult. Sulfur oxide control proved more expensive and harder to perfect than was expected when sulfur oxide control rules were imposed. Therefore, U.S. law was changed in 1977 to impose barriers to shifting to low sulfur coals instead of using clean up devices with the coals previously burned. The wastes from these cleanup facilities can produce solid waste disposal problems.

The situation is complicated when all the pollutants involved are considered. A switch to nuclear power eliminates the fossil fuel specific dangers but produces risks of radiation discharge. Here, it should be noted that antinuclear critics differ widely in which of the several forms of "discharge" is most dangerous. The claimed threats include contributing to a governmental bomb program, allowing private terrorists to secure radioactive material, the effects of the normal operation of nuclear plants, the effects of accidents, and leakages of stored wastes. As the ability to deal with the other problems became more evident, concentration focused on waste. The critical need is now alleged to be a permanent solution to waste disposal. Nuclear supporters contend that this is largely politics; satisfactory solutions are known, but political opposition prevents their implementation.

Within fossil fuels, the reduction in sulfur and particulate emission associated with a switch to oil or gas is associated with increases in nitrogen oxides and unburned hydrocarbons.

Cataloging what is upset and what consequences might arise is a formidable task. The externalities are often in realms in which measurement is nearly impossible. For example, the readily measured impacts of land disturbance and most forms of waste disposal are much smaller than the costs of abatement. The costs associated with a large oil spill, the harm to the productivity of lands adjacent to surface mines, and the property damages from air and pollution turn out to be far smaller than the estimated abatement costs.

In every case, less tangible environmental damages might be involved. The Appalachian Regional Commission's (1969) pioneering study of acid mine drainage and the Brock and Brooks (1968) case study of the damages of a surface mine suggested that the unmeasured demand for unspoiled rivers and landscapes must be substantial to make abatement efficient. (Both studies seemed skeptical that such additional aesthetic and recreational benefits were sufficient to justify controls. Policy makers accepted this view about acid mine drainage but imposed stringent surface mine reclamation laws.)

In contrast, the case for air pollution control rests on the existence of extensive measurable damages. The principal concerns are the health effects Landy, Roberts, and Thomas (1990) fear are overemphasized. The difficulties of determining such effects are formidable. Too many discussions have relied on the pioneering estimates by Lave and Seskin (1977) without recognition of the problems with the data. Critics have suggested that Lave and Seskin's estimates are biased upwards by such defects as inadequate control for other influences. The fullest critiques that I have seen emanate from industry-sponsored research. The only discussion of which I am aware from a clearly disinterested party is a brief statement by Ramsay (1979). Conversations with other disinterested environmental economists, however, confirmed Ramsay's views.

Wilson, et. al. (1980) point out the simultaneous occurrence of several pollutants precluded determining the exact culprit. In particular, the close association between sulfur dioxides and particulates hinders isolating the role of each. Wilson et. al. suggest that particulates may be more culpable than believed and that public policy may have unwisely overemphasized sulfur dioxides and inadequately treated particulates. Since much U.S. low sulfur coal has high particulate content, a shift to such fuel to lower sulfur levels can increase particulate emissions and be harmful.

Similarly, the discussion of "acid rain" was misleading. The evidence suggests that the much cited damages to lakes and forests produced by acid raid are far less costly than controls. At least one discussion from the Office of Technology Assessment of the U.S. Congress (OTA, 1984a) has argued that additional health benefits suffice to justify control. OTA bases its findings on the Lave-Seskin (1977) estimates upon which prior legislation was based. The OTA assertion would be correct only if prior regulation had failed to meet its purported goal of attaining an efficient degree of health improving controls.

A particularly questionable aspect of the 1990 Clear Air Amendments was to add a large number of "toxic" chemicals to the substances whose emissions must be controlled. These chemicals tend to create damages far smaller than the abatement costs. Another problem is that the law of conservation of matter ensures that problems are transferred rather than solved. Preventing the discharge of air pollutants means the wastes go elsewhere. Then we have concerns about more toxic wastes in landfills. Questions exist about whether the dangers of what is presently in such landfills justify the elaborate program enacted to clean up these landfills.

We are again back to Coase's concerns about public solutions. The evidence is insufficient to negate (or confirm) the arguments for intervention. It is clear that the problems of measurement are inadequately recognized.

Recreation, Land Preservation and Federal Management Revisited: The Issues and the Appraisal

Much economic writing on public land ownership combines externality and internality arguments. This section tries to sort out the issues. The case for preventing commercial uses of land involves both a preference for recreational use and belief that serious externalities are involved in nonrecreational use. The case for recreation is made with varying degrees of sophistication. At the popular level, much stress is placed on dubious arguments of the ethical value of making recreation available more cheaply.

As noted above, some economists still argue that public provision is justified because the uncrowded resource argument applies to recreation. The uncrowded resource argument is that when the capacity to produce exceeds the amount that would be consumed if no charges were levied, it is inefficient to charge. A competitive market would produce a zero price, but land owners possessing a monopoly on the resource would charge a nonzero price. (The argument traces back to an 1844 article by a French engineer, Jules Dupuit.) Transaction costs considerations add the modification that if the demand justifies a price that is less than the cost of levying charges, it is preferable not to charge.

The uncrowded facility is an extreme case of a decreasing-cost industry. The literature on optimum public-utility prices applies. Writings on uncrowded resources stress the fixed charge approach to financing. Construction and upkeep would be financed by taxes or individual subscriptions that would not vary with the amount of use. The choice between the tax or subscription route is another where Coase's analysis applies.

These arguments are excessively applied. Crowded parks are at least one example in which a nonzero price is desirable; so are the roads and bridges with which Dupuit was concerned. The complaint of the environmental movement is that crowding does prevail. U.S. national parks and other recreational areas are being trampled because of fees too low to limit access to efficient levels and failure to spend adequately on maintenance (see Baden and Leal 1990). Allocation of water resources similarly is hindered by failure to allow free sale of rights and by often subsidizing access. Journalists then are scandalized by efforts to evade the limits placed on water receipts. Low tolls lead to congested waterways.

In short, many policies are clear failures to take advantage of available possibilities to use markets or allocation by price. The case for markets in chapter 2 implies access fees are the best way to limit use, and the revenues from such fees could make private provision of parks profitable. A private firm would also be more motivated to use the revenues to maintain the facility. Much of the arsenal of market failure weapons is invoked to bolster the case for wilderness preservation. Conversely, all the tools of government failure arguments are employed in reply. The two most critical are alleged imperfections in the ability to predict demands and imperfect capital markets for financing recreation.

Krutilla's (1967) analysis of the case for land preservation mixes together diverse arguments of variable merit.[2] Krutilla created confusion by simultaneously adding two externalities to a dubious recreation preservation argument involving concern about the ability of consumers to forecast demands. This last is essentially another shaky imperfect capital market argument. He also noted the pleasure that consumers have from knowing that amenities are preserved and the actual environmental damages such as destruction of valuable biological resources introduced by land use. The last is precisely the type of problem long agreed to be policy relevant, but existence values are a questionable basis for policy. Only the possible publicness of the biota seems to justify public retention.

(Again practice suggests that, even so, implementation is difficult. In 1991, it was found that some cancers might be cured by a drug presently producible by cutting down many trees. Concerns were immediately raised about whether the losses, whatever they might prove to be, were small enough to allow actually employing the valuable resource.)

Valuing pleasures is a morass that should be avoided. Consideration of the value of pleasures about the existence of a good poses unmanageable policy problems. The existence of pleasures or pains at the status of others potentially arises with the consumption of every public and private good. Policy making to incorporate all these effects would be intolerably intrusive. Stressing the likings of the affluent for rarefied recreational activities and high culture is dubious welfare economics.

Hanke's (1982) case for privatizing land rests on greater faith in private ventures. This is Coase's lighthouse principle appropriately extended. Objections to these proposals suffer from inadequate attention to Coase's warnings that evaluations should be based on what is possible from actual institutions. Mismanagement, as noted, is chronic with recreational facilities on public lands. The limited experience of management of land by private environmental groups, in contrast, appears to have produced efficient outcomes. Private management of recreation areas even where amenities are critical (e.g., ski resorts) similarly seems more efficient than

---

[2]The commentary on Krutilla is extensive, stresses the preservation of options issue, and includes Arrow and Fisher (1974), R. C. Bishop (1982), Bohm (1975), Cicchetti and Freeman (1971), Conrad (1980), Cory and Saliba (1987), Freeman (1984), D. A. Graham (1981, 1984), Mendelsohn and Strang (1984), Schmalensee (1972, 1975), and K. Smith (1982). Krutilla's drew upon Weisbroad (1964), a generally clearer analysis.

government actions. As an implicitly Coasian solution, Hanke, therefore, suggested the environmentalists be given the parks to manage.

Hanke's proposal for transfer of all such resources to environmental organizations has been opposed by such groups. This could reflect a correct appraisal of the limits of their abilities. As the scale of private operations increases, the difficulties of financing and operating these preserves could rise to a point at which the incremental private operations would be worse run than if they had remained public. However, this would imply applicability of market failure arguments such as imperfect capital markets that chapter 3 viewed skeptically.

An alternative view is that the conservationists recognize that they have persuaded government to preserve an inefficiently high level of parks and wilderness. The real objection is to the state of private tastes (on which, recall the discussion above of Stigler 1984 on taste). Amenities may not be preserved because demand is too weak. Privatization would remove the subsidies and force land with low social value in recreation into more efficient uses. Yet another explanation is that conservationists misunderstand or distrust Hanke's reasoning. The reluctance that the environmentalists displayed to accept Hanke's offer is another reason to suspect the soundness of arguments for preservation. The private sector has profitably provided a wide variety of recreation. If parks are so desirable, why do these environmentalists fear competition from Walt Disney?

The defense of public ownership by environmentalists, as noted, also seems to involve an equity argument that easy access to public land is an essential civil right. This inherent right of access to public lands makes use of prices unfair. This argument suffers from the usual flaws of singling out any particular good as too important to be left to the market. Moreover, favoring recreation is subsidizing amenities and raising prices of essentials such as the food that keeps us alive. Such policies are unfair by any reasonable definition. We raise the cost of the basic commodities produced on public lands to protect them for recreation by people who typically have high incomes. The arguments previously made against using regulation of individual markets to redistribute income strongly apply. It is questionable that substantial benefits accrue to the poor who get and employ greater access. Director's law of income distribution applies.

The critical practical questions concern the applicability of preservationist arguments, particularly when the policy under consideration is the one prevailing in the U.S. of severely limiting transfer of public land to private ownership and preserving almost all allegedly unique species. Chapter 11 indicates that much federal land is used for predominantly private uses such as grazing and forestry. Little or no publicness is involved. What little publicness that prevails would probably be better preserved by dealing with private owners than by continued public possession. Possibly, but not necessarily, government policy might be needed to ensure public-good provision. However, again private deals may be preferable.

Adam Smith's warnings apply to this whole debate; every interest group that fails to succeed as much as it desires in the marketplace judges that the market is wrong. Here too intervention is usually ill-advised because it seeks to lessen the burden of scarcity borne by the interest group. Environmentalists are an interest group. However noble the cause may seem, its advocates are not immune from often presenting, consciously or unconsciously, economically unsound positions. Only the extent of the excess is unclear.

Conclusions

In sum, a well established economic theory shows what is required to regulate externalities and how difficult is the implementation of these requirements. Nevertheless, elaborate policies have been imposed. The experience suggests that the warnings against hasty action were appropriate. This widely admired policy realm is problem plagued. More serious attention to these problems is yet another need. This chapter has stressed that economic analysis clearly indicates that, at a minimum, the form of environmental regulation employed is unsatisfactory. Experience suggests that many goals are questionable. More critically, sincerity and fervor are never guarantees of validity. The environmentalists, must meet the standards of proof normally applied to other policy advocates.

Chapter 11

Land Policy as a Case Study in Excess Intervention

Chapter 6 stressed the importance of well-defined, securely protected property rights to ensuring efficient markets. Efficient private resource use depends upon the unambiguous granting to one entity of the right to use land and other resources. The experience viewed here suggests that attaining and maintaining private ownership too often is unjustifiably restricted. The efficiency of markets, in turn, affects the optimality of land law.

As with much intervention, valid rationales exist for some public land ownership. As the discussion of fairness in chapter 9 suggested, concerns also exist over windfall profits earned from possession of an inherently superior resource. Publicness, however, can preclude efficient private ownership and justify government ownership. Since a principal conclusion of this study is that valid justifications for regulation often are misapplied, this chapter concentrates on examples of excessive statism in land policy.

Disputes perennially arise over land use. Throughout the world inefficient interventionist land policy prevails. These programs have been widely examined. Policies affect both land and facilities, particularly rental housing. Rent and other price controls and farm subsidies, as noted, are invincible policies to politicians but are widely condemned by economists. Comparable inefficiencies in public land policy, in contrast, are failings known only to land law specialists. Even in the economics literature, belief that valid market-failure arguments exist for government intervention in land is widespread. The arguments have become virtually irresistible and almost totally eliminated effective opposition to public ownership. Maintaining extensive public land is a powerful secular religion that misinterprets ample evidence of government failure.

The posture prevails even though advocates of public ownership demonstrate the previously noted tendency to be the most vocal critics of the deficiencies of actual practices. Again belief that better management can overcome the problem prevails even among economists. Only those familiar with land law adequately recognize the limitations of public ownership and believe faith in public management is misplaced. It is widely agreed that public ownership is excessive; the discord is on the degree of excess. This experience thus provides an unfamiliar illustration of the arguments of this book.

Perpetuating public land ownership involves extensive nontotalitarian planning of the forms Hayek (1976, 1978) correctly predicted would produce failures of implementation. Administration is assigned to entrenched bureaus in the U.S. Departments of Interior and Agriculture. As Coase (1988) warned, these agencies do not secure sufficient funds to attain their legislative responsibilities. Those involved also have fought so many charges of carelessness and corruption that fear of controversy overly affects behavior. The administrators worry excessively about market failures. To do otherwise invites inquisitions.

The interaction between the law and economic principles is particularly relevant to land law. Clear economic advice can be given and should be heeded. Land law has been a blatant example of situations in which bad legislation hinders desirable activity. The history of land law confirms the arguments of economists stressing the importance of efficient systems of property rights. Unsatisfactory systems of assigning property ownership have been adopted. In such circumstances, the law, not its enforcement, should be changed to encourage private ownership. Little attention, if any, is given solving the problem by eliminating the misassignment of property ownership. Instead, the regulators resort to another undesirable practice often noted by critics of statism of adding worse restrictions. For example, rules that set special conditions under which land could be acquired or leased were often imposed. The Homestead Act only allowed small-scale farmers to acquire ownership. The Mining Act made land available to discoverers of mineral properties. When the law prevented those with more profitable uses from acquiring the land, fraudulent claims were made that the land was being used for an allowed purpose. The preferable approach is to permit free access to anyone wishing to use the land for the purpose the claimant believes is most profitable. Actual "reform" was limited to preventing diversion of land into uses not favored by Congress.

U.S. public land policies, thus, moved to reject the principles favored for the rest of the economy and once stressed in land law. Until the late nineteenth century, public land practices were oriented toward facilitating private ownership. In the subsequent century, unwise pressures arose to reverse these policies. This culminated in the 1970s with legislation that explicitly favored federal land retention. In the 1990s, environmental groups are calling for similarly altering the Mining Act. The experience is a good example of the perils of abandoning private property.

The issue of appropriate assignment of property rights for energy and mineral extraction has been extremely controversial. Many well-documented cases exist. A widespread tendency occurs to separate mineral property rights from those to other uses of the land. Private owners can and do sever and separately sell mineral and surface rights. Often government ownership of these separated mineral rights prevails. Some governments reserve all mineral rights for the state. The U.S. government adopted a practice of retaining mineral rights to some lands it sold to private owners. Also, governments often tax energy and minerals production.

Any country with extensive mineral resources faces problems of setting rules for exploitation. Important experience also has arisen in Great Britain, Australia, Canada, and South Africa. The United States has a history of varied involvement in regulation of access to land. Its land ownership pattern is one of the most complex. The modes range from complete private ownership of the land and subsurface to complete government ownership and operation. In the U.S., three or four levels of government prevail--national, state, municipalities, and in most cases, subregions usually called counties. Each level owns land.

The discussion here emphasizes U.S. government policy toward development of federal government owned coal resources. Note is also taken of the policy difficulties produced by the migratory qualities of oil and gas. The coal case has a compact, well-documented history. Most of the critical principles are in a short 1976 law. These concepts were introduced more gradually into policies for other minerals. The debates over coal were most pronounced in the 1971-1984 period. Moreover, special problems arise in managing coal leases, at least in the view of U.S. Department of the Interior officials.

An extensive literature reviewed below has arisen about U.S. public land. The writing indicates that the problems observed in coal arise in every other area of public land management. The oil experience in the U.S. and abroad has received extensive attention. The issue emphasized internationally is dealings between the governments of less developed countries (LDC) and companies from industrialized countries able and desirous of developing mineral resources particularly oil in the Middle East. (On international oil, see Hartshorn 1967, Penrose 1968, Sampson 1975, Shwadran 1973, Yergin 1991, and Adelman 1972, 1993a. McDonald 1979 and the contributions of Walter Mead et. al. 1985 cover U.S. issues.)

In viewing oil policy in OPEC countries, it suffices here to note that a long struggle of the host countries for higher revenues culminated in nationalization of the oil industry. The history of oil development in many countries, particularly the less developed countries, with potential for substantial exportable production has three phases. (1) Initially foreign companies were invited to develop the resources. (2) As profitability proved high, governments increased the taxes levied on producers. (3) In the wake of the upheavals in country-company relations of the 1970s, the countries assumed ownership and often operation of the oil industry. A growing concern is the harm to supply development caused by the deficiencies of state management.

Discussion begins with an overview of land policy issues including the problem of separation of property right to minerals from those over the surface. Key features of the history of U.S. land law are reviewed. U.S. mineral land law policy for oil and gas rights is surveyed. An extensive analysis is provided of the disparity between the economic theory of land taxation and its practice. The program for coal then is examined.

Principles of Mineral Law

As the prior section should have suggested, the basic issues in land law relate to defining rights including the critical ones of transferability and deciding who possesses them. The development of both the principles and practices of land ownership evolved over many centuries with many regional peculiarities. Emphasis in this section is on principles, not history.

All rights are inherently limited by conflicts with other rights, moral principles, and the requirements of maintaining the rule of law. Implementation problems arise from the difficulties of balancing. A particular difficulty with land law is that belief in the desirability of national management is better entrenched than for other aspects of economic life. The defects of this faith in central control of land are a major focus in this chapter.

A wide range of arrangements can and does prevail. One extreme is government ownership *and* utilization of land as in Soviet state-owned farms. The other is a system in which individuals can own the land, freely transfer it, and employ it for whatever legal activity the possessors feel most appropriate. Governments can allow private use of public land under many different arrangements and impose many restrictions on exercise of private property rights. A primary choice is among granting (1) ownership, (2) the right to operate, or (3) the right to enjoy the output of operation. Some government owned land is restricted for government use; much is devoted to government-run operations, particularly for recreation. Other land is made available by private use.

The other principal distinction is between allocation by price or by nonprice mechanisms. Competitive leasing systems similar to those discussed below may be devised; rights can be granted on a first-come-first-served basis or by lottery. Grants can be made by administrative judgments about who is most worthy. An important special consideration is subdividing rights such as separating mineral rights. Separate ownership of the land's subsurface and the surface severs an indivisible property and guarantees conflicts. The subsurface cannot be exploited without affecting the rights of the surface property owner. Defining and, more critically, implementing an acceptable system of surface-owner compensation is a major problem with government retention of mining rights. In particular, regulations strong enough to protect surface-owners from misuse of sovereign power may constitute de facto privatization of the mineral rights to surface owners.

Economists such as Shavell (1987) have shown that, in private disputes, suits to secure compensation for damages can produce efficient outcomes. (Recall chapter 10.) Governments can devise techniques, such as exempting themselves from liability, that preclude solutions by efficient damage suits. An alternative is to give surface landowners strong protection from damages such as by granting a veto power over access to minerals. For example, the U.S. Surface Mining Control and Reclamation Act of 1977 (SMCRA) contained a provision that increased the rights of many surface owners. Those who resided on the land or used it for farming or ranching had to give written permission before the coal could be leased. This veto power gave the surface property owner priority over the federal government in securing a payment for the right to lease and thus conflicted with the supposed goal of ensuring government primacy.

Another key distinction concerns the systems' true impact on sharing of the economic rents or "excess" income (defined more precisely below). Government ownership is neither necessary nor sufficient to ensure transfer of rents from landowners or users. Rent transfer is possible without government ownership. Taxation is an alternative way to shift rents. Rent taxation is widely discussed and employed in public finance. Too many commentators on land law at least implicitly neglect the tax option. A failure to charge specifically for access is treated as abdication of rent transfer powers. The probability that taxes will be imposed to offset the initial lenience is ignored. Conversely, governments often deliberately choose not to tax heavily and even to subsidize. Federal timber programs are widely criticized for subsidizing leaseholders.

Another option is to devise a method to transfer rents to consumers of minerals. The United States has used price controls on oil and gas to effect such transfers (see Bradley 1989, Deacon and Mead 1985, and Mancke 1974, 1976). These policies were imposed separately from and on top of traditional-rent collection processes. Others have required leaseholders to promise use of rents to subsidize output. British leases for offshore oil, for example, encouraged use of rents for further exploration. Important examples outside the land-law realm include performance requirements for regulated public utilities, radio and television stations, and cable television systems. Thus, land law is one element in the debate on sharing economic rents. A maze of competing programs exists and is difficult to reform.

An Overview of Public Land Policy

The United States effected a nearly total reversal in public land policy. Historical accident made the U.S. government a major landowner. The states ceded to the new federal government the unoccupied portion of the lands the British crown had granted to individual colonies. Annexations starting with Jefferson's Louisiana Purchase added more land.

Initially, public policy closely followed the guidelines of writers, such as the classic essays of John Locke, particularly chapter 5 of *The Second Treatise of Government*. Given the stress on limited government and the virtues of private property, facilitating private land acquisition, improvement, and utilization was U.S. policy. Citizens could and did acquire large parts of the country and employ their land to contribute to U.S. economic growth. Land was made available for the taking, and the federal government thus disposed of almost all of the original Northwest Territory and the Louisiana Purchase.

Starting in the late nineteenth century, particularly in Theodore Roosevelt's administration, concerns arose about the wisdom of the policy. A policy of federal retention emerged. Much of the present East Central States had been transferred to private ownership and development proceeded to the Mountain and Pacific States. The laws were designed for East Central Plains farming were incapable of handling the distinct geographic features of the Mountain and Pacific States. In particular, one could not legally secure the large tracts needed for efficient land utilization in such activities as grazing. Much land was economically unattractive.

These land developments were only one of the radical changes in the U.S. economy. Other striking developments included the rise of new industries such as in steel and oil and of large, national corporations in new and old industries. A new wave of immigration prevailed. Much criticism arose from many sources. As often is true of reaction to radical change, much of this concern reflected fears of new competition. Theodore Roosevelt's progressive movement represented the distillation of this discontent into action. The policies included attacks on big business in the East and a conservation movement to thwart big private landholdings in the West.[1] The first element faltered. Slowly, with little public scrutiny, concerns about the wisdom of public land wholesale disposals expanded and became more influential. The move to retaining federal ownership reached its acme in the Carter administration. Faith abounded that the federal government had a trust to maintain. It should retain ownership, ensure socially efficient use, and prevent excess profits. It became increasingly difficult to convert public land to private ownership. Ultimately, maintenance of federal ownership became dominant.

Samuelson's (1954, 1958, 1969) public-good argument is excessively applied to public lands. The literature on public lands often points out that much of the land is devoted to grazing and timber, goods best provided privately, and has no significant other use. In many other cases, the principal service is recreation in which severe crowding occurs because political pressures prevent efficient pricing.

---

[1]Barnett and Morse (1963) discuss these developments from a natural resource perspective; revised views appear in Kerry Smith (1979). Hofstadter's (1955) writings deal more broadly with the discontents. The big business issue is treated by the pertinent antitrust literature reviewed in chapter 4.

Until the late 1960s, DOI proceeded under long-extant and rarely changed laws. Under the 1872 Mining Act, mineral-bearing land could be claimed and owned outright by anyone who could prove that valuable minerals occurred on the land. Leshy (1987) reviews the implementation and modification of the 1872 law. He is excellent on details but weak in appreciation of property-right economics. Subsequently, some minerals, particularly oil, gas, and coal, were removed from the system by the 1920 Mineral Leasing Act. Leases could be acquired but not the land.

Since the late 1960s, Congress made profound changes in the legislation governing federal land management. Review is best handled by first examining these legislative changes and then turning to administrative developments. The 1969 National Environmental Policy Act (NEPA) proved a major influence. The Act required preparation of environmental impact statements (EIS) when the federal government undertook "major" actions. Resolving questions about the meaning of this requirement inspired extensive litigation. Environmental groups succeeded in getting courts to impose broad definitions of what constituted a major decision and to require extensive inquiries about impacts and how to mitigate them. For example, setting a basic leasing policy, holding a lease auction, and letting a mine begin operation are separate major actions. The EIS for any energy-related project had to discuss all other fuels and measures to reduce fuel use. (For an overview of the early history of NEPA, see F. R. Anderson 1973.)

The process generated opportunities to impose long delays in decision making. Environmentalists often succeeded in getting courts to rule that the evaluations were inadequate. The decision makers moved to undertake extensive, protracted studies to disarm critics. Court cases continued. Even the extensive studies were deemed inadequate. It cannot be ensured that when action ultimately is taken, it is materially improved. Courts can only evaluate the form of the report. It became possible to comply with hundreds of pages of meaningless information. Such delays, by raising costs, may discourage the actions. Thus the policy would have desirable results only if, as is not certain, the most dubious projects are also the most vulnerable to prevention by protracted delays. In any case, the NEPA EIS system is an awkward way to proceed.

A 1976 act--the Federal Land Policy and Management Act, FLPMA--established provisions for land use planning on all public lands. FLPMA also made retention of public lands the preferable policy goal. Another clause made environmental preservation, recreation, and "human occupancy and use" the primary goals. As is typical, the provision explicitly uses the word environmental and also lists other "values" such as protecting air and water quality that are usually considered environmental.

Federal management is ineffective either at ensuring that federal lands are devoted to their socially most productive use or in promoting the efficient use of land in the activity allowed. Arbitrary procedures determine allowable uses. The choice is often based on the historical accidents by which land was or was not dedicated to specific uses. New commercial uses are now difficult to establish, but existing private rights are preserved if the use is not altered.

The government exhibits worse performance than does the private sector. The absence of strong property rights discourages efficient private operation of leased lands. Federal directives often increase inefficiency (Stroup and Baden 1983 and Truluck 1983). The literature on every area of end use--grazing (Libecap 1981), timber production (Deacon and Johnson 1985), recreation (Baden and Leal 1990, a case study of Yellowstone) and mining--argues that policies have produced inefficiency.[2] The timber companies of the United States with clear title to forest lands have proved better than the U.S. Forest Service at efficiently supplying timber and pulpwood.

A consensus exists among public land economists that land used primarily for commercial purposes, such as grazing and timber production, should be transferred to the private sector. The extensive review of land policy by the Land Law Review Commission led to advocacy of selling grazing land. This proposal failed to get support in Congress. This rejection reflected the triumph of faith in continued ownership over the vestiges of belief in disposal when appropriate.

Steve Hanke (1982, 1985), a particularly vigorously critic of government intervention, contends that all land services should be provided privately. He suggests that even amenity protection would be more satisfactory under private ownership. His contentions are a special case of Coase's argument discussed in chapter 6. Hanke effectively argues that public land is another case in which government failure has produced worse results than would market failure.

The record suggests his proposal is less extreme than it might appear. Clawson's (1983) effort to weigh the retention and antiretention cases were viewed by Hanke (1985) as too sympathetic to public retention.[3] However, Clawson's presentation of the antiretention case is more convincing than his exposition of the retention case. Clawson, for example, identifies the defects of Krutilla's (1967) widely cited defense of preservation (see chapter 10). Clawson recognizes that Krutilla's analysis is another example of the tendency incorrectly to ignore the crowding prevailing on public lands. Clawson's proposals include suggestions about ways in which sales of public land could be increased. Thus, Hanke exaggerates Clawson's timidity.

In his study of coal leasing, Nelson (1983) presents a fuller view of the pressures toward elaborate government planning. His stress is on the history of DOI decision making and the challenges to that arose to its actions. He treats coal leasing administration as a case study of faith in the impartial expert. He recalls how reformers believed that good government could be produced by assigning responsibility to disinterested specialists isolated from political pressures. It has long been realized that policy makers cannot be isolated. Moreover, the Hayek problem limits how much can be accomplished. While these problems were well known when coal policy was formed in the 1970s, Nelson shows that DOI opted for elaborate planning and the courts still required that the procedures be more elaborate than Interior proposed. (See Tarlock 1985 for a postmortem on the policy.) Clawson and Nelson implicitly provide considerable support for the privatization case.

When the Reagan administration proposed modest sales of federal lands, the environmental movement was able to prevent the sales. The extent of the disposals was overstated in these attacks. The case was not helped by Secretary of Interior James Watt's stridency and by the administration's confusion over whether the

---

[2]This material largely comes from libertarian groups, particularly the Pacific Institute.

[3]Clawson, the former head of the Bureau of Land Management and the long-time head of a program at Resources for the Future dealing with land policy, provides a thoughtful balanced discussion. The main difference between Clawson and Hanke is that the former wants to move slowly with disposal and the latter wants instant disposal of everything. A companion volume of essays edited by Brubaker (1984) is a useful supplement. Barnett and Morse's (1963) earlier book contains a discussion of conservation that points to its faults.

preferable policy was true privatization or mere transfer of land to the states. The Reagan privatization effort also was greatly harmed by introducing revenue-raising considerations into the argument. Rather than producing support from those wishing to reduce deficits, the call simply fostered opposition from current leaseholders. Nevertheless, the Clinton administration repeated this error.

The problem is more fundamental. The reluctance to change land policy arises from the absence of effective unified opposition to environmentalism. Severe difficulties, moreover, arise in privatizing. Two widely accepted aims are in conflict in this and all other aspects of federal land management. A desire exists to ensure that the federal government be properly compensated for the land. Another concern is protecting those who have long been economically dependent upon leasing federal land.

A federal policy of seeking payment for privatizing land can harm long-time leaseholders in several ways. The most obvious is by losing the lease. In addition, given sufficiently secure leases, the holders will have undertaken investments in land improvement that increase the market value. Transfer of the land will involve securing the benefits, not just of the inherent productivity of the land, but of the enhancements made by the established leaseholder. Thus, bidders will be willing to pay a price equal to the present value of using the improved land. To outbid rivals, the leaseholders must match the bids of newcomers reflecting the value of upgrading. Unless, as is unlikely, the federal government compensates the leaseholders for their investment, selling improved land at auction confiscates the value of assets created by leaseholders.

These tensions hinder action. Significant forces support both federal ownership and rent transfers. The demand for payment can be traced to the conservation movement's attacks on giveaways. Modern environmentalists are more flexible on the subject. Giveaways are sometimes attacked; so are some efforts to oust existing lessors. Moreover, many people worry about giveaways as an independent problem. This can reflect fear of monopoly or desire to lower the federal deficit. Locke again may be instructive. He can be extended to infer that no real conflict exists. The long-run benefit to society and its government is greatest when the land is most productively used.

The narrow focus on receipts from a specific sale should yield to fostering economic growth. Expansion increases the ability to undertake many more ventures including financing government. In the many cases in which the best uses are private, private ownership should be encouraged. Efforts to secure high-immediate compensation should be radically reduced. The sole explicit objective of competitive bidding should be to select among rival claimants to the land. For reasons discussed more fully below, a byproduct of such a system would be to effect rent transfers more efficiently than the present system.

That system has unwisely harmed production and rent collection. Efforts to insist that the adequacy of payments is well verified have proved undesirable. Under the best of circumstances, confirmation is difficult. Several practical forces aggravate the problem. Payment adequacy, at best, can be determined only after a long history of operations accumulates. At the time of leasing, critics can and do adopt assumption about probable future profits that imply that giveaways occurred. Such allegations are a good way for those opposed on other grounds to thwart the action. Attacks on the payments are also an effective device for casting suspicion on the political opponents.

Thus, a major element in U.S. land policy is the inability to secure transfers of land to private use even when that employment is preferable. In addition, the concerns for how the land is utilized have been a major element in U.S. environmental legislation from the 1960s. This has imposed both a more complex decision-making structure and more stringent rules to govern the decisions.

Congress introduced into federal lands the attenuation of property rights widely practiced abroad but previously avoided in the United States. U.S. specialists on public land economics believe this termination of the sale of U.S. public land was a grave error. The historical process of rapid transfer to the private sector served everyone better. It was more productive to the land users and society. It also contributed more revenue. Fees on public lands even fail to repay the costs of administration. Private landowners pay taxes.

The Problem of Mobile Resources: Property Right Definition in Oil and Gas

A major concern in U.S. oil and gas policy has been devising an efficient system of property rights. The system established by U.S. courts caused inefficient allocation of resources. In seeking the most apt precedent, courts unwisely applied principles applicable to wild beasts wandering onto individual property. The property owner had the right to capture the beasts. Should they migrate to a nearby property, they could be captured. It was decided that such a law of capture should apply to oil and gas resources. Migration was defined to include flows caused by removing oil and gas from adjacent land.

Waste was inherent. Undertaking or preventing capture is not an economically beneficial activity. Benefits arise only from making oil available. Outlays that only transfer incomes among landowners produce no mutual gains. The capturer takes money from the victim; both spend more than needed to produce efficiently. (Recall the discussion of monopoly in chapter 3.)

Years of discussion led to the conclusion that the preferable approach was an explicit switch to a system of property rights that encouraged unitization--the creation of a unified privately developed and implemented operating plan for each oil and gas field. The experience with trying to effect efficient production by regulation inspired severe criticism. (See the critiques by Lovejoy and Homan 1967 and by McDonald 1971 and also Weaver 1986 on Texas experience with unitization by regulatory coercion.) In the 1980s, Libecap and Wiggins wrote three articles (Libecap and Wiggins 1984, 1985, Wiggins and Libecap 1985) presenting empirical studies of private efforts to unitize. McGee (1988, 411), observing this literature, correctly notes that it provides too many explanations.

The large-numbers problem stressed in proregulation interpretations of the Coase theorem on social costs prevails. However, so do the political barriers to implementation of unitization, stressed by Coase. Many cooperative ventures have arisen in oil, and trading in leases is extensive. Therefore, the conclusion that only strong political pressures would have succeeded may be incorrect. It is unclear what weights should be given market and government failure in preventing private cooperation.

Coase's suggestion for analysis of whether and under what circumstances an efficient private solution would emerge had little impact on the debate. Earlier writers showed no awareness that Coase's analysis existed, and Libecap and Wiggins only briefly considered the question. They (Libecap and Wiggins 1984, 87; Wiggins and Libecap 1985, 368) emphasize the problems of contracting. Libecap and Wiggins uphold the more traditional view that unitization had to be forced by supporting legislation. Mention is also made that recalcitrant small firms went to the legislature for assistance. Another possibility is that refusal to intervene could have stimulated private cooperation.

The key conclusion remains that some method to encourage unitization is essential. Production controls are policies worse than the problem that they are supposed to solve. It is unclear whether unitization is easy enough to effect that Adam Smith's few words of encouragement are sufficient. Another possibility is that the legislation actually adopted was needed. Finally the Rothbard concept adopted by Bradley in a forthcoming history of U.S. oil and gas policy of homesteading, granting rights to the entire field to its discoverer, might be preferable. The experience with problems of identifying *the* discoverers and delineating fields suggests that the Rothbard concept would be unworkable as a reform of existing law. Adoption before the oil industry was established might have proved an efficient solution. I lean towards belief in simply avoiding establishment of barriers to unitization.

The Theory and Practice of Rent Transfer

The method of charging for rights of excess to those who extract minerals has long been debated by policy makers and economists. The three basic approaches to charges are preset fixed-total-sum bonus payments, royalties (or taxes) as a fixed amount per unit of output or percent of sales, and profit sharing. Each type has numerous variants, and actual charge systems may employ at least two of the basic systems. For example, U.S. fossil-fuel leasing policy involves requiring both bonus payments and royalties.

Economic analyses of these methods concentrate on securing as much government revenue as possible without inefficiently reducing production. Many terms exist for this maximum income. Whatever its name, it consists of the differences between revenues and the social costs including the necessity to earn the required rate of return on investment. (See below for more details.) Two standard terms for the annual flows are excess profits or economic rents.

Fair market value is the legal term used to determine the appropriate price to be paid in the purchase and sale of property by government agencies. The concept needs explanation. A manual entitled *Uniform Appraisal Standards for Federal Land Acquisitions* (U.S. Interagency Land Acquisition Conference 1973) is widely used as the guide to all types of U.S. government fair market value determinations. The manual's definition is that fair market value is what a willing, knowledgeable, voluntary buyer would pay an equally willing and knowledgeable seller. This seems a restatement of the definition of a competitive market price. In a 1943 Supreme Court decision cited in the Appendix on the legal definition of fair market value in the Coal Leasing Commission report, it was argued "The term 'fair' hardly adds anything to the phrase 'market value'...(1984, 618)." Despite the similarity between fair market value and a competitive market price, many observers claim the former concept is mystifying. Viewing the definition and efforts to implement it suggests that the concept is clear, but politically invulnerable measurement can be difficult for rarely traded assets.

Public data must exist on going prices and the values assigned to differences in characteristics among properties. Problems arise when vigorous markets, data about them, or both are unavailable. Where vigorous markets exist and information is available, the level of a competitive price is clear. This would be true for commodities principally traded on organized exchanges and also for regularly traded goods on which other forms of reporting are available, such as the reporting to local governments of real estate transfers. A problem that causes discontent with the bid levels is that good data on other transactions are difficult to find. Where evidence is deficient, *determination* of fair market value seems difficult. What constitutes an adequate appraisal seems unclear. We thus have another illustration of Coase's point about the problems of responding to transaction costs.

As noted in chapter 7, the critical principle in asset valuation is the present value of expected future net income. This approach adjusts for the requirement that any investment worth taking must yield an adequate return on investment. Calculation starts with estimates of the gross inflows and outflows in each period in which the assets are used. Then a "discount" factor is employed to adjust for the loss of interest incurred by waiting for a payoff. The present value is the amount that must be invested now to secure a given future income.

The appraisal manual suggests three valuation methods--comparable worth, reproduction cost, and income. Comparable worth involves looking at available data about sales of similar properties and adjusting for the differences between the other properties and that being valued. For a capital asset, comparable worth is the market-determined estimate of the present value of future incomes. Reproduction cost is applicable only to assets that the decision maker could create for itself and thus irrelevant to a mineral or lease or sale. Income is shorthand for an estimate of the present value of the income generated from the assets. The choice of valuation methods for minerals or land lies between comparable worth and present value. The appraisal manual expresses a preference for comparable worth. This is implicitly based on the economics of worth determination. Competition, as noted, makes the market price of an asset equal its present value. Private owners are likely to have better information than a government agency about the present value. The comparable worth method then takes advantage of the superiority of market prices over administrative determinations as a measure of present value.

Hayek's (1945) observations about information imply severe barriers to governmental estimates of present value. A correct estimate requires accuracy about costs, benefits, and future interest rates. Thus, error is inevitable from whoever makes the estimate. Calls, nevertheless, are made for governments to undertake elaborate evaluation studies. Determining fair market value involves considerable practical difficulties under the best of circumstances. Policy makers lack, not only clearly satisfactory measures of fair market value, but even a crude indicator of how bad are the available figures. Bitter arguments arise about the appropriate degree of effort to stimulate greater payments for assets sold or leased by the federal government.

Requests for high degrees of sophistication in appraisal are unrealistic. Sometimes the problem is naiveté. Excessive caution is another factor. A more important influence is sophisticated recognition that pushing for strict interpretation of the appraisal requirements is another effective tactic to prevent action. Environmentalists routinely use charges of failure to comply with regulations as a means to prevent action. This strategy deliberately takes advantage of the fundamental flaw in the Congressional tendency to demand extensive review of the consequences of policy decisions. These demands are precisely the types of actions Hayek (1945) and Coase (1988) have suggested governments cannot do well. The studies always will be inadequate, and obstructionists can always thwart action by noting the inadequacy. The salvation is that ultimately courts implicitly recognize the difficulties and tacitly stop taking the laws literally.

The assumptions of efficient markets and the absence of market or government failures have important implications for the determination of the net present value of exploiting a resource. An efficient market is one in which private, profit-oriented decision making ensures attainment of the desirable outcomes described in chapter 2. The owner of the resource will be paid an amount equivalent to the net present value of exploiting the resource (see below).

The implications to the conclusions of market failures too unclear to suggest policy responses. Six aspects of an efficient market are critical. The first requirement is that markets for the products produced from the land be vigorously competitive. Second, similarly vigorous competition must prevail for securing a particular lease. (The distinction is made here to reflect DOI's belief that the first condition, but not the second, prevails. See below.) A third requirement of efficient markets is that private investors can accurately appraise future prospects. Fourth, the firms' estimate of the cost of capital must be close to that of the true social cost of capital. Fifth, a mechanism must exist to charge for the environmental damages produced--a proposition that needs no further elaboration here. The last requirement is that the government not impose inefficient rules. While this requirement is self-explanatory, it is often violated. Examples of inappropriate requirements imposed include a statutory minimum-required payment on all leases and restrictions on what is produced or on the timing, level, or method used in this production.

The first two conditions are particularly vital. The definition of competition implies that firms are forced to pay the full expected value. A bid less than the full worth of the property will attract rivals who will offer more and win. This basic outcome will occur whether the arrangement is an outright sale or a lease.

Acquisition of ownership implies the ability to secure and, consequently, pay for all the income the property ever generates. The amount paid will decline if the lease makes the period of occupancy less than the optimal duration of operations. Such a lease necessarily yields the lesser income secured over part of the economic lifetime of the venture, is less valuable, and thus will be bought for less than either a lease without such limits or a transfer of ownership.

A further critical implication is that the competitive process leads to determining the most profitable uses of the property and utilizing the most efficient technologies for those uses. A competitive price is determined by the interaction of many buyers and sellers. All participation is voluntary, and all participants base their decisions on their knowledge of the situation. Therefore, the competitive market price is the best available measure of the present value of a resource.

Ample, if often disputed, evidence exists that vigorous competition exists in the U.S. mineral industries. Competition in U.S. energy is a perennial issue and inspired many studies after the 1973-1974 oil price increases. Among the first works in this period was a survey of competition in all fuels undertaken for the Ford-Foundation funded Energy Policy Project (see Duchesneau 1975). The Federal Trade Commission conducted coal (1978), uranium (Mulholland, Haring, and Martin 1979), and natural gas (Mulholland 1979) studies. Competition in coal market has been extensively studied with other discussants including the General Accounting Office (1977a), the Department of Energy (1981a, 1981b), and the Department of Justice. A 1976 law required Justice to issue an annual report on coal competition, but after six reports, Justice found that only a perfunctory updating was required. These studies concluded that competition among U.S. energy producers is vigorous.

Since they refute rather than affirm the existence of practices, these analyses necessarily are not conclusive. Evidence might have been overlooked. However, if serious problems were apparent, many were eager to provide it. Despite considerable effort, no one has produced a satisfactory demonstration that private energy monopolies prevail. Three decades of literature search has failed to unearth properly documented claims of private energy monopoly. Attacks on energy monopolies are universally either shoddy or actually attacks on the well-recognized formerly extant power of the industry to get government protection.

As far as competition for leases is concerned, oil-and-gas leasing experience suggests that by organizing continual large-scale leasing of tracts, each of interest to several bidders, vigorous competition for leases can be assured. Many studies (particularly those of Walter Mead et. al. 1985) show that the U.S. government has captured the net value of offshore oil and gas. (Also see Rockwood 1983.)

However, the applicability of these results to coal is challenged, at least by DOI. Studies of competition in the coal industry, such as those just cited, suggest that many well-financed participants operate. Since coal resources are better delineated than those for oil and gas, it should be possible for private firms to make good value estimates when many tracts are involved. Coal leasing was suspended from 1971 to 1981 and resuspended in 1983. During the brief period of resumed leasing, every offering attracted few bidders. Considerable concern, therefore, exists on whether competition for leases is adequate. This creates a reluctance to undertake the vigorous leasing that might establish experience including price information. A true Catch 22, a policy that builds in the impossibility of implementation, prevails. Oil and gas leasing stays free from crippling objections to the amounts paid because continuing leasing establishes a record of successful sales. However, it is retarded by environmental objections (see chapter 10). Interior issued many studies on the coal problem (1975, 1979, 1985, 1986a, and 1986b).

The predictable effect of pre-1920 outright grants of coal bearing land, extensively leasing, and severing coal from surface ownership was fragmentation of property rights. Difficulties are caused by the grants of land to railroads, past leasing of coal, and past accords with surface owners. An important element was the construction incentive given to railroads by granting large amounts of land surrounding areas where new lines were built. That land had been divided into square mile sections, and the railroads received every other section. Given the appearance of the holdings on a map, the policy has been characterized as checker-boarding the West. Other public land was dedicated to nonmining use, often with transfer of the surface to private ownership. Much coal is already controlled.

Therefore, the parcels of federal coal available for leasing often could be used most profitably by those with rights to adjacent coal resources. DOI fears that fragmentation severely reduces the willingness to bid. DOI believes no one is as capable of bidding as those with rights to adjacent land.

Arbitrage may be standard economics but is still too radical a concept for the scandal-shy leasing officials to recognize. As chapter 2 indicated, arbitrageurs ensure that every financial asset or commodity selling on more than one securities or commodity exchange sells for the same price in all exchanges. Specialists exist to eliminate price disparities that, if continued, would produce windfall profits. A tendency to underpay for leases would inspire arbitrageurs to participate in the leases. If the bidders best able to use the land bid far less than the value, others may begin to bid against them. These rivals will hope to resell at a price close to the value to the firm best able to exploit the resource.

The successful bidders for coal leases were companies who should possess the requisite sophistication to recognize arbitrage possibilities. DOI must ignore the role of arbitrage because no evidence exists of its extensive use in coal leasing. It is always possible to recognize when rival bidders appear. We cannot be sure whether their absence is due to failure to recognize the profit potential, to bids so high that additional bidders are unnecessary, or to political barriers discussed below. The fear of bidding by speculators could force the mine operator to bid as if it will encounter competition at the auction. Such reliance on the potential for additional bids seemed politically infeasible in the prevailing climate.

The third requirement of efficient markets, that private investors be able accurately to appraise future prospects, does not require accurately predicting the value of any one property. Investors only must know enough about the resources so that on average, the valuation equals the actual total net worth of the resources being sold.

The fourth requirement, that the firms' estimate of the cost of capital must be close to that of the true social cost of capital, stems from the imperfect capital market argument discussed in chapter 3. Theoretical economics, as noted in that chapter, stresses that private institutions may not provide enough devices to hedge risks. Risk-averse investors may demand too high a rate of return. Imperfect capital markets also may inefficiently limit access to funds and make the opportunity cost of funds to some firms greater than the social cost of capital. In addition, taxes on return on investment and other incomes distort decision making. The assumption about discount rates is critical because using an incorrect interest rate leads to a misestimate of the present value.

Concerns also exist about the feasibility of administering the system and ensuring public faith in the integrity of the system. With the many possible circumstances surrounding a given lease or sale and the several, conflicting policy goals, consensus on choice is difficult to attain. Having gone this far in discussing the implications of efficient markets, it seems appropriate to pause and complete the argument by dealing with the implications for sale timing and with the impacts of inefficiencies.

If markets are efficient, leasing delays can only be inefficient. By the principles of efficiency, any private firm making a lease or purchase before it is efficient to utilize the property will wait until the socially most desirable exploitation date. It is possible to lease too late. Resources may not be made available to a qualified operator until after the most desirable time for exploitation.

The competitive market value is determined by the existence of the mineral, not its ownership. Failure to realize this basic principle results in concerns about adequate payments. The land sale or lease transfers control without altering supply. With sufficient rationality among potential operators and the expectation that land will be made available on a timely basis, the existence of the land affects present values independently of when the transfers are made. Where resource ownership is concentrated as in federal mineral holdings, greater selling or leasing can increase efficiency. *Increased* leasing is the cure for all forms of monopoly in the product market. The excess profits the federal government could obtain by restricting supply are prevented. Restriction by definition is the failure to lease all properties that could be profitably exploited. The federal government would be inadvertently collecting monopoly profits by reducing production below its socially best level.

Another Coase contribution to economics is a 1972 study of the problem of the optimum policy for the monopolistic owner of a durable asset such as land. It inspired other work (recapitulated in Tirole 1988 and Krouse 1990). The fundamental problem is overcoming buyer concerns that arise if more supplies can be added in future periods (whether in the case of land purely from inventories or with reproducible goods also from new production). Once a sale is made (or a once and for all lease bonus is received), the original supplier has less interest in what happens in the market. Selling more is attractive because the original owner reaps the benefits from the sale and others suffer the loss to new competition. Buyers recognize this possibility and reduce their bids accordingly. Coase suggested that fears of further sales are best alleviated by leasing and requiring payments over the life of the lease. The original owners' resulting dependence on the future income generated by the durable asset restores the interest in output control and profit levels that diminishes with outright sale. While Coase used public land as his example, economists appraising public lands have not applied his insights to evaluating public land policy. Those attempting to expand on Coase's analysis have not looked at experience with public land.

Obsession with fictitious problems has probably produced the dangerous outcome critics of statism fear--government exercise of its monopoly power by unconsciously taking Coase's advice. The exercise may have been excessive even from a federal government perspective. The U.S. government's caution about how much to lease may restrict supply more than would be appropriate for exploiting monopoly power. Curtailment below the monopoly level necessarily keeps leases below the even higher efficient competitive market level of leasing. The principal corrective is that so much coal was leased before the excessive fears of giveaways arose.

The final problem with market failures is that their policy implications are unclear at best. Control of lease levels is difficult and, in many ways, undesirable. Even if DOI were right about inadequacy of competition for leases, this inadequacy would diminish receipts whenever the leasing is held. The profitability of the sale depends on the vigor of competition for the lease. This competition depends on largely unchanging ownership positions. Similarly, the need to protect the environment depends only on the nature of each lease and does not vary with leasing levels. Any failures to make firms adequately responsible for environmental damages would persist even if leasing were delayed.

Limiting leasing levels, therefore, does not directly contribute either to ensuring receipt of a competitive market price or to protecting environmental amenities. It can be argued that delays in leasing can be advantageous because they also may serve provide time to increase competition and more effectively evaluate environmental impacts. These contentions are also dubious.

Devices exist with potential to promote competition. For example, intertract leasing has been proposed to offset the alleged inadequacy of competition for leases. Several tracts of similar characteristics would be offered simultaneously. It would be announced that only a preset proportion of the leases would be granted. The separate bids would be compared, and awards would be made to those bidding highest. Thus, if six out of ten tracts were offered, the six highest bidders would get leases. A principal problem is finding comparable leases to offer together.

Environmental improvement might occur in two ways. First, a slower pace would presumably allow enough time for the Office of Surface Mining thoroughly to investigate and control more effectively undesirable environmental impacts. However, if overly rapid decisions are taken, this would be a general problem better cured by altering surface mine regulation. Second, with sufficient time, BLM may overcome the inadequacies of those with primary responsibility for surface reclamation. The argument is implausible. It implies that the specialists in the Office of Surface Mining and state agencies are incompetent or underfunded and that follow-up by BLM is the preferable solution. It is unlikely that using the less relevant expertise of BLM is the optimum cure. This is an example of the chronic government failure of trying to deal with problems with many inadequate mandates instead of a single vigorous policy. It also can be interpreted as another example of how the environmental movement likes to impose multiple barriers.

Severe problems exist with responding to any difficulties that might exist of imperfect capital markets and imperfect knowledge. The most important drawback of regulation is that since the capital-market problem is not confined to mineral leases, a solution confined to mineral leasing introduces distortions of the choice between mineral and other investments. These new distortions could be greater than the existing ones that the problem was designed to reduced. Another difficulty is that even the qualitative effects of poor foresight and improper interest rates are not readily determined. It is not clear whether expectations at any moment are too optimistic or too pessimistic. Not only is the direction of the error in estimating the social cost of capital uncertain, but the impact of an error in either direction is ambiguous.

In particular, at a higher interest rate, the present value of a given net income stream is lower. Thus, the fair market value is lower and an incentive exists to speed production to lower the interest costs of waiting. However, a higher interest rate also lowers net receipts by raising the costs of repaying investments in the facility. This discourages production for highly profitable deposits, the lowering of the present values of the profits would be the more important effect. For a barely profitable deposit, the cost raising effects of a higher interest rate might be the dominant influence (Gordon 1966).

Finally, the policy must be practically implementable. Correction would require that leasing be delayed or speeded to correct for undue or inadequate private willingness to operate. In addition, rules of optimal operation would have to be imposed on private firms. The usual arguments against centralized planning are particularly applicable here. The long lead times and limited staffing in leasing preclude efficient correction of incorrect foresight or inefficient interest rates. Inadequate foresight and incorrect interest rates, therefore, are problems whose reality is suspect and whose correction in mineral leasing is impractical. If efficient markets prevail, the competitive market value is obtained on the lease bonus from competitive bidding. When the assumptions are violated, no simple means are available to determine or offset the impacts on receipt of competitive market value.

With efficient markets, the preferred method is to rely entirely on bonus payments. A lease bonus--a single payment made when the lease is implemented--is the simplest form of a preset total payment. Options involve spreading the payments over varying time periods. These could range from a few years up to the expected life of the mine as presumed in the Coase-inspired analysis of durable good asset markets. The prior argument indicated that efficient markets ensure transfer of the net present value of the economic rents from utilizing the property in its most efficient fashion.

The bonus-bid has the additional advantage of not influencing any of the postlease decisions of the firm. The bonus by definition cannot be altered by any action of the firm, and no decisions can be affected by having paid a bonus. In economic jargon, the bonus is thus a sunk cost. The case for bonuses is reinforced by the defects of the alternatives. The widely used system of basing payments on output creates a disincentive to produce (explained in textbook discussions of sales taxes). Both more complex charging schemes that lessen output distortion and profit sharing are expensive to administer. Moreover, the methods involve the uncertainties of outcome that normally produce criticism of DOI.

The Case of Coal Leasing: An Overview

The U.S. government owns many of the nation's most economically attractive coal resources. In particular, it is the dominant owner of coal in such western states as Wyoming, Montana, Colorado, Utah, North Dakota, and New Mexico. Much of U.S. coal output growth since 1970 occurred in those states. Coal leasing law and its administration changed little from 1920 to 1971. Leases were freely granted under the provisions of the 1920 Mineral Leasing Act. These policies allowed satisfaction of most desires for leases. Coal leasing proceeded quietly and modestly until the late sixties, when it spurted. At least retrospectively, the 1960s leasing surge is explicable by anticipation of the expansion of western output that actually occurred. The prospects were evident in the late sixties.

Starting in the late 1960s, both the legislative and administrative processes changed radically. Congress passed a series of laws directly or indirectly affecting coal leasing. Federal coal policy became so polarized that a hiatus in leasing has prevailed through most of the period from 1971 to the time of writing. In 1971, Interior became concerned over an acceleration of leasing without a concomitant increase in output. The result is that coal leasing ceased from 1971 to 1981, resumed briefly in 1981, was stopped in 1983, and its resumption remained indefinite as of 1994. Almost two years of preparation are required for a lease sale so that resumption in the twentieth century is unlikely. (A few leases are granted to cover emergency needs.)

A better but still questionable rationale for Interior's leasing moratorium is that the prior system paid little or no attention to how much revenue was being collected by DOI. Given that concern was rising about the adequacy of payments for leaseholding, Interior might have wanted to ensure higher yields on future leases.

The reluctance to resume leasing arises because the amount of coal already leased appears sufficient to meet predicted consumption levels for several more decades. Established producers feel they possess reserves sufficient for their future operations. Other justifications have not gained support sufficient to inspire resumed leasing. One such argument is that new leases would raise the number of leaseholders and increase competition in the coal market. The unwillingness of established producers to endorse extensive leasing suggests that competition was feared. It is also contended that some attractive reserves remain unleased. The available data are inadequate to confirm or refute these and many other controversial views about coal leasing. No powerful group is interested in fighting for resumption of coal leasing.

Prevailing legislation assures that the availability of federal coal cannot continue without either new leasing or new legislation. In 1976, coal leasing rules were comprehensively changed.

The Coal Leasing Amendments

The Coal Leasing Amendment Act of 1976 radically altered coal leasing policy. The central components of the Act were: (1) requiring competitive bidding on all leases (section 2), (2) requiring the receipt of fair market value on all leases (section 2), and (3) requiring a royalty of at least 12.5 percent of the selling price on all surface mined coal with the Secretary of the Interior given discretion to set a lower rate on underground mined coal (section 7a). (The section numbers shown relate to sections of the Amendments rather than to the section of the mining act that was amended.) Many ancillary provisions were provided, but full review (as in Gordon 1988) is not critical here. The provision that proved to have the greatest practical relevance was that requiring forfeiture of any lease that was not developed within ten years (the due diligence requirement). President Ford vetoed the act, but the veto was overridden.

The problems with the three main provisions were noted above. The Coal Leasing Commission devoted considerable attention to the effects on federal government of revenue sharing with the states. The clearest impact is that basing the share on gross revenues creates a conflict of interests. The states get all the benefits but pay none of the costs of efforts to increase gross receipts. Thus, states lobby for federal enforcement that extends past the point at which costs exceed benefits.

Initially, loss of lease for lack of diligence was also to occur ten years after the Act was passed with the possibility of a five year extension (OTA 1981, 238-40). However, DOI conservatively interpreted the time when the due diligence clause became applicable to leases issued before the 1976 law. In 1982, DOI decided that loss of pre-1976 leases would occur ten years after the expiration of the twenty year term of the lease. (See Coal Leasing Commission, 292-302.)[4]

Since most leases antedate the 1971 moratorium, few can last past 2001 unless they are being exploited. According to the U.S. Office of Technology Assessment (1981, 49), only 18 percent of the leased acreage is in pre-1960 leases; another 20 percent was leased from 1960 to 1965, with 56 percent between 1965 and 1975. Thus, lease forfeitures are not likely to be extensive until the 1990s but then could become substantial.

Penalties for delayed development and maximum recovery rules are undesirable if efficient markets and reliance only on lease bonuses prevail. Four outcomes are possible with a diligence requirement. Two are innocuous, but two are harmful. The optimum starting date may be before the expiration of the diligence deadline; the redundancy of the requirement then renders it harmless. Similarly, if the requirement is not met, the lease is forfeited, and DOI reissues the lease soon enough for

---

[4]Earlier policies are reviewed in the 1981 OTA report (238-49). The OTA report appraises the prospects of lease forfeiture under the then prevailing interpretation that no unexploited lease could be retained past 1991.

development to occur in the optimal time, only harm that occurs is higher transaction costs. Injury is produced when premature development is more profitable than surrender or when reissue by DOI of a surrendered lease is delayed past the optimum time for starting mining. Again, it is unrealistic to believe that leasing can be controlled to avoid these defects.

Diligence requirements have undesirable effects on arbitrage in bidding and on prevention of mining when superior private uses exist. If lease lengths were unlimited, the leaseholder could refrain forever from mining the land. Someone who believed that other uses were more profitable than mining could prevent mining the land by buying the lease and not mining it. This would be superior to land use planning for determining whether other uses were more profitable. Privatization would be even better since reliance on markets would be effected. The limited term of the lease lowers the willingness to pay of someone wishing to obtain the land for other purposes. Only the present value of the income obtained from another use over the term of the lease would be paid. Lease length limits prevent increasing bids to reflect additional revenues from continuing the other activity after the expiration of the lease. Similarly, the risk of loss to diligence requirements lessens the willingness of arbitrageurs to participate.

Diligence requirements and maximum production rules offset to a degree the production retarding of royalties. The correction, at best, is incomplete. Delays are reduced, but disincentives to production remain. Feasible diligence and production rules are unlikely to be based upon estimates of socially efficient patterns and so are unlikely to correct optimally. Thus, unlimited leases and the abolishment of diligence requirements would allow for more profitable private use of the land.

The Coal Leasing Amendment Act established too many layers of restrictions in an effort to alleviate the consequences of the basic requirements. This classic problem with regulation of preferring increased complexity to elimination of undesirable restrictions proliferates. Diligence requirements seek to offset the stimulus to holding caused by the compulsory royalties. The type of land use planning required is precisely the type that is best done by the marketplace. The effort to determine administratively whether other private land uses are harmed also, as noted, is a consequence of the diligence requirement. Similarly, diligence requirements make bidding by arbitrageurs more risky and may necessitate development of other ways to ensure higher bids. Where the controls were well defined as in the diligence requirements, they threatened to be too restrictive. Where advice was limited to ordering programs, the problem was, again confirming Coase, that such programs could or would not be implemented. The amendments' shift of all leasing to competitive bidding removed the incentive to private exploration provided by the previously available alternative of noncompetitive grants to those making discoveries. A requirement of federal exploration was included in the amendments to offset the effects on private exploration. The program was never funded.

As noted, coal leasing has ceased despite all the safeguards imposed. This suggests that land management has become so controversy bound that even when unreasonably stringent safeguards are in place, the critics remain dissatisfied. The prevalence of such implacable opposition is typical of what is being challenged here. All this illustrates the cumbersome way in which the policy of federal land retention has been implemented. This in turn is just one of many examples of how land law around the world stresses rent taxes over efficiency.

Conclusions

The experience with U.S. mineral land management provides considerable ammunition for the free market case. What the public has been led to believe is ideal government intervention turns out to be a defective system. Elaborate requirements are imposed by legislators aware that adequate resources for implementation will not be provided. It is an approach designed to guarantee undesirable results. The system cannot even be excused as the best possible way of preserving resources for future generations. A large element consists of indiscriminate grants of access. Such defects justify rethinking views about public lands and are precisely the sorts of policy failures that stimulate broad concerns about government failure and advocacy of government withdrawal. Therefore, privatization deserves consideration as the most feasible reform. Certainly, the experiments proposed by Clawson are the minimum change worth implementing.

Chapter 12

The Critiques of Intervention Reconsidered

Extensive criticisms of government regulation have appeared in the economics literature for more than two centuries. Economics as a formal discipline began in the eighteenth century as an attack on ill-advised controls. Ever since, traditional economics has stressed the desirability of fostering competition and limiting government interference, particularly in the markets for individual commodities. The fervor for free markets of the century after Adam Smith eventually weakened and many commentators turned to stress market imperfections. The tradition of skepticism about government, nevertheless, remains a powerful force in economic analyses. The classic arguments of Hume, Smith, and their successors, therefore, have proved among the most valuable and enduring contributions to human knowledge. The need to reform ill-advised government policies remains the area over which the greatest consensus exists in the economics literature.

On the basis of this tradition, George J. Stigler ([1959] 1965, 51-65) notes "my thesis is that the professional study of economics makes one politically conservative." Recognizing the ambiguity of the term conservative, he notes, "I shall mean by a conservative in economic matters a person who wishes most economic activity to be conducted by private enterprise and who believes that abuses of private power will usually be checked, and incitements to efficiency and progress usually provided, by the forces of competition."

The theme of this book essentially is that Stigler was correct. It is nearly impossible simultaneously to accept standard economic theory and not be highly critical of, at least, the practice of government intervention. Study of economics forces radical reappraisal of views and at least increases admiration for markets.

Resistance to full commitment to such ideas often prevails. Economists of all viewpoints often point out that they entered the field to promote reform, usually through more active government. Klamer and Colander's (1987, 1990) survey of students in six leading graduate programs in economics suggests that students enter their programs supporting the modern concept of liberalism (1990, 14). The students wish to use economics to affect policy, presumably by increasing intervention (1990, 15). Similarly, many critics of intervention note that they held contrary views before studying economics.

Outside economics, support of interventionist government is strong. Admission of "conservatism" certainly invites unpopularity, and many may be reluctant to admit their position. The result all too often is excessive effort to disclaim affinity with the vigorous advocates of a market-oriented approach. A countertheme espoused by the most vociferous advocates of free markets is exaggeration of how original and beleaguered they are.

Adam Smith was a mild critic by modern standards. His treatment of what governments should do makes concessions that subsequent writings have challenged. While some suggest this shows Smith was more realistic, others argue that the problem was the primitive nature of his analysis. With this tradition and the clear defects of much dirigisme, many economists were ready, willing, and able to contribute to the criticisms of prevailing public policy in the late twentieth century.

Adam Smith, David Ricardo, and their many successors believed that free trade in goods, services, and ideas was a liberating force. This vision looks even better given the prevailing expanded ability to trade. Efforts are better directed at removing government barriers to trade than concentrating on the elimination of private efforts to restrict markets. Undesirable government actions are far more visible and obviously pernicious than private ones.

In the twentieth century, extensive efforts were made to strengthen the earlier views of the classical liberals. A group associated with the University of Chicago makes its points mainly through articles in scholarly journals (including law reviews). As a result, the group has maintained a reputation for a scholarly approach and consequently muted the criticism received. Leaders include Coase, Stigler, Demsetz, Peltzman, Telser, McGee, Bork, and Posner. In addition, numerous more polemical works by other economists were addressed to nonprofessional audiences. Writers such as Mises, Hayek, Schumpeter, Knight, and Milton Friedman represent the second group. (Milton Friedman, while the most celebrated Chicago economist, has not contributed to the Chicago analysts of market regulation. Friedman's more technical work has largely been in monetary economics, and his writings on market regulation are largely directed at noneconomists.) Perhaps because the work of the latter group was targeted at a wider audience, it provoked more counterattacks. This response may be another confusion of form with substance. The substance of the Chicago approach often presents stronger antidirigism than any of the polemicists. Coase, in particular, has mounted a broader challenge to intervention than many of the polemicists. Coase also named more of those he considered in error than did many polemicists. The Chicago approach also has greatly advanced the economic theory of government failure.

The Chicago group is less subject to (but far from immune to) attack than the more polemical writers. As already noted above, a critical misrepresentation of these positions consists of contentions that the conclusions come from excessive, often totally intellectual, belief in free markets. The proponents of lessened intervention warn of the inappropriateness of looking at defects of only the market or only of governments. This case against intervention involves comparing actual performances of *both* the public and private sector. The Chicago work stresses the inefficiency of governments and the adaptability of markets. Easterbrook (1984) well sums up the position with his argument that governmental errors are less likely to be eliminated than monopolistic practices.

Chicago ideas thus are in many ways simultaneously stronger attacks on intervention than those of the ideologues but less deviant than either the advocates or critics are willing to admit (see chapter 4 for an example). The vigor of the anti-intervention arguments of Stigler and Coase is often neglected. Few appreciate the ways in which Coase's widely cited and accepted analyses are more anti-interventionist than those of Mises and Hayek. Coase's work on transaction costs is often applied, ignoring all his caveats about the drawbacks of a public solution. Coase and Stigler have made formidable contributions to economic analysis. As a result, those who disagree with them do so by omission or by deflecting criticism. Attacks are saved for secondary figures such as Demsetz, McGee, and Bork. Similar deficiencies arise in responding to challenges to Keynesian economics.

One aggressive group of polemicists espouses what they term Austrian economics. University of Vienna trained economists such as Schumpeter, Mises, and Hayek were among the most forceful expositors of the importance of the division of labor and of technical progress and, thus, of the advantages of a market economy. Austrian economics consists of consciously building on Austrian views, particularly those of Mises. (Many link themselves to this tradition, but none seems to match their masters. The Cato Institute is good at commissioning applications of the ideas such as Boaz and Crane 1993. Hughes 1991 represents an anti-intervention discussion that eschews ideology.) Their arguments may actually say considerably less than even their developers believe. They and similar writers, however, are much less extreme, much closer to more standard economics, and much more correct than many economists admit.

The Austrian opponents of statism appear too confident about the exact form the reductions should take. Hayek's view that the economic system is too complex to comprehend fully should be taken very literally. Humility about policy proposals is the appropriate reaction to imperfect comprehension. However, to provide an effective exposition, Hayek had to adopt the paradoxical approach of being certain that uncertainty prevailed.

Although Austrians basically have updated David Hume and Adam Smith, the Viennese versions are particularly unattractive to many of those who admire Adam Smith. Supporters of economic liberalism have come from outside the Austrian tradition. While the substance of their argument is consistent with the views expressed here, the Austrians can be overly arrogant. Therefore, a more appropriate term might be Scottish economics or simply liberalism. Those objecting to strong anti-intervention views, moreover, have not maintained the balanced and restrained moderation purportedly supported. Few economists critical of market-oriented writings have bothered to respond with anything approaching the depth of the challengers. This failure is inherent. The anti-intervention case is more central to economics than its critics wish to admit.

Mises, Hayek, and similar writers encounter frequent misstatements about economic issues (and themselves). Hayek (1978, 305) has argued that his efforts to stimulate a reasoned debate of the issues must be refuted by more than personal attacks on the writers. (See Hayek 1978, 309 for examples of how two other Nobel laureates, Myrdal and Leontief, displayed ignorance of Hayek's work; Leontief claimed Hayek was not qualified to write on planning; Myrdal contended Hayek was ignorant of epistemology.) Hayek's complaint was often confirmed.

Too often in the economics literature, writers attack the ideologues while adopting their ideas. Many writers endorse Hayek's views about the impossibility of securing adequate data to allow effective regulation but too readily dismiss as extremist his assertions about the implications. Prior discussion here suggested Hayek's critiques deserve careful consideration.

This book ignores the leading U.S. advocates of expanded government. These critics are omitted because their attacks on market economies involve conscious rejection by self-proclaimed rebels against the economic principles that all those discussed here (and I) accept.

A Note on the Meaning of Liberalism

Many economists with policy views similar to Stigler's reject his willingness to be considered a conservative. Schumpeter, Mises, Hayek, and Milton Friedman have insisted that the correct term for their outlook is liberalism. (Stigler's choice of terms may reflect the origin of the article as a talk at Harvard; the attribution of conservatism would have had more impact on his audience than that of perversion of liberalism.)

Schumpeter (1954), for example, identifies "removing fetters from the private-enterprise economy" with Economic Liberalism. He quickly adds "the term has acquired a different--in fact almost the opposite--meaning since about 1900 and especially since about 1930: as a supreme, if unintended, compliment, the enemies of the system of private enterprise have thought it wise to appropriate its label (1954, 394)." This is discussed further in chapter 13 in which the argument that liberalism is the best term is endorsed.

Hayek (1960) has an appendix called "Why I Am Not a Conservative"; Friedman (1962, 5) makes similar points. Mises does likewise in the 1962 preface (xvi) to the English translation of his 1927 *Liberalismus* and the 1963 foreword (v) to the revised edition of *Human Action*. Mises was so concerned about the changing meaning of liberalism that the original title given the translation of *Liberalismus* was *The Free and Prosperous Commonwealth*; the 1986 edition is called *Liberalism: In the Classical Tradition*.)

"Austrian" Economics Reconsidered

The main problem with the Austrians is their aggressive stance. This is a problem particularly with Mises. His propensity to overstate his case troubles even his admirers. Some aspects of his exposition seem indefensible. His *Human Action* denounces empirical analysis, use of mathematics, and other tools many other economists find useful. The overall impression given is that Mises believes he is the only sound economist and that the way to truth is to trust him.

Mises inspired considerable animosity even among other critics of etatism. For example, Frank Knight (1956, 170) dismisses a characterization by Hutchinson of Mises as the "leader of contemporary Economic Liberalism." Knight says this description is untrue "unless this means the academic opponent of socialism most conspicuous for the extremism of his position." Even admirers such as Butler (1988) and Rothbard (1988) recognize Mises's tendency towards scathing attacks. This nastiness is unattractive and inspires unwillingness to give Mises unqualified endorsement or accept him as one's prime inspiration. To ignore him, however, seems equally inappropriate. Once the invective is scraped away, much value remains.

His works still are critiques unavailable elsewhere of the defects of statism and of the virtues of a market economy. Such defenses of the market system are welcome because so much of economics is concerned with evaluating regulation rather than explaining the market alternative. Even the more analytic discussions associated with the Chicago school are more attacks on dirigisme than defenses of a spontaneous market order. Mises also made major contributions to the attack on intervention.

conduct of debates suggest that Mises's methodological arguments contain valuable insights. Mises's contention that economic relationships change too rapidly to be captured by conventional statistical techniques nicely epitomizes still prevalent problems. Had he been more circumspect, Mises might be hailed as the anticipator of criticisms that formal theoretical and statistical studies are far less conclusive than their developers promised. Satisfactory analyses had to be left to those such as Lucas, able and willing to master the intricacies of econometrics (statistical analyses of economic problems).

Mises also was objecting to the attack on theoretical economics based on the contention associated with the German historical approach that principles could be inferred from observation (see, e.g., Schumpeter 1954, 800-24). Empirical studies originally were guided by that principle. Mises failed to note that, as shown here in chapter 4, a theory-based approach to applied analysis had emerged when *Human Action* first appeared. He recognized that the most conclusive appraisals would be ignored by those unwilling to relinquish prior views. Moreover, his practice was better than his explanation. His concept of "apriorism" (e.g., 1966, chapter 2) suggested that ideas emerge by deduction. He created the impression that this deduction was guided solely by instinct. An enormous amount of observation of experience and of other writings actually fills his work.

Another troubling aspect of the Austrian movement is the feuding between Mises and Schumpeter. As the quotation above from Schumpeter on liberalism suggests and further reading confirms, the differences of substance among Schumpeter, Mises, and Hayek are small. The points on which Schumpeter differs most from the other two are the least satisfactory in his arguments.

Schumpeter contributed major elements in the current promarket case-- recognition of the superiority of private markets in promoting economic progress, indication that such innovations disturb equilibrium, and warning of the rise an intellectual class ignorant of and opposed to a market economy.

The critical dispute among the Austrians was over how to appraise the problems of capitalism. Schumpeter (1950) contends that these difficulties are so deep and irreversible that socialism is inevitable. Capitalism is seen as routinized, bureaucratized, and hemmed in by statism. His (1950) economic theory of democracy as competition for votes (see chapter 6) proved more insightful, prophetic, and useful than his analysis of capitalism and socialism.

Schumpeter (1950) chose to side with Lange (1936-7) in the debate with Hayek and Mises about whether a socialist state could establish efficient prices. Lange claimed that a planning board could compute such prices. (Recall the treatment of Lange in chapter 6) By accepting Lange's premise, Schumpeter could conclude that workable socialism was possible. A critical requirement is that many responsibilities be delegated to the bureaucracy (Schumpeter 1950, 293-4). His discussion ends with hints of concerns over the attainability of this ideal. The remainder of his book treats socialist practice. While he avoids broad condemnation, he also notes disturbing experiences with socialist practice. (With hindsight, these remarks can be dismissed as watered down Mises.)

One possible explanation of this analysis is that Schumpeter felt that something more subtle than Mises's frontal attacks was needed. *Capitalism, Socialism, and Democracy* may be an effort of an admirer of capitalism to show that even after ceding the feasibility-of-socialism argument to Lange, the resulting socialist society still would have unattractive features and not improve on true capitalism.

Other, not necessarily mutually exclusive, explanations are possible. Schumpeter's (1954) review of economic thought is notorious for dissents with standard evaluations of famous economists. In particular, he is very critical of Adam Smith and, as in prior writings, very admiring of Karl Marx. These views follow from Schumpeter's decision to make originality of thought the criterion of merit. This may reflect a tendency to excessive admiration of cleverness. To Schumpeter, a correct synthesis is less interesting than an incorrect brilliant new argument. Mises may not have been an innovative thinker, but his syntheses attracted attention because they were effective.

Mises ironically ended up as a key influential synthesizer of prior arguments, many of which were from Schumpeter. Thus, commentators on Mises such as Butler (1983) and Rothbard (1988) stress Mises's concern with the very Schumpeterian themes of innovation and disequilibrium. The citations Butler and Rothbard provided and a comparison of *Human Action* with *Liberalism* suggest that emphasis on these concepts was added late in the development of Mises's thought. In effect, after Schumpeter muted his support of capitalism and joined in repudiating Mises's critique of socialism, Mises responded by strengthening his defense by more explicit use of Schumpeter's insights. Mises's disciples went on to stress Schumpeter's later enthusiasm for economic formalism over his contributions to Austrian thought.

Schumpeter's analysis of the struggle between capitalism and socialism obviously now seems less satisfactory than those of Mises and Hayek. Discontent with Schumpeter indeed arose when the Iron Curtain fell over Eastern Europe. Direct attacks on intervention and explicit defenses of the liberal market system have greater intrinsic appeal. Mises and Hayek provide a better framework than Schumpeter's.

One critical defect seems to be Schumpeter's theory of bureaucratization. Neither the prediction that capitalism would become routinized and hidebound nor the faith in management by civil service proved valid. Ample evidence exists that innovative capitalism is thriving. Those of us who lived through the postSchumpeter era witnessed profound changes through innovation (for a formal review, see, e.g., Porter 1990). Many observers have recognized that faith in an impartial bureaucracy was misplaced (see, e.g., Nelson 1987 and for an excellent study of the milieu in which the faith developed, Hofstadter 1955). Schumpeter's key concession to the interventionists thus proved acceptance of a concept that has proven untenable.

Hayek seems to have been even more seriously misunderstood by friends as well as foes. Perhaps his writings are so extensive that few have examined enough to recognize the complexity of his views. Others might argue he is unclear. Hayek was well aware, at least in his later writings, that much intervention was intended to be limited and arose from nonideological sources. He also recognized the more germane point that policies of this type also could be unsound.

Hayek is best thought of as warning that stated policy goals can be attained only by intolerably repressive policies. He is aware that one possible outcome (the one regularly observed in U.S. practice) is enforcement too restrained to meet the goals. This is most clearly seen in his critique of the U.S. planning rage of the 1970s ([1976] 1978). He notes that interference can be futile or disastrous. Thus, tyranny lies not in dalliance but determination.

Ambiguity, more typical of Hayek than is recognized, arises precisely because he is not a doctrinaire ideologue. He relies on his professional judgment about what seems likely, rather than propounding more extreme, totally clear positions. We must look to others for more concrete proposals. Milton Friedman's (1962) great contribution of presenting a well-developed program of specific reforms represents a leading effort to provide such a supplement.

The view that Hayek is not an extremist has at least one distinguished supporter outside the enthusiasts. Viner's review (reprinted in Viner 1991) of *The Constitution of Liberty* correctly notes how much government action is endorsed. Starting with a 1927 essay on Adam Smith, the 1991 reprinted essays of Viner frequently note that Smith and the leading nineteenth century advocates of a market economy defined laissez-faire to mean the limitation rather than the elimination of government. Rothbard (1988) denounces these concessions by Hayek as an unfortunate break from Mises's superior vision rather than sensible moderation (see below).

Some, including admirers, suggest Hayek goes further and contends that intervention cannot be kept limited. Samuelson's examination of Hayek's policy views concentrate on the alleged deficiencies of *The Road to Serfdom*. Samuelson (1986, 791) accuses Hayek's book of arguing that "partial reform was the sure path to total tyranny." The book actually endorses several interventions such as social insurance (Hayek 1944, 120-1) and public utility regulation (Hayek 1944, 198). Given Samuelson's sweeping attacks and apparent neglect of Hayek's later work, Samuelson may be overreacting to the success of the book when his concept of a neoclassical synthesis (see below) was struggling to become established.

In a laudatory précis of Hayek's thought, Butler (1983) often makes comments similar to Samuelson's about fears of the danger of involvement in planning (e.g., 1, 10, 85). (These comments also share with Samuelson a failure to cite specific statements by Hayek making this point.) Butler writes, "...the most modest dalliance with these ideas would lead to disaster if they were pursued consistently (1)." Given Hayek's recognition noted above that disaster could be avoided by inconsistent pursuit, the last two words are more critical than Butler indicates.

None of the market-oriented authors except Mises, argue for a literal interpretation of laissez-faire or even, for the minimal watchman or caretaker state. Laissez-faire is an unfortunate term since most relentless opponents of statism recognize the need for a state at least to protect law and order. Aaron Director (1964, 1) states "Laissez-faire has never been more than a slogan in defense of the proposition that every extension of state activity should be examined under a presumption of error."[1] Similarly, a narrow view of the caretaker state as one that only protects law and order may be too limited.

Hayek's main target was not modest reform, but the excessive influence of those insensitive to the dangers of dirigisme--nineteenth century reactionaries and twentieth century fellow travelers. His choice of heroes and villains has survived well. Concern over the divergence between criticisms of the book and my reaction has inspired several reexaminations. Each strengthens my convictions. A look at

---

[1] This quote was used by Bork (1989, 225) in his discussion of the proper role of a judiciary. Director's article, when examined, proved to present the remark incidentally to a discussion of problems of appropriate policies outside the marketplace. In reading another book, I learned J. S. Mill's *Principles of Political Economy* (950 in the still in print Ashley edition) states "Laissez-faire, in short, should be the general practice: every departure from it, unless required by some great good, is a certain evil." The qualification nearly vitiates Mill's statement. Such equivocation is why to many commentators Mill is a prime source of the decline of classical liberalism.

those attacked shows they include the Webbs, Harold Laski, E. H. Carr, Bertrand Russell, Thomas Carlyle, and Werner Sombart. These are hardly moderate reformers.

Counterattacks: The Case of Paul Samuelson

While anti-intervention economics is often viewed warily, the most accessible critiques appear in various articles in Paul Samuelson's (esp. 1977 and 1986) collected papers. In this book as in much of the economics literature, Samuelson plays an important, but ambiguous role. His contributions made him a critical positive influence on modern economics. He produced invaluable theoretical work and showed strong understanding of the virtues and limitations of economics. His 1948 introductory text provided the model on which most of its successors are based. He ventured into applied areas later leading theorists ignored and made frequent efforts to present his views to general readers. In the last, he did better at more analytic matters such as sound personal investing than at policy analysis.

Samuelson (e.g., 1977, 876; 1986, 271, 315) simultaneously supports Hayek in the socialist calculation debate and, as shown, denounces Hayek's policy views. Samuelson tries to support the belief that interference can be tamed. He argues that limits can be set on involvement, processes can be made more impartial, and monitoring can be more careful. In practice, Samuelson accepts many of the criticisms of specific policies.

His overall efforts were described as providing a neoclassical synthesis. The goal was to modify traditional economic theory to allow active efforts by governments at least to lessen unemployment and inflation. A further proposal, with much earlier antecedents, was for governments to act more forcefully to lessen inequalities in individual incomes. This was to be combined with the traditional views about the proper roles of governments and private firms in individual markets. The synthesis sought to retain proper appreciation of the virtues of markets and the drawbacks of government. Whether it succeeded is the key issue. Such a view can understate the concerns of economists over excesses of government. Sound economic judgment may be sacrificed to prevailing intellectual fashions.

Mises and Hayek seemed enemies of a neoclassical synthesis. This synthesis proposed various weakenings in the anti-intervention tradition. Growing concerns about the synthesis made Mises and Hayek seem less antiquated. As discussed in chapter 8, the case for economic stabilization policy, about which Mises and Hayek were critical, is under increasing challenge. Appreciation of the operation of markets has increased. As is only briefly examined here, programs to alleviate poverty have proved more difficult to implement than their advocates expected.

Comments scattered in Samuelson's writings (e.g., 1986, 790) suggest that another influence may be the effect of the unhappy experience in dealing with American communism in the decade after World War II. Samuelson felt "Worshippers of laissez-faire...were insensitive and on the whole unsympathetic toward the rights and personal freedoms of scholars." Samuelson indicated that his conclusions emerged from the outcomes of private conversations. The public record is clearest in showing that some noneconomist admirers of Austrian economics were guilty of Samuelson's charges. Evidence is not readily available that the Austrians themselves were suppressing anyone's freedoms. In fact, their admirers complain that Mises and Hayek were not granted academic positions commensurate with their ability. Hayek was only affiliated with a general education program at the University of Chicago. Special private funding supported Mises in teaching night courses at New York University's Business School. In other writings, Samuelson identified a clearer source of villainy, the exclusionary policies prevailing in faculty hiring in all fields at U.S. universities. Mason (1982) gives a good sense of how this problem operated at Harvard.

The fundamental problem with Samuelson is that he had tried unsuccessfully to reconcile his admiration for conflicting views. A reading of his statements on policy and the history of economics suggest that he was profoundly influenced by traditional market-oriented economics. He also was an advocate of government action to stabilize the economy and redistribute income. He was an enthusiast of Adam Smith, Walras, Schumpeter, and Keynes. Samuelson tried to evade the conflicts among these views. The resurgence in classical economics is response to the failures of moderate controls. Undesirable misguided etatism can occur without evil.

A large subjective element prevails in determining what is the correct vision of what a modern economy should be. U.S. and British economists trained from the thirties through the sixties probably were guided by a perception that too much reluctance to intervene prevailed. The Keynesian revolution of the 1930s and its ascendancy in the years immediately after World War II accelerated a tendency among economists toward lessening opposition to interference.

Mises, Hayek, and similar people had histories profoundly different from those of their critics. Mises and Hayek were heavily influenced by their ordeal with the Nazis. The last version of Mises's *Socialism* (1981) makes evident the impact of his encounters. His criticisms treat Prussian state socialism, Nazism, and Soviet communism as part of the same disease (see, e.g., the discussions of State Socialism, 212-20, compulsory social insurance, 429-32, the welfare state, 520-1, and Nazism, 528-32). The danger of excess interference seemed the key concern. In retrospect, those concerned with tyranny had identified the more lasting problem.

Another influence is that writings for noneconomists must provide detail and repetition that no trained economists believe they need. Ennui occurs. This explanation, however, is inappropriate for similar attacks on the more formal criticisms of intervention discussed above.

A Digression on Libertarianism: the Elimination of the State

Some advocates of free markets suggest considering narrowing the scope of the state even further. Concepts of free market law and order have been proposed (see Becker and Stigler 1974, its review in Posner 1986, and Benson 1990). Here theory may be imitating fiction. Robert A. Heinlein's *The Moon is a Harsh Mistress* (1966) portrays the moon as a penal colony with free-market justice. (The book is also the source of converting a slangy version of the infamous slogan that supposedly epitomizes economics "there ain't no such thing as a free lunch" into the acronym Tanstaafl. As chapter 2 notes, the aphorism ignores how markets increase individual welfare by lowering prices. It is not only that we must pay a price that matters.)

Some extreme libertarians go further and propose abolishing the state. Market alternatives would be adopted for every government activity. Murray Rothbard (1978) is the strongest exponent of this position. His view suffers from excess confidence and reliance on a shared-guilt explanation of the cold war to minimize the problem of national defense. A later Rothbard (1988) effort, his sketch of the contribution of Mises, provides particularly clear evidence of Rothbard's excessive zeal. Rothbard pillories Hayek for insufficient loyalty mainly because of Hayek's stress on the unplanned. Rothbard is concerned in the first case about neglect of the heroic role of entrepreneurs. Hayek is dealing with a different problem about which Mises was also concerned of the limits to individual influence. Mises regularly noted his heroes continuously faced failure.

Even worse is Rothbard's (1988) dubious descriptions of Hayek, the man who wrote (1960) of "The Myth of the Welfare State" as an advocate of the welfare state, and of Haberler and Machlup as Keynesians. No reader of *Prosperity and Depression* would confuse Haberler as a Keynesian, and Machlup also seems too classically liberal to qualify. Rothbard's implicit contention that Mises had a narrower concept of the proper state than did the three former students seems correct. However, Mises's view also is not Rothbard's either (see the chapter on war in Mises 1966, 821-32). Hayek and Rothbard diverged from Mises in opposite ways. Hayek adopted the more traditional approach, recognized by Viner (1991), of qualifying the anarchy plus a watchman view held by Mises; Rothbard wants to abolish the watchman.

David Friedman (1989) provided a more satisfactory approach. He admits the need for national defense instead of using Rothbard's evasion. As David Friedman (1989, 146-7) points out, the concept of limited government fails in theory and practice to indicate exactly where government activity should cease. Nothing will work except challenging everything. He is careful to recognize the difficulties involved, and while the effort may fail, he still considers it desirable.

Rothbard and David Friedman expose a disturbing neglected point. The strong tradition, dating back at least to Aristotle, that governments are indispensable, heavily influences discussions including most of those denounced as extremist. Once the validity of government action is questioned, the only logically consistent position is that everything must be appraised. Whether this logic is sensible is less clear. The advocates, particularly Rothbard, seem unduly confident about what the outcome will be. They adopt a far stronger position than is necessary here. The milder argument, that much intervention is obviously undesirable, is being made. To criticize clearly inefficient, protectionist arguments, pushing the promarket case to its logical extreme is unnecessary.

However, candor and logical consistency require admission that Rothbard and David Friedman have unearthed a problem in the criticisms of government. Arguments, rather than going to extremes, are restrained by tradition. Such caution is prudent. No economic principle has been demonstrated conclusively. Professional judgment is employed to reach conclusions. Reliance on this consensus has made economics an effective, useful discipline. Acceptance of David Friedman's research program is different from expecting it to prove that it is possible to eliminate government.

A Note on the Illusions of Indicative Planning and Coordinated Policy

Observers of public policy often decry its prevailing state and call for a coordinated policy or plan to alleviate the deficiencies. Concerns, for example, are expressed over the entire natural resource realm or some subareas, such as public lands, all minerals (in the popular sense that includes fossil fuels), energy, and nonenergy minerals.[2] This is often a call for some general, nonsocialist national plan. Such proposals inspired the Hayek discussion of ineffective planning treated above. While broad planning never caught on, sectorial plans are often proposed, and this tendency is particularly persistent with energy and minerals. The experience should provide ample warning of the drawbacks of the idea. However, the persistence of failure to learn from this experience was what inspired this book. Supporters of coordination profess to believe that policy could consist of agreeing to return significant amounts of decision making to the private sector. The sincerity of this contention is questionable.

The difficulties are illustrated by U.S. experience. The U.S. government is vigorously devoted to formal study of policy issues. Congress has several special agencies whose sole role is preparing studies; the National Research Council regularly undertakes policy review assignments; parts of the executive branch are often asked to conduct investigations; many independent commissions (inevitably dubbed blue-ribbon panels) are created. As part of this process, the United States has conducted many studies relating to natural resource policy.

Similar efforts have occurred in other countries. Since the inception of the European Economic Community in 1959, the member countries tried unsuccessfully to develop rational agricultural and energy policies. A subsequent search for a better steel policy emerged (see, e.g., Mény and Wright 1986). The difficulties of removing unwise policies inspired a push to Europe 1992--a program to attain many of the thus-far thwarted policy objectives by 1992. The limitations of the initiative are demonstrated by the incompleteness of attainment by 1994.

Some government policy studies have led to changes in the details of public policy. None have produced anything faintly resembling the radical transformations purportedly desired. The record suggests that, at least in the U.S., studies are a substitute for action. To avoid a controversial decision, a group is appointed to contemplate the issues. Long after interest has waned, a report emerges and is ignored. In contrast, the ending of the mass of controls on U.S. energy during the 1980s was effected piecemeal and very quietly. Elaborate studies were avoided. This record reflects widespread practical recognition of the defects of the calls for coordination.

Using the term coordination.to serve as the rallying point for a better policy strains credulity. The concept of coordination is at best vague and tainted by the close identity between it and protectionism. The term "coordinated policy" too often means vigorous continuing government involvement. Claims that inaction is a possible "policy" would be more plausible if we could believe that advocates of coordination would seriously consider a market alternative. Calls for coordination most often come from either those ideologically committed to statism or from groups seeking protection of their interests. Those advocating reduced regulation prefer to use terms such as policy reform or deregulation that convey clear opposition to dirigisme.

As with Hayek's concern over the welfare state and social justice, acceptance of the term coordination may bias the discussion. The counterargument is that this

---

[2]A strict mineralogical definition of minerals confines them to inorganics with defined structures. Here an energy and mineral distinction is used only because energy policy has become more separate from those for nonfuel minerals.

makes too much of a fuss over form. The implication is that no one can oppose coordination because it is such an encompassing concept. While this argument is formally correct, its sincerity is suspect for the reasons just stated. We should shift to frank comparison between dirigisme and free markets. To reiterate the earlier discussion, the gigantic literature (see chapter 6) on the defects of massive intervention is applicable to (and supported by experience with) regulation of specific sectors.

At least two other difficulties are involved with designing and implementing a coordinated intervention policy of any sort. First, bitter discord about what comprises appropriate reform created the prevailing policy deficiencies and precludes reform. Protectionists, for example, battle with free traders. As the French Nobel laureate economist, Maurice Allais, stressed in 1962, advocates of coordination ignore such problems of producing consensus. He proved prophetic in his chosen case, energy. European energy policy in 1994 is still fragmented and filled with unwise intervention.

Another problem is defining the coverage of policy. The appropriate scope of an energy or mineral policy is unclear. This was illustrated by the experience in creating the U.S. Department of Energy (DOE). Failure occurred in developing a fresh, comprehensive, undiluted approach to energy (see Ogden 1978). Many, probably most, critical decisions affecting energy were not transferred to DOE. The Department of the Interior (DOI) continued to administer leasing or claiming energy minerals on public lands; the Environmental Protection Agency and the states still regulated air pollution; the Nuclear Regulatory Commission kept responsibility for licensing nuclear plants; federal regulation of natural gas and electricity continued to be handled by an independent agency. (The agency had its name changed from the Federal Power Commission to the Federal Energy Regulatory Commission, was given control of oil pipelines, and was placed within the Department of Energy without losing its independence.)

In every case, the issues were felt to belong primarily to another realm. Leasing, for example, was effectively considered primarily a land management issue; pollution, an environmental matter.

DOE proved largely an amalgamation of the hastily erected new energy regulatory and analytic groups of the Federal Energy Administration with the Energy Research and Development Administration (ERDA). ERDA, in turn, was created largely to assume the military and civilian nuclear development responsibilities of the Atomic Energy Commission (AEC); much smaller fossil fuel programs were transferred from DOI. Despite the two changes, the AEC tradition is heavily influential. Nuclear weaponry is still a major concern. The national laboratories created to facilitate bomb development were asked to play a major role in civilian nonnuclear research. DOE may be a bomb maker that considers energy on the side.

Conclusions

This chapter examined critical aspects of the strong attacks on statism. The basic proposition is that such attacks largely are standard principles vigorously stated. The Chicago school uses academic journals to develop its attacks on intervention. By muting their polemicism, the Chicago economists succeed at presenting stronger cases than do its ideologues without provoking the denunciations heaped on the latter. The Austrians and other polemicists overstate but not to the extent their critics cases than do its ideologues without provoking the denunciations heaped on the latter. The Austrians and other polemicists overstate but not to the extent their critics assert. The Austrian case for markets and against dirigisme is closer to standard economics that its attackers recognize. Chicago and the Austrians both revitalize the case for Adam Smith's form of liberalism. Conversely, Samuelson's efforts to find a middle ground proved unconvincing, and indicative planning is doomed to failure. Hayek is correct that successful planning would be tyrannical and unrepressive plans would fail. The stateless society is intellectually fascinating, but the world must first abolish clearly bad policies before experimenting with market alternatives to services traditionally considered governmental.

Chapter 13

Conclusions

Excessive intervention remains the primary defect of policy making. Noneconomists have strong interventionist instincts. Democratic governments too often think that their restraint is sufficient to avoid error. The evidence refutes this.

Economists often understate their concerns about limited intervention. This book presents the arguments against statism, widely accepted, but inadequately expressed by economists. In this chapter, the key points are reiterated and related to classic liberalism. I conclude that classic liberalism is the best guide ever devised for a free, progressive society.

This book begins with remarks about attitudes among economists about regulation of markets. Attention turns to what economic theory says about markets, nationally or internationally. Then responses to the complexities of actual markets are appraised. These approaches prove so effective that government policies to stabilize markets are unnecessary. The next chapters deal with economic instability, income distribution, environmental problems, and land-law experience. The policy views in economics are examined more fully.

Here the key specific conclusions are reiterated and applied to broader issues. The themes of chapters 1 and 12 are that:

1. Unwise intervention is widespread.
2. The defects of regulation are less well understood by noneconomists than the apparent virtues.
3. Skepticism about intervention is central to economics.
4. Economists emphasizing the defects of etatism are expressing concerns widely held in the discipline.
5. Other economists are too reluctant to admit their concerns about excessive regulation.

Chapter 2 sketches several key propositions about markets. Differences among households and firms in the appraisal of the benefits of changing the composition of their existing wealth create opportunities for mutually beneficial trade. Trade, in turn, leads ultimately to a reallocation in which no further changes are worth taking. Market prices are the signals by which opportunities for trade are indicated. Money is used to simplify trading. Participation in a market economy encourages specialization and innovation. Thus, people benefit themselves and others by learning to do a few things well. Rewards are attained by devising new products or processes with wide appeal.

Modern economics recognizes that markets and governments are complex entities. To make the analysis manageable, many separate models are used. The key model is of general equilibrium. It covers the simplest possible economy with multiproduct production, trade, and consumption. This suffices to convey the essential points.

The differences that justify dealing are recognized. The process of trading goods for a standard of value and using that standard of value to secure other goods is described. The attainment of equilibrium is explained. In this simple model, equilibrium is synonymous with undertaking all mutually beneficial reallocations of resources.

Numerous analyses deal with the complications that the general equilibrium model ignores. Several principles guide these extensions. A primary influence is consideration of the expenses of decision making, transaction costs. Such costs limit profitable public and private action. Transaction costs often make inaction by both the public and private sectors the efficient policy. Even if action is efficient, the preferability of public over private action, however, still depends on the specific situation in every case. Coase's warning that appraisals give too little weight to the drawbacks of government deserves more attention.

The concerns relate especially to the transaction costs of knowledge (and information exchange) about production technology and market conditions. This was the focus of Hayek's work. The division of labor in a private market economy is a superior system for dealing with these problems. Another closely related consideration is that proper assignment of property rights is critical to easing the transaction cost problem. Property-law reform is an attractive, often neglected way to increase efficiency.

Given the implications of transaction costs, problems termed market failure (treated in chapters 3, 4, and 5) and government failure (in chapter 6) can arise. These include providing commodities such as national defense and environmental amenities that are consumed simultaneously by all members of society, monopoly, distorting taxes, and imperfect capital markets. Given the focus of this book, discussion of collective consumption only covers externalities. The difficulties of resolving the problem are noted. Coase's contention that the rationale is overused is viewed sympathetically. Similarly, little is said about taxes. While they probably are the source of more distortions than all the prevailing market failures of inefficiency, tax problems are so well treated in many books by specialists in the field that discussion here is redundant. Capital market imperfections are dismissed for a quite different reason. The contentions seem implausible. Capital markets function better than theorists admit.

Stress is on an issue critical to this study, monopoly, the focus of chapter 4. It is argued that in practice the apparently heated debates over monopoly are over fine points. Many economists doubt that private monopoly is widespread or that anticompetitive tactics such as predation are widely used. Some observers seem primarily concerned with the remaining monopolies and their tactics. Others only fear government policies to undermine competition. Here, the last view is considered more plausible. Such issues in international economics as optimum policy, use of national monopoly power, fostering new industry, and preventing dumping are examined in chapter 5. It is concluded again that the free trade tradition remains valid.

Problems arise in the practical application of the public good, its externality variant, and other market-failure arguments. As discussed in chapter 6, the information problems that are involved with public goods are problematic for public as well as private solutions. Uncertainty about how much market failure exists is great. Economic theories of political decision making explain the incentives for adopting inefficient policies (chapter 6). Governments fail because of pressure group activities and the problems of controlling the bureaucracy. Economic theories of vote

seeking, regulation, and bureaucratic behavior conclude that it is beneficial to
politicians to adopt economically inefficient policies.

These problems are not easily overcome. The record of groups purporting to
represent broader viewpoints is depressing. The environmentalists are prone to
elitism and rigidity. Public interest crusaders are generally enemies of free markets
and want to impose their wills. Traditional conservatives only wanted to reallocate
the benefits of statism. This is why classic liberals so often denied being
conservatives. While the limits of minimum government remain to be determined, it
is clear that the best reform of many policies is abolition.

Many devices are available to facilitate adaptation to changing market
conditions. These include long-term contracts, commodity exchanges, brokers,
inventories, and flexible organizations. Chapter 7 examines the existence and use of
such devices. Discussion begins with a review of the problems in defining markets
and commodities. Stress is given the nature of contracting. Energy and mineral
experiences are used to illustrate how reorganization and contract adjustment arose to
ease adjustment to gyrations in the markets. The principles also are used to challenge
the conduct of public-utility regulation. The possibility that inaction is the best
feasible policy is so great that more serious discussion of deregulation is essential.
Commodity stabilization schemes including the U.S. oil stockpile are considered
indefensible.

The issues of economic stabilization are examined in chapter 8. It is suggested
that critics of active stabilization policy have clearly succeeded in convincing many
economists that ambitions about controlling overall economic performance should be
limited. The critics failed to agree among themselves about the best alternative. This
naturally leads to an inability to convince others about what is best. It is agreed that
regulating markets is not a satisfactory way to stabilize an economy.

Another difficult issue is the appropriate sharing of wealth (chapter 9). A
balance must be struck among individual rights to property, the need for economic
incentives, and concerns for the poor. Satisfactory criteria of desirable goals do not
exist. Those who sought to provide them invariably failed. Regulating markets is a
poor way to improve the distribution of income. At best, more distortions are
introduced than occur with direct aid. Intervention in markets, moreover, tends to aid
the less deserving.

The theory and practice of environmental policy and of regulating health, safety,
and similar problems are reviewed in chapter 10. It is suggested the experience with
regulatory approaches is again less satisfactory than popularly recognized. Chapter
11 uses the experience in energy to argue that U.S. government land management is
defective and unlikely to be improved. The tradition of encouraging transfer to
private ownership should be revived.

The discussion in chapter 12 supports the statement in chapter 2 on economic
attitudes. Economic theory is not a clear vigorous defense of laissez-faire. Economics
also provides the most powerful available rationales for *intervention*. The long list of
market failures discussed in chapter 3 can be and has been used to justify much
regulation. Analysis suggests that only monopoly and publicness justifications for
regulating markets meet even minimal standards of reasonability. Their precise
implication in theory and practice is unclear.

Resolving these issues has defied the greatest minds in economics. Economic
analysis has proved incapable of settling these issues. The extensive theorizing about
market failures has produced the standard theoretic conclusion that impacts depend

upon actual conditions. Resolution depends on the facts, and the Hayek principle suggests they are prohibitively expensive to obtain. Thus, heavy reliance is placed on professional judgment. Faults as well as virtues should be recognized. Skepticism about everything including the validity of one's own arguments should be maintained. (The prior statement implies that it is suspect itself--a difficulty that commonly arises in trying to explain unresolvable problems.)

Considerable evidence was found that the judgments about intervention involve great distrust of government controls. Economic theory and experience produce suspicion of government. The distrust arises, not from subservience to any persons or ideologies, but from disillusion with those whom we hoped would implement desired reforms. Too many policies satisfy none of the economic rationalizations for action. Many others might be, but in practice are not, justifiable by economic principles. The true rationale is that some group has enough influence to receive protection. As noted, rarely are the influential clearly deserving.

This book advocates the removal of clearly defective policies. The examples were selected by observing historical experience. The observation motivated very belated appreciation of anti-intervention writings. Both the vigorous critics of regulation and those seeking to moderate their views contribute to confusion over what constitutes clearly defective government policies. The consensus about the extent of clearly undesirable intervention is obscured. Given the political resistance, decades of effort are needed to remove the policies that are almost universally condemned in the economics literature. Others have more ambitious agendas, and they may or may not be right. The case for massive privatization is impressive but not conclusive.

Several viewpoints on the true state of actual markets coexist in the economics literature. Part of these divergences of appraisal is that what some see as market failures others perceive as adaptation to transaction costs. A more important influence is differences of opinion about what is critical. Some see excess intervention as the primary evil. Others are more concerned about residual market failures.

Those who stress lessened intervention start with the premise that given the clear costs of regulation, it should not be imposed unless clear evidence of its necessity prevails. Director's (1964) strengthening of Mill's (1848) dictum about the meaning of laissez-faire clearly expresses this view. The advocates of intervention implicitly counter that since the costs of market failure are so hard to measure, the presumption of innocence should not be adopted without strong evidence.

I believe the first position is the correct one. However, the more modest argument that much clearly bad regulation prevails suffices. Considerable evidence exists that many specific claims of market failure are suspect. Case studies of regulation usually indicate it works badly and is difficult, if not impossible, to reform. Even policies attempting to correct real inefficiencies may worsen things. Comparable evidence of important neglected examples of market failures is unavailable. The alleged market failure often does not exist.

It is premature to expect that anyone can conclusively determine exactly which government regulations make positive contributions. Worse, even when good justification seems to exist, as in the pollution realm, it is not clear that actual policies are beneficial. Concerns with government failure increased in the 1980s. For example, even advocates of public-utility regulation recognize existing controls are too rigid. The dangers of etatism are illustrated by the difficulties arising in maintaining interest in deregulation.

It is now time to provide a list of what reforms seem essential. The first is the abandonment of all traditional forms of protection. These include most barriers to international trade, price controls, and subsidy programs. Possible exceptions in international trade might arise with munitions and specialized technologies with direct military applications.

Protection of industries should end. Stress should be on ceasing to retard the contraction of declining sectors. Free-market agriculture should be established everywhere. All rent controls should be abolished. Minimum wage laws and laws requiring payment of locally prevailing wages should terminate. Tariffs and subsidies for industries should be ended. The candidates include steel everywhere, automobiles in the U.S., and coal in Germany and Britain. The French should abandon their mania for investing in unprofitable advanced technologies.

Government policy toward monopoly should be restrained. The perversion of economic principles to protect weak competitors should be abandoned. Price fixing should continue to be at least legally unenforceable and probably banned. Efforts to restructure industry seem no more urgent than they were in the first century of the Sherman Act. The efforts of the 1980s to lessen restrictions on mergers seem largely beneficial. For instance, the anticompetitive effects of even such monster mergers as General Electric with RCA were limited by growing linkages of markets.

The scope of natural monopoly policy should be reduced. At most, a few industries such as electric power and local gas and water distribution might be monopolistic enough to merit control. Regulation is preferable to ownership. If maintained, major reforms are needed in this regulation.

Deregulation probably is preferable to feasible regulation. Our regulators wasted seventeen years of opportunities to provide regulations adaptable to shocks to the system. Fixation was over avoiding rate increases. Construction of capacity that could reduce oil and gas use was discouraged. Several nearly completed and even one completed plant were blocked. Undue faith was placed on conservation and alternative energy. All industries in which no problems of publicness arise should be privatized. This would include farming, mining, mineral processing, retail banking, airlines, and manufacturing.

Conversely, U.S. reluctance to allow industry-wide cooperative ventures seems desirable. The growing literature on Japan with input from first-hand observers (especially Porter 1990) suggests the importance and success of cooperation were exaggerated. Even if the criticisms are overstated, the lessons are probably not to be exportable anywhere and particularly not to the United States.

Other countries have an unhappy history of concentrating on allowing dying industries to secure outrageous subsidies. The U.S., unfortunately, also shows a greater tendency to unwise aid than to promoting emerging industries. The failure in the U.S. to realize the dream of an impartial bureaucracy precludes attainment of the vision of a Japanese style planning that sagely improves the evolution of the economy. The evidence suggests the planning did not even work that way in Japan. Stopping declines was always a concern.

It is doubtful that the needed insulation can be provided within U.S. traditions. Our politicians love to make sweeping attacks. Our journalists delight in reporting this. Careful discussions of the issues are rarely written and read even less. (The sales of serious books and even the leading policy-oriented magazines are depressingly small.) These traditions have served us and the rest of the world well. I prefer to preserve our openness and avoid policies that require its alteration.

The U.S. government's greatest successes were in fostering development of technologies to meet our military needs. Ventures into other areas were more often disastrous. Farm subsidies, rent controls, price controls on oil and natural gas, protection of steel and automobiles, and subsidy of synthetic-fuels production are typical programs.

The U.S. government owns too much land. This land never will be well managed by DOI. The minimum desirable reform is adoption of the proposal of the Public Land Law Review Commission that grazing and farming land be privatized. Experiments should be conducted with turning some national parks over to private ownership. The fixation over giveaways must cease. Long-time lessors should be given the land. Pre-lease estimation of values should be abandoned. When bidding is needed to chose among claimants, the highest bid should be accepted without question.

The process of subjecting regulations to more intensive benefit-cost analysis should be strengthened. Opponents have too easily convinced the etatist-minded that the difficulties of abatement benefit appraisal cause a bias towards undervaluing controls. The present system proceeds on the assumption that the benefits of abatement always are greater than the costs. This has produced a climate in which relentless pressure to regulate succeeds often even after evidence accumulates that the steps are unwise.

All health, safety, and environmental regulations need review. The belief that markets handle internalities less efficiently than government agencies is questionable. The records of the federal job, health, and safety agencies and of the Food and Drug Administration are unimpressive. The Food and Drug Administration is so obsessed with preventing the introduction of drugs with dangerous side-effects that the U.S. lags the world in drug introduction. A private system of banking insurance seems feasible. Certainly, it could have done better in policing savings and loan banks than the actual regulators hemmed in by Congressional affection for the industry.

Every energy conservation standard should be repealed, and all energy demand management programs should be eliminated.

Suspicions that environmental goals are too ambitious are widely supported by the specialists. Even if this view is wrong, existing policies need simplification.

Freer immigration is desirable.

All these proposals are deliberately uncompromising. I err on the side of avoiding making concessions that are usually misused.

Economic Intervention and Classic Liberalism: The Case for the Market

The central proposition of anti-intervention economics is that markets and other decentralized institutions are benign institutions, but governments, while probably essential, are prone to malfunction. The poor performance of governments is unquestionably the critical inspiration for this view. The limitations of markets are understood. They are thought lesser and more readily correctable than government failure. Thus, intervention does not seem the preferable cure. Intervention in markets is likely to make things worse.

Different restraints prevail. While firms must provide desired goods and services to survive unaided, governments are inherently dangerous since sovereignty removes accountability. Great restraint should be exercised in extending government action. At a minimum, incompetence is less apparent and thus harder to eliminate in government than in profit-oriented firms. Power is abused, and incompetence could turn into tyranny. This has been largely avoided in the Western world, but much damage still occurs. Government mishandling of policy is widespread. It is essential to recognize that government policy implementation will be flawed and thus advocate further restraints on action. Zeal in enforcement can tyrannize many individuals.

Representative government cannot adequately resist demands for special privilege. As economic analyses of political processes discussed above stress, parochial concerns often are more forcefully advocated than are the interests of the rest of society. All is not hopeless; apparently economists have sufficiently convinced other people that protectionism is an evil that dubious market failure arguments now are concocted to provide respectability.

The power to own and use property under a well-defined rule of law is essential. Transfers of control of the use of property to the state reduce the efficient use of resources. Intervention restricts freedom by reducing both the options open to us and our ability freely to choose among them. More generally, the minimum problem is that regulation employs scarce resources and their cost should be considered. In particular, while we know that many unwise policies exist, the exact situation is unclear. Whatever government action is retained should be undertaken using measures that accomplish their goals as unobtrusively as possible. This generally means reliance on systems of direct financial aids or penalties, not complex, detailed regulations.

Well-functioning markets are liberating because they are both less coercive and more productive than other systems. More resources are available, and greater opportunity to use them is allowed. As Mises and Hayek point out, the critical role of market rewards to success is to encourage people to undertake socially useful activities. The emphasis is on greater individual responsibility.

Success in markets could be and, in most cases, would be attained through voluntary transactions in which participants proved themselves by providing more value. The market test of success, profitability, is the most effective incentive available. The rewards encourage innovative behavior. The risk of ruin imposes prudence. Dishonesty is attributable to human frailty, can arise anywhere, and is less harmful and less likely to persist in markets than in governments. The large number of participants limits the ability to tyrannize.

Conversely, government often promotes dishonesty by prohibiting activities for which strong demands exist. The undesirability of these bans is clearest with the criminal sanctions associated with policies criticized here that inhibit activities such as food production uniformly recognized as desirable. The trickiest issues arise in dealing with widely disapproved activities in the area sometimes described as victimless crimes. Bitter debates exist whether bans on uncontrolled sales of narcotics are desirable on balance. Economists have conjectured that decriminalization would be preferable. The undesirable effects in creating violent crimes with victims and in eliminating corruption are clear. Whether drug use would rise or fall is unclear because criminalization creates incentives to drug use such as the challenge to thrill-seekers and high profits to sellers.

These arguments were often dismissed as proclaiming a freedom to starve and be monopolized. The evil of poverty arises from the existence of scarcity. The right question then is what system best reduces scarcity. The essence of liberalism is the assertion that the market economy far outperforms socialism in producing greater and more widely shared prosperity and freedom. In 1994, it suffices to compare any free-market economy to the former Soviet Union.

The limitation of antigovernment views is that their implications are less precise than the advocates' enthusiasm suggests. Distinguishing precisely the areas where government action is undesirable remains difficult. Several examples are given here in which Hayek is more supportive of intervention than other observers including me. Hayek, in any case, seems to accept more regulation than would Mises who, in turn, accepted more than does Rothbard.

Economists excessively blame themselves for the confusion on intervention. The real problem is resistance to economic analysis. It undermines preconceptions, particularly those about aiding parochial interests. The greatest limitation *and* virtue of the economic vision is that it does not provide assurances about exactly what needs to be done. It is the etatists who are the ideologues with precise agendas. Classical liberals face the impossible situation of trying to be confident about uncertainty. A valid argument must stop short of trying to resolve all the problems of implementation and leave room to adapt to specific problems.

Schumpeter's criticisms (1954, 410) of Carlyle well summarize the difficulty:

> Completely incapable of understanding the meaning of a theorem, overlooking the fact that *all* science is 'dismal' to the artist, he thought he had got hold of the right boy to whip. A large part of the public applauded, and so did some economists who understood no more than he did what a 'science' is and does.

Schumpeter added the contention that Carlyle was right in criticizing utilitarianism and attacked Ruskin for not adhering to the standards of careful research that made him a great art historian in his discussions of economics. That my references to Carlyle and Ruskin are to secondary sources reflects the irony of their efforts. The original attacks have not remained as accessible as the economic writings being attacked. The immortality of the disparagement is attributable largely to tendencies among economists to self-flagellation.

The proposition that our knowledge of how economies and government agencies work is imperfect implies that the ideal balance among public policy and markets is unclear. This open-endedness produces less coherence, and it is an advantage over socialism and other interventionist approaches. The consistency of dirigiste arguments involves unwillingness to adapt to emerging evidence. For reasons confirmed by the events of 1991, many were skeptical that the Soviet Union could be restructured by committed communists. Concerns then rose about how fast former communists could learn appropriate new behavior. Reform probably is too slow rather than too fast.

If this analysis is correct, the advocates of lessened statism are the true liberals. Liberalism is advocating institutions that advance freedom. Conservatism is a preference for prevailing conditions that historically, although not currently, has meant indifference to existing evils. Schumpeter's (1954) assertion was correct that it is a perversion that, particularly in the U.S., the enemies of true liberal principles could claim the label.

Those defining liberalism as intervention have not produced a new, more realistic view of the desirable extent of government. Quite the contrary, they have inadequately recognized the still valid classic liberal warnings of the drawbacks of mercantilism. The advocacy of protectionism by "liberal" Democrats is particularly striking evidence of the validity of Schumpeter's appraisal. Historically, it also is a radical reversal of political positions. Until the 1970s, the Democrats resisted Republican tendencies to protectionism.

Conversely, no satisfactory alternative term is available for the original version of liberalism. The objections raised to the conservative label seem appropriate. The major changes proposed hardly correspond to the every day meaning of conservative. Libertarian and neoconservative are problematic labels because they are associated with special positions not endorsed by all classic liberals. Too many libertarians tried to evade the problem of national defense by claiming the dangers are overstated. The neoconservatives are too often former enthusiasts of intervention, inadequately appreciative of economics and markets, and too anxious to substitute bad new regulations for bad old policies. Milton Friedman (in Block, Brennan, and Elzinga, 455) similarly criticizes the neoconservatives and notes that originally but "probably no longer" they came from "the rather far Left." The neoconservatives, for example, do not adequately understand that it is possible to support their social views without endorsing legislative enforcement. They have already been forced to reconsider aid to the arts. Perhaps they will someday rethink drug control and abortion. When *Commentary* shifted from a modern liberal to a neoconservative stance, it replaced economist bashing by interventionists with attacks by libertarians.

Classic liberal arguments call for abandoning deep-seated traditions. Liberalism in the sense used here was always an ideal being advocated against fierce pressure. The essence of the concept is an attack on special privilege. Nobles, landlords, tenants, entrepreneurs, and unions have been attacked. Heavy opposition arose since privilege is often sought and secured.

If the principles have any bias, it is to favor ambitious newcomers over established groups. One cause of the umbrage taken at characterizing the approach as conservative is that conservatives often approve of protecting whatever interest groups they prefer. The reform proposals, moreover, involve extensive changes rather than conserving present practice.

The market process is praised because of its overall effects. Liberalism is not unqualified admiration of capitalists. Their vigorous performance in conducting ever more productive businesses is admired. It is also recognized and deplored that capitalists can and regularly do succumb, as does everyone else, to the temptation to lessen market pressures by securing government protection. That capitalists are the worst enemies of capitalism is a well-established commonplace.

The positive side of this argument often gets neglected. Dealing with the private sector is more lucrative, less frustrating, and less confining than working with government. Excellent people work in government. Their dealings with outsiders are circumscribed by regulations that treat everyone as a scoundrel. Incredible pettiness occurs. Government officials go to ridiculous lengths to avoid lunches because of (unwarranted) embarrassment at the inability to get compensated for treating a guest. The positive connotation of businesslike and the negative implication of bureaucratic reflect these realities.

Liberalism warns that all searches for government protection are undesirable. Many would be victimized and even those supposedly aided could be harmed because the aid is so badly designed. The inherent constraints to total support noted by Peltzman (1976) are reinforced by the drawbacks of government and the tendency noted by other observers of lobbying expenditures to eat up the gains.

Aid might not attain its stated goals or it might have side effects such as reduced output that offset the direct benefits. A better share of a less productive regulated economy might be inferior to a lower share of a more protective economy. Ten percent of four trillion is better than 15 percent of one trillion.

The search for political favors should be replaced by greater trust in the impersonal workings of market forces. The advocacy of sacrifice is difficult to encourage under the best of circumstances. Long-standing condescending attitudes toward commercial activities and disbelief in decentralized decision making further retard acceptance of relying on markets. Markets are considered mundane at best, often corrupt, and too chaotic to work.

A freedom particularly promoted by liberalism is political diversity. Much of the response may prove illiberal. A vast but diffuse literature exists on this point. Hayek presents in his treatises an analysis of rational attacks on liberalism from those who believe it is possible consciously to order society. As he and many others are aware, several interrelated types of irrational objections also are involved. These include envy of the successful, fear of foreigners, and the ancient belief that nothing occurs without conscious effort--the conspiracy theory. Schumpeter (1950) is the basic source of the envy theory, but many others extended it. Great stress is placed on alienation. People may feel themselves inadequately esteemed in the liberal social order.

Schumpeter's treatment (1950, 61-163) of envy is part of his discussion of how the success of capitalism will lead in various ways to self-destruction. The clearest concerns are with opposition by the intellectual classes (145-51). In his critique of Carlyle and Ruskin (1954, 409-11), Schumpeter shows that one type of opposition comes from those who favor the precapitalist order. His 1950 exposition stresses critics seeking to develop a new order. He concentrates on Marx. He also remarks on the conflicts between the bourgeois and new and old political establishments.

Mises (1956) wrote a short book discussing criticisms of capitalism. He digresses from development of a complete, coherent description of the opposition to reiterate his responses. He, nevertheless, provides some interesting extensions of Schumpeter's points and adds another explanation. In particular, Mises's (176) discussion of Ruskin makes more apparent than does Schumpeter's the reactionary nature of Ruskin's view. Mises points out that liberalism holds that everyone is free to strive to achieve their best in a market economy (1950, 11-15). Failure occurs because of personal deficiency. This obviously is not a pleasing idea to those who do not do as well as they had hoped. He also adds the further observation that rich but inactive, intellectually alienated heirs of prominent capitalists often become supporters of anticapitalist activities (25-33).

The distrust of markets often involves particularly reprehensible forms of "envy," fear of outsiders. This issue is widely touched upon but rarely confronted bluntly. Liberalism advocates freedom for everyone to participate. Some writers have conjectured, not always approvingly, that often those who were oppressed by the old order are the most willing and able to take advantage of these opportunities.

Many examples exist and since the problem is so poorly recognized, a range of illustrations seems worth providing. Outsiders of every type are attacked. Hobson (1938) is a particularly interesting case because his prejudices long were ignored. Hannah Arendt's (1958) survey of totalitarianism, for example, despite its concern for anti-Semitism among despots was very restrained about the obvious bias in Hobson. In contrast, Paul Johnson's *Modern Times* bluntly states "...Hobson was also an anti-Semite...(1991, 152)." (Arendt was Jewish but reticent about strong identification, and Johnson is a Roman Catholic. This lesser assertiveness unfortunately is quite common among Jewish writers.)

This is not the only prejudice expressed. Other villains were selected. For example, Hofstadter's (1955) excellent history of populism and the progressive movement makes clear its xenophobic aspects. Indians in Africa and the overseas Chinese in many places in Asia are often attacked. Distinct indigenous groups are distrusted--the Kurds in Turkey, Iraq, and Iran and the Sikhs in India. India was divided because its Muslims feared Hindu rule. The Muslims who remain in India saw these fears confirmed. Tribal rivalry plagues Africa. Bigotry may be one reason why Japan is the most criticized U.S. trading partner. Simple aloofness can invite attacks on such bodies as the Trilateral Commission. Fear of the Jesuits has arisen in Catholic as well as Protestant countries. The Free Masons have also been suspect.

Finally, unending searches occur to find the conspiracies behind mysterious events such as political assassinations, sudden deaths, and disasters. Among the many other examples of the strength of this idea are the views on presidential assassinations. The unending efforts to find conspiracies behind the Kennedy assassination are only slightly more intense than those about Lincoln.

Conspiracy theories may not be linked with bigotry, but all too often they are. While the alleged leaders may be from the core of society, some hated minority is more likely to be blamed. Many minorities do use the market economy to improve their status. Their successes even in backbreaking, modest efforts often provoke envy.

As a once avid reader of suspense fiction, I encountered many variants on the conspiracy motif that proved the basis of the first Sherlock Holmes book--*A Study in Scarlet*. The crime proved the murder of apostates from a U.S. sect greatly resembling the Mormons. Conan Doyle returned to this theme at least twice including the introduction of the master criminal Professor Moriarty who appeared in only a few of Conan Doyle's writings but dominated dramatizations. Many later writers such as Agatha Christie, Ian Flemming, and Sax Rohmer devised variations with even more unattractive features. Rohmer's Fu Manchu novels were particularly noxious. They pitted inept caricatures of Holmes and Watson against "the yellow peril incarnate." Christie and Flemming seem to have indulged in at least unconscious anti-Semitism. In a different vein, it might be argued that another defect of *Atlas Shrugged* is belief that a cabal can restore capitalism.

The search for the conspirators causing events is widely recognized For example, those even vaguely aware of psychoanalysis know that Freud and Jung devoted considerable attention to the irrational basis of cravings for explanation of the inexplicable. It is an obvious next step to point out that a spontaneous market order is a concept that would be rejected by those believing that everything is consciously planned. Fear of markets is part of the general fear of the unknown.

Similarly, as Schumpeter (1950) stressed, the liberal order is intellectually boring. Economic theories of competition cannot be as rich as those dealing with market imperfections simply because competition comes in far fewer forms than do imperfections. Politicians have less about which to worry if the world is competitive. Artistic tirades about the evils of capitalism become less convincing as poverty lessens markedly from participation in the market economy.

Hayek's great triumph was to have recognition of the inferiority of planning sweep the world. It is now more widely recognized that what is critical to eliminate poverty is mastery of the available knowledge about how to promote the wealth of nations. Thus, a framework to encourage acquiring that knowledge is the key to poverty elimination. Hayek's formula seems by far the best to follow

Perhaps even more critically, the call of liberalism is for a degree of farsightedness much easier to secure in private than in public affairs. In the political process, instant gratification is sought without concern for long-run consequences. These prove to include failure of the intervention to do what was hoped and the incentives for creating further bad programs. Thus, a chasm separates the teachings of economics on markets from popular beliefs.

Given envy and the reliance on an invisible hand and similar forces, support for economic liberalism would be difficult to maintain even if we were confident the claims of liberalism were valid. Such validity is still not adequately established. The liberal concern over the evils of excess government, however, is far more demonstrable than fears of market failures. That proposition is sufficient for the study here of unjustified policies.

As the prior discussion tried to argue, we should rely much more heavily on markets. How far to go is neither clear nor critical. Given the slow pace of education and action, ending all clearly undesirable intervention in market economies will take many generations. Much effort also is needed to maintain past deregulations and resist unwise new policies. The rapidity with which deregulation is attacked (often successfully) is evidence of the difficulties.

We will not soon reach the point at which deregulation will terminate desirable rather than undesirable policies. The continuing problem still will be overuse of market regulation. The difficulty of implementing and preserving the deregulations that are almost universally advocated in the economics literature shows how formidable is the "easy" part of deregulation.

We are not choosing between poles, but seeking the proper balance. Neither a totally planned nor a totally market-driven economy seems optimal or feasible. Big brother cannot choose what everyone will buy. Collective consumption must be provided for, and institutions must be established to provide secure property rights. The wrong balance prevails. Intervention is vastly overused. More reliance on markets and less on regulation is clearly needed.

Appendix

Methodological Debates in Philosophy and Economics--Substance Behind the Form?

Among the developments in economics encountered in the research is increasing interest in what is variously termed methodology, epistemology, and philosophy of science. Attention seems desirable because so much of the discussion is intended to influence policy appraisals.

The interest per se is curious, and the ideological application is even more problematic. Discussions in this realm involve enormous difficulties and appear at best capable only of raising interesting points. One critical drawback is one often pointed out in the literature that the analyses are after the fact efforts to explain how things were done. It is questionable whether these explanations will help others or even will be followed by those who propose them. This position, for example, is strongly advocated by the philosopher Feyerabend (1975). Such economic writers on methodology as Caldwell (1982) and McCloskey (1985) present proposals that are more moderate warnings about the problems of proscription.

Another basic impediment is that immortalized in Alice's encounter with Humpty Dumpty in *Through the Looking-Glass*: "When I use a word," Humpty Dumpty said, in a rather scornful tone, "it means just what I choose it to mean-- neither more nor less."

Lewis Carroll was the pseudonym of Charles Lutwidge Dodgson, a mathematical logician. The cited passage nicely epitomizes the lack of firm definitions of many terms and the need to provide such definitions and thus is much quoted in the literature on economic methodology. (The annotated edition prepared by Martin Gardner contains an extensive note on how Dodgson handled this issue in his writings on logic--by allowing authors to choose and specify their preferred definitions, 268-70.) The discussions of methodology suffer from imprecise, changing, or nonexistent definition of terms.

Yet another problem is the inordinate knowledge required to appraise properly the methodological debates. The least that is required is familiarity with the leading efforts by economists to discuss methodology. A fully adequate study appears to require deep knowledge of philosophy, natural science, mathematics, and economics, i.e., more knowledge than can be acquired in a single lifetime.

It is thus no wonder that distinguished support can be found for rejecting methodology. Schumpeter's essay in the first issue of *Econometrica* ([1933] 1989) rejects "general discussion on scientific method" because "We know it leads nowhere...(106)." Others continue to disagree, and their use of epistemology to appraise economics merits review.

The economics literature on methodology seems to concentrate on a few philosophers--Popper (1965, 1968, 1972), Kuhn (1970), Lakatos (1978a, 1978b), Feyerabend (1975), and Polanyi (1962). However, reading all of these writers and the economic commentaries suggests that far more philosophers made relevant

195

pronouncements. Probably all the major figures and certainly at least Hume, John Stuart Mill qua philosopher, John Dewey, Wittgenstein, and the "logical positivists" of the Vienna circle discussed the issues. Conversely, Bartley (1990, 185-201) contends that Popper is esteemed outside philosophy and largely ignored within it. The favorites of economic writers apparently were chosen through their impact on pioneering economic methodologists. The influence of Popper and his associates, for example, was promoted by both Hutchinson's early advocacy of Popper's approach and the personal ties between Popper and Hayek.

Economic discussions themselves range widely in form and substance. Several such as Blaug (1992), Caldwell (1982), Hausman (1992) (a philosopher), and Redman (1991) are efforts broadly to survey general discussions of methodology and their application to economics. Others such as Mises (1960, 1966), Hayek, McCloskey (1985), Machlup (1978, 1991), Mirowski (1988, 1989), Boland (1989a, 1989b) Robbins (1932), and Hutchinson (1960, 1977) develop personal methodological positions derived independently or under the influence of a particular philosopher. For example, Hutchinson (1960, 1977) has long been an advocate of applying Popper's methods to economics.

Mirowski (1988, 1989) claims that the constrained maximization model central to modern economics is too uncritically adopted from nineteenth century physics. He has produced two books demonstrating the borrowing and the inability of Walras and others to understand why mathematicians and physicists objected to the approach. However, no examples are given of how this has made the approach misleading. D. A. Walker's (1991) devastating review adds the criticism that Mirowski's attack on the ties to physics is full of inconsistencies such as charges of both full acceptance and misunderstanding. Walker suggests that Mirowski is contending that no useful propositions emerge from economic theory and that avoidance of specific illustrations occurs because the invalidity of the sweeping attack would be more evident if examples were provided.

Others have concentrated on the views of particular economists. One notable example is Hirsch and de Marchi's (1990) effort to explain Milton Friedman's (1953) methodology. Friedman's own work is an example of yet another approach of short, casual discussions inserted in a collection of essays in economic analysis. Finally, many symposiums have been held on the issues.

For present purposes, it seems sufficient to survey the most influential work. Discussion begins by presenting what seems the essence of the views of the five most cited philosophers and a few of the leading economic commentators. Then, closer examination is given Friedman's controversial approach and Hirsch and de Marchi's attempt to resolve the controversies inspired by Friedman's pronouncements. The objective is first to argue that while the form of Feyerabend's argument is objectionable, the substance is essentially correct. Second, the record clearly shows that methodology is not a good form of ideological debate. Only works actually examined are cited; some things read are not cited.

Philosophers Economists Read

Popper is noted for arguing that (1) theories can be refuted but not proved, (2) induction can never prove anything, and (3) the potential for refutation is what makes a field scientific. His first point seems widely accepted. One can never be sure that some counterexample has been overlooked. The attack on induction makes a tricky distinction about the role of evidence. Investigation may suggest a theory or provide a refutation. It can never settle anything because of what Popper terms infinite regress--no matter how many successful steps may be taken in induction, the last still leads to requiring another step. Refutation remains more problematic. His critics stress that strictly speaking every theory fails to resolve fully the issues covered. His defenders, particularly Lakatos (1978b, 8-101, 139-61; 1978a, 170-210), suggest that, nevertheless, Popper is on the right track in suggesting that we search for serious errors and omissions in the analysis. (For a good summary, see Blaug 1992, 12-4.)

Kuhn's main contribution is the contention that science is subject to periodic revolutions in which the governing principle that he terms a paradigm is replaced. This term has become widely and probably excessively used. Kuhn identifies the paradigm with a major conceptual breakthrough. He also distinguishes between revolutions and the quieter periods of refinement that he terms normal science. Important cases have occurred in physical science in which an earlier theory was disproved. His critics wonder how much progress takes this form.

The history of economics more typically has involved extensions rather than refutations. Even Walras's development of general equilibrium extended, rather than disputed, prior work. Samuelson (1986, 272) suggests that the approach to economic instability inspired by Keynes is an example of an economic paradigm shift. Keynes's work was revolutionary, but many feel that this was more a disadvantage than a benefit.

Lakatos's (1978a, 1978b) contributions to analysis of methodology in physical sciences include refinements of Popper's concept of refutation and criticisms of what he views as Kuhn's overemphasis of revolutions and paradigms. Lakatos (1978b, 8-101) suggests we alter the emphasis from paradigms to research programs and study how they evolve. The philosophers leave considerable latitude in determining what constitutes a fatal flaw and its identification. Clearly deciding whether refutation is potentially attainable or actually has been attained seems a more formidable task than Popper or Lakatos admit. This implies that identifying what is scientific is also difficult.

Polanyi (1962) takes an introspective approach. He stresses the critical role of professional judgment--which seems best interpreted as developing insights suggested by prior training and observation of past practice without using formal rules. The Popperian Bartley (1990) warns that in the cartelized academic world, prevailing views may arbitrarily discourage discussions. Bartley (1990, 205) refers to Polanyi only in passing but seems to recognize that Polanyi's vision specifically renounced such parochialism. These arguments indicate that subjectivity while dangerous is also unavoidable. Proper skepticism must be retained.

Feyerabend (1975) provides a deliberately intemperate attack on prior efforts. He starts with the point cited above and develops it extensively. He is most useful at warning of the defects of sweeping arguments. He appropriately contends that we do not know enough about how knowledge is advanced to restrict methods of inquiry. He also punctures excessive claims about what science has achieved. Feyerabend seems to be on the right track in suggesting that being scientific, whatever it may mean, does not guarantee success. He also correctly warns that the relationship between actual practice and the pronouncement of epistemologists is tenuous.

Feyerabend pushes his anything-goes argument further than seems appropriate. In particular, he clearly wants to be taken literally. The inability precisely to state what is unacceptable, however, does not prevent practical judgments that certain ideas are nonsense. Feyerabend crosses the line between open-mindedness and abandonment of professionalism. He also understates the desirability of striving for logical consistency, careful analysis, and efforts at refutation. Feyerabend went beyond the role of useful skeptic by appearing overly sympathetic to dubious ideas. Whether he intends to or not, he sounds very much like a cheerleader for the antirationalism of the 60s.

For good reason, he has disturbed many of his readers including Lakatos (1978b 166) and Blaug (1992) by this excessive enthusiasm for free form. Given the way books are presaged by articles, this defect in Feyerabend was noted by Lakatos whose criticism well summarizes the problem. Lakatos's death preceded the completion of Feyerabend's *Against Method*, which originally was supposed to be a debate between Feyerabend and Lakatos. Lakatos (1978b, 166) described Feyerabend as "the anarchist darling of the New Left." Blaug (1992, 40) similarly sees a devotion to flower power. Redman (1991) counters that Feyerabend is a superrationalist and that, quite correctly, his exposition is motivated by a conviction that scholars are too pompous.

In economics, Blaug (1992), Caldwell (1982), and Redman (1991) provide particularly valuable analyses of the contribution of the philosophers to methodology. Each offers a review of what they consider the key arguments. Blaug uses the survey as the basis of an examination of how sound were the methodologies used in various economic inquiries. Caldwell goes on to examine various methodological pronouncements by economists. Redman ends up arguing her analysis demonstrates racism and sexism in economics. Blaug is sympathetic to Popper and Lakatos but stresses the desirability of prediction that is central to Milton Friedman's (1953) methodological pronouncements. Caldwell tends to view the efforts by philosophers and economists as interesting but inconclusive. He urges eclecticism.

Friedman's Positive Economics and Its Assessors

Before discussing any further surveys, it is desirable to examine the approach of Milton Friedman. Much attention is given his 1953 sketch of the principles of a "positive" approach to economics--one in which the analyst explained without judging. The term long antedates the logical positivists and, as far as I can tell, has nothing to do with their views. Reviewers tend to discuss the essay as if it were a tightly reasoned, detailed treatise. It is only a sketch that inadequately develops the definitions of the imprecise concepts advocated. It was after all only an introduction to other essays and not intended as a definitive position paper.

Critics focus on the assertion that useful predictions rather than realism should be the test of theory. (Some suggest this view comes from the positivists.) Friedman's dismissal of realism seems no more than stating the widely-recognized point that all theories must simplify and thus, as Popper's critics note, necessarily are false. Friedman's (1953) call for prediction is best seen as stressing the importance of testing and choosing theories that clearly help explain observed behavior. The critiques are curiously backward. Too much fuss is made about the easier to settle issue of realism; the more troublesome concept of his view of prediction is inadequately treated.

Commentators have assigned meanings to the arguments that are not the only plausible ones and, more critically, are not ones most consistent with the ample evidence provided by Friedman's massive contribution to theory and practice. The depth of the ambiguity is illustrated by two radically different views of the essay, those critiques discussed below by Samuelson (1966) and McCloskey (1985).

Hirsch and de Marchi (1990) try directly to tackle these problems. They start with recognition of the incompleteness of Friedman's exposition and seek to deduce from his other work exactly what his intentions were. (They note that Friedman read the manuscript but do not indicate what he said.) However, his long-time associate, Anna J. Schwartz (1992) considered the book unfair to Friedman. In her strongest response, she calls the interpretation of Friedman's methodological essay "arrant pedantry." Whatever the validity of the attributions to Friedman, the principles stated are useful additions to the debate. Hirsch, and de Marchi suggest five propositions:

1. Adopt an "outside" view of behavior.
2. Start with observation.
3. Test implications, continuously, although not in order to falsify.
4. Use the best knowledge available as a framework in doing empirical research.
5. Do not look for answers 'in principle', but address concrete problems.

The first proposition indicates that one key aspect of Friedman's rejection of realism is that no satisfactory method exists to verify realism. Subjective decisions are made. The fifth point relates to the argument that some complications are not worth adding to the analysis. Hirsch and de Marchi describe the primary point as preference for Marshall over Walras. Marshall is judged correct in suggesting that the connections among parts of the economy should be ignored in practice. The decision is based on the inability to consider these connections in applied analyses. Assuming that this is not taken too literally, this is sound advice. Marshall's single product concept is too vague, but the widely used alternative of considering only a group of close substitutes is essential to keep analyses manageable. Hirsch and de Marchi, however, may have overstated Friedman's criticism. This issue was not central to Friedman's work.

Friedman, clearly accepted the Chicago view that considering the complexities of differentiated competition does not contribute to better empirical analysis. This once controversial Chicago position has prevailed because efforts to implement Chamberlin's techniques have not succeeded.

Since Friedman's view of realism appears correct, his proposals seem valid for applied work. The other propositions reflect an effort to develop a methodology that properly states the roles and rules of observation, testing, and theorizing. Friedman is seen as rejecting Popper's scorn for induction and search for refutation while simultaneously neither accepting total reliance on induction nor rejecting hypothesis testing. Instead one moves from observation to theory formulation to tests. As suggested above, the Hirsch-de Marchi treatment of Popper may involve misunderstanding of the attack on induction as a method of proof. The attack does not reject making observations; the complaint is about trusting nothing but such observations.

The idea that we should mix observation, theorizing, and testing is more acceptable than the extremes of waiting for regularities to emerge as the historical school allegedly wanted or of Mises's stated preference for apriorism. The drawback is that the suggestion is not much more concrete than Feyerabend's call for anarchy and about the same as Caldwell's proposing diversity.

For good reason, Hirsch and de Marchi are least satisfactory on the most cryptic aspect of Friedman's argument--his stress on prediction. In fact, none of his technical writings provide the sorts of precise quantitative estimates that constitute forecasts in the physical sciences. Prior to reading Hirsch and de Marchi, I hypothesized that Friedman's practice suggested that he had tacitly redefined forecasts to mean qualitative estimates of impacts. The rationale is simply that this definition of forecasts corresponds with what Friedman's formal work typically provides. Economists are good at providing such qualitative predictions and bad at quantification. Reading Hirsch and de Marchi reinforced my views. Hirsch and de Marchi chose to seek examples of more quantitative forecasts. They observe that to find such forecasts it is necessary to consult his popular writings, particularly the columns that he contributed to *Newsweek*.

They find Friedman's record and his response to it problematic. Hirsch and de Marchi find such forecasts as "The most likely pattern for the year is a mild recession." Given Friedman's views on the state of usable knowledge, they point out "a question arises whether, if the connection between money and nominal income is as imprecise as it seems to be (on his acknowledgment), Friedman should be predicting at all, let alone predicting with such confidence (266)." This critique neglects the qualitative nature of the prediction.

Hirsch and de Marchi also cite but fail to comment on "forecasts" more akin to Friedman's pronouncements in more technical works such as Inflation is always and everywhere a monetary phenomenon. This type of statement is the quintessence of the qualitative judgments that I assert are what Friedman considered technically valid forecasts.

McCloskey's Rhetoric

With this view of Friedman in mind, a better appraisal of McCloskey (1985) is possible. McCloskey proposes using "rhetoric" as defined by writers such as Booth (1974) and Toulmin (1958). McCloskey's rhetoric turns out to be sound reasoning that will supplement precise tests of hypotheses with judgment. Here he relies on writers such as Kuhn (1970) and Polanyi (1962) who insist that professional judgment has always been a major influence. Critics such as the contributors to the symposium in the April 1988 *Economics and Philosophy* fear that McCloskey's principles leave too much room for sophistry. This seems incorrect. McCloskey is aware of the difference between sound and specious reasoning. McCloskey's appeal for clearer exposition with stress on effectively conveying the critical points was useful.

However, McCloskey's method of justifying his proposals and particularly his placing so much blame on Friedman's essay seem unsatisfactory. A simple statement that in practice economists have gotten away from clearly presenting useful advice and some examples would have been preferable. Instead, he presents propositions that he claims constitute economic "modernism" and makes his case a refutation of this modernism. His definition of modernism encompasses concepts of testing, quantification, prediction, and objectivity. It is questionable that this modernism is preached as widely as McCloskey contends; indeed his criticisms include the observation that the principles are not practiced.

McCloskey describes Friedman's paper as "the central document of modernism in economics (1985, 9)." As both Hirsch and de Marchi's analysis and the vehemence of Samuelson's (1966, 1772-8) critiques suggest, Friedman's practice seems much closer to what McCloskey would desire than that of the economists who regularly attack Friedman. Friedman seems actually a master of rhetoric in both his technical and popular writings. McCloskey is attacking the way others have interpreted Friedman or worse improperly blaming Friedman for outlooks formed elsewhere.

Somehow Friedman's views have been taken as a defense of highly abstract theorizing and stress on econometric analyses of empirical developments. McCloskey's emphasis on discrediting the principles is not the optimal one for overcoming objections that McCloskey, Friedman, and many others share about the priority given to the form of the analysis. A more direct criticism of the practice of excessive formalism would have been preferable. The change would have made McCloskey's case for better approaches more palatable.

Friedman's (and Blaug's) stress on prediction was severely criticized by McCloskey who contends prediction is impossible. He is clearly stressing the failures in quantitative forecasting. As suggested above, one interpretation of Friedman is that his advocacy of predictions is a call for qualitative principles. That economists can produce such statements is a commonplace in appraisals of the usefulness of economics. The oddity is that so many experienced observers invite confusion by taking the argument for granted.

Samuelson versus Machlup

To complete this literature review, note should be taken of Samuelson's (1966, 1978) methodological pronouncements and the response made by Machlup (1978 481-4). Samuelson has generated a vast, diverse contribution to economics well sampled by his collected papers. While no critiques as systematic as those of Friedman exist, Samuelson increasingly is made the scapegoat for an alleged excess of formalism in economics. This too is an unfair attack that ignores Samuelson's formidable contribution to making economics comprehensible. His methodological writings largely consist of brief scattered statements. Among the most famous ones are the call in the *Foundations* for testable hypotheses and his vehement condemnation (1966, 1772-8) of Friedman's rejection of realism. In the latter case, Samuelson takes the shaky position that Friedman intended to say more than that all theories simplify.

While Samuelson is an enthusiastic Walrasian, the *Foundations* also contains recognition that while more prone to misuse, Marshallian analysis can be very effective in empirical work. Similarly, Samuelson's admiration for monopolistic competition has never extended to its extensive employment.

Among the responses Samuelson provoked was that of Machlup that pure analysis can be valuable. An avowedly unrealistic model that produces no clear predictions may still increase comprehension of practical problems. Machlup (1978, 482-3) proceeded to show that one of Samuelson's most influential contributions, the analysis of "factor price equalization" in international trade (1966, 847-887), was a prime example. This work that shaped how the theory of international trade is presented. Samuelson delineated the conditions under which international trade equalized international wage rates, rents, and payments to other inputs to production. The proof suggested the many ways actual economies could deviate from the required conditions and fail to equalize factor prices.

As Machlup did not indicate, the analysis and its extensions well illustrates the difficulties of deciding whether predictions are made. Equalization occurs if the Samuelson assumptions are satisfied. Many different results arise depending upon what alternatives to the Samuelson assumptions are considered. Given the lack of established evaluation criteria, this situation could be described as providing an array of predictions or as being too unrestrictive. Perhaps even better examples are the persistence of the assumption of rational behavior to avoid the unbounded behavior possible under irrationality and the continued use of an avowedly oversimplified general equilibrium model.

Conclusions

All this suggests first that the eclecticism of a Caldwell or a McCloskey seems preferable to the dogmatism of a Mises or a Hutchinson. Speculation is not enough. As I argued in chapter 12, Mises observed closely, and his intent seems primarily to argue that broadly applicable theories can be derived analytically.

Second, the Humpty-Dumpty problem runs rampant. Testing is desirable but, as Popper, Lakatos, Polanyi, Feyerabend, and McCloskey warn in different ways, the concept of what constitutes a satisfactory test is unclear. Realism, rationality,, objectivity, and science are elusive concepts. Realism might be presumed to be synonymous with refutability and rationality with the search for refutation. In logic, subjectivity is unavoidable since assumptions by definition are untestable.

Those who talk about objective analysis and the possibility of "positive" rather than normative analysis probably are trying to express their recognition of the difference between subjective and controversial. The subjective view that logic is preferable to ill-logic is less controversial than the various theories of what constitutes fairness. Objectivity then is an unfortunate term for belief in the existence of both a core of generally accepted principles of analysis upon which one can build and a cadre of trained professionals capable at least in principle of fairly appraising ideas. Finally, given all these problems, no rules are available to determine what is truly "scientific", but presumably it involves at least satisfying some concepts of realism, rationality, objectivity, and refutation.

Thus, given the uncertainty about what it means to be scientific and about the desirability of being scientific, too much effort has been devoted to proving economics is a science. Scientific can mean many things ranging from reliance on theoretical principles to meeting rigid achievement criteria. Since the choice of definition determines whether economics is a science, analysts can reach whichever answer they prefer a priori. The simpler, more readily treated question of whether economics is useful is more germane. As should have been made apparent, the position here is resoundingly affirmative.

The consequences of the unavoidability of subjectivity should not be exaggerated. The lessons of experience remain relevant. Properly, the economic literature still stresses careful, logically consistent, well documented arguments. Economics has benefited from continued resistance to free form. Few of us still have direct contact with the historical and institutional approaches, but the lessons of their failure still exerts a strong influence. The imperfections of the efforts to organize economic inquiries seem less important than the virtues.

It matters little what we call the process. The content counts. Those characteristics to stress are open-mindedness, respect for facts, careful observation, and the use of proven analytic methods.

Annotated Bibliography

Only selected items are explained; many entries have self-explanatory titles; others are discussed in the text.

Adams, Walter, ed. 1990. *The Structure of American Industry*. 8th ed. New York: Macmillan Publishing Company. Long-lived collection of case studies on leading industries following the structure, performance, conduct framework.

Adelman, M. A. 1948. "Effective Competition and the Antitrust Laws." *Harvard Law Review* 61 (8): 1289-1350. Pioneering view of the conflicting goals of antitrust enforcement.

Adelman, M. A. 1949. "Integration and Antitrust Policy." *Harvard Law Review* 63 (1): 27-77.

Adelman, M. A. 1951. "The Measurement of Industrial Concentration." *Review of Economics and Statistics* 33 (4): 269-96. Reprinted in Heflebower and Stocking, eds. 1958, 3-45. Classic refutation of the Berle-Means view of concentration. Numerous critiques and rebuttals appeared in later issues of the *Review*.

Adelman, M. A. 1955. "Concept and Statistical Measurement of Vertical Integration." In *Business Concentration and Price Policy*, National Bureau of Economic Research, 281-330. Princeton: Princeton University Press.

Adelman, M. A. 1959. *A&P: A Study in Price-Cost Behavior and Public Policy*. Cambridge, Mass.: Harvard University Press. Synthesis of numerous prior articles arguing that the case attacked the virtues of A&P as a stimulator of competition.

Adelman, M. A. 1960. "Some Aspects of Corporate Enterprise." In *Postwar Economic Trends in the United States*, edited by Ralph E. Freeman, 289-308. New York: Harper.

Adelman, M. A. 1972. *The World Petroleum Market*. Baltimore: Johns Hopkins University Press for Resources for the Future. The classic refutation of the impending shortage theory and a presentation of the argument that consuming country desires to protect domestic energy producers were the chief barrier to competition.

Adelman, M. A. 1973. "Is the Oil Shortage Real? Oil Companies as OPEC Tax-Collectors." *Foreign Policy* 9: 69-107. Prophetic warning that the 1983 Tehran agreements initiated monopolizing forces in world oil.

Adelman, M. A. 1993a. *The Economics of Petroleum Supply: Papers by M.A. Adelman 1962-1993*. Cambridge, Mass.: The MIT Press. A collection of penetrating analyses of oil developments

Adelman, M. A. 1993b. "Modelling World Oil Supply." *The Energy Journal* 14 (1): 1-32.

Allais, Maurice. 1962. "Les Aspects Essential de la Politique de l'Énergie--Synthèse et Conclusions." In *La Politique de l'Énergie.*, edited by M. Allais. Paris: Imprimerie Nationale (reprinted from *Annales des Mines*). The volume reproduces papers presented at Professor Allais's seminar by participants in various aspects of French energy. Contains Allais's comments on each

guest's paper, a summary of the discussion, and a long essay by Allais
summing up.

Anderson, Frederick R. 1973. *NEPA in the Courts: A Legal Analysis of the National
Environmental Policy Act.* Baltimore: Johns Hopkins University Press for
Resources for the Future. Summary of the court decisions leading to a broad
interpretation of the act.

Anderson, Terry L., ed. 1993. *NAFTA and the Environment.* San Francisco: Pacific
Institute for Policy Analysis (jointly sponsored with the Fraser Institute and
the Political Economy Research Center).

Anderson, Terry L. and Donald R. Leal. 1991. *Free Market Environmentalism.* San
Francisco: Pacific Institute for Public Policy and Boulder: Westview Press.

Appalachian Regional Commission. 1969. *Acid Mine Drainage in Appalachia.*
Washington, D.C.: U.S. Government Printing Office. Demonstration that
control benefits were much smaller than costs.

Areeda, Phillip. 1980. *Antitrust Analysis, Problems, Texts, Cases.* 3d ed. Boston:
Little, Brown. One of the standard texts in field.

Areeda, Phillip and Donald F. Turner. 1975. "Predatory Pricing and Related
Practices under Section 2 of the Sherman Act." *Harvard Law Review* 88 (4):
697-733. A proposal to simplify the law that provoked many responses to
which the authors often reacted.

Areeda, Phillip and Donald F. Turner. 1976. "Scherer on Predatory Pricing: A
Reply." *Harvard Law Review* 89 (5): 891-900.

Areeda, Phillip and Donald F. Turner. 1978. "Williamson on Predatory Pricing." *The
Yale Law Journal* 87 (7): 1337-1352.

Arendt, Hannah. 1958. *The Origins of Totalitarianism.* 2d enlarged ed. Cleveland:
World Publishing Company Meridian Books. A survey of the various roots
of totalitarianism.

Armentano, Dominick T. 1990. *Antitrust and Monopoly: Anatomy of a Policy
Failure.* 2d ed. New York: Homes and Meier for The Independent Institute.
Modest revision of book published by Wiley in 1982; this, in turn, was an
updating a 1972 book. Concludes from standard criticisms of the
implementation of antitrust that repeal is the only feasible cure.

Arrow, Kenneth J. and Anthony C. Fisher. 1974. "Environmental Preservation,
Uncertainty, and Irreversibility." *Quarterly Journal of Economics* 88 (2):
312-19. Arrow's collected papers are available from the Harvard University
Press.

Arrow, Kenneth J. and Tibor Scitovsky, eds. 1969. *Readings in Welfare Economics.*
Homewood: Richard D. Irwin.

Baden, John A. and Donald Leal, eds. 1990. *The Yellowstone Primer: Land and
Resource Management in the Greater Yellowstone Ecosystem.* San
Francisco: Pacific Institute for Public Policy Research. Essays attacking
mismanagement and the ability of the Park Service to mute criticism.

Bailey, Ronald. 1993. *Eco-Scam: The False Prophets of Ecological Apocalypse.*
New York: St. Martins Press (A Cato Institute book). Reviews such
advocates of global disaster as Forrester, the Meadows, Ehirlich, and
Commoner as evidence that environmentalism involves concerns with
issues economists consider unimportant, notably mineral exhaustion.

Bain, Joe S. 1949. "A Note on Pricing in Monopoly and Oligopoly." *American Economic Review* 39 (1): 448-64. Reprinted in Heflebower and Stocking, eds. 1958, 220-35. His basic article on limit pricing.

Bain, Joe S. 1954. "Economies of Scale, Concentration, and the Conditions of Entry in Twenty Manufacturing Industries." *American Economic Review* 44 (1): 15-39. Reprinted in Heflebower and Stocking, eds. 1958, 46-68. Summary of the 1956 book arguing scale economies did not justify the size of major U.S. firms.

Bain, Joe S. 1956. *Barriers to New Competition: Their Character and Consequences in Manufacturing Industries.* Cambridge, Mass.: Harvard University Press. Analysis of causes of market structure.

Bain, Joe S. 1968. *Industrial Organization.* 2d ed. New York: John S. Wiley & Sons. A pioneering effort to organize the material in the field, organized around the structure, conduct, performance framework.

Barnett, Harold J. and Chandler Morse. 1963. *Scarcity and Growth: The Economics of Natural Resource Availability.* Baltimore: Johns Hopkins Press for Resources for the Future. A demonstration that scarcity of minerals had decreased over time and a short history of the conservation movement.

Barro, Robert J. 1972. "A Theory of Monopolistic Price Adjustment." *Review of Economic Studies* 39 (1): 17-26. This effort to formalize the economics of optimal price variation is more cited in macroeconomics than in microeconomics.

Bartley, William Warren, III. 1990. *Unfathomed Knowledge, Unmeasured Wealth: On Universities and the Wealth of Nations.* La Salle: Open Court. Reversing the usual stress, he urges the use of economic principles in epistemology.

Bator, Francis. 1958. "The Anatomy of Market Failure." *Quarterly Journal of Economics* 72 (3): 351-79. Classic survey of the defects of markets.

Bauer, P. T. 1981. *Equality, the Third World and Economic Delusion.* Cambridge, Mass.: Harvard University Press. A selection of essays on Bauer's belief that foreign aid is harmful and inequitable.

Baumol, William J. 1952. "The Transactions Demand for Cash: An Inventory Theoretic Approach." *Quarterly Journal of Economics* 66 (4): 545-56. One of several efforts to provide a simple model of optimal inventory holding; it is applicable to things other than cash.

Baumol, William J. 1959. *Economic Dynamics: An Introduction.* New York: Macmillan. A survey of issues of growth and cycles and the related mathematics.

Baumol, William J. 1977. "Quasi-Permanence of Price Reductions: A Policy for Prevention of Predation." *The Yale Law Journal* 89 (1): 1-26. A proposal to limit predation by forcing maintenance of price cuts; a contribution to the Areeda-Turner debate.

Baumol, William J. 1986. "Williamson's *The Economic Institutions of Capitalism.*" *Rand Journal of Economics* 17 (2): 279-86.

Baumol, William J. and Wallace E. Oates. 1975. *The Theory of Environmental Policy: Externalities, Public Outlays, and the Quality of Life.* Englewood Cliffs, N.J.: Prentice-Hall. A mathematical development of the analysis. The difficulty and quality are variable but it is by far the best available. The revision is an improvement.

Baumol, William J. and Wallace E. Oates. 1979. *Economics, Environmental Policy, and the Quality of Life.* Englewood Cliffs, N.J.: Prentice-Hall. A good but now obsolete discussion of practices.

Baumol, William J. and Wallace E. Oates. 1988. *The Theory of Environmental Policy.* 2d ed. Cambridge: Cambridge University Press.

Baumol, William J. and Janusz A. Ordover. 1985. "Use of Antitrust to Subvert Competition." *Journal of Law and Economics* 28 (2): 247-65.

Baumol, William J., John C. Panzar, and Robert D. Willig. 1982. *Contestable Markets and the Theory of Industry Structure.* New York: Harcourt Brace and Jovanovich. A controversial effort to provide a more rigorous formulation of the relationship between size and diversity of operation and costs and analyze the impacts on behavior of the threat of entry given various combinations of cost situations and exit potential.

Baumol, William J. and James E. Tobin. 1989. "The Optimal Cash Balance Proposition: Maurice Allais' Priority." *Journal of Economic Literature* 27 (3): 1160-2.

Becker, Gary S. 1968. "Crime and Punishment: An Economic Approach." *Journal of Political Economy* 76 (2): 169-217. Reprinted in Stigler, ed. 1988, 537-92. A study of how crime might be deterred by increased probability of punishment.

Becker, Gary S. 1983. "A Theory of Competition Among Pressure Groups for Political Influence." *Quarterly Journal of Economics* 98 (3): 371-400.

Becker, Gary S. and George J. Stigler. 1974. "Law Enforcement, Malfeasance, and Compensation of Enforcers." *The Journal of Legal Studies* 31 (1): 1-18. Reprinted in Stigler, ed. 1988, 593-611. Further discussion of the effect of punishment on crime.

Benson, Bruce L. 1990. *The Enterprise of Law: Justice Without the State.* San Francisco: Pacific Institute for Public Policy. Fuller development of the case for free-market justice with discussions of its practical implementation by arbitration and private security forces.

Berg, Sanford V. and John Tschirhart. 1988. *Natural Monopoly Regulation: Principles and Practice.* Cambridge: Cambridge University Press. Largely mathematical review of a wide range of issues in the area.

Berle, Adolph A. and Gardiner C. Means. [1932] 1968. *The Modern Corporation and Private Property.* Rev. ed. New York: Harcourt Brace and World. Purports to find a growing separation between owners and managers and agonizes over consequences; stresses potential for deceit.

Bhagwati, Jagdish N. 1971. "The Generalized Theory of Distortions and Welfare." In *Trade, Balance of Payments and Growth, papers in International Economics in honor of Charles P. Kindleberger,* edited by Jagdish N. Bhagwati, Ronald W. Jones, Robert A. Mundell, and Jaroslav Vanek, 69-90. Amsterdam: North-Holland Publishing Co. Reprinted in Bhagwati, ed. 1981, 171-89 and Bhagwati, 1983, 73-94. Terse summary of the full theory. Five volumes of Bhagwati's collected papers are available from the MIT Press.

Bhagwati, Jagdish N. 1983. *The Theory of Commercial Policy: Essays in International Economic Theory,* Vol 1. Edited by Robert C. Feenstra. Cambridge, Mass.: The MIT Press.

Bhagwati, Jagdish N. 1989. *Protectionism.* Cambridge, Mass.: The MIT Press.

Bhagwati, Jagdish N. 1991. *The World Trading System at Risk*. Princeton: The Princeton University Press.

Bhagwati, Jagdish N., ed. 1981. *International Trade: Selected Readings*. Cambridge, Mass.: The MIT Press.

Bhagwati, Jagdish N. and V. K. Ramaswami. 1963. "Domestic Distortions, Tariffs, and the Theory of Optimum Subsidy." *Journal of Political Economy* 71 (1): 44-50. Reprinted in Caves and Johnson, eds. 1968, 230-9.

Bhagwati, Jagdish N. and T. N. Srinivasan. 1983. *Lectures on International Trade*. Cambridge, Mass.: The MIT Press. Difficult mathematical development.

Bishop, Richard C. 1982. "Option Value: An Exposition and Extension." *Land Economics* 58 (1): 1-15.

Bishop, Robert L. 1960. "Duopoly: Collusion or Warfare?" *American Economic Review* 50 (5): 933-61. A particularly clear presentation of the issues using algebra.

Blanchard, Olivier Jean and Stanley Fischer. 1989. *Lectures on Macroeconomics*. Cambridge Mass.: The MIT Press. Discussion of a variety of advanced models in field with a "new Keynesian" outlook. For the specialist. It assumes knowledge of statistical tools unfamiliar even to many economists.

Blaug, Mark. 1985. *Economic Theory in Retrospect*. 4th ed. Cambridge: Cambridge University Press. A good history.

Blaug, Mark. 1992 *The Methodology of Economic or How Economists Explain*, 2d edition Cambridge: Cambridge University Press. Reviews philosophy, advocates prediction, and applies the principles to various examples.

Block, Walter, Geoffrey Brennan, and Kenneth Elzinga, eds. 1985. *Morality of the Market: Economic and Religious Perspectives*. Vancouver: The Fraser Institute.

Block, Walter and Irving Hexham, eds. 1986. *Religion, Economics and Social Thought*. Vancouver: The Fraser Institute. These two volumes present papers by economists, theologians, philosophers, and others showing broad disagreements prevail in each field and no clear interdisciplinary differences arise.

Bloom, Allan. 1987. *The Closing of the American Mind*. New York: Simon and Schuster. Best seller on fears that valid traditions in culture are being undermined by unsound ideas, often involving replacement of teaching with propaganda. Suffers from excessive belief in the central importance of the humanities as traditionally taught.

Boaz, David and Edward H. Crane, eds. 1993. *Market Liberalism: A Paradigm for the 21st Century*. Washington: The Cato Institute.

Bohi, Douglas R. 1990. *Energy Price Shocks and Macroeconomic Performance*. Washington: Resources for the Future. Argues that the evidence is inadequate to support contention that oil shocks are so bad for the economy that oil taxes are desirable.

Bohi, Douglas R. and W. David Montgomery. 1982. *Oil Prices, Energy Security, and Import Policy*. Washington, D.C.: Resources for the Future, Inc. An earlier treatment advocating oil taxes and a large government-owned stockpile.

Bohm, Peter. 1975. "Option Demand and Consumer's Surplus: Comment." *American Economic Review* 65 (4): 733-36.

Bohn, Roger E., Bennett W. Golub, Richard D. Tabors, and Fred C. Schweppe. 1984. "Deregulating the Generation of Electricity Through the Creation of Spot Markets for Bulk Power." *The Energy Journal* 5 (2): 71-91.

Bohn, Roger E., Fred C. Schweppe, and Richard D. Tabors. 1983. "Using Spot Pricing to Coordinate Deregulated Utilities, Customers, and Generators." In *Electric Power Strategic Issues*, edited by James Plummer, Terry Ferrar, and William Hughes, 265-82. Arlington, Va.: Public Utilities Reports and Palo Alto, Calif.: QED Research. These articles and the book listed under Schweppe suggest that technology allows spot pricing of electricity to large customers and this would facilitate deregulated generation.

Boland, Lawrence A. 1989a. *The Methodology of Economic Model Building: Methodology after Samuelson*. London: Routledge.

Boland, Lawrence A. 1989b. *The Principles of Economics: Some Lies My Teachers Told Me*. London: Routledge.

Bonbright, James C., Albert L. Danielson, and David R. Kamerschen. 1988. *Principles of Public Utility Rates*. 2d ed. Arlington: Public Utility Reports. Substantial revision by last two authors of work by long-time observer of regulation; recognizes limitations of regulation and problem of attaining economic efficiency under regulation.

Booth, Wayne C. 1974. *Modern Dogma and the Rhetoric of Assent*. Chicago: University of Chicago Press.

Bork, Robert H. 1954. "Vertical Integration and the Sherman Act: The Legal History of an Economic Misconception." *The University of Chicago Law Review* 22 (1): 157-201. His earliest attack on the misunderstandings of vertical integration.

Bork, Robert H. 1965. "The Rule of Reason and the per se Concept: Price Fixing and Market Division, Part I." *Yale Law Journal* 74 (5): 775-847. His fullest development of his case that resale price maintenance should not be banned.

Bork, Robert H. 1966a. "Legislative Intent and the Policy of the Sherman Act." *Journal of Law and Economics* 9: 7-48. Reprinted with deletions in Sullivan, 1991. Contention that efficiency, not preservation of small business, was the goal.

Bork, Robert H. 1966b. "The Rule of Reason and the per se Concept: Price Fixing and Market Division, Part 2." *Yale Law Journal* 75 (3): 373-475.

Bork, Robert H. 1978. *The Antitrust Paradox, a Policy at War with Itself*. New York: Basic Books. Summary of his views that enforcement has been contaminated by failure to concentrate on efficiency issues.

Bork, Robert H. 1989. *The Tempting of America: The Political Seduction of the Law*. New York: Free Press. A summing up of his legal philosophy and response to the attacks that prevented his appointment to the U.S. Supreme Court.

Bovard, James. 1991. *The Fair Trade Fraud*. New York: St. Martins Press. Attack on protectionist policies.

Bradley, Robert L., Jr. 1989. *The Mirage of Oil Protection*. Lanham: University Press of America. Attack on policy by a overt libertarian.

Brander, James A. 1986. "Rationales for Strategic Trade and Industrial Policy." In *Strategic Trade Policy and the New International Economics*, edited by Paul R. Krugman, 23-46. Cambridge Mass.: The MIT Press.

Breyer, Stephen G. 1982. *Regulation and Its Reform*. Cambridge, Mass.: Harvard University Press. Good survey of the issues in various areas.

Broadman, Harry G. and Michael A. Toman. 1986. "Non-price Provisions in Long-Term Natural Gas Contracts." *Land Economics* 62 (2): 111-18.

Brock, Samuel M. and David B. Brooks. 1968. *The Miles Job Mine: A Study of Benefits and Costs of Surface Mining in Northern West Virginia*. Morgantown: Appalachian Center, West Virginia University. Case study showing costs exceed measurable benefits.

Brodley, Joseph F. and George A. Hay. 1981. "Predatory Pricing: Competing Economic Theories and the Evolution of Legal Standards." *Cornell Law Review* 66 (4): 738-803. Yet another effort to sort out the issues.

Bromley, Daniel W. 1991. *Environment and Economy: Property Rights and Public Policy*. Oxford: Basil Blackwell. Rexamination of issues including discussion of the circumstances under which common ownership can be efficient.

Brown, Stephen J. and David S. Sibley. 1986. *The Theory of Public Utility Pricing*. Cambridge: Cambridge University Press. Fairly short but with material not available elsewhere on problems of efficiency in sales to industrial firms.

Brubaker, Sterling, ed. 1984. *Rethinking the Federal Lands*. Washington: Resources for the Future. Good presentation of a range of views.

Buchanan, James M. and Gordon Tullock. 1962. *The Calculus of Consent: Logical Foundation of Constitutional Democracy*. Ann Arbor: University of Michigan Press. Classic study of how best to solve the public good issue. Warns of dangers of majorities oppressing minorities, producing excess government spending and urges legal restraints to avoid the outcome.

Bull, Clive. 1987. "The Existence of Self-Enforcing Implicit Contracts." *Quarterly Journal of Economics* 102 (1): 147-59.

Burns, Malcolm R. 1986. "Predatory Mergers and the Acquisition Cost of Competitors." *Journal of Political Economy* 94 (2): 266-99. Suggests American Tobacco may have used predation to get rivals to sell out more cheaply.

Butler, Eamonn. 1983. *Hayek: His Contribution to the Political and Economic Thought of Our Time*. New York: Universe Books.

Butler, Eamonn. 1988. *Ludwig von Mises: Fountainhead of the Modern Microeconomics Revolution*. Aldershot: Gower Publishing Company. Both books are largely sympathetic surveys of the writings of the two subjects.

Caldwell, Bruce J. 1982. *Beyond Positivism: Economic Methodology in the Twentieth Century*. London: George Allen & Unwin. An excellent review of the work in philosophy and economics, concluding that diversity is appropriate.

Carliner, Geoffrey. 1986. "Industrial Policies for Emerging Industries." In *Strategic Trade Policy and the New International Economics*, edited by Paul R. Krugman, 147-68. Cambridge Mass.: The MIT Press.

Carlton, Dennis. W. 1984. "Futures Markets: Their Purpose, Their History, Their Growth, Their Successes and Failures." *Journal of Futures Markets* 4 (3): 237-71.

Carlton, Dennis. W. 1986. "The Rigidity of Prices." *American Economic Review* 76 (4): 637-58.

Carlton, Dennis. W. 1989. "The Theory and Facts of How Markets Clear: Is Industrial Organization Valuable for Understanding Macroeconomics?" In *Handbook of Industrial Organization*. Vol. 1, edited by Richard

Schmalensee and Robert D. Willig, 909-46. Amsterdam: North-Holland. These articles review the problem of price rigidity and its optimality.

Carlton, Dennis W. and Glenn C. Loury. 1980. "The Limitations of Pigouvian Taxes as a Long-Run Remedy for Externalities." *Quarterly Journal of Economics* 98 (4): 559-66.

Carlton, Dennis W. and Glenn C. Loury. 1986. "The Limitations of Pigouvian Taxes as a Long-Run Remedy for Externalities: An Extension of Results." *Quarterly Journal of Economics* 101 (3): 631-4.

Carlton, Dennis W. and Jeffrey M. Perloff. 1990. *Modern Industrial Organization*. Glenview: Scott Foresman/Little Brown. Good presentation stressing fairly accessible presentations of the relevant theory.

Carpenter, Paul, Henry D. Jacoby, and Arthur W. Wright. 1987. "Adapting to Change in Natural Gas Markets." In *Energy: Markets and Regulation*, edited by Richard L. Gordon, Henry D. Jacoby, and Martin B. Zimmerman, 1-29. Cambridge, Mass.: The MIT Press.

Carroll, Lewis. 1960. *The Annotated Alice: Alice's Adventures in Wonderland and Through the Looking Glass*, with an introduction and notes by Martin Gardner. New York: Clarkson N. Potter. Reprint edition Cleveland: World Publishing. 1963.

Caves, Richard E. 1960. *Trade and Economic Structure: Models and Methods*. Cambridge, Mass.: Harvard University Press. Classic review of the state of theory at the time.

Caves, Richard E. and Harry G. Johnson, eds. 1968. *Readings in International Economics*. Homewood, Ill.: Richard D. Irwin.

Chamberlin, Edward H. 1962. *The Theory of Monopolistic Competition: A Reorientation of the Theory of Value*. 8th ed. Cambridge, Mass.: Harvard University Press. Classic and controversial effort to develop a more complete analysis of types of market structure and how they operate. Famous for formalizing analysis of competition on product quality and by advertising and for predicting oligopolies would achieve the monopolistic solution.

Chandler, Alfred D., Jr. 1962. *Strategy and Structure: Chapters in the History of the Industrial Enterprise*. Cambridge, Mass.: The MIT Press.

Chandler, Alfred D., Jr. 1977. *The Visible Hand: The Managerial Revolution in American Business*. Cambridge, Mass.: Harvard University Press. Discussions of the emergence of large firms.

Chandler, Alfred D., Jr. 1990. *Scale and Scope: The Dynamics of Industrial Capitalism*. Cambridge, Mass.: Harvard University Press. Comparisons of the development from the middle 19th century to the middle of the twentieth century of large firms in the United States, United Kingdom, and Germany.

Cheung, Steven N. 1969. "Transaction Costs, Risk Aversion, and the Choice of Contractual Arrangements." *Journal of Law and Economics* 12 (1): 23-45

Cheung, Steven N. 1978. *The Myth of Social Cost*. London: The Institute of Economic Affairs. Reprinted with additional foreword San Francisco: Cato Institute, 1980.

Cheung, Steven N. 1983. "The Contractual Nature of the Firm." *Journal of Law and Economics*, 26 (1): 1-22

Cicchetti, Charles J. and A. Myrick Freeman III. 1971. "Option Demand and Consumer Surplus: Further Comment." *Quarterly Journal of Economics* 85 (3): 528-39.

Clawson, Marion. 1983. *The Federal Lands Revisited.* Baltimore: Resources for the Future. A careful survey of theory and practice expressing concern over excess centralization.

Cline, William R. 1992. *The Economics of Global Warming.* Washington: Institute for International Economics. Tries to refute Nordhaus's criticism of immediate action by considering impacts of assumptions more favorable to action. Cline still recognizes uncertainties necessitate a review at least after some action is tried.

Coase, Ronald H. 1937. "The Nature of the Firm." *Economica* NS 4 (4): 386-405. Reprinted in Stigler and Boulding, eds. 1952, 331-51; Coase 1988; and Williamson and Winter 1991. Classic brief discussion of the application of marginal analysis to the organization of the firm.

Coase, Ronald H. 1960. "The Problem of Social Costs." *Journal of Law and Economics* 3: 1-44. Reprinted in Coase 1988. Discussion with extensive empirical examples of the problems of controlling externalities

Coase, Ronald H. 1972. "Durability and Monopoly." *Journal of Law and Economics* 15 (1): 143-9. While Coase left this out of his collected essays, some writers act as if it were his most important article. He raises the question of how can a monopolist whose goods have long durability and have not been completely sold avoid the effects of expectations of future sales. He used the example of federal lands.

Coase, Ronald H. 1988. *The Firm, the Market and the Law.* Chicago: University of Chicago Press. A collection of what he considers his most important articles.

Cohen, Linda R. and Roger C. Noll with Jeffrey R. Banks, Susan A. Edellman, and Roger M. Pegram. 1991 *The Technology Pork Barrel.* Washington: The Brookings Institution.

Collinge, Robert A. and Wallace E. Oates. 1982. "Efficiency in Pollution Control in the Short and Long Runs: A System of Rental Permits." *Canadian Journal of Economics* 15 (2): 346-54.

Conrad, Jon M. 1980. "Quasi-option Value and the Expected Value of Information." *Quarterly Journal of Economics* 94 (4): 813-20.

Cooper, Edward H. 1974. "Attempts and Monopolization: A Mildly Expansionary Answer to the Prophylactic Riddle of Section Two." *Michigan Law Review* 72 (3): 375-462.

Corden, W. M. 1971. *The Theory of Protection.* Oxford: Oxford University Press. Good survey of issues including controls on intermediate goods.

Corden, W. M. 1974. *Trade Policy and Economic Welfare.* Oxford: Oxford University Press. An extensive, clear treatment of the limits of trade restrictions as a means to secure policy goals.

Cory, Dennis C. and Bonnie Clubby Saliba. 1987. "Requiem for Option Value." *Land Economics* 63 (1): 1-11.

Cournot, Augustin A. [1838] 1927. *Researches into the Mathematical Principles of the Theory of Wealth.* London: Macmillan. (Translation originally appeared in 1897 and apparently reprinted in 1927. That version, in turn, war reprinted by Richard D. Irwin in 1963.)

Crocker, Keith J. and Scott E. Masten. 1988. "Mitigating Contractual Hazards: Unilateral Options and Contract Length." *Rand Journal of Economics* 19 (3): 327-43.
Darby, Michael R. 1982. "The Price of Oil and World Inflation and Recession." *American Economic Review* 72 (4): 738-51. A skeptical view of the concerns.
Deacon, Robert T. and M. Bruce Johnson, eds. 1985. *Forestlands: Public and Private*. Cambridge Mass.: Ballinger Publishing Company for Pacific Institute for Public Policy Research. Critique of defects of federal management
Deacon, Robert T. and Walter J. Mead. 1985. "The Oil and Gas Industry: Regulation and Public Policy." In *Economics of the Mineral Industries*. 4th ed., edited by William A. Vogely, 483-531. New York: American Institute of Mining, Metallurgical, and Petroleum Engineers, Inc.
Deese, David A. and Joseph S. Nye, eds. 1981. *Energy and Security*. Cambridge, Mass.: Ballinger Publishing Company. Review of measures with great faith in stockpiling if better administered.
Demsetz, Harold. 1968. "Why Regulate Utilities?" *Journal of Law and Economics* 11 (1): 55-65. Reprinted in Stigler, ed. 1988, 267-78. Reprinted with postscript in Demsetz 1989, 75-90. Famed proposal for government ownership of facilities and bidding to operate efficiently.
Demsetz, Harold. 1969. "Information and Efficiency: Another Viewpoint." *Journal of Law and Economics* 12 (1): 1-22. Reprinted in Demsetz 1989, 3-24.
Demsetz, Harold. 1973a. "Industry Structure, Market Rivalry, and Price Policy." *Journal of Law and Economics* 16 (1): 1-10.
Demsetz, Harold. 1973b. "Joint Supply and Price Discrimination." *Journal of Law and Economics* 16 (2): 389-405.
Demsetz, Harold. 1974. "Two Systems of Belief About Monopoly." In *Industrial Concentration: The New Learning*, edited by Harvey J. Goldschmid, H. Michael Mann, and J. Fred Weston, 164-84. Boston: Little Brown. Reprinted in Demsetz 1989, 91-111. The efficiency-based justification.
Demsetz, Harold. 1988. *Ownership, Control and the Firm, the Organization of Economic Activity*. Vol. 1. Cambridge Mass. and Oxford: Blackwell.
Demsetz, Harold. 1989. *Efficiency, Competition and Policy, the Organization of Economic Activity*. Vol. 2. Cambridge Mass. and Oxford: Blackwell.
Demsetz, Harold. 1991. "The Theory of the Firm Revisited." In *The Nature of the Firm: Origins, Evolution and Development*, edited by Oliver E. Williamson and Sidney G. Winter, 144-65. New York: Oxford University Press. Preprinted in Demsetz 1988.
Destler , I. M. 1992. *American Trade Politics*, second edition. Washington: Institute for International Economics and New York: Twentieth Century Fund. A nonideological appraisal.
Dewey, Donald. 1969. *The Theory of Imperfect Competition: A Radical Reconstruction*. New York: Columbia University Press. Summarizes the theory and develops a large numbers analysis of limit pricing.
Dewey, Donald. 1974. "The New Learning: One Man's View." In *Industrial Concentration: The New Learning*, edited by Harvey J. Goldschmid, H. Michael Mann, and J. Fred Weston, 1-14. Boston: Little Brown.

Diamond, Peter A. and Eric Maskin. 1979. "An Equilibrium Analysis of Search and Breach of Contract." *Bell Journal of Economics* 10 (1): 282-316.

DiLorenzo, Thomas J. 1990. "The Origins of Antitrust: Rhetoric vs. Reality." *Regulation* 13 (3): 26-34.

Director, Aaron. 1964. "The Parity of the Marketplace." *Journal of Law and Economics* 7: 1-10.

Dornbusch, Rudiger and Stanley Fischer. 1987. *Macroeconomics*. 4th ed. New York: McGraw-Hill Book Company. (Revised in 1990). One of the leading texts.

Dornbusch, Rudiger and James M. Poterba, eds. 1991. *Global Warming: Economic Policy Responses*. Cambridge, Mass.: The MIT Press. Various writers including such regulars as Nordhaus, Jorgenson, and Manne and Rickels present papers.

Downs, Anthony. 1957. *An Economic Theory of Democracy*. New York: Harper and Row. Expands on Schumpeter's view of competition for votes.

Duchesneau, Thomas D. 1975. *Competition in the U.S. Energy Industry*. Cambridge, Mass.: Ballinger Publishing Company. Contains appendixes by various specialists; concludes competition is vigorous.

Dupuit, Jules. [1944] 1966. "On the Measurement of the Utility of Public Works." Reprinted in Arrow and Scitovsky 1966, 255-83. The translation first appeared in 1952 in *International Economic Papers* 2, 83-110.

Dye, Ronald A. 1985. "Costly Contract Contingencies." *International Economic Review* 26 (1): 233-50.

Easley, David, Robert T. Masson, and Robert J. Reynolds. 1985. "Preying for Time." *Journal of Industrial Economics* 33 (4): 445-60. Contention that aggressive behavior is an effective way to intimidate rivals.

Easterbrook, Frank H. 1981. "Predatory Strategies and Counterstrategies." *The University of Chicago Law Review* 48 (2): 263-337. Another skeptical treatment of predation.

Easterbrook, Frank H. 1984. "The Limits of Antitrust." *Texas Law Review* 63 (1): 1-40. Suggests erring on the side of caution because court errors are more permanent than monopolies.

Eaton, B. Curtis, and Richard C. Lipsey. 1989. "Product Differentiation." In *Handbook of Industrial Organization*. Vol. 1, edited by Richard Schmalensee and Robert D. Willig, 723-68. Amsterdam: North-Holland.

Ellis, Howard S. and Lloyd A. Metzler, eds. 1950. *Readings in the Theory of International Trade*. Philadelphia: The Blakiston Company (subsequently Homewood: Richard D. Irwin).

Fellner, William. 1949. *Competition among the Few: Oligopoly and Similar Market Structures*. New York: Alfred A. Knopf. Summary of the literature; probable source of most people's knowledge of Stackelberg.

Feyerabend, Paul. 1975. *Against Method, Outline of an Anarchistic Theory of Knowledge*. London: Verso. Advocacy of freer approach to methodology.

Fisher, Franklin M. 1989. "Games Economists Play: A Noncooperative View." *Rand Journal of Economics* 20 (1): 113-24. Expresses skepticism about contribution of game theory.

Fisher, Franklin M., John J. McGowan, and Joen E. Greenwood. 1983. *Folded, Spindled, and Mutilated Economic Analysis and U.S. v. IBM*. Cambridge, Mass.: The MIT Press. Consultants to IBM contend the case based on severe misunderstanding of competition and the problems of measuring it.

Fisher, Irving, 1930. *The Theory of Interest*. New York: Macmillan Publishing Company. Classic treatment of interest using a two commodity general equilibrium model.

Frankland, E. Gene and Donald Schoonmaker. 1992. *Between Protest and Power: The Green Party in Germany*. Boulder: Westview Press. Examination of an extreme example of how environmentalism goes far beyond internalizing externalities.

Freeman, A. Myrick III. 1984. "The Sign and Size of Option Value." *Land Economics* 60 (1): 1-13.

Frieden, Bernard J. 1979. *The Environmental Protection Hustle*. Cambridge, Mass.: The MIT Press. Discussion of exclusionary zoning and growth limitation policy in California.

Friedman, David D. 1989. *The Machinery of Freedom: Guide to a Radical Capitalism*. 2d ed. La Salle: Open Court. A collection of short essays arguing trying to eliminate all government.

Friedman, David D. 1990. *Price Theory: An Intermediate Text*. 2d ed. Cincinnati: South-Western Publishing. Well discusses the standard subjects from a libertarian viewpoint.

Friedman, James. 1977. *Oligopoly and the Theory of Games*. Amsterdam: North-Holland.

Friedman, James. 1983. *Oligopoly Theory*. Cambridge: Cambridge University Press.

Friedman, James. 1990. *Game Theory with Applications to Economics*, 2nd ed. New York: Oxford University Press.

Friedman, Milton. 1948. "A Monetary and Fiscal Framework for Economic Stability." *American Economic Review* 38 (2): 245-64. Reprinted in Friedman 1953 and Lutz and Mints, eds. 1951, 369-93.

Friedman, Milton. 1953. *Essays in Positive Economics*. Chicago: University of Chicago Press. Collected essays, mostly on monetary economics but starting with a controversial brief statement of principles.

Friedman, Milton. 1962. *Capitalism and Freedom*. Chicago: University of Chicago Press. Essays for the nonspecialists on the defects of selected policies.

Friedman, Milton. 1968a. "The Role of Monetary Policy." *American Economic Review* 58 (1): 1-17. Reprinted in Friedman, 1987.

Friedman, Milton. 1968b. *The Optimum Quantity of Money and Other Essays*. Chicago: Aldine Publishing Company.

Friedman, Milton. 1984. "Monetary Policy for the 1980s." In *To Promote Prosperity: U.S. Domestic Policy in the Mid-1980s*, edited by John H. Moore. Stanford: Hoover Institution Stanford University.

Friedman, Milton. 1987. *The Essence of Friedman*. Edited by Kurt R. Leube. Stanford: Hoover Institution Stanford University.

Friedman, Milton and Rose Friedman. 1980. *Free to Choose*. New York: Harcourt Brace Jovanovich. More general critiques of policies; the elaboration of his television series.

Friedman, Milton and Anna J. Schwartz. 1963. *A Monetary History of the United States, 1867-1960*. Princeton: Princeton University Press.

Furubotn, Eirik G. and Svetozar Pejovich, eds. 1974. *The Economics of Property Rights*. Cambridge, Mass.: Ballinger Publishing Company. Essays by various leading figures in the market-oriented school

Fudenberg, Drew and Jean Tirole. 1984. "The Fat-Cat Effect, The Puppy-Dog Ploy, and the Lean and Hungry Look." *American Economic Review* (Papers and proceedings) 74 (2): 311-6. Classification of possible images firms can convey to improve competitive position.

Fudenberg, Drew and Jean Tirole. 1989. "Noncooperative Game Theory for Industrial Organization: An Introduction and Overview." In *Handbook of Industrial Organization*, Vol. 1, edited by Richard Schmalensee and Robert D. Willig, 259-327. Amsterdam: North-Holland.

Fudenberg, Drew and Jean Tirole. 1991. *Game Theory.* Cambridge, Mass.: The MIT Press.

Galbraith, John Kenneth. 1952. *American Capitalism: The Concept of Countervailing Power.* Boston: Houghton Mifflin. Contends that to a degree that interaction of powerful sellers such as unions and large manufacturers with large buyers such as big processing firms and retailing chains lessens monopoly.

Galbraith, John Kenneth. 1958. *The Affluent Society.* Boston: Houghton Mifflin. Contends too little is spent on government.

Galbraith, John Kenneth. 1967. *The New Industrial State.* Boston: Houghton Mifflin. Contends large corporations can plan their future without restraint.

Gaskins, D. 1971. "Dynamic Limit Pricing under Threat of Entry." *Journal of Economic Theory* 3 (3): 306-22. Classic extension of the Bain analysis.

Giersch, Herbert, Karl-Heinz Paqué, and Holger Schmeiding. 1992. *The Fading Miracle: Four Decades of Market Economy in Germany.* Cambridge: Cambridge University Press. Examination of conflicting forces at work.

Gilbert, Richard J. 1981. "Patents, Sleeping Patents and Entry Deterrence." In *Strategy, Predation, and Antitrust Analysis*, edited by Stephen C. Salop. Washington: U.S. Federal Trade Commission.

Gilbert, Richard J. 1989. "Mobility Barriers." In *Handbook of Industrial Organization.* Vol. 1, edited by Richard Schmalensee and Robert D. Willig, 475-535. Amsterdam: North-Holland.

Globerman, Steven and Michael Walker, eds. 1993. *Assessing NAFTA: A Trinational Analysis.* Vancouver: The Fraser Institute.

Goldberg, Victor P. 1976. "Regulation and Administered Contracts." *Bell Journal of Economics* 7 (2): 426-45.

Goldberg, Victor P. and John R. Erickson. 1987. "Quantity and Price Adjustment in Long-Term Contracts: A Case Study in Petroleum Coke." *Journal of Law and Economics* 30 (2): 369-98.

Goldschmid, Harvey J., H. Michael Mann, and J. Fred Weston, eds. 1974. *Industrial Concentration: The New Learning.* Boston: Little Brown. Confrontations between classic fears of monopoly and more optimistic views.

Golub, Bennett W., Richard D. Tabors, Roger E. Bohn, and Fred C. Schweppe. 1983. "An Approach for Deregulating the Generation of Electricity." In *Electric Power Strategic Issues*, edited by James Plummer, Terry Ferrar, and William Hughes, 59-92. Arlington, Va.: Public Utilities Reports; Palo Alto, Calif.: QED Research.

Goodhart, C. A. E. 1989. *Money, Information and Uncertainty.* 2d ed. Cambridge, Mass.: The MIT Press. Good review of the monetary side of macroeconomics; reasonably accessible.

Goodwin, R.M. 1955. "A Model of Cyclical Growth." In *The Business Cycle in the Post-War World*, edited by Erik Lundberg. London: Macmillan. Reprinted in Robert Aaron Gordon and Lawrence R. Klein, eds. 1965, 6-22.

Gordon, Richard L. 1963. "Coal Price Regulation in the European Community." *Journal of Industrial Economics* 10 (3): 188-203. Early critique of the defects.

Gordon, Richard L. 1965. "Energy Policy in the European Community." *Journal of Industrial Economics* 13 (3): 219-34. Warning that the search for coordination would fail.

Gordon, Richard L. 1966. "Conservation and the Theory of Exhaustible Resources." *Canadian Journal of Economics and Political Science* 32 (3): 319-26. First known demonstration that the effect of interest rates on exhaustion was undetermined in general.

Gordon, Richard L. 1967. "A Reinterpretation of the Pure Theory of Exhaustion." *Journal of Political Economy* 75 (3): 274-86. An attempt to treat (with varying degrees of success) neglected elements of Hotelling's theory. Reintroduced his general model, correctly indicated its implications, failed to present the analysis as elegantly as other were to do. Incorrectly postulated inefficiency of decentralized management and erred about implications of rapid growth.

Gordon, Richard L. 1969. "Without Rudder Compass or Chart--The Problem of Energy Policy Guidelines." In *The Political Economy of Energy and National Security*, edited by S. H. Hanke. Published as *Quarterly of the Colorado School of Mines* 64 (4): 29-51. Shows that a market failure justification did not exist for U.S. energy policy.

Gordon, Richard L. 1970. *The Evolution of Energy Policy in Western Europe: The Reluctant Retreat from Coal*. New York: Praeger Special Studies in International Economics and Development. More elaborate review of experiences with coal-based energy policy.

Gordon, Richard L. 1974a. "Mythology and Reality in Energy Policy." *Energy Policy* 2 (3): 189-203.

Gordon, Richard L. 1974b. "The Optimization of Input Supply Patterns in the Case of Fuels for Electric Power Generation." *Journal of Industrial Economics* 23 (1): 19-37. First known survey of electric utility coal and oil buying practices, includes link to Coase theory of the firm.

Gordon, Richard L. 1975. *U.S. Coal and the Electric Power Industry*. Baltimore: Johns Hopkins University Press for Resources for the Future.

Gordon, Richard L. 1976a. "Government Controls of Competition in the Mineral Industries." In *Economics of the Mineral Industries*. 3d ed., completely revised and rewritten, edited by William A. Vogely, 712-34. New York: American Institute of Mining, Metallurgical, and Petroleum Engineers, Inc. Completely revised and rewritten.

Gordon, Richard L. 1976b. "Government Policies for Mineral Development and Trade." In *Economics of the Mineral Industries*. 3d ed., completely revised and rewritten, edited by William A. Vogely. New York: American Institute of Mining, Metallurgical, and Petroleum Engineers, Inc., 735-78.

Gordon, Richard L. 1978a. "The Hobbling of Coal: Policy and Regulatory Uncertainties." *Science 200* 14 April: 153-58. Reprinted in Philip H. Abelson and Allen L. Hammond, eds. *Energy II: Use Conservation and*

Supply, a special *Science* compendium. Washington: American Association for the Advancement of Science, 1978.

Gordon, Richard L. 1978b. "Hobbling Coal--Or How to Serve Two Masters Poorly." *Regulation* 2 (4): 36-45.

Gordon, Richard L. 1979. "Problems of Fair Market Value Estimation." In *Final Report Observations on Fair Market Value for Federal Coal Leases*, ICF Inc., submitted to the Fair Market Value Task Force, U.S. Department of the Interior.

Gordon, Richard L. 1981a. *An Economic Analysis of World Energy Problems*. Cambridge, Mass.: The MIT Press. Surveys energy use, exhaustion, and government regulation.

Gordon, Richard L. 1981b. *Federal Coal Leasing Policy, Competition in the Energy Industries*. Washington, D.C.: American Enterprise Institute for Public Policy Research.

Gordon, Richard L. 1981c. "Nuclear Power, The Uranium Industry, and Resource Development." With Appendixes on "Background on the Uranium Industry and the Use of Nuclear Energy." and "Summary of Selected Uranium Procurement Contracts." In *Uranium Resource Assessment.*, edited by John J. Schantz, Jr. (Resources for the Future Inc.), 135-208 and 222-75. Springfield, Va.: National Technical Information Service. Also in 1982, *Issues in Uranium Availability*, edited by John J. Schantz, Jr., Samuel S. Adams, and Richard L. Gordon. Washington, D.C.: Resources for the Future (Discussion paper D-84).

Gordon, Richard L. 1982. *Reforming the Regulation of Electric Utilities*. Lexington, Mass.: Lexington Books, D.C. Heath. Attacks lethargy in regulation and calls for radical reform.

Gordon, Richard L. 1983. "The Economics of Optimal Self-sufficiency and Energy Independence, Mineral Wars and Soft Energy Paths. "*Materials and Society* 7 (2): 225-35.

Gordon, Richard L. 1984a. "Reforming Regulation of Electric Utilities in the U.S.A.: Priorities for the 1980s." *Energy Policy* 12 (2): 146-56.

Gordon, Richard L. 1984b. "Access to Federal Lands for Profit Making Purposes--An Economic Overview." *Materials and Society* 8 (4): 699-718. A call for a shift towards encouraging production instead of worrying about windfall profits.

Gordon, Richard L. 1985a. "Energy Policy Issues." In *Economics of the Mineral Industries*. 4th ed., edited by William A. Vogely, 535-91. New York: American Institute of Mining, Metallurgical, and Petroleum Engineers, Inc.

Gordon, Richard L. 1985b. "Levies on U.S. Coal Production." *The Energy Journal*. Special Tax Issue, 6: 241-54.

Gordon, Richard L. 1985c. "The Production of Mineral Commodities." In *Economics of the Mineral Industries*. 4th ed., edited by William A. Vogely, 99-159. New York: American Institute of Mining, Metallurgical, and Petroleum Engineers, Inc. A survey of production economics.

Gordon, Richard L. 1986. "Perspectives on Reforming Electric Utility Regulation." In *Electric Power: Deregulation and the Public Interest*, edited by John C. Moorhouse, 447-75. San Francisco: Pacific Research Institute for Public Policy.

Gordon, Richard L. 1987a. "Coal in U. S. Land Policy." In *Planning for Changing Energy Conditions*, edited by John Byrne and Daniel Rich, 139-72. New Brunswick, N.J.: Transaction Books, Inc.

Gordon, Richard L. 1987b. "Using Markets to Solve Natural Resource Problems." In *Resources and World Development*, edited by D. J. McLaren and B. J. Skinner, 453-72. New York: John Wiley & Sons. Discusses market failures and why they do not justify prevailing interventions in mineral markets.

Gordon, Richard L. 1987c. *World Coal: Economics, Policies and Prospects*. Cambridge: Cambridge University Press.

Gordon, Richard L. 1988. "Federal Coal Leasing: An Analysis of the Economic Issues." Discussion Paper EM88-01, Washington, D.C.: Resources for the Future, Energy and Materials Division, July.

Gordon, Richard L. 1990. "Timidity in Electric Utility Deregulation." *Resources and Energy* 12 (1): 17-32.

Gordon, Richard L. 1992a. "EEC Hard Coal in a Restructured Europe." *Coping with the Energy Future: Markets and Regulations*. Proceedings of the 15th Annual International Conference, International Association for Energy Economics, H-21-H-28.

Gordon, Richard L. 1992b. "Energy Intervention After Desert Storm." *Energy Journal* 13 (3): 1-15.

Gordon, Richard L. 1992c. "The Public Utility Holding Company Act: The Easy Step in Electric Utility Regulatory Reform." *Regulation* 15 (1): 58-65.

Gordon, Richard L., Henry D. Jacoby, and Martin B. Zimmerman, eds. 1987. *Energy: Markets and Regulation*. Cambridge, Mass.: The MIT Press.

Gordon, Robert Aaron and Lawrence R. Klein, eds. 1965. *Readings in Business Cycles*. Homewood, Ill.: Richard D. Irwin.

Gordon, Robert J. 1990. *Macroeconomics*. 5th ed. Glenview: Scott-Foresman. Another standard text in the field.

Gore, Senator Al (sic). 1992. *Earth in the Balance: Ecology and the Human Spirit*. Boston: Houghton Mifflin. Calls for sweeping action against externalities of widely different credibility and for actions on other fronts.

Graham, Daniel A. 1981. "Cost-Benefit Analysis under Uncertainty." *American Economic Review* 71 (4): 715-25.

Graham, Daniel A. 1984. "Cost-Benefit Analysis under Uncertainty: Reply." *American Economic Review* 74 (5): 1100-2.

Graham, Frank D. 1923. "The Theory of International Values Re-examined." *Quarterly Journal of Economics*, 27 (4): 54-86. Reprinted in Howard S. Ellis and Lloyd A. Metzler, eds. 1950. *Readings in the Theory of International Trade*. Philadelphia: The Blakiston Company (subsequently Homewood, Ill.: Richard D. Irwin), 301-30. Brief development of his analysis of the problems of determining prices in a Ricardian model of trade.

Gray, John. 1984. *Hayek on Liberty*. New York: Basil Blackwell.

Grossman, Gene M., 1986. "Strategic Export Promotion: A Critique." In *Strategic Trade Policy and the New International Economics*, edited by Paul R. Krugman, 47-68. Cambridge Mass.: The MIT Press.

Grossman, Gene M. and Elhanan Helpman. 1991. *Innovation and Growth in the Global Economy*. Cambridge Mass.: The MIT Press.

Grossman, Sanford J. and Oliver D. Hart. 1986. "The Cost and Benefits of Ownership: A Theory of Vertical and Lateral Integration." *Journal of Political Economy* 94 (4): 691-719. Interesting view of the possibilities for extensive disintegration.

Haberler, Gottfried. 1950. "Some Problems in the Pure Theory of International Trade." *Economic Journal* 60 (238): 230-40. Reprinted in Caves and Johnson, eds. 1968, 213-29. Widely cited critique of the excessive support then given protectionism.

Haberler, Gottfried. 1958. *Prosperity and Depression.* 4th ed. Cambridge, Mass.: Harvard University Press. Classic survey and synthesis of the literature.

Haberler, Gottfried, ed. 1944. *Readings in Business Cycle Theory.* Homewood, Ill.: Richard D. Irwin.

Hamilton, James D. 1983. "Oil and the Macroeconomy since World War II." *Journal of Political Economy* 91 (2): 228-48. Claims oil prices were very influential.

Handler, Milton, assisted by Joshua F. Greenberg. 1967. *Cases and Materials on Trade Regulation.* 4th ed. Brooklyn, N.Y.: Foundation Press. Another standard text.

Hanke, Steve H. 1982. "The Privatization Debate: An Insider's View." *The Cato Journal* 2 (3): 652-62. Calls for complete transfer of public lands to private ownership. Proposes giving parklands to environmental groups.

Hanke, Steve H. 1985. "*The Federal Lands Revisited* by Marion Clawson." *Land Economics* 61 (2): 221-4. Criticizes Clawson for inadequate support of privatization.

Hanke, Steve H., ed. 1987. *Privatization and Development.* San Francisco: Institute for Contemporary Studies.

Hartshorn, J. E. 1967. *Politics and World Oil Economics.* Rev. ed. New York: Frederick A. Praeger. (U.S. edition of *Oil Companies and Governments.* London: Faber and Faber). Careful sensible review of the then prevailing situation. Good way to see how different things have become.

Hart, Oliver D. and John Moore. 1988. "Incomplete Contracts and Renegotiation." *Econometrica* 56 (4): 755-85.

Hausman, Daniel M. 1992. The Inexact and Separate Science of Economics. Cambridge: Cambridge University Press.

Hausman, Daniel M., ed. 1984. *The Philosophy of Economics: An Anthology.* Cambridge: Cambridge University Press. Covers most of the main figures in appendix A and many others.

Hayek, Friedrich A. 1944. *The Road to Serfdom.* Chicago: University of Chicago Press. An attack on the ill-conceived views of the British Labour Party widely misinterpreted as an attack on all intervention. (Hayek's British publisher long has been Routledge, formerly Routledge and Keegan Paul.)

Hayek, Friedrich A. 1945. "The Uses of Knowledge in Society." *American Economic Review* 35 (4): 519-30. Reprinted in Hayek 1948 and 1984. Widely cited explanation of how markets process information more efficiently than planning boards.

Hayek, Friedrich A. 1948. *Individualism and Economic Order.* Chicago: University of Chicago Press. (Collected Articles)

Hayek, Friedrich A. 1960. *The Constitution of Liberty.* Chicago: University of Chicago Press. Updating of policy views to object to newly emerging errors.

Hayek, Friedrich A. 1973, 1976, and 1979. *Law, Legislation and Liberty*. 3 vols. Chicago: University of Chicago Press. Extension of 1960 views.

Hayek, Friedrich A. 1976. "The New Confusion about 'Planning'." *Morgan Guaranty Survey* January: 4-13. Reprinted in Hayek 1978. Argues planning can be inept instead of dangerous.

Hayek, Friedrich A. 1978. *New Studies in Philosophy, Politics Economics and the History of Ideas*. Chicago: University of Chicago Press. (Collected Articles)

Hayek, Friedrich A. 1989. *The Fatal Conceit: The Errors of Socialism*. Chicago: University of Chicago Press. Summation of views; apparently drastically edited from sprawling first draft.

Hayek, Friedrich A. 1984. *The Essence of Hayek*. Edited by Chiaki Nishiyama and Kurt R. Leube. Stanford: Hoover Institution Stanford University.

Hay, George A. 1981. "A Confused Lawyer's Guide to the Predatory Pricing Literature." In *Strategy, Predation, and Antitrust Analysis*, edited by Stephen C. Salop. Washington: U.S. Federal Trade Commission.

Heflebower, Richard B. and George W. Stocking, eds. 1958. *Readings in Industrial Organization and Public Policy*, Homewood, Ill.: Richard D. Irwin.

Helpman Elhanan and Paul R. Krugman. 1985. *Market Structure and Foreign Trade: Increasing Returns, Imperfect Competition, and the International Economy*. Cambridge, Mass.: The MIT Press. Technical discussion of issues listed in title.

Helpman Elhanan and Paul R. Krugman. 1989. *Trade Policy and Market Structure*. Cambridge, Mass.: The MIT Press.

Heinlein, Robert A. 1966. *The Moon is a Harsh Mistress*. New York: G. P. Putnam. Novel in which the moon is a penal colony in which everything including justice is provided on a free market basis.

Hirsch, Abraham and Neil de Marchi. 1990. *Milton Friedman: Economics in Theory and Practice*. Hemel Hempstead: Harvester Wheatsheaf and Ann Arbor: University of Michigan Press.

Hobson, J. A. 1938. *Imperialism: A Study*. London: George Allen & Unwin. An overrated classic that gives the facts on imperialism and an inadequate explanation marred by anti-Semitism.

Hofstadter, Richard. 1955. *The Age of Reform: From Bryan to F.D.R.* New York: Alfred A. Knopf. (Vintage paperback edition, 1960) An excellent review of this history with appreciation of the defects as well as the virtues.

Hofstadter, Richard. 1963. *Anti-intellectualism in American Life*. New York: Alfred A. Knopf. (Vintage paperback edition, 1966)

Hofstadter, Richard. 1965. "What Happened to the Antitrust Movement?" In *The Paranoid Style in American Politics and Other Essays*, Richard Hoftstadter. New York: Alfred A. Knopf (Vintage paperback edition, 1967; University of Chicago paperback 1976); revised from earlier version in *The Business Establishment*, edited by Earl F. Cheit. New York: John Wiley & Sons, 1964. Reprinted with deletions in Sullivan 1991.

Holmstrom. Bengt R. and Jean Tirole. 1989. "The Theory of the Firm." In *Handbook of Industrial Organization*. Vol. 1., edited by Richard Schmalensee and Robert D. Willig, 61-133. Amsterdam: North-Holland.

Horwich, George and David Leo Weimer. 1984. *Oil Price Shocks, Market Response, and Contingency Planing*. Washington: American Enterprise Institute for Public Policy Research. Critical of controls but supportive of stockpiles.

Hotelling, Harold. 1931. "The Economics of Exhaustible Resources." *Journal of Political Economy* 39 (2): 137-75. The classic discussion; all the relevant cases are treated but the treatment of the general case was sketchy.

Houthakker, H. S. 1957. "Can Speculators Forecast Prices?" *The Review of Economics and Statistics* 39 (2): 143-51. Shows they can.

Houthakker, H. S. 1959. "The Scope and Limits of Futures Trading." In *The Allocation of Economic Resources*, edited by M. Abramovitz et al., 134-59. Stanford: Stanford University Press. Pioneering effort to sort out how and why it operates.

Howell, Thomas R., William A. Noellert, Jesse G. Kreier, and Alan Wm. Wolff. 1988. *Steel and the State: Government Intervention and Steel's Structural Crisis*. Boulder: Westview Press. Sponsored by leading U.S. steel companies, it documents state aid to steel around the world and claims that retaliation is appropriate.

Hufbauer, Gary Clide and Jeffrey J. Schott. 1992. *North American Free Trade: Issues and Recommendations*. Washington, DC: Institute for International Economics.

Hufbauer, Gary Clide and Jeffrey J. Schott. 1993. *NAFTA: An Assessment* Washington, DC: Institute for International Economics.

Hughes, Jonathan R. T. 1991. *The Governmental Habit Redux: Economic Controls from Colonial Times to the Present*. Princeton: Princeton University Press.

Hume, David. 1985. *Essays: Moral, Political, and Literary*. Indianapolis: Liberty Classics. This firm prepares beautifully printed, carefully edited versions of what it considers the classics supporting its viewpoint; this collection provides all of Hume's essays including his pioneering work in economics.

Hurwitz, James D., William E. Kovacic, Thomas A. Sheehan III, and Robert H. Lande. 1981. "Current Legal Standards of Predation." In *Strategy, Predation, and Antitrust Analysis*, edited by Stephen C. Salop. Washington: U.S. Federal Trade Commission.

Hutchinson, T. W. [1938] 1960. *The Significance and Basic Postulates of Economic Theory*. New York: Augustus M. Kelley. (Includes a 1960 preface by author.) One of the earliest proposals to apply Popper's then untranslated arguments to economics.

Hutchinson, T. W. 1977. *Knowledge and Ignorance in Economics*. Chicago: University of Chicago Press. Further views.

Ingrao, Bruna and Giorgio Israel. 1990. *The Invisible Hand: Economic Equilibrium in the History of Science*. Cambridge, Mass.: The MIT Press. Excellent history of the influence of the model, perhaps unduly concerned with the existence, stability, and uniqueness problem.

International Energy Agency. 1993. *Energy Policies of IEA Countries: 1992 Review*. Paris: Organisation for Economic Co-operation and Development.

Isaac, R. Mark and Vernon L. Smith. 1985. "In Search of Predatory Pricing." *Journal of Political Economy* 93 (2): 320-45. Smith, following the example set by Chamberlin, has sought to test the validity of economic theory by having small groups act out various cases of market behavior. Here, the experiment showed that participants did not adopt predatory pricing.

Ito, Takatoshi. 1992. *The Japanese Economy*. Cambridge Mass.: The MIT Press.

Jacquemin, Alexis and Margaret E. Slade. 1989. "Cartel, Collusion, and Horizontal Merger." In *Handbook of Industrial Organization*. Vol. 1, edited by Richard Schmalensee and Robert D. Willig, 415-73. Amsterdam: North-Holland.

Johnson, Harry. 1965. "Optimal Trade Intervention in the Presence of Domestic Distortions." In *Trade, Growth, and the Balance of Payments*, edited by Robert G. Baldwin (and 15 others), 3-34. Chicago: Rand McNally.

Johnson, Harry. 1977. "Commodities: Less Developed Countries' Demands and Developed Countries' Responses." In *The New International Order: The North-South Debate*, edited by Jagdish N. Bhagwati, 240-51. Cambridge, Mass.: The MIT Press.

Johnson, Paul. [1983] 1991. *Modern Times: The World from the Twenties to the Eighties*. Revised second edition. New York: Harper & Row. (U.S. edition of *A History of the Modern World: From 1917 to the 1980s*. Revision consists of new chapter on later developments.) Johnson takes a classic liberal view of the record.

Joskow, Paul L. 1977. "Commercial Impossibility, the Uranium Market and the Westinghouse Case." *The Journal of Legal Studies* 6 (1): 119-76.

Joskow, Paul L. 1985. "Vertical Integration and Long Term Contracts: The Case of Coal-burning Electric Generating Plants." *Journal of Law, Economics and Organization* 1 (1): 33-88.

Joskow, Paul L. 1987. "Contract Duration and Relationship-Specific Investments: Empirical Evidence from Coal Markets." *American Economic Review* 77 (1): 168-85.

Joskow, Paul L. 1988. "Price Adjustment in Long-Term Contracts: the Case of Coal." *The Journal of Law and Economics* 31 (1): 47-83.

Joskow, Paul L. 1990. "The Performance of Long-Term Contracts: Further Evidence From Coal Markets." *Rand Journal of Economics* 21 (2): 251-74. These articles subject published contract information to statistical analysis and show that the patterns correspond with theoretic expectations.

Joskow, Paul L. and Alvin K. Klevorick. 1979. "A Framework for Analyzing Predatory Pricing Policy." *The Yale Law Journal* 89 (2): 213-70. They propose a miniature appraisal of the vigor of competition to screen charges of predation.

Joskow, Paul L. and Richard Schmalensee. 1983. *Markets for Power: An Analysis of Electric Utility Deregulation*. Cambridge, Mass.: The MIT Press. Argues that improving the operation of regulatory commissions is preferable to radical reform.

Kahn, Alfred E. 1970. *The Economics of Regulation: Principles and Institutions*. 2 vols. New York: John Wiley & Sons. (Reprinted in 1988 without revision; bound in one volume with foreword by Paul L. Joskow and introduction by Kahn. Cambridge Mass.: The MIT Press.) A massive study of regulation practices.

Katz, Michael L. 1989. "Vertical Contractual Relations." In *Handbook of Industrial Organization*. Vol. 1, edited by Richard Schmalensee and Robert D. Willig, 655-721. Amsterdam: North-Holland.

Kaysen, Carl and Donald F. Turner. 1959. *Antitrust Policy: A Economic and Legal Analysis*. Cambridge, Mass.: Harvard University Press. A proposal for extensive deconcentration. See Sullivan, 1991 for an excerpt.

Kemp, Murray C. 1964. *The Pure Theory of International Trade*. Englewood Cliffs: Prentice Hall.

Kemp, Murray C. 1969. *The Pure Theory of International Trade and Investment*. Englewood Cliffs: Prentice Hall. Two difficult but excellent mathematical developments of the theory.

Keynes, John Maynard. 1936. *The General Theory of Employment, Interest, and Money*. London: Macmillan and Company. (Available in the Royal Economics Society collected works series.) The influential effort to provide a better analysis of depressions.

Klamer, Arjo and David Colander. 1987. "The Making of an Economist." *Journal of Economic Perspectives* 1 (2): 95-111.

Klamer, Arjo and David Colander. 1990. *The Making of an Economist*. Boulder: Westview Press. The results of surveys of the attitudes and ambitions of students at leading graduate schools; expresses concern about inadequate interest in applications. The book adds excerpts from interviews with students and separate reflections by each author.

Klein, Benjamin. 1980. "Transaction Cost Determinants of Unfair Contractual Relationships." *American Economic Review* (Papers and proceedings) 70 (2): 356-62.

Klein, Benjamin, Robert G. Crawford, and Armen A. Alchian. 1979. "Vertical Integration, Appropriable Rents, and the Competitive Contracting Process." *Journal of Law and Economics* 22 (2): 297-326. Case studies used to discuss the choice of procurement methods.

Klein, Benjamin and Keith B. Leffler. 1981. "The Role of Market Forces in Assuring Contractual Performance." *Journal of Political Economy* 89 (4): 615-41. Deals with the problems of quality assurance; shows that without explicit guarantees, assurance is expensive to obtain.

Klein, Lawrence R. 1947. *The Keynesian Revolution*. New York: Macmillan. One of the leading early post-war efforts to clarify the theory.

Knight, Frank H. 1956. *On the History and Method of Economics, Selected Essays*. Chicago: University of Chicago Press.

Knight, Frank H. [1947] 1982. *Freedom and Reform: Essays in Economics and Social Philosophy*. Indianapolis: Liberty Press. (Reprint of 1947 Harper & Brother publication.) Views of a classic liberal.

Koller, Roland H. II. 1971. "The Myth of Predatory Pricing--An Empirical Study." *Antitrust Law and Economics Review* 4 (4): 105-23. More case studies on the absence of predation.

Komiya, Ryutaro, Mashahiro Okuno, and Kotaro Suzumura, eds. 1988. *Industrial Policy of Japan*. Tokyo: Academic Press.

Kornhauser, Lewis A. 1983. "Reliance, Reputation, and Breach of Contract." *Journal of Law and Economics* 26 (2): 691-706.

Krattenmaker, Thomas G. and Steven C. Salop. 1986. "Anticompetitive Exclusion: Raising Rivals' Costs to Achieve Power over Price." *Yale Law Journal* 6 (2): 209-93. Develops Salop's earlier work on tactics to scare rivals.

Kreps, David M. 1990. *A Course in Microeconomic Theory*. Princeton: Princeton University Press, 1990. An effort to combine standard general equilibrium, models of uncertainty, and new models of oligopoly and the firm. The last is more successful than the other.

Kreps, David M. and Robert Wilson. 1982. "Reputation and Imperfect Information." *Journal of Economic Theory* 27 (2): 253-79. Another model of how to discourage competition.

Krouse, Clement G. 1990. *Theory of Industrial Competition*. Cambridge Mass.: Basil Blackwell. A review of formal models of imperfect competition.

Krugman, Paul R. 1989. "Industrial Organization and International Trade." In *Handbook of Industrial Organization*. Vol. 2, edited by Richard Schmalensee and Robert D. Willig, 1179-1123. Amsterdam: North-Holland.

Krugman, Paul R. 1990. *Rethinking International Trade*. Cambridge Mass.: The MIT Press.

Krugman, Paul R., ed. 1986. *Strategic Trade Policy and the New International Economics*. Cambridge Mass.: The MIT Press. A range of views on the potential for managed trade.

Krutilla, John V. 1967. "Conservation Reconsidered." *American Economic Review* 57 (4): 777-86. Recitation of the case for preserving land.

Kuhn, Thomas. 1970. *The Structure of Scientific Revolutions*. 2d ed., enlarged. Chicago: University of Chicago Press. Widely cited theory of science ruled by basic principles (paradigms) that are periodically overthrown in revolutions.

Kukathas. Chandran. 1989. *Hayek and Modern Liberalism*. Oxford: Oxford University Press. Views Hayek as a political philosopher and stresses the failure to reconcile support of naturally occurring process with criticism of existing practices.

LaCasse, Chantale and André Plourde. 1992a. "Oil and the Macroeconomy since World War II." *Journal of Political Economy* 91 (2): 228-48.

LaCasse, Chantale and André Plourde. 1992b. "Towards an Operational Definition of Security of Oil Supply." *Coping with the Energy Future: Markets and Regulations*. Proceedings of the 15th Annual Conference, International Association for Energy Economics, F39-46.

Laffont, Jean-Jacques and Jean Tirole. 1993. *A Theory of Incentives in Procurement and Regulation*. Cambridge Mass.: The MIT Press. Highly theoretic analysis.

Lakatos, Imre. 1976. *Proofs and Refutation: The Logic of Mathematical Discovery*. Cambridge: Cambridge University Press.

Lakatos, Imre. 1978a. *Mathematics, Science and Epistemology*. Philosophical Papers, Vol. 2. Cambridge: Cambridge University Press.

Lakatos, Imre. 1978b. *The Methodology of Scientific Research Programs*. Philosophical Papers Vol. 1. Cambridge: Cambridge University Press. Develops a modification of Popper's view that theories are refuted, not proved.

Landes, William M. and Richard A. Posner. 1981. "Market Power in Antitrust Cases." *Harvard Law Review* 94 (5): 937-86. Discussion of how to measure market power.

Landy, Marc K, Marc J. Roberts, and Stephen R. Thomas. 1990. *The Environmental Protection Agency: Asking the Wrong Questions*. New York: Oxford University Press. The heart of the book is five case studies involving decisions in the Carter administration. Participants were interviewed, mostly in 1981.

Lange, Oscar. 1936-1937. "On the Economic Theory of Socialism." *Review of Economic Studies* 4: 53-71 and 123-42. Frequently reprinted. First in 1938. *On the Economic Theory of Socialism.*, edited by B. E. Lippincott. Minneapolis: University of Minnesota Press. See, e.g., 1971. *Price Theory*, edited by Harry Townsend, 32-56. Harmondsworth: Penguin Books. Also 1972. *Socialist Economies*, edited by Alec Nove and D. M. Nuti, 92-112. Harmondsworth: Penguin Books. The classic defense that a planning board can set efficient prices.

Lave, Lester B. and Eugene P. Seskin. 1977. *Air Pollution and Human Health.* Baltimore: Johns Hopkins University Press for Resources for the Future. A pioneering effort to measure costs of health damage by pollution; now criticized for overstating health damages.

Leijonhufvud, Axel. 1968. *On Keynesian Economics and the Economics of Keynes: A Study in Monetary Theory.* New York: Oxford University Press. Contends that Keynes had a more sophisticated model than that presented in the texts.

Leshy, John D. 1987. *The Mining Law: A Study in Perpetual Motion.* Washington: Resources for the Future. Reviews the history of the law and calls for a more sensible one.

Letwin, William. 1965. *Law and Economic Policy in America: The Evolution of the Sherman Antitrust Act.* New York: Random House. (Now University of Chicago Press) Broad survey of the Act and its early history.

Levy, David. 1984. "Testing Stigler's Interpretation of 'The Division of Labor Is Limited by the Extent of the Market'." *Journal of Industrial Economics* 32 (3): 377-89. Presents confirming evidence.

Libecap, Gary D. 1981. *Locking Up the Range: Federal Land Controls and Grazing.* Cambridge Mass.: Ballinger Publishing Company for Pacific Institute for Public Policy Research. Shows defects of administration.

Libecap, Gary D. and Steven N. Wiggins. 1984. "Contractual Response to the Common Pool Problem: Prorationing of Crude Oil Production." *American Economic Review* 74 (1): 87-98.

Libecap, Gary D. and Steven N. Wiggins. 1985. "The Influence of Private Contractual Failure on Regulation: The Case of Oil Field Unitization." *Journal of Political Economy* 93 (4): 690-714. These discuss why regulation was adopted.

Lind, Robert C. (with Kenneth J. Arrow, Gordon R. Corey, Partha S. Dasgupta, Amartya K. Sen, Thomas Stauffer, Joseph E. Stiglitz, J. A. Stockfisch, and Robert Wilson). 1982. *Discounting for Time and Risk in Energy Policy.* Washington, D.C.: Resources for the Future.

Lindzen, Richard S. 1992. "Global Warming: The Origin and Nature of the Alleged Scientific Consensus." *Regulation* 15 (2): 87-98. Views of a meteorologist deeply engaged in attacking the claims of severe global warming problems.

Little, I. D. M. 1957. *A Critique of Welfare Economics.* 2d ed. Oxford: Oxford University Press. One of the better discussions.

Locke, John. 1688. *Two Treatises of Government.* (available in numerous reprints.)

Lott, John R., Jr. 1992. "Goring the U.S. Economy." *Regulation* 15 (3): 76-80. (Review of Senator Al Gore, *Earth in the Balance: Ecology and the Human Spirit.*) Indicates the defects of Gore's sweeping concerns.

Lovins, Amory B. 1977. *Soft Energy Paths: Toward a Durable Peace*. Cambridge, Mass.: Ballinger Publishing Company. Suggests use of simpler more decentralized approaches.

Lovejoy, Wallace F. and Paul T. Homan. 1967. *Economic Aspects of Oil Conservation Regulation*. Baltimore: Johns Hopkins Press for Resources for the Future. History of state regulation.

Lowry, S. Todd. 1976. "Bargain and Contract Theory in Law and Economics." *Journal of Economic Issues* 10 (1): 1-22.

Lucas, Robert E., Jr. 1981. *Studies in Business Cycle Theory*. Cambridge, Mass.: The MIT Press. Collected articles by Lucas (some coauthored) on the rational expectations approach; some are accessible to nonspecialists and give a good introduction to his approach.

Lucas, Robert E., Jr. and Thomas J. Sargent, eds. 1981. *Rational Expectations and Practice*. Minneapolis, Minn.: University of Minnesota Press. Collected largely highly technical articles by numerous authors.

Lutz, Friedrich A. and Lloyd W. Mints, eds. 1951. *Readings in Monetary Theory*. Philadelphia: Blakiston (subsequently Homewood, Ill.: Richard D. Irwin).

MacAvoy, Paul W. 1987. "The Record of the Environmental Protection Agency in Controlling Industrial Air Pollution." In *Energy: Markets and Regulation*, edited by Richard L. Gordon, Henry D. Jacoby, and Martin B. Zimmerman, 107-36. Cambridge, Mass.: The MIT Press. Contends, EPA, if anything, hindered the trend towards air quality improvement.

Macbean, Alasdair I. 1966. *Export Instability and Economic Development*. Cambridge Mass.: Harvard University Press and London: George Allen & Unwin. Showed defects in contention that poor countries could benefit from commodity price stabilization schemes.

McCloskey, Donald N. 1985. *The Rhetoric of Economics*. Madison: University of Wisconsin Press and Brighton: Harvester Press. Expands a journal article, largely by presenting various case studies.

McDonald, Steven. 1971. *Petroleum Conservation in the United Stars: An Economic Analysis*. Baltimore: Johns Hopkins Press for Resources for the Future. Excellent review of state policies.

McDonald, Steven. 1979. *The Leasing of Federal Lands for Fossil Fuels Production*. Baltimore: Johns Hopkins University Press, for Resources for the Future. Solid survey of issues.

McGee, John S. 1958. "Predatory Price Cutting: The Standard Oil (N.J.) Case." *Journal of Law and Economics* 1: 137-69. Widely cited discussion of the general drawbacks of predation as a strategy with argument that the record of the Standard Oil case does not support the belief that Standard engaged in predation.

McGee, John S. 1965. "Some Economic Issues in Robinson-Patman Land." *Law and Contemporary Problems* 30 (3): 530-51.

McGee, John S. 1971. *In Defense of Industrial Concentration*. New York: Praeger Publishers. Discusses problems of measuring loss to monopoly and argues the efficiency case for big firms is correct.

McGee, John S. 1974. "Efficiencies and Economies of Size." In *Industrial Concentration: The New Learning*, edited by Harvey J. Goldschmid, H. Michael Mann, and J. Fred Weston. Boston: Little Brown, 55-97. More on the efficiency case for big firms.

McGee, John S. 1980. "Predatory Pricing Revisited" *Journal of Law and Economics* 23 (2): 289-329. Summary evaluation of Areeda-Turner and their critics.

McGee, John S. 1988. *Industrial Organization*. Englewood Cliffs: Prentice Hall. Text stressing the optimistic view of actual competition from his prior writings.

McGee, John S. and Lowell R. Bassett. 1976. "Vertical Integration Revisited." *Journal of Law and Economics* 19 (1): 17-38. Points out that only one monopoly profit exists, the issue is how best to obtain it, and integration is not necessarily the best approach.

Machlup, Fritz. 1978. *Methodology of Economics and Other Social Sciences*. New York: Academic Press. Collected Articles.

Machlup, Fritz. 1991. *Economic Semantics*, second edition. New Brunswick: Transaction Publishers. Earlier anthology reissued.

Mancke, Richard B. 1974. *The Failure of U.S. Energy Policy*. New York, NY: Columbia University Press.

Mancke, Richard B. 1976. *Squeaking By: U.S. Energy Policy Since the Embargo*. New York, NY: Columbia University Press. Two surveys of the defects up to the time of writing.

Mankiw, N. Gregory and David Romer, eds. 1991. *New Keynesian Economics*. 2 vols. Cambridge Mass.: The MIT Press. A collection of articles updating the argument that price rigidities are major cause of economic instability.

Mariger, Randall. 1978. "Predatory Price Cutting: The Standard Oil of New Jersey Case Revisited." *Explorations in Economic History* 15 (4): 341-67. Supports McGee.

Marshall, Alfred. 1920. *Principles of Economics*. 8th ed. London: Macmillan and Company. (A two volume Variorum edition edited by C. W. Guillebaud was published by Macmillan in 1961). This was the classic basic text in economics for many years.

Mason, Edward S. 1957. *Economic Concentration and the Monopoly Problem*. Cambridge, Mass.: Harvard University Press. Collected articles on antitrust, natural resources, and economic development.

Mason, Edward S. 1982. "The Harvard Department of Economics from the Beginning to World War II." *Quarterly Journal of Economics* 97 (3): 383-433.

Masten, Scott E. and Keith J. Crocker. 1985. "Efficient Adaptation in Long-Term Contracts: Take-or-Pay Provisions for Natural Gas." *American Economic Review* 75 (5): 1083-1092.

Mead, Walter J. 1969. "Federal Public Lands Leasing Policies." *Quarterly of the Colorado School of Mines* 64 (4): 181-214. First of his many demonstrations that the federal government is well paid for oil leases.

Mead, Walter J. 1978. "Political-Economic Problems of Energy: A Synthesis." *Natural Resources Journal* 18 (4): 703-23.

Mead, Walter J., Asbjorn Moseidjord, Dennis D. Muraoka, and Philip E. Sorensen. 1985. *Offshore Lands: Oil and Gas Leasing and Conservation on the Outer Continental Shelf*. San Francisco: Pacific Institute for Public Policy Research. A summing up of the work

Mead, Walter J., Philip E. Sorensen, Russell O. Jones, and Asbjorn Moseidjord. 1980. *Competition and Performance in OCS Oil and Gas Lease Sales and Lease Development, 1954-1969*. Reston, Va.: U.S. Geological Survey.

Meade, J. E. 1955. *Trade and Welfare, The Theory of International Economic Policy.*
    Vol. 2. London: Oxford University Press. A solid, somewhat dull verbal
    discussion.
Means, Gardiner. 1939. *The Structure of the American Economy.* Washington:
    National Resources Council. The pioneering study of market share data.
Means, Gardiner. 1972. "The Administered-Price Thesis Reconfirmed." *American
    Economic Review* 62 (3): 292-306. A summing up of the contention that
    some firms administer prices not to respond to changing market conditions.
Meier, Gerald M. 1968. *The International Economics of Development, Theory and
    Policy.* New York: Harper & Row. An early survey of the limits of
    intervention.
Mendelsohn, Robert and William J. Strang. 1984. "Cost-Benefit Analysis under
    Uncertainty: Comment." *American Economic Review* 74 (5): 1096-1099.
Mény, Yves and Vincent Wright, eds. 1986. *The Politics of Steel: Western Europe
    and the Steel Industry in the Crisis Years (1974-1984).* Berlin: Walter de
    Gruyter. Useful surveys.
Michaels, Patrick J. 1992. *Sound and Fury: The Science and Politics of Global
    Warming.* Washington: The Cato Institute. A meteorologist's dissent over
    the assertion of certainty of warming.
Milgrom, Paul and John Roberts. 1982. "Predation, Reputation and Entry
    Deterrence." *Journal of Economic Theory* 27 (2): 280-312. Another model
    of how competitors might be intimidated.
Milgrom, Paul and John Roberts. 1987. "Informational Asymmetries, Strategic
    Behavior, and Industrial Organization." *American Economic Review.*
    (Papers and proceedings) 77 (2): 184-93.
Mill, John Stuart. [1848] 1909. *Principles of Political Economy with Some of Their
    Applications to Social Philosophy.* Edited by Sir William Ashley. London:
    Longman Green. Reprinted Fairfield: August M. Kelley. 1989.
Mirowski, Philip. 1988. *Against Mechanism: Protecting Economics from Science.*
    Totowa: Rowman & Littlefield.
Mirowski, Philip. 1989. *More Heat than Light: Economics as Social Physics:
    Physics as Nature's Economics.* Cambridge: The Cambridge University
    Press. Attacks economics for reliance on a model that by slavishly imitating
    nineteenth century physics presumes "conservation"; fails to indicate why
    this is bad and what to do about it.
Mises, Ludwig von. 1956. *The Anti-Capitalist Mentality.* Princeton: Van Nostrand.
    (Available with periodically added material from Libertarian Press, Spring
    Mills, Pa.) Rambling discussion of attacks on capitalism and reiteration of
    his defenses.
Mises, Ludwig von. 1960. *Epistemological Problems of Economics.* Princeton: Van
    Nostrand. (Translation of 1933 German book. 1976 edition with foreword
    by Ludwig M. Lachmann, New York: New York University Press) The
    initial presentation of the view that the theory is a priori; he apparently only
    means that neither confirmation or refutation is possible.
Mises, Ludwig von. 1966. *Human Action: A Treatise on Economics.* 3d rev. ed.
    Chicago: Henry Regnery Company. (Now published by Contemporary
    Books Inc., Chicago) A long defense of capitalism into which many attacks
    on other people's approaches to economics are interpolated.

Mises, Ludwig von. 1980. *The Theory of Money and Credit*. Indianapolis: Liberty Classics. (Reprint of the 1953 2d English ed., published by the Yale University Press. The original German language version appeared in 1912; the 2d German ed. in 1924; the first English translation in 1934.) His extensive review of the critical contribution of money to efficient economy.

Mises, Ludwig von. 1981. *Socialism: An Economic and Sociological Analysis*. Indianapolis: Liberty Classics. His classic review of the varieties of socialism and their defects.

Mises, Ludwig von. 1985. *Liberalism: In the Classical Tradition*. San Francisco: Cobden Press. A shorter, less digression-marred defense of capitalism.

Modigliani, Franco. 1958. "New Developments on the Oligopoly Front." *Journal of Political Economy* 66 (3): 215-32. A review of limit pricing theories.

Mork, Knut Anton and Robert E. Hall. 1980a. "Energy Prices and the U.S. Economy in 1979-1981." *The Energy Journal* 1 (2): 41-53.

Mork, Knut Anton and Robert E. Hall. 1980b. "Energy Prices, Inflation and the Recession in 1974-1975." *The Energy Journal* 1 (3): 31-63. An examination of the macroeconomic impacts that assumes many of the key results.

Mueller, Dennis C. 1989. *Public Choice II: A Revised Edition of Public Choice*. Cambridge: Cambridge University Press. A review of proposed solutions to the public good problem; excellent but technical.

Mulherin, J. Harold. 1986. "Complexity in Long-term Contracts: An Analysis of Natural Gas Contractual Provisions." *Journal of Law Economics and Organization* 2 (1): 105-17.

Mulholland, Joseph P. 1979. *Economic Structure and Behavior in the Natural Gas Production Industry, Staff Report to the Federal Trade Commission*. Washington, D.C.: U.S. Government Printing Office. Argues the industry is competitive.

Mulholland, Joseph P., John Haring, and Stephen Martin. 1979. *Staff Report on an Analysis of Competitive Structure in the Uranium Supply Industry*. Washington, D.C.: U.S. Government Printing Office. (Also draft version on file in the Federal Trade Commission Library). Argues the industry is competitive.

Muth, John F. 1961. "Rational Expectations and the Theory of Price Movements." *Econometrica* 29 (3): 315-35. Reprinted in Lucas and Sargent, eds. 1981. The first presentation of the concept.

Nahata, Babu, Kryzsztof Otaszewski, and P. K. Sahoo. 1990. "Direction of Price Changes in Third-Degree Price Discrimination." *American Economic Review* 80 (5): 1254-8.

Neale, A. D. and D. G. Goyder. 1980. *The Antitrust Laws of the United States of America, A Study of Competition Enforced by Law*. 3d ed. Cambridge: Cambridge University Press. Good survey but now needs updating.

Neff, Thomas L. 1984. *The International Uranium Market*, Cambridge Mass.: Ballinger Publishing Company. Excellent review of an inadequately studied industry.

Nelson, Robert H. 1983. *The Making of Federal Coal Policy*. Durham, N. C.: Duke University Press. An insider's view with stress on the lessons provided on the unrealism the belief in the desirability planning entrusted to impartial experts.

Nelson, Robert H. 1984. "Ideology and Public Land Policy: the Current Crisis." In *Rethinking the Federal Lands*, edited by Sterling Brubaker, 275-98. Washington: Resources for the Future.

Nelson, Robert H. 1987. "The Economics Profession and the Making of Public Policy." *Journal of Economic Literature* 25 (1): 49-91.

Nelson, Robert H. 1991. *Reaching for Heaven on Earth: The Theological Meaning of Economics*. Savage: Rowman & Littlefield Publishers. Uses religious and philosophical metaphors to show the critical role of policy advocacy in economics. He tries to divide people into two camps, but the framework is not ideal.

Neuhaus, Richard. 1971. *In Defense of People: Ecology and the Seduction of Radicalism*. New York: Macmillan Company.

Newbery, David M. G. and Joseph E. Stiglitz. 1981. *The Theory of Commodity Price Stabilization: A Study in the Economics of Risk*. Oxford: Oxford University Press. A highly technical survey.

Newlon, Daniel H. and Norman V. Breckner. 1975. *The Oil Security System: An Import Strategy for Achieving Oil Security and Reducing Oil Prices*. Lexington: Lexington Books, D.C. Heath. After admitting the barriers to private stockpiling are government made, the authors suggest how to improve government policy.

Niskanen, William A., Jr. 1971. *Bureaucracy and Representative Government*. Chicago: Aldine-Atherton. Argues decision making is governed by a search for power.

Nordhaus, William D. 1991. "The Cost of Slowing Climate Change: a Survey." *The Energy Journal* 12 (1): 37-65. One of his numerous articles arguing controls do not appear worth their costs.

Nozick, Robert. 1974. *Anarchy, State, and Utopia*. New York: Basic Books. Vigorous statement of the case for noncoercive government.

Ogden, Daniel M., Jr. 1978. "Protecting Energy Turf: The Department of Energy Organization Act." *Natural Resources Journal* 18 (4): 845-57. Shows how the Department deliberately was not given total control of energy.

Ohlin, Bertil. 1933. *Interregional and International Trade*. Cambridge, Mass.: The Harvard University Press.

Ohlin, Bertil. 1967. *Interregional and International Trade*. Rev. ed. Cambridge, Mass.: The Harvard University Press. Classic review of the many influences on international trade. The revision modifies the discussion by deleting material invalidated by Samuelson's analysis of factor price equalization.

O'Neill, Richard, Joan Heinkel, and Ruth Stokes. 1981. *Natural Gas Pipeline/Producer Contracts: A Preliminary Analysis*. Washington: U.S. Department of Energy, Energy Information Administration.

Ordover, Janusz A. and Garth Saloner. 1989. "Predation, Monopolization, and Antitrust." In *Handbook of Industrial Organization*. Vol. 1, edited by Richard Schmalensee and Robert D. Willig, 537-96. Amsterdam: North-Holland.

Ordover, Janusz A. and Robert D. Willig. 1981a. "An Economic Definition of Predation: Pricing and Product Innovation." *Yale Law Journal* 91 (8): 8-53.

Ordover, Janusz A. and Robert D. Willig. 1981b. "An Economic Definition of Predatory Product Innovation." In *Strategy, Predation, and Antitrust Analysis*, edited by Stephen C. Salop Washington: U.S. Federal Trade

Commission. These articles propose incorporating review of product innovation into studies of predation.

Panzar, John C. 1989. "Technological Determinants of Firm and Industry Structure." In *Handbook of Industrial Organization*. Vol. 1, edited by Richard Schmalensee and Robert D. Willig, 3-59. Amsterdam: North-Holland.

Patinkin, Don. 1948. "Price Flexibility and Full Employment." *American Economic Review* 38 (4): 543-64. Reprinted in Lutz and Mints eds., 1951.

Patinkin, Don. 1965. *Money, Interest and Prices*. 2d ed. New York: Harper and Row. (Available minus appendixes from MIT Press) The article and book discuss problems of interpreting Keynesian economics. Technical but excellent.

Peck, M. J. Richard Levin, and Akira Goto. 1987a. "Picking Losers: Public Policy Toward Declining Industries in Japan." *Journal of Japanese Studies* 13 (1): 79-123.

Peck, M. J., Richard Levin, and Akira Goto. 1987b. "Picking Losers: Public Policy Toward Declining Industries in Japan." In *Government Policy Towards Industry in the United States and Japan*. Proceedings of a Conference co-organized by Chikahii Moriguchi and John B. Shoven and sponsored by the Center for Economic Policy Research of Stanford University and the Sunatory Foundation of Japan, edited by John B. Shoven, 195-239. Cambridge: Cambridge University Press. Interesting paper on conscious shrinking program.

Peltzman, Sam, 1971. "Pricing in Public and Private Enterprises: Electric Utilities in the United States." *Journal of Law and Economics* 14 (1): 109-47.

Peltzman, Sam. 1976. "Towards a More General Theory of Regulation." *The Journal of Law and Economics* 19 (2): 211-40. Reprinted in Stigler, ed. 1988, 234-66. Develops a model of balancing pressures from the regulated and others.

Peltzman, Sam. 1977. "The Gains and Losses from Industrial Concentration." *Journal of Law and Economics* 20 (2): 229-63.

Peltzman, Sam. 1980. "The Growth of Government." *Journal of Law and Economics* 23 (2): 209-87. Reprinted in Stigler, ed. 1988, 3-84.

Penrose, Edith. 1968. *The Large International Firm in Developing Countries: The International Petroleum Industry*. London: James Allen & Unwin; Cambridge, Mass.: MIT Press. Develops the concept that bigness and integration are essential.

Penrose, Edith. 1980. *The Theory of the Growth of the Firm*. White Plains: M. E. Sharp.

Perry, Martin K. 1989. "Vertical Integration: Determinants and Effects." In *Handbook of Industrial Organization*. Vol. 1, edited by Richard Schmalensee and Robert D. Willig, 183-255. 1989. Amsterdam: North-Holland.

Phillips, Charles F., Jr. 1984. *The Regulation of Public Utilities: Theory and Practice*, Arlington: Public Utility Reports. Exhaustive study of regulatory practice.

Pigou, A. C. 1952. *The Economics of Welfare*. 4th ed. London Macmillan. Famed for its pioneering but now outmoded discussions of externalities and price discrimination.

Plott, Charles. 1981. "Theories of Industrial Organization as Explanations of Experimental Market Behavior." In *Strategy, Predation, and Antitrust*

234 Regulation and Economic Analysis

Analysis, edited by Stephen C. Salop. Washington: U.S. Federal Trade Commission.

Plummer, James L., ed. 1982 *Energy Vulnerability*. Cambridge, Mass.: Ballinger Publishing Company. Largely a review of the problem of stockpiling.

Plummer, James, Terry Ferrar, and William Hughes, eds. 1983. *Electric Power Strategic Issues*. Arlington, Va.: Public Utilities Reports; Palo Alto, Calif.: QED Research. Regulatory reform, diversification, and other alternatives are reviewed.

Polanyi, Michael. 1962. *Personal Knowledge: Towards a Post-Critical Philosophy*. Chicago: University of Chicago Press. Stresses the role of professional opinions and develops the argument informally.

Popper, Karl R. 1965. *Conjectures and Refutations: The Growth of Scientific Knowledge*. New York: Harper & Row. Further essays on refutation.

Popper, Karl R. 1966. *The Open Society and Its Enemies*. 2 vols., 5th ed. Princeton: Princeton University Press. The enemies are Plato, Aristotle, Hegel, and Marx.

Popper, Karl R. 1968. *The Logic of Scientific Discovery*. New York: Harper & Row. A tightly reasoned first statement of the concept that science involves refuting theories.

Popper, Karl R. 1972. *Objective Knowledge: An Evolutionary Approach*. Oxford: Oxford University Press. Further essays on refutation with stress on the invalidity of inductive reasoning.

Porter, Michael E. 1981. "Strategic Interaction: Some Lessons from Industry Histories for Theories and Antitrust Policy." In *Strategy, Predation, and Antitrust Analysis*, edited by Stephen C. Salop. Washington: U.S. Federal Trade Commission.

Porter, Michael E. 1980. *Competitive Strategy: Techniques for Analyzing Industries and Competitors*. New York: The Free Press. Industrial organization concepts used to organize efforts of firms to improve their position.

Porter, Michael E. 1985. *Competitive Advantage: Creating and Sustaining Superior Performance*. New York: The Free Press. Further discussion of how to use the concepts.

Porter, Michael E. 1990. *The Competitive Advantage of Nations*. New York: The Free Press. Case studies of successful industries in different countries.

Portney, Paul R., ed. 1978. *Current Issues in U.S. Environmental Policy*. Baltimore: The Johns Hopkins University Press for Resources for the Future.

Portney, Paul R., ed. 1990. *Public Policies for Environmental Protection*. Washington: Resources for the Future.

Posner, Richard A. 1969. "Natural Monopoly and Its Regulation." *Stanford Law Review* 21 (February): 548-643. Extends prior criticisms to conclude regulation is unnecessary.

Posner, Richard A. 1974. "Theories of Economic Regulation." *Bell Journal of Economics and Management Science* 5 (2): 335-8. Another view of how political pressures lead to inefficiencies.

Posner, Richard A. 1975. "The Social Costs of Monopoly and Regulation." *Journal of Political Economy* 83 (4): 807-27. Reprinted in Stigler, ed. 1988, 279-300.

Posner, Richard A. 1976. *Antitrust Law: An Economic Perspective*. Chicago: University of Chicago Press.

Posner, Richard A. 1979. "The Chicago School of Antitrust." *University of Pennsylvania Law Review* 27: 925-52. Reprinted with deletions in Sullivan, 1991. Claims a distinct Chicago stress on theory and promoting efficiency.

Posner, Richard A. 1986. *Economic Analysis of Law.* 3d ed. Boston: Little Brown. A classic on how economic principles can improve legal decisions.

Posner, Richard A. and Frank H. Easterbrook. 1981. *Antitrust: Cases, Economic Notes, and Other Materials.* 2d ed. St. Paul, MN: West Publishing Company. Another standard text.

Posner, Richard A. and Andrew M. Rosenfield. 1977. "Impossibility and Related Doctrines in Contract Law: An Economic Analysis." *The Journal of Legal Studies* 6 (1): 83-118.

Pratt, Joseph A. 1980. "The Petroleum Industry in Transition: Antitrust and the Decline of Monopoly Control in Oil." *Journal of Economic History* 40 (December): 828-31.

Primeaux, Walter J., Jr. 1975. "A Reexamination of the Monopoly Market Structure for Electric Utilities." In *Promoting Competition in Regulated Markets,* edited by Almarin Phillips, 175-200. Washington, D.C.: The Brookings Institution.

Primeaux, Walter J., Jr. 1986. *Direct Electric Utility Competition: The Natural Monopoly Myth.* New York: Praeger Publishers. Both publications claim multiple electricity distribution companies are efficient.

Ramsay, William. 1979. *Unpaid Costs of Electrical Energy: Health and Environmental Impacts from Coal and Nuclear Power.* Baltimore: Johns Hopkins University Press for Resources for the Future.

Rawls, John. 1971. *A Theory of Justice.* Cambridge, Mass.: Harvard University Press. Controversial effort to establish better rules for income distribution.

Ray, Dixy Lee with Lou Guzzo. 1990. *Trashing the Planet: How Science Can Help Us Deal with Acid Rain, Depletion of the Ozone, and Nuclear Waste (Among Other Things).* Washington: Regnery Gateway.

Ray, Dixy Lee with Lou Guzzo. 1993. *Environmental Overkill: Whatever Happened to Common Sense?* Washington: Regnery Gateway. A natural scientist and one-time head of the Atomic Energy Commission criticizes intervention

Redman, Deborah A. 1989. *Economic Methodology: A Bibliography with References to Works in the Philosophy of Science, 1860-1988.* New York: Greenwood Press.

Redman, Deborah A. 1991. *Economics and the Philosophy of Science.* New York: Oxford University Press.

Reinganum, Jennifer F. 1989. "The Timing of Innovation: Research, Development, and Diffusion." In *Handbook of Industrial Organization.* Vol. 1., edited by Richard Schmalensee and Robert D. Willig, 849-908. Amsterdam: North-Holland.

Ricardo, David. 1817. *The Principles of Political Economy and Taxation.* (Available in many editions including a volume in the Royal Economic Society's series of collected works of Ricardo published by the Cambridge University Press.) Classic most famous for presenting the comparative advantage principle.

Riordan, Michael H. 1984. "Uncertainty, Asymmetric Information and Bilateral Contracts." *Review of Economic Studies* 51 (1): 83-93.

Robbins, Lionel. 1932. *An Essay on the Nature and Significance of Economic Science*. London: Macmillan and Company Ltd. Survey of methodological issues centering on the central role in economics of choice.

Roberts, John. 1986. "A Signalling Model of Predatory Pricing." *Oxford Economic Papers* 38 (Supplement-November): 75-93.

Robinson, Joan. 1933. *The Economics of Imperfect Competition*. London: Macmillan and Company. Classic study of monopoly and monopsony with and without discrimination.

Rockwood, Alan. 1983, "The Impact of Joint Ventures on the Market for OCS Oil and Gas Leases." *Journal of Industrial Economics* 31 (4): 453-68.

Rogerson, William P. 1984. "Efficient Reliance and Damage Measures for Breach of Contract." *Rand Journal of Economics* 15 (1): 39-53.

Rothbard, Murrary N. 1971. "Freedom, Inequality, Primitivism and the Division of Labor." *Modern Age* 15 (3): 226-45. Reprinted in Kenneth S. Templeton, Jr., ed. 1977. *The Politicization of Society*. Indianapolis: Liberty Press, 83-126 and in George A. Panichas, ed. 1988. *Modern Age: The First Twenty-Five Years*. Indianapolis: Liberty Press, 103-23.

Rothbard, Murrary N. 1978. *For a New Liberty: The Libertarian Manifesto*. Rev. ed. New York: Libertarian Review Foundation. A strong antigovernment position.

Rothbard, Murrary N. 1988. *Ludwig von Mises: Scholar, Creator, Hero*. Auburn: Ludwig von Mises Institute. Short sketch.

Saloner, Garth. 1987. "Predation, Mergers, and Incomplete Information." *Rand Journal of Economics* 18 (2): 165-86.

Salop, Stephen C., ed. 1981. *Strategy, Predation, and Antitrust Analysis*. Washington: U.S. Federal Trade Commission. Useful collection of articles and discussions on the predation debate.

Sampson, Anthony. 1975. *The Seven Sisters: The Great Oil Companies and the World They Shaped*. New York: Viking Press. Despite his anti-industry bias, Sampson accurately reports the history.

Samuelson, Paul A. 1939. "Interactions between the Multiplier Analysis and the Principle of Acceleration." *Review of Economic Statistics* 21 (2): 75-8. Reprinted in Haberler, ed. 1944, 261-69 and Samuelson 1966, Vol. 2, 1107-1110. Classic business cycle model.

Samuelson, Paul A. 1948a. *Economics*. New York: McGraw-Hill. (The book went through 11 editions, the last in 1980, under the sole authorship of Samuelson and then with the 12th edition of 1985 became a collaboration with William Nordhaus.)

Samuelson, Paul A. 1948b. "International Trade and the Equalization of Factor Prices." *Economic Journal* 48 (2): 163-84. Reprinted in Samuelson 1966, Vol. 2, 847-85.

Samuelson, Paul A. 1949. "International Factor-Price Equalization Once Again." *Economic Journal* 49 (2): 181-97. Reprinted in Samuelson 1966, Vol. 2, 869-79. The two articles provide demonstrations of the circumstances under which trade equalizes factor prices.

Samuelson, Paul A. 1954. "The Pure Theory of Public Expenditure." *Review of Economics and Statistics* 36 (4): 387-89. Reprinted in Samuelson 1966, Vol. 2, 1223-25 and Kenneth J. Arrow and Tibor Scitovsky, eds. 1969. *Readings in Welfare Economics*. Homewood, Ill.: Richard D. Irwin, 179-82.

Samuelson, Paul A. 1955. "Diagrammatic Exposition of a Theory of Public Expenditure." *Review of Economics and Statistics* 37 (4): 350-56. Reprinted in Samuelson 1966, Vol. 2, 1226-1232. Discusses publicness and how to deal with it.

Samuelson, Paul A. 1957. "Intertemporal Price Equilibrium: A Prologue to the Theory of Speculation," *Weltwirschaftliches Archiv* 79 (2): 181-219. Reprinted in Samuelson 1966, Vol. 2, 946-84. Discusses price behavior of goods with major seasonal variations in demand or supply; proves to lead to a rule similar to Hotelling's rule for a constant cost exhaustible resource industry.

Samuelson, Paul A. 1958. "Aspects of Public Expenditure Theories." *Review of Economics and Statistics* 40 (4): 332-38. Reprinted in Samuelson 1966, Vol. 2, 1233-9. Further discusses publicness and how to deal with it.

Samuelson, Paul A. 1966. *The Collected Scientific Papers of Paul A. Samuelson.* 2 vols. Edited by Joseph E. Stiglitz. Cambridge, Mass.: The MIT Press.

Samuelson, Paul A. 1967a. "Indeterminacy of Governmental Role in Public-good Theory." *Papers on Non-Market Decision Making.* 8 (3): 47. Reprinted in Samuelson 1972a, 521.

Samuelson, Paul A. 1967b. "Pitfalls in the Analysis of Public Goods." *Journal of Law and Economics* 10: 199-204. Reprinted in Samuelson 1972a, 522-27.

Samuelson, Paul A. 1969. "Pure Theory of Public Expenditures and Taxation." In *Public Economics*, edited by J. Margolis, and H. Guitton, 98-123. New York: St. Martins Press. Reprinted in Samuelson 1972a, 492-517. Further discusses publicness and how to deal with it.

Samuelson, Paul A. 1972a. *The Collected Scientific Papers of Paul A. Samuelson.* Vol. 3. Edited by Robert C. Merton. Cambridge, Mass.: The MIT Press.

Samuelson, Paul A. 1972b. "Liberalism at Bay." *Social Research* 39 (1): 16-31. Reprinted in Samuelson 1977, 865-80. Discusses attacks on the active government concept of liberalism of the twentieth century and in passing awards victory to Hayek in the debate over socialist planning.

Samuelson, Paul A. 1977. The *Collected Scientific Papers of Paul A. Samuelson.* Vol. 4. Edited by Hiroaki Nagatani and Kate Crowley. Cambridge, Mass.: The MIT Press,

Samuelson, Paul A. [1947] 1983. *Foundations of Economic Analysis*. Expanded edition. Cambridge, Mass.: Harvard University Press. A mathematical development of production, consumption, and welfare theory.

Samuelson, Paul A. 1981. "Schumpeter's *Capitalism Socialism and Democracy.*" In *Schumpeter's Vision: Capitalism, Socialism and Democracy After 40 Years*, edited by Arnold Heertje, 1-21. London: Praeger. Reprinted in Samuelson 1986, 328-48.

Samuelson, Paul A. 1982. "Schumpeter as an Economic Theorist." In *Schumpeterian Economics*, edited by Helmut Frisch, 1-27. London: Praeger. Reprinted in Samuelson 1986, 301-27.

Samuelson, Paul A. 1983a. "My Life Philosophy." *The American Economist* 27 (2): 5-12. Reprinted in Samuelson 1986, 789-96.

Samuelson, Paul A. 1983b. "The World Economy at Century's End." In *Human Resources, Employment and Development: Vol. 1., The Issues*, edited by Shigeto Tsuru, 58-77. London: Macmillan. Reprinted in Samuelson 1986, 881-900.

Samuelson, Paul A. 1986. *The Collected Scientific Papers of Paul A. Samuelson.* Vol. 5. Edited by Kate Crowley. Cambridge, Mass.: The MIT Press.

Samuelson, Paul A. and Robert M. Solow. 1960. "Analytic Aspects of Antiinflation Policy." *American Economic Review* 50 (2): 177-94. Reprinted in Samuelson 1966, Vol. 2, 1336-1353. An adaptation of the Phillips's tradeoff analysis to the United States.

Scherer, F. M. 1974. "Economies of Scale as a Determinant." In *Industrial Concentration: The New Learning*, edited by Harvey J. Goldschmid, H. Michael Mann, and J. Fred Weston, 15-54. Boston: Little Brown. The case against big corporations.

Scherer, F. M. 1976a. "Predatory Pricing and the Sherman Act: A Comment." *Harvard Law Review* 89 (5): 869-90. Discussion of the drawbacks of Areeda and Turner.

Scherer, F. M. 1976b. "Some Last Words on Predatory Pricing." *Harvard Law Review* 89 (5): 901-3.

Scherer, F. M. 1980. *Industrial Market Structure and Economic Performance.* 2d ed. Chicago: Rand McNally College Publishing Company. (Republished Boston: Houghton-Mifflin Co.)

Scherer, F. M. and David Ross. 1990. *Industrial Market Structure and Economic Performance.* 3d ed. Boston: Houghton-Mifflin Co. A classic text with good view of theory and exhaustive literature review. Views monopoly with concern.

Schmalensee, Richard. 1972. "Option Demand and Consumer's Surplus: Valuing Price Changes under Uncertainty." *American Economic Review* 62 (5): 13-24.

Schmalensee, Richard. 1973. "A Note on the Theory of Vertical Integration." *Journal of Political Economy* 81 (2) part 2: 442-49. Further examination of the inefficiencies of monopolized earlier stages.

Schmalensee, Richard. 1975. "Option Demand and Consumer's Surplus: Reply." *American Economic Review* 65 (4): 737-39.

Schmalensee, Richard. 1979. *The Control of Natural Monopolies.* Lexington, Mass.: Lexington Books, D.C. Heath. Excellent survey of limits of regulation.

Schmalensee, Richard. 1981. "Output and Welfare Implications of Monopolistic Third-Degree Price Discrimination." *American Economic Review* 71 (1): 242-47. Analyzes when discrimination produces welfare improvement.

Schmalensee, Richard. 1989. "Inter-Industry Studies of Structure and Performance." In *Handbook of Industrial Organization.* Vol. 2, edited by Richard Schmalensee and Robert D. Willig, 951-1009. Amsterdam: North-Holland.

Schmalensee, Richard and Robert D. Willig, eds. 1989. *Handbook of Industrial Organization.* 2 vols. Amsterdam: North-Holland.

Schumacher, E. F. 1973. *Small is Beautiful: Economics as if People Mattered.* New York: Harper & Row. Contends a smaller scale technology is needed for poor countries.

Schumpeter, Joseph A. 1934. *The Theory of Economic Development: An Inquiry into Profits, Capital, Credit, Interest, and the Business Cycle.* Cambridge, Mass.: Harvard University Press. Classic study of innovation in capitalism.

Schumpeter, Joseph A. 1950. *Capitalism, Socialism, and Democracy.* 3d ed. New York: Harper & Brothers. Discussion of threats to the persistence of capitalism and of how socialism could be made tolerable.

Schumpeter, Joseph A. 1954. *History of Economic Analysis*. New York: Oxford University Press. Patched together from incomplete notes, this is a massive survey with views on many economists. His judgments often are idiosyncratic.

Schumpeter, Joseph A. 1989. *Essays on Entrepreneurs, Innovations, Business Cycles, the Evolution of Capitalism*. Edited by Richard V. Clemence, with a new introduction by Richard Swedenberg. New Brunswick: Transaction Publishers. (Reprint of 1951 publication by Addison-Welsey Press containing all of Schumpeter's published articles.)

Schumpeter, Joseph A. 1991. *The Economics and Sociology of Capitalism*. Edited by Richard Swedenberg. Princeton: Princeton University Press. Assorted essays ranging from the long available classics "Imperialism" and "Social Classes" to the previously unpublished; the editor provides a long introduction.

Schwartz, Anna J. 1992. "Review of Milton Friedman: Economics in Theory and Practice by Abraham Hirsch and Neil de Marchi." *Economic Journal* 102 (4): 959-61. Sees book as marred by misunderstanding of Friedman.

Schweppe, Fred C., Michael C. Caramanis, Richard D. Tabors, and Roger E. Bohn. 1988. *Spot Pricing of Electricity*. Boston: Kluwer Academic Publishing. Definitive review of the prospect spot pricing of electricity to large consumers.

Shapiro, Carl. 1989a. "Theories of Oligopoly Behavior." In *Handbook of Industrial Organization*. Vol. 1, edited by Richard Schmalensee and Robert D. Willig, 329-414. Amsterdam: North-Holland.

Shapiro, Carl. 1989b. "The Theory of Business Strategy." *Rand Journal of Economics* 20 (1): 125-37. Defends game theory models from attack by Franklin Fisher.

Sharkey, William W. 1982. *The Theory of Natural Monopoly*. Cambridge: Cambridge University Press. Short well done but not the first choice.

Shavell, Steven. 1980. "Damage Measures for Breach of Contract." *Bell Journal of Economics* 11 (2): 466-90.

Shavell, Steven. 1984. "The Design of Contracts and Remedies for Breach." *Quarterly Journal of Economics* 99 (1): 121-48.

Shavell, Steven. 1987. *Economic Analysis of Accident Law*. Cambridge, Mass.: Harvard University Press. These publications develop the case for private cures.

Sherman, Roger. 1989. *The Regulation of Monopoly*. Cambridge: Cambridge University Press. Short well done but not the first choice.

Shubik, Martin. 1959. *Strategy and Market Structure: Competition, Oligopoly, and the Theory of Games*. New York: John Wiley & Sons. Early presentation of the approach.

Shwadran, Benjamin. 1973. *The Middle East, Oil and the Great Powers*. 3d ed. Jerusalem: Israel Universities Press. Extensive details on this history; little analysis.

Sidak, Joseph Gregory. 1983. "Debunking Predatory Innovation." *Columbia Law Review* 83 (5): 1121-49.

Slutsky, Eugene. 1937. "The Summation of Random Causes as the Source of Cyclic Processes." *Econometrica* 5 (2): 105-46. Famous demonstration that random variations may seem to have a pattern.

Smith, Adam. 1978. *Lectures on Jurisprudence.* The Glasgow edition of the Work and Correspondence of Adam Smith. Oxford: Oxford University Press and Indianapolis: Liberty Classics. Students notes of lectures most notable for anticipation of the *Wealth of Nations.*

Smith, Adam. 1979a. *An Inquiry into the Nature and Causes of the Wealth of Nations.* The Glasgow edition of the Work and Correspondence of Adam Smith, Oxford: Oxford University Press and Indianapolis: Liberty Classics. (The most widely available alternative is the Cannon edition long in the Modern Library and now from the University of Chicago Press. A Penguin edition also exists.) The classic on the case for lessened government intervention.

Smith, Adam. 1979b. *The Theory of Moral Sentiments.* The Glasgow edition of the Work and Correspondence of Adam Smith. Oxford: Oxford University Press and Indianapolis: Liberty Classics. His effort to propound a theory of ethics based on sympathy.

Smith, V. Kerry. 1982. "Option Value: A Conceptual Overview." *Southern Economic Journal* 48 (3): 654-68.

Smith, V. Kerry, ed. 1979. *Scarcity and Growth Reconsidered.* Baltimore: The Johns Hopkins University Press for Resources for the Future. Debates whether the Barnett and Morse analysis still is valid.

Solow, Robert M. 1956. "A Contribution to the Theory of Economic Growth." *Quarterly Journal of Economics* 70 (1): 65-94. Reprinted in Stiglitz and Uzawa, eds. 1969, 58-87. Classic contribution adding input substitution to growth models.

Solow, Robert M. 1992. *An Almost Practical Step Toward Sustainability.* Washington: Resources for the Future. A distinguished economist endorses the case for conserving resources.

Spencer, Barbara J. 1986. "What Should Trade Policy Target?" In *Strategic Trade Policy and the New International Economics,* edited by Paul R. Krugman, 69-89. Cambridge Mass.: The MIT Press.

Spence, A. Michael. 1981. "Competition, Entry and Antitrust Policy." In *Strategy, Predation, and Antitrust Analysis,* edited by Stephen C Salop. Washington: U.S. Federal Trade Commission.

Spulber, Daniel F. 1989. *Regulation and Markets.* Cambridge Mass.: The MIT Press. Survey of public utility, environmental, health and safety, and antitrust regulation. Examines both firm behavior and interactions between regulators and firms. Heavily mathematical with extensive commentary.

Statistik der Kohlenwirschaft E.V. 1993. *Der Kohlenbergbau in der Energiewirschaft der Bundesrepublik Deutschland im Jahre 1992.* Essen.

Stern, Jonathan P. 1982. *East European Energy and East-West Trade in Energy.* London: Policy Studies Institute.

Stern, Jonathan P. 1984. *International Gas Trade in Europe: The Politics of Exporting and Importing Countries.* London: Heinemann Educational Books.

Stern, Jonathan P. 1985. *Gas's Contribution to UK Self-sufficiency.* London: Heinemann Educational Books.

Stigler, George J. 1947. "The Kinky Oligopoly Demand Curve and Rigid Prices." *Journal of Political Economy* 54 (5): 185-93. Reprinted in Stigler 1968, 208-34. Attack on the belief in rigid oligopoly prices.

Stigler, George J. 1949. "A Theory of Delivered Price Systems." *American Economic Review* 39 (6): 1143-59. Reprinted in Stigler 1968, 147-64.

Stigler, George J. 1950. "Monopoly and Oligopoly by Merger." *American Economic Review* (Papers and proceedings), 40 (2): 23-34. Reprinted in Stigler 1968, 95-107. Discusses mergers that lessened competition.

Stigler, George J. 1951. "The Division of Labor is Limited by the Extent of the Market." *Journal of Political Economy* 59 (3): 185-93. Reprinted in Stigler 1968. Argues that in larger markets, more input suppliers can operate and perils of open-market dealing decreases.

Stigler, George J. 1957. "Perfect Competition Historically Contemplated." *Journal of Political Economy* 64 (1). Reprinted in Stigler 1965, 234-67.

Stigler, George J. 1958. "The Economies of Scale." *Journal of Law and Economics* 1: 54-71. Reprinted in Stigler 1968, 71-94.

Stigler, George J. 1959. "The Politics of Political Economists." *Quarterly Journal of Economics* 73 (4): 522-32. Reprinted in Stigler 1965, 51-65. Argues professional economists are more appreciative than noneconomists of markets.

Stigler, George J. 1961. "The Economics of Information." *Journal of Political Economy* 69 (3):. Reprinted in Stigler 1968, 171-90.

Stigler, George J. 1964. "A Theory of Oligopoly." *Journal of Political Economy* 72 (1): 44-61. Reprinted in Stigler 1968, 39-63. Analysis of the problems of sustaining collusion when imperfect information hinders distinguishing price cutting from random market fluctuations.

Stigler, George J. 1965, *Essays in the History of Economics*. Chicago: University of Chicago Press.

Stigler, George J. 1966. The Economic Effects of Antitrust Laws." *Journal of Law and Economics* 9: 225-58. Reprinted in Stigler 1968, 259-95.

Stigler, George J. 1968. *The Organization of Industry*. Homewood, Ill.: Richard D. Irwin (available as a paperback from the University of Chicago Press).

Stigler, George J. 1971. "The Theory of Economic Regulation." *Bell Journal of Economics and Management Science* 2 (1): 3-21. Reprinted in Stigler 1975, 114-41. Develops the theory of capture of regulators by the regulated industry.

Stigler, George J. 1975. *The Citizen and the State: Essays on Regulation*. Chicago: University of Chicago Press.

Stigler, George J. 1982. *The Economist as Preacher and Other Essays*. Chicago: University of Chicago Press.

Stigler, George J. 1984. *The Intellectual and the Marketplace*. Enlarged edition. Cambridge Mass.: Harvard University Press. Stigler's title article dates back to 1962 when it appeared in a short-lived, University-of-Chicago-based magazine *The New Individualist Review*. All the 21 issues are reprinted in a volume issued by Liberty Press. A collection of short, often satirical essays on assorted subjects; the title essay suggests bad taste is inherent and markets merely reflect it.

Stigler, George J. 1986. *The Essence of Stigler*. Edited by Kurt R. Leube and Thomas Gale Moore. Stanford: Hoover Institution Stanford University.

Stigler, George J. 1987. *The Theory of Price*. 4th ed. New York: Macmillan Publishing Company. A classic text; somewhat less comprehensive than more recently initiated efforts but far more penetrating and witty.

Stigler, George J. 1988. *Memoirs of an Unregulated Economist.* New York: Basic Books.

Stigler, George J. and Claire Friedland. 1962. "What Can Regulators Regulate?: The Case of Electricity." *Journal of Law and Economics* 5: 1-16. Reprinted in Stigler 1975, 61-77. Shows that regulation had no statistically significant effects.

Stigler, George J. and Robert A. Sherwin. 1985. "The Extent of the Market." *Journal of Law and Economics* 28 (3): 555-85. Further tests confirming the applicability of Stigler's analysis.

Stigler, George J., ed. 1988. *Chicago Studies in Political Economy.* Chicago: University of Chicago Press. Major studies in the Chicago tradition.

Stigler, George J. and Kenneth E. Boulding, eds. 1952. *Readings in Price Theory.* Homewood, Ill.: Richard D. Irwin.

Stiglitz, Joseph E. 1989. "Imperfect Information in the Product Market." In *Handbook of Industrial Organization.* Vol. 1, edited by Richard Schmalensee and Robert D. Willig, 769-847. Amsterdam: North-Holland.

Stiglitz, Joseph E. and G. Frank Mathewson, eds. 1986. *New Developments in the Analysis of Market Structure.* Cambridge Mass.: The MIT Press.

Stiglitz Joseph E. and Hirofumi Uzawa, eds. 1969. *Readings in the Modern Theory of Economic Growth.* Cambridge Mass.: The MIT Press. Collected articles including most of the classics.

Stolper, Wolfgang and Paul A. Samuelson. 1941. "Protection and Real Wages." *Review of Economic Studies* 9 (1): 58-73. Reprinted in Ellis and Metzler 1949, 333-51 and Samuelson 1966, Vol.. 2, 831-46. Demonstration of relationship between good and factor prices.

Stroup, Richard L. and John A. Baden. 1983. *Natural Resources Bureaucratic Myths and Environmental Management.* San Francisco: Pacific Institute for Public Policy Research. Overview of the defects of public land management.

Sugden, Robert. 1984. "Reciprocity: The Supply of Public Goods Through Voluntary Contributions." *The Economic Journal* 94 (4): 772-87.

Sullivan, E. Thomas, ed. 1991. *The Political Economy of the Sherman Act: The First One Hundred Years.* New York: Oxford University Press. A collection of shortened selected articles on antitrust. Better than half the book is devoted to alternative explanations of the motives behind the Sherman Act--roughly Bork versus his critics. The rest relates to practice and is roughly Posner's case for Chicago and its critics.

Svensson, Lars E. O. 1984. "Oil Prices, Welfare and the Trade Balance." *Quarterly Journal of Economics* 99 (4): 649-72.

Sylos-Labini, Paolo. 1969. *Oligopoly and Technical Progress.* Rev. ed. Cambridge, Mass.: Harvard University Press. Discussion of the limit price concept.

Tarlock, A Dan. 1985. "The Making of Federal Coal Policy: Lessons for Public Lands from a Failed Program, An Essay and Review." *Natural Resources Journal* 25 (April): 349-71

Tamari, Meir. 1987. *"With All Your Possessions": Jewish Ethics and Economic Life.* New York: The Free Press.

Telser, L. G. 1960. "Why Should Manufacturers Want Fair Trade?" *Journal of Law and Economics* 3: 86-105. Argues that either better control of marketing or facilitating price discrimination may be involved.

Telser, L. G. 1966. "Cutthroat Competition and the Long Purse." *The Journal of Law and Economics* 9 : 259-77. Argues long purses are not critical.

Telser, L. G. 1965. "Abusive Trade Practices: An Economic Analysis." *Law and Contemporary Problems* 30 (3): 488-505.

Telser, L. G. 1980. "A Theory of Self-enforcing Agreements." *Journal of Business* 53 (1): 27-44.

Tex Report Ltd. Annual. *Coal Manual.* Tokyo. Elaborate compendium of data on Japanese coal trade.

Thorelli, Hans B. 1955. *Federal Antitrust Policy: Origination of an American Tradition.* Baltimore: John Hopkins Press. Good review of the enactment and early history of the Sherman Act.

Tirole, Jean. 1986. "Procurement and Renegotiation." *Journal of Political Economy* 94 (2): 235-59.

Tirole, Jean. 1988. *The Theory of Industrial Organization.* Cambridge, Mass.: The MIT Press. Formal models of the subject.

Tobin, James. 1956. "The Interest Elasticity of Transactions Demand for Cash." *Review of Economics and Statistics* 38 (3): 241-7.

Tocqueville, Alexis de. 1848. *Democracy in America.* Vintage Book ed. 2 vol. New York: Vintage Books, 1954.

Toulmin, Stephen Edelston. 1958. *The Uses of Argument.* Cambridge: Cambridge University Press.

Train, Kenneth E. 1991. *Optimal Regulation: The Economic Theory of Natural Monopoly.* Cambridge Mass.: The MIT Press. Covers the standard topics with discussions simpler than in many other texts. Still requires knowledge of economics.

Truluck, Phillip N., ed. 1983. *Private Rights and Public Lands.* Washington, D.C.: The Heritage Foundation and San Francisco: Pacific Institute for Public Policy Research.

Tucker, William. 1982. *Progress and Privilege: America in the Age of Environmentalism.* Garden City: Anchor Press/Doubleday.

Tucker, William. 1990. *The Excluded Americans: Homelessness and Housing Policies.* Washington: Regnery Gateway.

Tugwell, Rexford G. 1957. *The Democratic Roosevelt: A Biography of Franklin D. Roosevelt.* Garden City: Doubleday. Reprinted Penguin Books 1969.

Tussing, Arlon R. and Connie C. Barlow. 1984. *The Natural Gas Industry: Evolution, Structure, and Economics.* Cambridge, Mass.: Ballinger.

Tyson, Laura d'Andrea. 1992. *Who's Bashing Whom?: Trade Conflict in High-Technology Industries.* Washington, DC: Institute for International Economics. A qualified endorsement of aiding critical industries.

U.S. Commission on Fair Market Value Policy for Federal Coal Leasing. 1984. *Report of the Commission.* Washington, D.C.: U.S. Government Printing Office.

U.S. Congress. 1976. *Federal Coal Leasing Amendments Act of 1975.* Washington, D.C.: U.S. Government Printing Office.

U.S. Congress. General Accounting Office. 1977a. *The State of Competition in the Coal Industry.* Washington, D.C. Another report concluding competition is vigorous.

U.S. Congress. General Accounting Office. 1977b. *U.S. Coal Development: Promises, Uncertainties.* Washington, D.C.

U.S. Congress. General Accounting Office. 1983. *Analysis of the Powder River Basin Federal Coal Lease Sale: Economic Improvements and Legislative Changes Needed*, Washington, D.C.: U.S. Government Printing Office.

U.S. Congress, House of Representatives, Committee on Appropriations, Surveys and Investigations Staff. 1983. *A Report to the Committee on Appropriations, U.S. House of Representatives on the Coal Leasing Program of U.S. Department of Interior*.

U.S. Congress, Office of Technology Assessment. 1981. *An Assessment of Development and Production Potential of Federal Coal Leases*. Washington, D.C.: U.S. Government Printing Office.

U.S. Congress, Office of Technology Assessment, 1984a, *Acid Rain and Transported Air Pollutants: Implications for Public Policy*. Washington, D.C.: U.S. Government Printing Office.

U.S. Congress, Office of Technology Assessment. 1984b. *Environmental Protection in the Federal Coal Leasing Program*. Washington, D.Ç.: U.S. Government Printing Office.

U.S. Department of Energy. 1981a *Coal Competition: Prospects for the 1980s, Draft Report* (with Technical Appendix). Another report concluding competition is vigorous.

U.S. Department of Energy. 1981b. *Coal Competition: Prospects for the 1980s*. Springfield, Va.: National Technical Information Service. Another report concluding competition is vigorous.

U.S. Department of the Interior. 1979. *Secretarial Issue Document Federal Coal Management Program*. Washington, D.C.

U.S. Department of the Interior, Bureau of Land Management. Annual. *Federal Coal Management Report*.

U.S. Department of the Interior, Bureau of Land Management. 1975. *Final Environmental Impact Statement Proposed Federal Coal Leasing Program*. Washington, D.C.: U.S. Government Printing Office.

U.S. Department of the Interior, Bureau of Land Management. 1979. *Final Environmental Statement: Federal Coal Management Program*. Washington, D.C.: U.S. Government Printing Office.

U.S. Department of the Interior, Bureau of Land Management. 1985. *Federal Coal Management Program: Final Environmental Impact Statement*.

U.S. Department of the Interior, Bureau of Land Management. 1986a. *Competitive Coal Leasing*, BLM Manual Handbook 3420-1.

U.S. Department of the Interior, Bureau of Land Management. 1986b. *Guide to Federal Coal Property Appraisal*.

U.S. Department of Justice. Annual since 1978. *Competition in the Coal Industry*. Washington, D.C.: U.S. Government Printing Office. (The last extensive report was in 1983; now replaced by statement in the annual Bureau of Land Management review of coal leasing.) These reports also conclude competition is vigorous.

U.S. Federal Trade Commission, Bureau of Economics. 1978. *Report to the Federal Trade Commission on the Structure of the Nation's Coal Industry 1964-1974*. Washington, D.C.: U.S. Government Printing Office. (Draft version available in FTC library). Another report concluding competition is vigorous.

U.S. Interagency Land Acquisition Conference. 1973. *Uniform Appraisal Standards for Federal Land Acquisitions*. Washington, D.C.: U.S. Government Printing Office. Rules for determining fair market value.

U.S. Public Land Law Review Commission. 1970. *One Third of the Nation's Land*.

U.S. Task Force on Antitrust Policy. 1968. "Task Force Report on Antitrust Policy." in *Congressional Record--Senate*, May 27, 1969, p. 5642-5659.

U.S. Tennessee Valley Authority (Herbert S. Sanger and William E. Mason). 1977. *The Structure of the Energy Markets: A Report of TVA's Antitrust Investigation of the Coal and Uranium Industries*, 3 vols. Knoxville, Tenn.

U.S. Tennessee Valley Authority (Herbert S. Sanger and William E. Mason). 1979. *The Structure of the Energy Markets: A Report of TVA's Antitrust Investigation of the Coal and Uranium Industries, 1979 update*. Knoxville, Tenn. Disjointed efforts to prove monopoly exists.

Varian, Hal R. 1985. "Price Discrimination and Social Welfare." *American Economic Review* 75 (4): 870-5. Further appraisal of the welfare effects of discrimination.

Varian, Hal R. 1987. *Intermediate Microeconomics: A Modern Approach*. New York: W. W. Norton.

Varian, Hal R. 1989. "Price Discrimination." In *Handbook of Industrial Organization*. Vol. 1 edited by Richard Schmalensee and Robert D. Willig, 597-654. Amsterdam: North-Holland. Summary appraisal of the welfare effects of discrimination.

Varian, Hal R. 1992. *Microeconomic Analysis*. 3d ed. New York: W. W. Norton. Excellent advanced text.

Verleger, Philip K., Jr. 1982. *Oil Market in Turmoil*, Cambridge Mass.: Ballinger Publishing Company for Pacific Institute.

Verleger, Philip K., Jr. 1987. "The Evolution of Oil as a Commodity." In *Energy: Markets and Regulation*, edited by Richard L. Gordon, Henry D. Jacoby, and Martin B. Zimmerman, 161-86. Cambridge, Mass.: The MIT Press.

Verleger, Philip K., Jr. 1993. *Adjusting to Volatile Energy Prices*. Washington: Institute for International Economics.

Viner, Jacob. 1931. "Cost Curves and Supply Curves." *Zeitschrift für Nationalokonome* 3 (1): 23-46. Reprinted with supplemental note in Stigler and Boulding, eds. 1952, 198-232. Classic presentation of the analysis.

Viner, Jacob. 1991. *Essays on the Intellectual History of Economics*. Edited by Douglas A. Walker. Princeton: Princeton University Press. Argues classic liberalism and Hayek allowed for many exceptions to nonintervention.

Walker, D. A. 1991. "Review Article: *Economics as Social Physics*." *Economic Journal* 101 (3): 615-31.

Walker, Gordon and David Weber. 1984. "A Transactions Cost Approach to Make or Buy Decisions." *Administrative Science Quarterly* 29 (3): 373-91.

Walras, Leon. 1954. *Elements of Pure Economics or the Theory of Social Wealth*. (translation by William Jaffé of 1926 edition of book first published in 1874). London: George Allen and Unwin. First full presentation of the general equilibrium model.

Weaver, Jacqueline Lang. 1986. *Unitization of Oil and Gas Fields in Texas: A Study of Legislative, Administrative, and Judicial Policies*. Washington, D.C.: Resources for the Future. Demonstrates how extralegal pressures by regulators forced unitization in absence of supporting law and calls for passage of the law.

Weisbrod, Burton A. 1964. "Collective Consumption Services of Individual Consumption Goods." *Quarterly Journal of Economics* 78 (3): 471-77. Pioneering article of the publicness externalities of some goods such as recreation; extended by Krutilla to cover other justifications for intervention.

Weiss, Leonard W. 1974. "The Concentration-Profits Relationship,and Antitrust." In *Industrial Concentration: The New Learning*, edited by Harvey J. Goldschmid, H. Michael Mann, and J. Fred Weston, 185-233. Boston: Little Brown. A contention that oligopoly does seem to raise profits.

Weiss, Leonard W. 1975. "Antitrust in the Electric Power Industry." In *Promoting Competition in Regulated Markets*, edited by Almarin Phillips, 138-173. Washington, D.C.: The Brookings Institution. A proposal, widely endorsed by economists, to separate generation from transmission and distribution and deregulate generation.

Weitzman, Martin L. 1974. "Prices vs. Quantities." *Review of Economic Studies* 41 (4): 477-91. Analysis of the comparative merits of regulating by price setting or quantity setting given imperfect information.

Wiggins, Steven N. and Gary D. Libecap. 1985. "Oil Field Unitization: Contractual Failure in the Presence of Imperfect Information." *American Economic Review* 75 (3): 368-85.

Wildavsky, Aaron. 1962. *Dixon-Yates: A Study in Power Politics*. New Haven: Yale University Press. Review of fight to allow the Tennessee Valley Authority to build coal-fired plants instead of allowing entry of private companies.

Williamson, Oliver E. 1967. *The Economics of Discretionary Behavior: Managerial Objectives in the Theory of the Firm*. Chicago: Markham Publishing Company. (Earlier edition Engelwood Cliffs: Prentice-Hall, 1964.) Formal analysis of how managerial control might alter the level and disposition of profits.

Williamson, Oliver E. 1975. *Markets and Hierarchies: Analysis and Antitrust Implications*. New York: Free Press. Discussions of barriers to open-market purchases encouraging integration.

Williamson, Oliver E. 1977. "Predatory Pricing: A Strategic and Welfare Analysis." *The Yale Law Journal* 87 (2): 284-340. Another critique of Areeda and Turner.

Williamson, Oliver E. 1979a. "Transaction Cost Economics: The Governance of Contractual Relationship." *Journal of Law and Economics* 22 (2): 233-61.

Williamson, Oliver E. 1979b. "Williamson on Predatory Pricing II." *The Yale Law Journal* 88 (6): 1183-1200.

Williamson, Oliver E. 1983. "Credible Commitments: Using Hostages to Support Exchange." *American Economic Review* 83 (4): 519-40.

Williamson, Oliver E. 1985a. "Assessing Contract." *Journal of Law, Economics, and Organization* 1 (1): 177-85.

Williamson, Oliver E. 1985b. *The Economic Institutions of Capitalism: Firms, Markets, Relational Contracting*. New York: The Free Press. A revised view, largely assembled from previously published articles, in which the virtues as well as the vices of open market buying are considered.

Williamson, Oliver E. 1989. "Transaction Cost Economics." In *Handbook of Industrial Organization*. Vol. 1 edited by Richard Schmalensee and Robert D. Willig, 135-82. Amsterdam: North-Holland.

Williamson, Oliver E. and Sidney G. Winter, eds. 1991. *The Nature of the Firm: Origins, Evolution and Development*. New York: Oxford University Press. A reprint of the Coase article, his reflections, and explorations of the argument by several economists prominent in the area. Except for the original Coase article and the introduction by Williamson, the material is taken from the Spring 1988 issue of the *Journal of Law, Economics, and Organization*.

Williams, Jeffrey. 1986. *The Economic Function of Futures Markets*. Cambridge: Cambridge University Press. Argues function is mainly to facilitate borrowing commodities (see text for further explanation).

Wilson, Richard, Steven D. Colome, John D. Spengler, and David Gordon Wilson. 1980. *Health Effects of Fossil Fuel Burning, Assessment and Mitigation*. Cambridge, Mass.: Ballinger Publishing Company. Challenges to estimates of pollution damages and identification of causes.

Woronoff, Jon. 1990. *Japan as--anything but--Number One*. Armonk: M. E. Sharpe, 1991. Originally: Tokyo: Yohan Publications. London: Macmillan Academic and Professional. A long-time observer of Japan chronicles its weaknesses.

Yamamura, Kozo. 1986. "Caveat Emptor: The Industrial Policy of Japan." In *Strategic Trade Policy and the New International Economics*, edited by Paul R. Krugman, 169-209. Cambridge Mass.: The MIT Press.

Yamey, B. S. 1972. "Predatory Price Cutting: Notes and Comments." *Journal of Law and Economics* 15 (1): 129-42.

Yergin, Daniel. 1991. *The Prize: The Epic Quest for Oil, Money, and Power*. New York: Simon & Schuster.

Zimmermann, Erich W. 1964. *Erich W. Zimmermann's Introduction to World Resources*. Edited by Henry L. Hunker Editor. New York: Harper & Row. (Updated and revised by the editor from Zimmermann's part I of *World Resources and Industries*.) Celebrated for its view that man creates resources.

Zimmerman, Martin B. 1981. *The U.S. Coal Industry: The Economics of Policy Choice*. Cambridge, Mass.: The MIT Press.

Zimmerman, Martin B. 1987. "The Evolution of Civilian Nuclear Power." In *Energy: Markets and Regulation*, edited by Richard L. Gordon, Henry D. Jacoby, and Martin B. Zimmerman, 83-106. Cambridge, Mass.: The MIT Press. Shows how government programs prolonged after private entry became extensive.

Zupan, Mark A. 1989. "The Efficacy of Franchise Bidding Schemes in the Case of Cable Television: Some Systematic Evidence." *Journal of Law and Economics* 32 (2) part 1: 401-56. Suggests that the barrier to efficient bidding is inefficient demands of municipalities.

Index

acid mine drainage, 143
acid rain, 144
Adams, Walter, 30, 35n
Adelman, M. A., 31-32, 33, 35n, 41, 93, 105, 137, 151
agency problem in economic relations, 69
agricultural subsidies, 2, 126-127
agricultural supply disruptions 107
agriculture, intervention in, 2, 42, 124, 126-127, 187
air pollution, 141-144
air pollution policies, 134, 138, 141-144
Alaska, harms by the Jones Act, 127
Alchian, Armen A., 71
Aluminum Corporation of America (Alcoa) antitrust case, 44-45, 47
Allais, Maurice, 83, 180
American Association of Retired People, 125
American Automobile Association, 125
American Economic Association, xiv
American Electric Power, 96, 97, 99
American Tobacco's competitive behavior, 37
Anaconda, 94
Anderson, Frederick R., 154
Anderson, Terry 137, 140
Anti-Semitism in attacks on liberalism, 193
antitrust, 29, 42-47, 63. *See also* Clayton Act, monopoly, Robinson Patman Act, and Sherman Act
Appalachian Regional Commission study of acid mine drainage, 143
appropriate technologies (Schumacher), 18
apriorism (von Mises), 173, 200
arbitrage, economic roles of, 12-13, 40, 79, 85, 114, 161-162, 167. *See also* brokers, commodity markets, futures markets, organized markets, speculation, and spot markets
Areeda, Phillip, 37-39, 43n
Arendt, Hannah, 193
Aristotle, 178
Armentano, Dominick, 47
Arrow, Kenneth J., 145n
Atlas Shrugged (Ayn Rand), 193
Australia, coal in, 83, 95, 97, 150
Austrian economics, 15, 70, 171-176, 181
Baden, John, 145, 154
Bailey, Ronald, 137
Bain, Joe S., 30, 31, 34-35, 39, 46
balance of payments equilibrium, 112-114. *See also* gold standard
Barlow, Connie C., 93
Barnett, Harold J., 28, 137, 153n, 155n
Barro, Robert J., 84
Bartley, William Warren III, 196-197
Bassett, Lowell R., 42

levels limits, 163-164
maximum production rules for mineral leases, 167
mineral land management, U.S., 168
mineral property rights and, 150
oil, 161
profit sharing in, 158
systems, 152
public property. *See* bonus payments, Coal Leasing Amendment Act, comparable worth, competitive bidding, competition for leases, diligence requirements, due diligence, economic rents, fair market value, federal coal leases, Federal Land policy and Management Act, government land management, land law, law of capture, lease bonus, maximum production requirements, Mineral Leasing Act, Mining Act, national parks, private property, privatization, property rights, public land, public land leasing, reproduction cost, royalties, separating mineral rights, surface owner compensation, U.S. Bureau of Land Management, U.S. Commission on Fair Market Value for Federal Coal Leases, U.S. Department of the Interior, U.S. Interagency Land Acquisition Conference, and U.S. Public Land Law Review Commission
Public Service Electric and Gas, 98
public utilities, 56, 67-68, 98-104. *See also* cable television regulation experience with franchise bidding, deregulated generation, franchise bidding, holding companies in U.S. public utilities, and natural monopolies
commissions and regulation, 65, 72-73, 80, 99, 101, 175, 186-187
quantity theory of money, 113
Queensland, Australia, electric utility coal procurement in, 97
quotas on imports, 50, 52, 54, 124
Ramsay, William, 143
rates of substitution, 11-13, 22
rational behavior, 9-10, 115, 202
rational expectations, 115
rational-expectations macroeconomists, 115-116
Rawls, John, 120-121
Ray, Dixy Lee, 137
RCA, 187
Reagan, Ronald, xii, 45, 55, 155-156
realism in Milton Friedman's methodology, 198-202
recreation, 22-23, 144-147
national parks, U.S., 144
park lands, 22-23
redistribution of income. *See* distribution of income
Redman, Deborah A.,196, 198
refutation of scientific theories, 196, 197, 199
regulation, xi-xiii, 1-7, 29-30, 42-47, 49-52, 55-57, 66-67, 99-109, 119, 123-127, 129, 133-141, 169, 184-194. *See also* government failure, intervention, nationalization, planning, and socialism
Reinganum, Jennifer F., 29n
renegotiation clauses in contracts, 87
rent controls, 2, 125, 187
rents (economic). *See* economic rents
reproduction cost value of public property, 159
research, 23
restructuring of industry. *See* structure of industry, reform of